The Limits of Heroism

THE BODY, IN THEORY   Histories of Cultural Materialism

The Subject as Action: Transformation and Totality in Narrative Aesthetics
by Alan Singer

Power and Knowledge: Astrology, Physiognomics, and Medicine under the Roman Empire
by Tamsyn S. Barton

Under the Sign: John Bargrave as Collector, Traveler, and Witness
by Stephen Bann

Simulacra and Simulation by Jean Baudrillard, translated by Sheila Faria Glaser

Philodemus in Italy: The Books from Herculaneum
by Marcello Gigante, translated by Dirk Obbink

The Tremulous Private Body: Essays on Subjection by Francis Barker

Picturing Silence: Emblem, Language, Counter-Reformation Materiality
by Karen Pinkus

The Abyss of Freedom / Ages of the World
by Slavoj Žižek / F. W. J. von Schelling, translated by Judith Norman

The Body and Physical Difference: Discourses of Disability
edited by David T. Mitchell and Sharon L. Snyder

Constructions of the Classical Body edited by James I. Porter

An Utterly Dark Spot: Gaze and Body in Early Modern Philosophy
by Miran Božovič

The Pedagogical Contract: The Economies of Teaching and Learning in the Ancient World
by Yun Lee Too

Cutting the Body: Representing Woman in Baudelaire's Poetry, Truffaut's Cinema, and Freud's Psychoanalysis by Eliane DalMolin

Staging Masculinity: The Rhetoric of Performance in the Roman World
by Erik Gunderson

The Culture of the Body: Genealogies of Modernity
by Dalia Judovitz

Stately Bodies: Literature, Philosophy, and the Question of Gender
by Adriana Cavarero, translated by Robert de Lucca and Deanna Shemek

The Limits of Heroism: Homer and the Ethics of Reading
by Mark Buchan

The Limits of Heroism

Homer and the Ethics of Reading

MARK BUCHAN

THE UNIVERSITY OF MICHIGAN PRESS
Ann Arbor

Copyright © by the University of Michigan 2004
All rights reserved
Published in the United States of America by
The University of Michigan Press
Manufactured in the United States of America
∞ Printed on acid-free paper

2007 2006 2005 2004   4 3 2 1

No part of this publication may be reproduced,
stored in a retrieval system, or transmitted in any form
or by any means, electronic, mechanical, or otherwise,
without the written permission of the publisher.

A CIP catalog record for this book is available from the British Library.

Library of Congress Cataloging-in-Publication Data

Buchan, Mark, 1966–
    The limits of heroism : Homer and the ethics of reading / Mark Buchan.
    p. cm. — (The body, in theory)
    Includes bibliographical references and index.
    ISBN 0-472-11391-7 (cloth : acid-free paper)
    1. Homer. Odyssey. 2. Odysseus (Greek mythology) in literature. 3. Epic poetry, Greek—History and criticism. 4. War—Moral and ethical aspects. 5. Ethics, Ancient, in literature. 6. Courage in literature. 7. Ethics in literature. 8. Heroes in literature. 9. Homer—Ethics. I. Title. II. Series.

PA4167.B64 2004
883′.01—dc22
                                                                    2004053741

To my parents

Acknowledgments

This book on the *Odyssey* has been long in the making and has accompanied me on my own voyage through four universities. Because of this, it bears the intellectual imprint of many friends, colleagues, and students who have had the energy and patience to read over parts or all of it in its various forms, as well as of the even more numerous who have argued with me in person over its central tenets. It is a book about the complicated process of desiring, about the way the Homeric poems complicate our everyday notions of what it means to want something, and about the strange way in which an individual's desire is inevitably and inextricably bound up in the desires of others. It is therefore a pleasure to be able to thank at least some of the fellow travelers who, by wanting me to write this book, have helped me to want to write it.

Ann Hansen, Sara Rappe, Sally Humphreys, Santiago Colas, and Gregory Nagy all read and commented on the full manuscript. Simon Goldhill, Stephen Hinds, Ruth Webb, John Kittmer, and Gina Soter read and discussed assorted parts with me, as did Tim and Emily Gowers. I also owe a great deal to the intellectual enthusiasm and support of many others: at Bristol, to Duncan Kennedy, Charles Martindale, Ellen O'Gorman, and Vanda Zajko; at the University of Washington, to Susan Lape and Cathy Connors; at Northwestern, to Ahuvia Kahane and Bob Wallace; at Princeton, to Andy Ford, Froma Zeitlin, Josh Katz, Giovanna Ceserani, and John Ma. I also benefited from the comments of two anonymous readers. Thanks also to Kirk Ormand and Denise McCoskey.

The book tries to revisit the central questions of the Homeric poems—the problems of human identity, the value of human life, the logic of heroic ideology. Perhaps because of this, most of the arguments I put forth here have sprung directly from debates in the classroom over the last decade, with both graduate and undergraduate students alike. Though I am happy to take responsibility for all that is said, this text now seems to me to be a composite, written version of all those classroom conversations. I am thus immensely grateful to the students who made it such a pleasure to teach and reteach these poems.

Finally, I would like to make special mention of James Porter. I have long stopped trying to puzzle out where his thinking ends and mine begins in this manuscript, but a thousand footnotes could not do justice to his influence. Thanks.

All citations in Greek of the Homeric texts are from the Oxford Classical Texts the *Iliad*, ed. David B. Monro and Thomas W. Allen, vols. 1 and 2 of *Homeri Opera* (Oxford: Clarendon Press, 1920) and the *Odyssey*, ed. Thomas W. Allen, vols. 3 and 4 of *Homeri Opera* (Oxford: Clarendon Press, 1917–19). I have used the translations of Richard Lattimore *The Iliad of Homer* (Chicago: University of Chicago Press, 1951) and *The Odyssey of Homer* (New York: Harper and Row, 1965), slightly modifying them in some instances. In the modified translations, italics denote modification.

Contents

Introduction *1*

1. Polyphemus: The Blinding of a Cyclops *18*

2. Phaeacia: The Impossible Choice of Subjectivity *36*

3. In the Beginning Was Proteus *50*

4. From Stones to Statehood: Sublime Objects in the *Odyssey* *72*

5. Metis and Monstrosity: Odysseus' and Demodocus' Battle of Wits *89*

6. The Limits of Heroism *107*

7. The *Odyssey* from the Perspective of Its Victims *133*

8. What Does a Phaeacian Woman Want? *181*

9. Penelope as *Parthenos* *206*

Notes *237*
References *269*
Index *275*

Introduction

The *Odyssey* is a poem of paradox. On the one hand, it is the "most teleological of epics,"[1] a story of a man's desire, long frustrated but finally satisfied, where what is lacking is finally restored. From the perspective of Odysseus, he regains his wife and household. From the perspective of the epic tradition itself, the final heroic *nostos* (the return trips of the Greek warriors from Troy) is told, and the story of the Trojan War is wrapped up. The fulfillment of these desires is, to be sure, deferred, but only to build up the significance of the climax, and everything moves toward the endgame on Ithaca. Such teleological readings have also brought with them a consensus concerning the poem's ideological impact. For the poem's ending is a thoroughly ideological resolution since it validates a certain mode of existence. To put it bluntly, we know that Odysseus is a good aristocrat, while the suitors are bad aristocrats. Penelope is good; Clytemnestra and Helen are bad. The poem shows us the triumph of the good, the destruction of the bad.[2]

On the other hand, the poem's teleological framework is in sharp contrast to the content of the poem. For the epic is made up of a long series of episodes charting the hero's miraculous escape from death, and so it has been easy to assimilate to the antiepic tradition of romance.[3] It is less a poem about closure and more one about the avoidance of closure, especially the closure implied by death itself. It is strange that such a romantic analysis of the poem has not tried to challenge its overall ideological force; that is, though one might expect these romantic tales of the conquering of death to be in some sort of tension with the imposition of a certain kind of social and moral order, this has not generally been advocated. If the *Odyssey* is about avoiding death and preserving life, the peculiar form that this life eventually takes—the normalized *oikos* (household)

[margin note: Importance of oikos]

that Odysseus restores—is generally taken to be the only kind of good life available. To be sure, there has, in recent years, been some effort to complicate this picture. Bakhtinian approaches have allowed us to see different ideological forces in competition throughout the poem, thus the "plural voices" of Homer. By emphasizing the actions of Penelope, feminist criticism has undermined accounts of the poem that center on Odysseus as fabricator of his own return: Penelope has become less an object Odysseus returns to and more a fellow agent aiding that return. Yet despite these complications, the major teleological logic stays in place.[4]

I want to shake up this critical consensus, which is at once too teleological and yet not teleological enough. It is too teleological because it identifies with a certain fantasy of social order that is certainly at the heart of the poem—that is, it follows closely the fantasy of Odysseus. Indeed, much analysis of the "world of Odysseus," as the phrase implies, suffers from too close an identification with Odysseus—as if the Homeric world simply *is* Odysseus' imaginary version of that world. Yet we need not be tied to this identification. For much of the force of the poem comes from the gap between Odysseus' own fantasy of Ithaca, on the one hand, and the world outside that seems to resist it, on the other. This gap means that the poem is always one step removed from any unproblematic depiction of reality—say, the telos of a restored *oikos* on Ithaca. On my reading, the *Odyssey* (and the *Iliad*, too) will be less about the social order itself and more about competing fantasies of that order.

Yet the critical consensus is also not teleological enough. For in following Odysseus' fantasy, too little attention is paid to the actual ending of the poem. So, following the advice of Herodotus' Solon, we need to "look to the end," where we find two well-known surprises. First, Odysseus' journey does not end with the poem; instead, he must embark on a second journey, in accordance with the prophecy outlined to him by Teiresias. Second, though peace is restored on Ithaca, it is only restored after an utter catastrophe is narrowly averted. Athena prevents Odysseus, together with his rejuvenated father and son, from killing the remaining adult males on the island. Though well known, these narrative surprises should still shock us each time we confront them, and they demand interpretation. So, in a properly teleological spirit, let us recount the last events at the beginning.

First, Athena intervenes to prevent the rejuvenated triad of Odysseus, Laertes, and Telemachus from massacring the remaining living men on Ithaca. This ending, in turn, provides some justification to the pithy summary of the actions of Odysseus by Eupeithes (father of the chief suitor, Antinous) earlier in the book.

> Friends, this man's will worked great evil upon the Achaians.
> First he took many excellent men away in the vessels
> with him, and lost the hollow ships, and lost all the people,
> and then returning killed the best men of the Kephallenians.
>
> (*Od.* 24.426–29)

Eupeithes' words should be read against the curiously selective version of Odysseus' return provided by the *Odyssey*'s proem. There, we find that the episode of the cattle of the sun, in a particularly violent synecdoche, is chosen to represent the death of all Odysseus' companions, who "died by their own recklessness" (*Od.* 1.7 ff.). In contrast to this foolish, self-destructive choice of a minority of the men, Eupeithes opposes the simple fact of all their deaths. What is at stake here is not simply two conflicting explanations of the same events—say, a selective, idealizing account of Odysseus' life as a hero compared to a more realistic one—a conflict that could be resolved by simply choosing between the explanations. Eupeithes' speech may very well be an example of a narrator encouraging us to cast a skeptical eye on what seems, with hindsight, to be the narrator's own unreliability in the proem. We may also be encouraged to view the idealization as an ongoing apology for real violence. But even this is not enough. It too easily separates ideology from reality, and it fails to see the way that the poem lays before us the success of a certain kind of fantasy of Odysseus. If the poem ends in a perturbing manner, it does so because the power of Odysseus' ideological vision for his homeland brooks no human resistance at all. Any opponents who do not play the proper role in restoring his version of paternal power on Ithaca—a paternal power multiplied threefold via the uncanny rejuvenation of the grandfather Laertes and the father Odysseus and the maturation of Telemachus—are on the point of being obliterated. So if there is something shocking at the poem's end, it is not so much that Odysseus nearly fails but that he comes all too close to succeeding. The gap between the "world of Odysseus" and the world as such is nearly closed by the almost total destruction of that world.

Thus the *Odyssey* leaves us with a difficult question: insofar as we have been lured into an identification with the hero, are we now to identify with the utter loss of the community he purportedly wants to rule?[5] If we choose to break this identification, it might allow us to shake up, with hindsight, our reading of the poem. For, as I hope to show, the human confrontation with complete destruction of the human is an ongoing motif of both the *Odyssey* and the *Iliad,* just as this fantasy of destruction lurks within the acts of the heroes of these poems, Odysseus and Achilles. But I will also argue that this process is a familiar one.

Unexpected disasters occur to other characters elsewhere in the poem, and these disasters offer us an invitation to rethink the kind of unreflective assumptions that produced them. A disaster is a sign that something has been misinterpreted or that a riddle or prophecy has been ignored—even if the correct reading of that sign may be only retroactively available. In short, the surprises of the ending of the poem itself can be better understood if we compare the ending to other tales of trauma and surprise within the poem.[6] There are a series of stories within the narrative that reflect on the dangers of certain fantasies of the self—on the fissures in self-understanding produced by these fantasies—and so provide an implied commentary on the central narrative of Odysseus' return. We should look to the poem's stories of reflective failure, available only with hindsight, as well as to its tales of success. By taking the former seriously, we will find a poem that is just as concerned with the breakdown of the self, with the failure of certain fantasies to render it coherent, as with any idealized restoration of a lost self. We must dare to read the narrative of Odysseus' *nostos* itself as an example of just this kind of retroactively available error. The *Odyssey* has generated plenty of Promethean readings, exploring the cunning and foresight of its hero; but we can also construct an Epimethean one, exploring the disasters that this same cunning unwittingly brings about.

Second, the end of the poem confronts us with its notorious endlessness. As we know from Teiresias' prophecy and as Odysseus reminds Penelope after their reunion, Odysseus' return to Ithaca will not be the end of his travels. Instead, he will soon leave the *oikos* he has struggled to regain. Of course, critics know this very well. Yet this knowledge has had relatively little impact on teleological interpretations. There is, it seems to me, a good reason for this. If critics know that the poem's end is not *the* end and yet act as if it is, they are simply continuing with the identification with Odysseus himself. For he hears Teiresias' prophecy but seems to act as if he has not heard it. Only when he has regained his home and after he has negotiated a tense recognition scene with Penelope does this repressed knowledge return. However, instead of endorsing or ignoring this form of disavowal (both strategies come to much the same thing), I suggest we view it as a central complicating truth about this poem: it is less an epic of return and more an epic about the complicated mechanisms involved in the desire for a return. For disavowal itself would be one way of keeping desire alive. So what remains to be examined is the complexity of the logic of desire itself.

This leaves us with a poem that is less about the return to a real place and more about the problems and complications of the desire for a return to that place. On the one hand, that might seem to turn the *Odyssey* into an exercise in manipulation—it encourages its readers (ancient and modern alike) to identify with its hero and to sympathize with his desire for home, only to lead Odysseus and us into disquieting ethical territory. More generously, it allows us to work through the significance of those nostalgic feelings and to question, retroactively, what they might mean. This would allow the *Odyssey* to be less a poem about *nostos* and more a poem about the allures and dangers of nostalgia. It is a truism of much of recent scholarship that Odysseus' world is vastly different in content from the modern world. Yet for the majority of the poem, the content of that world is put on hold, and we have the more abstract situation of the hero simply wanting what he does not have. As the poem lingers in this space, it allows—even encourages—readers to map on to the hero their own specific modes of desiring (their own fantasies of nostalgia and overcoming loss). For this reason, the poem encourages an entanglement of the fantasies of its central character and its readers. Odysseus' fantasies of return are thus inevitably overlaid with our own.[7]

To highlight this thematic nexus—catastrophe, loss, desire—is to venture onto terrain that is well charted by psychoanalysis, and my readings will be indebted to a psychoanalytically informed skepticism about desire. Rather than the Aristotelian picture of humans as creatures whose ultimate goal is happiness, I take seriously the Freudian possibility that humans do not want to be happy. Indeed, perhaps nothing provokes anxiety as much as getting what we want. Such a simple insight offers an opportunity to read the *Odyssey* in a different manner and might do justice to this "endlessness." Following Jacques Lacan, we can focus our attention away from any apparent content of the object that seems to be desired (in the case of Odysseus, his household on Ithaca) and instead see desire as intent on maintaining its own circuits, on keeping itself alive by avoiding satisfaction. Odysseus and Penelope might be just as interested in keeping the desire for the other alive as in any reunion, just as the desiring subject is interested less in satisfaction than in keeping at a safe distance the kind of overwhelming enjoyment that satisfaction promises.

To preview some of these psychoanalytic themes, in particular the contours of a relationship between desire and destruction, loss and obliteration, openness and closure, let me begin by turning to some well-known lines of the *Iliad*. In *Iliad* 9, in response to Odysseus' attempt to persuade him to return to the fighting, Achilles replies in words that have been understood to exemplify his character.

> Son of Laertes and seed of Zeus, resourceful Odysseus:
> without consideration for you I must make my answer,
> The way I think, and the way it will be accomplished, that you may
>   not

come one after another, and sit by me, and speak softly.
For as I detest the doorways of Death, I detest that man, who
hides one thing in the depths of his heart, and speaks forth another.

(*Il.* 9.308–13)

Achilles seems to voice both a hatred of deception and an accompanying desire for a world where moral problems are black-and-white. The likening of his hatred of the liar to death itself seems to expand on this notion. Achilles wants a world where the everyday matter of human communication is as irrevocable and absolute a matter as death itself.[8] One can even give the simile a subjective turn, understanding it to hint at the depths of Achilles' own commitment to such a world. Rather than live and be deceived, he would rather die, as he famously does—too early and tragically, in the name of an ethics of *kleos* (fame) that itself seems to put trust in the reliability of successful human communication across generations.

For the most part, this interpretation is relatively uncontroversial. But there is more to these lines. This interpretation views the reference to death as essentially passive. It is something that heroes—and axiomatically Achilles—suffer, much more than something they dish out. But this particular hero is already famed for his exploits in the active business of death, so we can see a veiled threat in this simile. The words come from the lips of a man who, before the death of his best friend, fantasizes about the destruction of all Greeks and Trojans (*Il.* 16.97 ff.) and, after his friend's death, begins a campaign of systematic killing. This suggests that suffering death may not be the only way of escaping the communicative impasses of human existence: extinguishing life may be another. In this light, the reference to the men who must not "come one after another" to him anticipates more than Achilles seems to know. It foreshadows the appeals of the Greeks less than the appeals of the Trojans, epitomized in the death of Lycaon. He will soon come with cooing, suppliant words, only to have such words ruthlessly ignored. Of course, these critical possibilities are only open if we partially break our identification with the tragedy of Achilles.[9]

From this reading, all sorts of paradoxes ensue. Achilles, as he voices his hatred of deception and ambiguity, utters words that are hopelessly polysemous. But what he says is also in complete contradiction with what he does—as Plato long ago realized.[10] But the paradox is not just that Achilles, the figure who supposedly exemplifies truth, is an objective liar—at least in the context of *Iliad* 9. It is that in this poem of action, the figure given the most power to choose his destiny, the well-known alternative between a short, famous life and a long anonymous one, makes no conscious choice at all. To be sure, after Patroclus' death, he will return to battle. But at that moment, nothing is further from his mind than fame. He gets it, to be sure, but neither chooses it nor cares about it. So the poem is less about the choice of Achilles and more about his failure to choose—and the tragic consequences are set in motion by this indecision itself. This conceptual place where he will say one thing but do another and thus attempt to cling to both—a self-conception as a man of action who gains the benefits of inaction, of not choosing—is Achilles' true home. Achilles refuses to fight, rejects the gifts of Agamemnon, and later allows Patroclus to dress up in his own armor; but all these acts are symptoms of his indecision and thus are hardly acts at all. There is a vast amount of scholarship on decision making in Homer, just as there is wide-ranging discussion of the normative contours of the *oikos* to which Odysseus returns. But there are perhaps other questions we should ask. Why, at the crucial moments, do Homeric heroes not choose, and why is their apparent desire so compromised? Here, once more, we have entered the terrain that psychoanalysis has mapped out as its own, analyzing a particular logic of doubt, of the failure to act, as crucial for attempts to understand human decision making. This also helps us link Achilles to Odysseus and link the extraordinary destruction caused by both. For Achilles' shift from passive acceptance of death to active causer of death mirrors a similar plot shift in the *Odyssey:* the passive loss of Odysseus' companions in the first half of the poem turns into the active destruction of the suitors. Both instances of destruction are intertwined with their respective hero's vacillation.

So much of this book is a literary-critical experiment, aided by the conceptual framework of psychoanalysis. What happens if we see the *Iliad* and the *Odyssey* as examing the psychological implications of how not to get what you want and if this is in tension with the thrust of the teleological structure that is so well known? This would suggest that the mass of deaths in the *Iliad* result less from Achilles' anger than from his indecision and that the deaths displayed at the end of the *Odyssey,* together with the near total destruction of the male community of Ithaca, would no longer be a kind of necessary collateral damage incurred because of Odysseus' commitment to a certain kind of civilization. Instead, they would be intimately related to the difficulties and dangers of keeping a certain kind of desire alive.[11]

We can begin to tease out the different kind of picture of the *Odyssey* that emerges from this perspective. The endlessness of the poem suggests there is something deathly about endings.[12] But the suspicious avoidance of closure can return us to the beginning of the poem and to Odysseus' situation there. He has spent seven years on Calypso's island, but in book 5 we see him looking out over the sea pining for Ithaca. After he is told that he can go home, Calypso questions the wisdom of his desire, precisely because he seems to want something worse than he already has. Here is Odysseus' reply.

> πότνα θεά, μή μοι τόδε χώεο· οἶδα καὶ αὐτὸς
> πάντα μάλ', οὕνεκα σεῖο περίφρων Πηνελόπεια
> εἶδος ἀκιδνοτέρη μέγεθός τ' εἰσάντα ἰδέσθαι·
> ἡ μὲν γὰρ βροτός ἐστι, σὺ δ' ἀθάνατος καὶ ἀγήρως.
> ἀλλὰ καὶ ὧς ἐθέλω καὶ ἐέλδομαι ἤματα πάντα
> οἴκαδέ τ' ἐλθέμεναι καὶ νόστιμον ἦμαρ ἰδέσθαι.
>
> [Goddess and queen, do not be angry with me. I myself know
> that all you say is true and that circumspect Penelope
> can never match the impression you make for beauty and stature.
> She is mortal after all, and you are immortal and ageless.
> But even so, what I want and all my days I pine for
> is to go back to my house and see my day of homecoming.]
>
> (*Od.* 5.215–20)

Odysseus rejects Calypso, even as he himself admits that she is the better choice. Humanist and romantic readings have taken for granted that, for all the apparent inferiority of Penelope, there is something essential about her that cannot be reduced to this series of qualities: Calypso may be better in every conceivable way than Penelope, but she is not Penelope, and it is this very thing that Odysseus wants. But it is better to take Odysseus at his word and emphasize that at the level of the content, he has absolutely no reason to go home. Here, a new possibility arises: rather than keeping him with Calypso, it could be this very insight that sends him off. He may be less interested in the apparent absence of the supposed object of the journey, Penelope, and more afraid of losing the desire for a return, the desire that itself made his stay on Calypso's island possible. So, rather than a hero who desires to go home to Penelope, the endlessness of the poem might let us see Odysseus as trapped between two women. They threaten him precisely because they offer to satisfy his desires.[13] At stake here would be not Ithaca itself but, rather, the fantasy of Ithaca, which is always a fantasy of somewhere else, just as his desire for a woman is always the desire of someone else. For it is precisely such a fantasy of Ithaca and Penelope that structures Odysseus' desire for them. What Odysseus is in danger of losing on Calypso's island is not the real Ithaca but this other, imaginary place.

By bracketing the content of what Odysseus desires, we can also undermine some of the force of those readings that see the *Odyssey* as enforcing a certain normative ideal—a certain family structure, social order, and so on. I do not wish to deny the salience of such dominant ideologies in the poem or the critical work that has been done in elucidating them. But I do emphasize the way their fragility is made manifest and, especially, how the complexities of the problem of desire threaten to undermine any such order. A certain social structure is dependent on the desire for such an order, and in the *Odyssey*, this will be a complicated matter. This emptying out of the content of desire in order to focus on its mechanisms can also change how we view the conventional villains of the *Odyssey*'s world. To return to the opening of the poem, rather than emphasizing the difference between Odysseus, already on his way back home, and the suitors who continue to eat up his household goods despite the warnings of Odysseus and Halitherses, consider what they have in common. Both eat huge amounts of food, and the supplies of it seem endless.[14] Both seem to want something (in Odysseus' case, to go home to Penelope; in the suitors' case, to marry Penelope), but both are curiously caught up in failing to achieve it.

Of course, no one really believes that the suitors are serious in their desire to marry Penelope; they seem to be enjoying Odysseus' involuntary hospitality all too well. But in focusing on the well-known eating excesses of the suitors (highlighted for us in and through the disapproving and selective language of Telemachus and Athena), we miss an equally important aspect of their behavior; they are curiously obsessed with justifying their presence in Penelope's household, constantly citing the need for Penelope to marry as a matter of due custom. As with Achilles, their world is also one of indecision. One could even say that their story, too, is a tragedy of timing, of an inability to extricate themselves in time from a similar kind of space where they seem to have their cake and eat it: they break certain kinds of customary law (eating the goods of Odysseus' household) *and* claim a principled allegiance to custom (demanding the marriage of Penelope). The suitors' relationship to any moral code of the world of the *Odyssey* is thus more complex than has been generally recognized.[15]

The similarity between the situation of Odysseus and the suitors at the start of the poem suggests that the narrative dramatizes a kind of race for survival between the two of them. The difference between Odysseus and the suitors is slight but crucial, and it is less about *who* they are than *when* they act: he decides to return just in time, whereas the suitors will react to the signals of their demise just too late.[16] This structural similarity is in tension with much of the rhetoric of separation between Odysseus and the suitors—say, the moral horror at the actions of the suitors that many of the poem's protagonists pay lip service to. The difference between Odysseus and the suitors is a matter of moments; Odysseus becomes dissatisfied with Calypso even as the suitors continue to enjoy the goods in his household, and it is only this victory in timing that allows us to sketch out any moral differences between them. Here, we have arrived at a well-known ethical motif in archaic culture, the need for actions to be performed "at the right time" *(kairos)*.[17] Success is all about a kind of timing. But there is a troubling correlative to this, which I think the poem invites us to explore: if ethics, the successful reclamation of an identity, and the ability to gain heroic fame all depend on actions performed at the right time, then this threatens to empty out the possibility of a moral or ethical world that would transcend this kind of impermanence. This has consequences for any fixed conception of the self. By arriving "just on time," Odysseus avoids the loss of his idealized conception of himself, the contours of the fantasy that drove him home in the first place, a fantasy that corresponds to the integrity of the narrative itself. In psychoanalytic terms, he avoids "subjective destitution"; in the language of the *Odyssey*, he flirts with the possibility that his most famous mask, that of "No one," might turn out to be real—he might become a man without any kind of social context to define the self.[18] The poem, then, is just as much about keeping Ithaca at the right distance, about preserving its place in fantasy, as it is about a return to Ithaca. To show this, we could trace out the likely alternate ending to another poem. If Odysseus had returned a little later, we might well *not* see an Ithaca where injustice had triumphed and where the goods of an *oikos* had been destroyed. Rather, there might simply be a place where life peacefully went on and where Penelope had married another man—the "world of Odysseus," but *without Odysseus*. But this, of course, would no longer be the *Odyssey*. The question of Odysseus' return thus marches hand in hand with the integrity of the narrative. The poem flirts with the possibility of its own self-destruction and, simultaneously, questions what the concept of such self-destruction might play in our psychic lives.

To focus on spaces of indecision in both texts is also part of an attempt to see what these texts share, rather than emphasizing the well-known thematic differences between the two—the *Iliad* as a poem of war, the *Odyssey* as a poem of economy and peace. For example, the general situation of Odysseus at the beginning of the *Odyssey*—a man between two *oikoi*, that of Calypso and that of Ithaca—is duplicated in interesting ways in the *Iliad*. For this poem, too—in its own way—is interested in interrogating the problem of what constitutes an *oikos*. Consider Achilles. His tent functions not only as the privileged space for his *martial* indecision (it is itself on the edge of the Greek army but not in the Greek army). It is also a place of his *marital* indecision. It is well known that Achilles lingers between the possibility of a long life after a homecoming and a short, glorious life in battle. But his indecision is also between two different kinds of brides and, thus, two differently constituted *oikoi*. On the one hand, there is his father, Peleus, who will grant him a bride should he return to Phthia (*Il.* 9.394). On the other is Patroclus, a surrogate father who, as we later find out, tried to take over Peleus' duties by making Bryseis his wife (*Il.* 19255 ff.). We should ponder what we mean when we say that the poem begins in medias res. After nine years of war, there is a conflict over two slave girls, Chryseis and Bryseis, that looks suspiciously like—indeed, is deliberately conflated with—a conflict over wives. The problem of the *oikos* is already under the spotlight because of the passage of time itself, and this, I suggest, is the exact dilemma of the opening of the *Odyssey*. When does a makeshift, impromptu *oikos* begin to replace, at the level of what people do, if not at the level of what they think, the *oikos* that has been abandoned in a separate place? This question can come into focus if we take the disjunction between saying and doing seriously.

We perhaps take too much for granted in the *Iliad* and the *Odyssey*—that the true *oikoi* of the Greeks are in Greece, as if this is a timeless truth independent of the desires of the actors. But both poems begin when this is the very thing in question, though from different perspectives. Odysseus wants to go to Ithaca—at the very moment that his home from home begins to look like home. Agamemnon, without knowing it, acts as if his permanent household is in Troy. Consider the way Agamemnon refers to Chryseis in *Iliad* 1.29–31.

τὴν δ' ἐγὼ οὐ λύσω· πρίν μιν καὶ γῆρας ἔπεισιν
<u>ἡμετέρῳ ἐνὶ οἴκῳ</u> ἐν Ἄργεϊ, τηλόθι πάτρης
ἱστὸν ἐποιχομένην καὶ ἐμὸν λέχος ἀντιόωσαν·

[The girl I will not give back; sooner will old age come upon her
in our own house, in Argos, far from her own land, going
up and down by the loom and being in my bed as my companion.]

How are we to read ἡμετέρῳ ἐνὶ οἴκῳ? "In our house" could simply be another way of saying "in my house." But Agamemnon talks of Chryseis as a substitute wife here, not as a slave girl, so the location of the *oikos* is in doubt. If "our house" comprises Agamemnon and Chryseis, it is at least possible that this *oikos* is whatever arrangement he already has at Troy. It takes his further, somewhat defensive clarification later in the line (ἐν Ἄργεϊ, τηλόθι πάτρης) to restore an official *Iliadic* discourse: he still thinks of his *oikos* as Argos, his wife as Clytemnestra. Thus, at the microlevel of a single line of the hexameter, we find the same general structure of the poems themselves—where uncertainty concerning what and where an *oikos* is will be retroactively canceled by the further acts of the heroes, just as the location of Agamemnon's *oikos* is clarified by "in Argos" [ἐν Ἄργεϊ]. The problem recurs later, when Agamemnon clarifies the attractions of Chryseis and claims that he wants to keep her at home (ἐπεὶ πολὺ βούλομαι αὐτὴν / οἴκοι ἔχειν·, 1.113–14). At first, it seems that

Agamemnon fantasizes that Chryseis will usurp the role of Clytemnestra in Argos, and this is what 'οἴκοι ἔχειν' refers to. But perhaps more perturbing, this may be a commentary on what he is already doing: for he is already keeping her in his makeshift home at Troy, and by so doing he puts his connection to all of Argos at stake. It is therefore not enough to say that the *Iliad* is the poem where warfare is preferred to the return home to an *oikos* of the *Odyssey*. Rather, both poems put into question the effects of time and place on the fantasies of what an *oikos* might be.[19]

The emphasis on desire and its logic can also help complicate a key motif in teleological readings of the poem: the apparent shift from ignorance to knowledge that the *Odyssey* offers. Again, there is much more at stake here than the simple knowledge of whether Odysseus will return and the suspense it generates within the narrative. For, as many have pointed out, there is a lot of social and ideological baggage in Odysseus' return: what is being recognized is not just an individual man but this man as representative of a whole way of life.[20] But what we know is always caught up in the desire to know, and this will mean that what we know of identity in the poem will also be victim to the vagaries of desire. Indeed, there is much in the poem to suggest that the passage from doubt to ignorance is not quite so smooth, and there is much more that questions the possibility of any sure knowledge of the self.

Consider a famous moment in the opening book. The disguised Athena arrives in Odysseus' palace and asks Telemachus about his parents. He expresses skepticism.

> τοιγὰρ ἐγώ τοι, ξεῖνε, μάλ᾽ ἀτρεκέως ἀγορεύσω.
> μήτηρ μέν τ᾽ ἐμέ φησι τοῦ ἔμμεναι, αὐτὰρ ἐγώ γε
> οὐκ οἶδ᾽. οὐ γάρ πώ τις ἑὸν γόνον αὐτὸς ἀνέγνω.
>
> (*Od*. 1.214–16)

[See, I will accurately answer all that you ask me.
My mother says indeed I am his. I for my part
do not know. Nobody really knows his own father.]

A plausible way of reading these remarks is to emphasize the impossibility of knowing one's genetic heritage for certain. Such ancient ignorance can be clarified by comparison to modern knowledge, since we now can make use of genetic testing to gain the certainty that Homer's protagonists seem to lack. The consequence of this ignorance is that Telemachus' mission to find his father, a social and cultural mission, is in part founded on the attempt to prove a biological connection. There is a fundamental split between female knowledge (the mother does know the birth of the child, as Athena grants: at least Penelope bore him) and paternal ignorance. Consider Katz' remarks on the identity of Telemachus: "[T]he biological 'fact' of his birth anchors his identity and provides the reference point for his assumption of the role of Odysseus' replacement."²¹ On the teleological reading of the poem, Telemachus' ignorance about his birth is overcome. Primarily, this is due to the nobility Telemachus shows in helping his father kill the suitors; but a hint at their genetic connection and its ideological importance is also offered by Helen, when she claims in book 4 that Telemachus is the spitting image of his father. The doubt that he is truly his father's son is retroactively dissolved, and the poem upholds a certain ideology in abolishing Telemachus' initial skepticism. Of course, it is possible to cling to that skepticism and maintain that there is forever a gap between the impossible knowledge that Telemachus proclaims in the opening book and his belief that he has attained that knowledge by the poem's end. But rather than follow this path, we can ask a more basic question: does the question of genetic identity exhaust Telemachus' skepticism at *Odyssey* 1.217?

οὐ γάρ πώ τις ἑὸν γόνον αὐτὸς ἀνέγω.

[No one recognizes *their own begetting*.]

(translation modified)

The problem is that knowing one's own "begetting," one's γόνος, is not simply a matter of knowing the identity of the parents. Imagine that Telemachus did have access to his birth. Imagine that a god told him, for certain, that Penelope and Odysseus had sex and that his birth was the consequence. Would that satisfy him? Would the brute physical fact of sex between two parents itself be enough to give him peace, restoring him to the aristocratic status he seems to question?²² What is elided here, by focusing on one aspect of the process of genetic inheritance, is the reason that the question is asked in the first place. Telemachus, who is on the point of manhood and is entering a social situation where his own role is far from clear, wants to know about his own begetting. But he surely wants this in order to a find a solution to the problem of what he should now do.²³ Telemachus' hope is less to find who sexually produced him and more to find out what his parents want from him, and that hope returns him to the origin of his being, the overlapping desires of the parents that brought him into the world. His desire, then, is not something that is merely his; it is always something searched for outside of himself, in what others want from him. Here, it is worth emphasizing that *not* knowing has benefits: it allows Telemachus to organize his life in step with what he believes to be the desires of others.

If we were to translate this scenario into psychoanalytic terms, we would say that Telemachus is confronted with the enigma of the Other's desire, with the question of what the Other (here, most obviously the elusive desire of his absent father) wants from him.²⁴ If there is an answer to that question, the riddle of his existence might be answered. Indeed, herein lies the force of the psychoanalytic concept of trauma. This has little to do with any physical form of wounding or physical loss—it is conceptually possible that a severe physical wound could be quite untraumatic—and is instead concerned with a different kind of absence: the absence of any sure response from the outside world to the problem of what human subjects want. In Lacan's language, there is no "Other of the Other," or "the Other lacks." The lack in the self (the origin of our desire) is thus correlative to a lack in the Other—since no symbolic system that promises to provide a sure place for the subject in the world can ever come to the subject complete, it always generates further questions. These concepts can point us in a useful interpretative direction. For in the Homeric poems, there are a series of stories that seem to relate a violent physical wounding to the more existential problem of what that wounding means. Indeed, I will suggest that humans, in the *Odyssey*, are constituted by the lack of any ultimate answer to the riddle of their existence, and the series of riddles of identity that confront us as we read the *Odyssey* are both an endorsement of this truth and a subtle attempt to veil it and render it bearable. Indeed, any answer might seem better than the terror of the insistent, enigmatic question, what does the Other want from me?²⁵

This book attempts to reread the Homeric poems in light of these shifts in critical emphasis. In chapters 1–3, I examine three tales in the *Odyssey* where characters undergo a physical loss that results in significant symbolic consequences. They are all narratives of trauma, of a primal wounding that defines the human condition by introducing desire into the self. They are also stories of surprise. For part of what is traumatic about the wound is that the victims fail to foresee it. The wounds are experienced not by humans but by a series of figures who are a curious mixture of the human and the divine: the Phaeacians, the Cyclopes, and the sea god Proteus. These strange creatures are forced to ask the kind of question that Telemachus confronts. What is crucial, in all three cases, is that these species believe themselves to be impervious to any wound to the self. They share a belief in their own infallibility and believe themselves to be perfect, self-sufficient, and thus free from desire. They lack a lack. This distinguishes them not only from humans but also from the ordinary Homeric gods, for even the most powerful of the gods, Zeus, is clearly vulnerable to deception and knows himself to be so. He can lie and be lied to in return.²⁶ Proteus, the Cyclopes, and the Phaeacians stand in sharp contrast to this. Proteus is characterized by his unerring prophetic knowledge (νημερτής); the Phaeacians have the uncanny ability to return every visitor home successfully, and they boast of the open relationship they have with the gods, who never deceive them; the asocial Cyclopes believe themselves to be superior to the gods. These beings are more "godlike" than the gods themselves, for they possess the sort of infallibility that it might be tempting to associate with an omnipotent god but that is clearly lacking in the anthropomorphic presentations of the dwellers on Olympus. This makes these figures worthy of special attention. But what is of particular importance is that all three stories revolve around the traumatic moment when these figures lose belief in their own infallibility. A physical wound thus cannot be divorced from its psychic consequences: it destroys not only the figures' idealized versions of themselves but also their trust in their ability to control the world around them.

These stories seem to depict the entrance of superhuman species into the incomplete and troubling human world. But, as fantastic beings, these species also are a kind of caricature of certain human ways of avoiding or ignoring this imperfect world. We should refuse any easy separation between the human and nonhuman, the realistic and the fantastic, in the *Odyssey*. Rather, we should see how the fantasized beasts provide clues to the underlying logic of human behavior. The *Odyssey* provides a series of "fantasies we live by."

The poem is also deeply aetiological, but in a more sophisticated and ambitious sense than is usually understood. For the "cause" that these narratives of trauma seek to pinpoint is the cause of our desire; the narratives seek to explain what human beings lack, not the origin of what they have. Rather than looking for an origin that can neatly explain how a present circumstance is linked to a past event, the *Odyssey* tries to show, in a series of mythical tales, the origin of the very desire to seek. It thus reflects on the problem that inspires aetiological searches. For these aetiological tales in the *Odyssey* explore the reasons behind a human tendency to seek aetiologies. These narratives can also be read as a commentary on the general mood of nostalgia that drives the poem. We see infallible creatures become human at the moment they start a search to recover something of themselves that has been lost. But because the narrative emphasizes the impossibility of this project, the possibility of any project of reclamation, including the return of Odysseus, is put into question.

The rest of this book builds on the insights of the opening three chapters. Once I have established the importance of the narrative of desire, I try to show how much of the actions of the *Iliad* and the *Odyssey* can be seen as a response to it. Desiring things is a way of domesticating the problem of desire itself— we desire something to keep at bay the impact of the fact that we desire. In chapter 4, I suggest that a concomitant truth to the narrative's concern with the role of human desire and fantasy in constructing our symbolic worlds is an awareness of the tenuousness and vulnerability of those worlds. I consider the role of stones in Odysseus' interactions with the Cyclopes and Phaeacians. I argue that stones appear at crucial moments in both narratives and function as a sign of the fragility of the human condition that awaits both groups. Stones signify the human separation from the realm of the inanimate but also remind us of our vulnerable, temporary hold on our animate existences. They are constant reminders of how our cultural existence is premised on the possibility of an absolute loss of culture itself. Stones in themselves are also utterly senseless and lacking in form yet are all the more fascinating because of this. "Homer's people"[27] are characterized by their confrontations with, and efforts to tame, this senselessness. In chapter 5, I try to rethink the significance of the *Odyssey*'s discourse of trickery, or *metis*, by examining its relationship to loss. Odysseus' trickery can only work by manipulating the desires of others. It is thus dependent on their own perception of their losses. But if the *Odyssey* allows us to indulge in the cleverness of Odysseus' tricks, it also hints at more unsavory aspects of this *metis*. Odysseus not only appears as a clever human figure but also closely resembles an all-powerful trickster who always wins. Because of this, his trickery seems to open up a possible world where there is no space for desire, because the failure of his tricks is unthinkable.

Chapters 6 and 7 try to link the problems of loss with the logic of Homeric violence—particularly the actions of Achilles after the death of Patroclus, but also the violence at the end of the *Odyssey*. They link the problems of trauma with the destructive impact of Odysseus' trickery. His ability to unify the troops in *Iliad* 2 and 10 is the subject of chapter 6; his success in the *Odyssey* in imposing his notion of order on his companions and, later, on the suitors is the subject of chapter 7. But I try to avoid the conventional humanist identification with the hero—preserving a belief in his good intentions—and read these episodes from the perspective of those who die as a result of Odysseus' leadership. *Metis*, in these chapters, becomes identified with a kind of ideological control, while Odysseus' success as a leader leads to the death of those around him. Indeed, Odysseus is persistently associated with death throughout both poems. This is the dark side of his cunning, the end point to which his cunning inexorably leads. He is eerily able to bring the concept of loss to others (the Phaeacians and Cyclopes, who believed themselves to be impervious to it), to manipulate others through their fears of loss, and ultimately to bring about their deaths because of this. This complex conflation of Odysseus' use of power with the effects of that power (the death of so many of those around him) can allow us to see the workings of ideology that keep the Greek communities together in the poems. But precisely because such workings are put on display, we are justified in seeing the poems as contributing to their critique.

The final two chapters consider the problem of gender in the *Odyssey* by examining the interdependence of sexual difference and sexual desire. I first argue that the fantasized, all-too-perfect world of Phaeacia is a world that is free of sexual difference and thus also free of desire. Indeed, it is only with the intervention of Odysseus as a possible husband of Nausicaa that desire as such enters Phaeacia, banishing the impossibly perfect universe of harmonious genders that seemed to exist before his arrival. Sexual difference itself, the desire for sexual harmony with another sex, becomes a sign of a lack that characterizes humans. The final chapter uses this insight to revisit the reunion of Penelope and Odysseus. I build on much of the recent scholarship that has paid close attention to what Penelope wants. If we have learned, from events on Phaeacia, that any perfect sexual harmony or idealized "like-mindedness" between two people is impossible, then this needs to be incorporated into our understanding of the encounter between Odysseus and his wife. The bed scene then becomes less about Odysseus' reclamation of Penelope and more about his belated recognition of the gap that separates the real Penelope (with her own desires, in all their enigmatic complexity) from Odysseus' fantasy of her. To gain one, he has to lose the other.

My reading of the poems may seem iconoclastic, taking away the kinds of comfort that certain sorts of teleological readings provide. But in offering an alternate and more complex picture of the ethics of these works, I hope they also become more interesting. For both poems do more than offer us a worldview; they show us a certain kind of worldview coming into being, faltering, and nearly dissolving. There is more to be learned from these poems if we pay attention to the details of this process.

I

Polyphemus

The Blinding of a Cyclops

The plot of the *Odyssey* depends on a single act of its hero: the blinding of the Cyclops. For the blinding creates the cosmic opposition between Poseidon and the rest of the gods that is responsible for the series of delays in arriving at Ithaca that *are* the poem—the loss of Odysseus' crew, the suffering of the hero, the prolonged attempt to regain his power in Ithaca. Odysseus, at the beginning of the poem, propels himself into a space between two women who promise to satisfy his desires (Penelope and Calypso). But this space, the space of the journey itself, is opened up by and linked to his encounter with the Cyclops. The Cyclops' anger at the loss of his own eye, followed by the Cyclops' curse on Odysseus, does not give Odysseus the object of his desire (Ithaca, his *oikos*, Penelope), but it does give him the space to desire those missing objects. It allows Odysseus not to have what he wants and thus to continue to desire it.

But rather than going directly to Odysseus' feelings and motivations in this encounter—the well-trodden path that involves trying to make sense out of the hero's motives and ultimate ethical responsibility for the blinding—I propose instead to look at the blinding from the perspective of its victim. For the critical emphasis on Odysseus might cause us to overlook the genuinely traumatic consequences of the blinding on the Cyclops. We can in part follow the lead of critics who see this episode as a strange perversion of the rituals of exchange. But the exchange is less one of objects than of loss itself; the episode stages acts of "negative reciprocity" that are nevertheless productive because they set desire in motion. The Cyclops loses an eye, which will never return to him, and is consequently given a desire for this lost object by Odysseus. Odysseus, in exchange, gets the deferred desire for Penelope and his fatherland. The encounter means radically different things to each party, and if we pay attenton to these differences, we can perhaps learn something about the *Odyssey*'s inquiry into the origins of human identity and the relationship of identity to desire.

Naming and Identity

We can begin with that most basic indicator of identity, the Cyclops' name. For when does Polyphemus become Polyphemus? When is Polyphemus named? Within book 9, the name of this Cyclops, *Poly-phemus*, does not appear until after his blinding by Odysseus, and it is far from clear that it even appears as a name at this point in the poem. At 9.403 we hear the word *Polyphemus* uttered for the first time, when the blinded Cyclops has just called out for help, prompting a surprised response from the other Cyclopes.

> Τίπτε τόσον, Πολύφημ', ἀρημένος ὧδ' ἐβόησας
> νύκτα δι' ἀμβροσίην, καὶ ἀΰπνους ἄμμε τίθησθα;
>
> (*Od.* 9.403–4)

[Why Polyphemos, what do you want with all this outcry through the immortal night and have made us all thus sleepless?]

This is the first time that the word *Polyphemus* is associated with this Cyclops. Only after the fellow Cyclopes call this out is the name *Polyphemus* applied to the single Cyclops blinded by Odysseus (9.407, 446). By contrast, within his narrative Odysseus never calls the Cyclops he blinds Polyphemus; in the run up to the blinding, he always addresses him as "Cyclops." This suggests that Odysseus is reacting to the single eye in the middle of the forehead of his adversary. There is thus an important change in the nomenclature of the Cyclops within *Odyssey* 9: before the blinding, Odysseus' adversary is a Cyclops; after the blinding, he is called Polyphemus.[1]

We should look more closely at the words of surprise uttered by the Cyclopes in response to the cry for help from the fellow member of their species. Why are the Cyclopes so surprised by this cry for help? The most convincing answer is that they have never before heard such a cry from another Cyclops. Indeed, why should they have? Odysseus, as narrator, has gone to some lengths to describe their self-sufficiency, which suggests that they never need help. Their surprise produces the naming of the Cyclops. We witness the moment when an adjectival cluster *(poly-phemus)* is first associated with the blinded Cyclops: the Cyclopes essentially call out, "Why on earth, Polyphemus, 'chatterbox,' 'man of much speech,' are you shouting?" The cluster is only then grafted, by the narrator Odysseus, as a name onto a referent: the helpless, blinded Cyclops. The Cyclopean surprise is a reaction to the first attempt at communication by one of their number, a breaking of a perennial Cyclopean silence. Their rude awakening by the blinded Cyclops is evidence not merely of a disturbed night's sleep but of an awakening from a much longer sleep. For Odysseus' tale stages both the first baptism of a Cyclops and, simultaneously, the Cyclopes' entrance as a species into the realm of linguistic exchange.²

The crucial point here is that we need not assume that the blinded Cyclops' plea for help is evidence of prior "minimal civilization norms."³ For this assumption cannot help us explain the surprise exhibited in their words at 9.403–4. Rather than repudiating the words of the narrating Odysseus about the Cyclopes, we should take them at face value.

> τοῖσιν δ'οὔτ' ἀγοραὶ βουληφόροι οὔτε θέμιστες,
> ἀλλ' οἵ γ' ὑψηλῶν ὀρέων ναίουσι κάρηνα
> ἐν σπέσσι γλαφυροῖσι, θεμιστεύει δὲ ἕκαστος
> παίδων ἠδ' ἀλόχων, <u>οὐδ' ἀλλήλων ἀλέγουσι</u>.
>
> (9.112–15)

[These people have no institutions, no meetings for counsels;
rather they make their habitations in caverns hollowed
among the peaks of the high mountains, and each one is the law
for his own wives and children, and cares nothing about the others.]

Before *Odyssey* 9, the Cyclopes are perfectly monadic. They are a species of ones who are self-sufficient and whose self-sufficiency makes communication unnecessary. This all changes when a certain unnamed Cyclops (though they are all unnamed, part of a species that has no need of names) meets Odysseus in his guise as Outis, "No one." After this meeting, in response to a cry for help, they no longer are heedless of each other. The phrase that once applied to them—<u>οὐδ' ἀλλήλων ἀλέγουσι</u> [they care nothing for each other]—no longer applies. In response to his blinding, one Cyclops resorts to an attempt to communicate with the others, which in turn functions as an attempt to gain help in healing his recent wound, the loss of his single eye.

The Cyclopes are one-dimensional beings and thus have no need for communication. This is reflected in their most significant physical feature, the single big eye in the middle of their forehead. Accordingly, they form an entirely static community of ones, whose self-sufficiency, in its perfection, renders them oblivious to any meaningful historical change. It is through their meeting with Odysseus/Outis—a figure of negativity—that this is forever altered. Just as the one eye of the one-eyed Cyclops is removed, poked out by the stabbing Odysseus,⁴ so, too, the monadic community of ones is destroyed, as the blindness leads the Cyclops to begin to forge a link with the fellow members of his species. The blinding thus anticipates a future when the Cyclopes will no longer be self-sufficient ones, alone on their separate mountaintops.

The blinding of the Cyclops, the removal of his central eye, destroys his wholeness and introduces him to a world beyond his previous self-sufficiency. An external negativity—in the shape of Odysseus as Outis—is transferred, in the act of blinding, into the center of the Cyclops. We can now see further significance in the new name of the Cyclops; because he has lost his one eye, he is no longer a *Kukl-ops*. His former singular identity as a monadic being is destroyed at the moment he is introduced into the realm of language. Though he is now a person "of much speech" *(polyphemos)*, there is as yet nothing positive we can say about him—though we can, at least, say what he is not. He is no longer one-eyed and thus is not a Cyclops.

We are now in a better position to reassess the significance of the name *Polyphemus*. For scholars have noticed the appropriateness of the meaning "much fame," inasmuch as the blinding portrayed in *Odyssey* 9 will provide Polyphemus (and Odysseus) with *kleos* (fame).⁵ We should be more precise. Polyphemus' access to *kleos* depends on his prior entrance to language, and this in turn is dependent on his loss of his eye.⁶ Here, by way of contrast, we can make use of Lynn-George's analysis of *kleos* in the *Iliad*. For Lynn-George, the crucial question of the *Iliad* is to what extent *kleos* helps balance the inevitability of loss. Lynn-George comments on the "language of Achilles" in *Iliad* 9:

> In the space of . . . [the] silence [of Achilles' language] the epic produces a statement which profoundly questions the conditions of its possibility as well as its worth. Hence it is here, beyond the limits of a restricted economy, beyond the achievements of plunder and the acquisition of possessions, that the language of Achilles finally confronts and tests the limits of language, life, and the music of the lyre—by questioning, implicitly, in relation to man's mortality, the possibility of any meaningful form of immortality in song, an epic "song" which this "language of Achilles" threatens to silence in the sailing for home. The *Iliad* thus structures itself as a question in celebration: does *kleos* ever balance the loss?⁷

The trauma narrative of *Odyssey* 9 suggests the need for a radical inversion of this *Iliadic* question; rather than asking whether *kleos* balances loss, it demonstrates that without loss there can be no language and therefore no *kleos;* language and, consequently, *kleos* are symptoms of this loss.⁸

We can now turn to classic structuralist (and, indeed, poststructuralist) interpretations of the episode and draw attention to what these interpretations overlook. Structuralists have emphasized that the Cyclopes violate a series of human laws, distinguishing their species from the realm of the human. Burkert, for example, provides four violations: man with weapon against unarmed savage, the sober against the drunkard, the seeing against the blind, the master of language against the stupid. Vidal-Naquet has drawn attention to the perversion of sacrifice and the Cyclopes' cannibalism as evidence of impiety.[9] The problem is that such criticism inevitably identifies (morally) with the position of Odysseus, which is in turn seen as representing Greek ethics as such. The Cyclopes are thus already judged by these ethical terms of reference, regardless of their position. But the Cyclopes reject these moral terms of reference *tout court*. What is overlooked in the tracing of this series of individual broken laws is that the Cyclopes are quite simply outside the law. This is represented in book 9 by their lack of concern for the supreme figure of authority, Zeus.

> οὐ γὰρ Κύκλωπες Διὸς αἰγιόχου ἀλέγουσιν
> οὐδὲ θεῶν μακάρων, ἐπεὶ ἦ πολὺ φέρτεροί εἰμεν.
>
> (*Od.* 9.275–76)
>
> [The Cyclopes do not concern themselves over Zeus of the aegis, nor any of the rest of the blessed gods, since we are far better.]

The rejection of this law cancels out any significance of the others, insofar as it means that the Cyclopes are a law unto themselves: θεμιστεύει δὲ ἕκαστος (*Od.* 9.114). They are not beholden to any law at all, insofar as the law is a necessarily social mechanism that regulates ties between people.

We are left with two interpretive possibilities. A critical identification with Odysseus and his moral universe is in and of itself not the problem; it is certainly a viable position. But not explicitly recognizing this position does lead to difficulties; for it too often brings with it assertions of an alleged morality of the "poem" or "poet" (or, more ambitiously, of the human) and fails to notice that this moral system is put into question by the completeness of the Cyclopes' rejection of it. This has meant that critics have generally ignored the significance of the words of the Cyclops about Odysseus—words that I will look at in detail later. For now, let us affirm that the Cyclopes' rejection of the law of Zeus is simply not of the same order as their other violations (cannibal against grain/meat eater, armed against not armed, etc.), which are properly differences that are traced from an identification with the perceived moral qualities of Odysseus. The rejection of the law of Zeus signposts the interchange between Odysseus and the Cyclops as a failed interchange. They themselves have no common terms of reference by which their respective behavior can be judged.¹⁰

The suggestion that the Cyclopes and Odysseus live in different moral universes is certainly less bold than my earlier suggestion that the blinding of the Cyclops announced the entrance of the Cyclopes to language as such. For the stronger thesis meets with an obvious objection: is it not self-evidently the case that the Cyclopes do have access to language? After all, the Cyclops who is soon to be blinded by Odysseus appears to have no trouble communicating with him, and his fellow Cyclopes respond to his cry for help, regardless of their surprise. Even if there is a failure to communicate in moral terms, the failure itself seems to be registered in language. In what follows, I try to defend the stronger thesis by taking a closer look at the Cyclopean language. For what sort of language can there be between members of a species that are self-sufficient and without any needs?¹¹ If the Cyclopes are speaking beings, they are so only to the extent that they speak a language that is completely irrelevant to their lives. Can a language that is not a social phenomenon be a language at all? Part of what the *Odyssey* is doing, in one of its most important episodes, is giving us a test case: can we imagine a world where language itself exists but is divorced from its habitual function as means of communication between members of a species? The Cyclops' language is used to keep other species out, not to communicate with members of the same species within.

Cyclopes and Psychoses

The deficiencies of this Cyclopean language will become clearer by contrast with the sort of words that Cyclops (now Polyphemus) utters after his blinding. But we can elaborate the deficiencies further by way of a theoretical detour into contemporary theories of naming, in particular the dispute between "descriptivism" and "antidescriptivism." The relevance of such theory for critics of the *Odyssey* has been admirably demonstrated in the work of John Peradotto.¹² It is from his book that I borrow a useful summary by John Searle of the essence of the descriptivist versus antidescriptivist controversy.

> According to the classical theory, names, if they are really names, necessarily have a reference and no sense at all. According to the Fregean theory, they essentially have a sense and only contingently have a reference. They refer if and only if there is an object that satisfies their sense. In the first theory proper names are *sui generis*, and indeed for Plato (in the *Theaetetus*) and Wittgenstein (in the *Tractatus*) they are the special connecting link between words and

world; in the second theory proper names are only a species of disguised definite descriptions: every one is equivalent in meaning to a definite description which gives an explicit formulation of its sense. According to the first theory, naming is prior to describing; according to the second, describing is prior to naming, for a name only names by describing the object it names.[13]

At first glance, the naming of Polyphemus might seem to provide evidence for the descriptivist position—the theory that argues that describing is prior to naming. For the theory of the antidescriptivists is dependent on an act of "primal baptism," whereby a name is contingently grafted onto a referent. All names, the antidescriptivist position argues, can be traced back via a causal chain of links to a series of such contingent baptisms. The baptism of Polyphemus, however, suggests just the opposite. His name surely comes from a set of descriptive features already there: he becomes Polyphemus because of his effusive wailings, and so the name makes sense. For the "sense" of his name exists independently of any referent, and the word *polyphemus* becomes a name when this contingent chatterbox fulfills the sense of that word. But before giving in to the descriptivist position, we should look at the theoretical dispute a little more closely. Let us do this by returning to a further argument on behalf of the descriptivist position by Searle himself, which I will follow with a psychoanalytic critique of it by Slavoj Zizek.[14]

To try to defeat the claims of antidescriptivists, Searle constructs a hypothetical tribe where every use of names fits descriptivist criteria.

> Imagine that everybody in the tribe knows everybody else and that newborn members of the tribe are baptized at ceremonies attended by the entire tribe. Imagine, furthermore, that as the children grow up they learn the names of people as well as the local names of mountains, lakes, streets, houses, etc., by ostension. Suppose also that there is a strict taboo in this tribe against speaking of the dead, so that no one's name is ever mentioned after his death. Now the point of the fantasy is simply this: As I have described it, this tribe has an institution of proper names used for reference in exactly the same way that our names are used for reference, but *there is not a single use of a name in the tribe that satisfies the causal chain of communication theory.*[15]

In this tribe, there is no act of "primal baptism" as such, no act that senselessly attaches name to referent because the former is the latter's name, but only public, open determination of referents (the naming ceremonies attended by the entire tribe) and naming by ostension. In this imaginary tribe, Searle has taken away the use of the "causal chain" to determine the names of its inhabitants.

Accordingly, no member of the tribe will ever lack a story he or she can tell about the names of objects, and no member will need to refer to a primal baptism. Because of this, Searle believes that he has proved that his descriptivist theory is logically prior to antidescriptivism. But what is the problem with this argument?

Zizek has emphasized that there is simply something missing in this tribe's language.

> If we are really concerned with language in the strict sense, with language as a social network in which meaning exists only in so far as it is intersubjectively recognized—with language which, by definition, cannot be "private"—then it must be part of the meaning of each name that it refers to a certain object *because it is this name*, because others use this name to designate the object in question: every name, in so far as it is part of common language, implies this self-referential, circular moment.[16]

The Lacanian term for this tautological moment is *master signifier,* a signifier that itself has no signified but that gives meaning to the other signifiers in the signifying chain by halting their slide. As Zizek argues, Searle's own example suggests an awareness of the need for such a master signifier in its prohibition of the naming of the dead. The prohibition is necessary in order to foreclose the entrance of such an antidescriptivist naming, a signifier that has no signified. In Lacanian terms, this prohibition rules out the replacement of the real, dead father with a symbol for him, a symbol that Lacan calls the "Name-of-the-Father." This ultimately provides entrance to the symbolic world of language that is our home as speaking beings. This Name-of-the-Father—straddling the subjective and objective modes of the genitive, belonging both to the father and to the child who is named by the father—produces a split between the human being who plays out the role of paternity and the symbolic mandate of paternity itself. The human being is always secondary to this idealized ability to regulate the social world, to pass on a name from generation to generation. In Searle's tribe, we have a world where communication between generations is short-circuited. But we can transfer this to Homer's world. In the terms of the shared ideology of heroes in the *Iliad,* Searle's taboo on uttering the name of the dead father is simply a rejection of the realm of *kleos aphthiton,* the world of "undying fame." This world both precedes heroes (the language/tales of the fathers of heroes) and holds out the promise of some kind of existence after their biological death. For "undying" fame is correlative to dying heroes.

Searle's tribe therefore has an impossible relationship to language, and its taboo is a symptom of this: a recognition *and* denial of that impossibility. For this very reason, it is illuminating for an analysis of conditions on the island of the Cyclopes. Let us extrapolate the possible consequences of this prohibition on the naming of the dead in Searle's tribe. Imagine what would happen to this tribe if an outsider arrived and simply named one of their dead ancestors or, alternatively, if one of the tribe overslept one day and missed a naming ceremony. Either of these acts would bring a dimension of trauma into their world, a world that had until then been built on a collective flight from just such a traumatic encounter. Perhaps they might even remember a prophecy, buried in the past, that foretold the emergence of just such a traumatic event, a prophecy that would be the first proper attempt to make sense out of and thus heal this trauma.[17] So, only after this element of trauma emerged would the tribe begin to recognize itself as a linguistic species.

It is also worth sketching the obvious differences in these tribes. Searle's tribe has an open language, where every act of naming is linked to sense. Homer's Cyclopean tribe has the exact opposite of this: there are no social institutions (the Cyclopes lack assemblies), and far from including all the members of the species in every naming ritual, the Cyclopes ignore each other.[18] But, ultimately, are not both these mythical species just different ways of avoiding the traumatic nature of the human encounter with language as such? The Cyclopes refuse to speak; the rituals of Searle's tribe ensure that any senseless dimension of language is taboo. No father in Searle's tribe will ever have to force his child to trust his words, and, correlatively, no father will ever have to use his authority in a traumatic way: "The object is called that *because I said so!*" If this authoritarian dimension is officially missing in this utopia, it is nevertheless implicitly recognized in the taboo.

This might make us look more closely at the workings of paternal authority among the Cyclopes. Ancient commentators at least as early as the time of Aristotle were extremely anxious concerning the parentage of the Cyclopes, particularly of Polyphemus: "[S]ince neither his father nor his mother is a Cyclops, in what sense can he be said to be one?"[19] The lack of generational normality is precisely what allows Polyphemus to remain oblivious of the law of Zeus. For the Cyclopean universe is a peculiar one. There are certainly fathers on the island—it is emphasized that their civilization is an amalgam of nuclear families—yet these fathers themselves have no fathers. There are thus only *real* fathers among the Cyclopes and no Name-of-the-Father—an ideal, symbolic figure of authority against which the Cyclopes could judge themselves. If human fathers are constantly plagued by their separation from the symbolic mandates they are required to fulfill, the Cyclopes have no such doubts. They can lay down the law, continue to say *"because I said so,"* but they need never remember a time when it was said to them.

We can now return to the apparent "descriptivism" suggested in the baptism of Polyphemus; for such a reading only works on a literal level. If we instead read the episode allegorically as announcing the entrance of Polyphemus (and then the Cyclopes) into language, we can emphasize that the blinding provides the conditions of possibility for language, by creating a void at the heart of Polyphemus and thus the possibility of a master signifier—a signifier that is attached to nothing more than this void. The name *Polyphemus* thus does indeed describe the speaking being, but this naming only occurs in response to the loss of the crucial defining feature of the Cyclops, his eye.[20] The naming is not a direct act of description but only occurs simultaneously with the creation of this void. As we will soon see, it is the role of any master signifier to try (but fail) to represent this void.

Need, Demand, Desire

Polyphemus, then, is introduced to language through his blinding. To help clarify the effects of this entrance, we can turn to Lacan's theoretical attempts to explain the consequences of the child's entrance to language by differentiating between need, demand, and desire. This Lacanian story about the child should also alert us to the strange way in which the story of the Cyclops' blinding manipulates the social roles of fathers and sons, turning a hyperautonomous adult (before the blinding) into a helpless child.

For Lacan, need functions at the level of the biological, as a child depends on others for its most elementary biological need. Need, then, always relates to something specific—a particular item (e.g., food)—that can of course be satisfied. However, an important change occurs when this need is mediated by language, when the child enters the symbolic. At this point, the request for the fulfillment of need is accompanied by a *demand* of the subject, a demand for recognition. Beyond any biological need articulated by the child, there is the demand for the love of the mother. This demand, in Lacan's words, "cancels out the particularity of anything which might be granted by transmuting it into a proof of love."[21] The child asks for food but wants the mother's love. At this point, at the failure of demand, desire appears, heralding a wish on the part of the subject for a (mythical) previous totality, wholeness; desire is a certain leftover of demand after all the specific, satisfied needs have been subtracted from it.

With this terminology in mind, let us return to our blinded Cyclops. After the removal of his eye, Polyphemus produces a loud wail—a wail that is worth a closer look.

> σμερδαλέον δὲ μέγ' ᾤμωξεν, περὶ δ' ἴαχε πέτρη,
> ἡμεῖς δὲ δείσαντες ἀπεσσύμεθ'. αὐτὰρ ὁ μοχλὸν
> ἐξέρυσ' ὀφθαλμοῖο πεφυρμένον αἵματι πολλῶι.
> τὸν μὲν ἔπειτ' ἔρριψεν ἀπὸ ἕο χερσὶν ἀλύων,
> αὐτὰρ ὁ Κύκλωπας μεγάλ' ἤπυεν, οἵ ῥά μιν ἀμφὶς
> ᾤκεον ἐν σπήεσσι δι' ἄκριας ἠνεμοέσσας.
>
> (*Od.* 9.395–400)

[He gave a giant horrible cry and the rocks rattled
to the sound, and we scuttled away in fear. He pulled the timber
out of his eye, and it blubbered with plenty of blood, then
when he had frantically taken it in his hands and thrown it
away, he cried aloud to the other Cyclopes, who live
around him in their own caves along the windy pinnacles.]

Crucial here is the move from the initial scream of pain to the cry to the other Cyclopes. The scream is the Cyclops' shuddering reaction to the loss of his eye; for the Cyclops, something is now missing and needs to be replaced; like a child, he recognizes his dependence.[22] However, in his second cry, to his fellow Cyclopes, this cry of pain immediately moves to an intersubjective level. Any prior self-sufficiency is destroyed, and the Cyclops looks to others in an attempt to heal his wound. At this point, the Cyclopean cry functions as a demand.[23] This is the import of the Cyclopean reply.

> εἰ μὲν δὴ μή τίς σε βιάζεται οἶον ἐόντα,
> νοῦσον γ' οὔ πως ἔστι Διὸς μεγάλου ἀλέασθαι·
> ἀλλὰ σύ γ' εὔχεο πατρὶ Ποσειδάωνι ἄνακτι.
>
> (*Od.* 9.410–12)

[If alone as you are none uses violence on you,
why, there is no avoiding the sickness sent by great Zeus;
so you had better pray to your father, the lord Poseidon.]

Several aspects of the Cyclopes' reply need to be emphasized. First, the thing that had always been avoided (Zeus) can no longer be avoided. Polyphemus is now subject to the law, the law of the father (represented by Zeus' sickness). Further, there is a nuanced use of the adjective οἶος, "alone." For in a profound way, the Cyclops is alone for the first time.[24] Since he is no longer self-sufficient, his loneliness—the possibility of needing help and having it rejected—is real. Before the blinding, the Cyclops was always on his own, in the perfection of his self-sufficiency, but only now is he truly alone, in that he recognizes that he is apart from others on whom he is dependent—in that he feels lonely. Finally, and most importantly, his new subjection to this "sickness of Zeus" means that he must pray to his father. This supplication needs to be considered in detail.

Fathers and Fallibility

We can best understand Polyphemus' appeal to his fellow Cyclopes, his prayer to his father, and his recollection of the prophecy of Odysseus' arrival if we recognize their fundamental similarity. For they are all a series of attempts to patch over the loss of the eye, an attempt on the part of the Cyclops to stabilize himself. In the terms outlined in the preceding section of this chapter, they are demands. The fellow Cyclopes cannot provide any help, and he looks elsewhere. Here, we encounter the problem of the father. The Cyclopes, in response to Polyphemus' cry, tell him to appeal to Poseidon, and this is exactly what he does.

> ἀλλ' ἄγε δεῦρ', Ὀδυσεῦ, ἵνα τοι πὰρ ξείνια θείω
> πομπήν τ' ὀτρύνω δόμεναι κλυτὸν ἐννοσίγαιον·
> τοῦ γὰρ ἐγὼ πάϊς εἰμί, πατὴρ δ' ἐμὸς εὔχεται εἶναι.
> αὐτὸς δ', αἴ κ' ἐθέλῃσ', ἰήσεται, οὐδέ τις ἄλλος
> οὔτε θεῶν μακάρων οὔτε θνητῶν ἀνθρώπων.
>
> (*Od.* 9.517–21)

[So come here, Odysseus, let me give you a guest gift
and urge the glorious Shaker of the Earth to grant you conveyance home. For I am his son, he announces himself as my father.
He himself will heal me, if he will, but not any other
one of the blessed gods, nor any man who is mortal.]

Here, we should avoid any simple reading that would suggest that he merely turns to a father who was always/already there; rather, the blinding in a crucial sense *creates* the concept of father for the Cyclops, a concept he never needed before. How?

I have already suggested that the universe of the Cyclopes is static: we can also explain this in terms of its relation to patriarchy. If the Cyclopes have no fathers and do not talk to each other, they nevertheless do have families:

θεμιστεύει δὲ ἕκαστος / <u>παίδων ἠδ' ἀλόχων</u>, οὐδ' ἀλλήλων ἀλέγουσι (*Od.* 9.114–15) [each one is the law for his own wives and children, and cares nothing about the others]. But since adult Cyclopes have no fathers but do have sons, they are in the (impossible) position of being fathers but not sons. Here, we should turn to the workings of the zero-sum game of patriarchy that is the framework for the poem itself. The Cyclopes are a fantasized solution to an endemic patriarchal tension between father and son. There is no generational tension in their society, because there is no generation; they represent a perfectly stable *oikos* frozen in time and place.[25] Within this context, Polyphemus' appeal to Poseidon as father is yet another first. For it is the first time that one of the Cyclopes has ever played the subordinate role of son.

If this passage tells us that a Cyclops is a son for the first time, we still need to explore the relationship between father and son in the *Odyssey*. Here, we can return to the relationship between Telemachus and Odysseus and to Telemachus' famous protestation about the impossibility of knowing one's father.

> τοιγὰρ ἐγώ τοι, ξεῖνε, μάλ' ἀτρεκέως ἀγορεύσω.
> μήτηρ μέν τ' ἐμέ φησι τοῦ ἔμμεναι, αὐτὰρ ἐγώ γε
> οὐκ οἶδ'. οὐ γάρ πώ τις ἑὸν γόνον αὐτὸς ἀνέγνω.
>
> (*Od.* 1.214–16)

[See, I will accurately answer all that you ask me.
My mother says indeed I am his. I for my part
do not know. Nobody really knows his own father.]

Telemachus' words illustrate how the question of paternity has much wider symbolic significance. For this wholehearted skepticism about the figure of the father tells us about the nature of paternal authority. Paternal authority does not in any way give the lie to Telemachus' skepticism; it is rather the other side of the same coin. For if skepticism functions as a pure challenge to all forms of authority, denying that authority any sustenance through rational argumentation (it doubts everything), paternal authority is, conversely, a pure authority that cannot be justified through argument. Because one can never know who one's father might be, any respect for the authority of a father qua father must be a complete leap of faith. This is clearly represented within the *Odyssey* through the uniqueness of the recognition between Telemachus and Odysseus. Though Odysseus can rely on tokens and scars to prove his identity to others, no such proofs can help him with Telemachus.

The link between skepticism and paternity can help explain the recognition scene between Telemachus and Odysseus in book 16, which is highlighted by a debate over whether or not Odysseus is a god. Here is Odysseus' denial.

οὔ τίς τοι θεός εἰμι· τί μ᾽ ἀθανάτοισιν ἐΐσκεις;
ἀλλὰ πατὴρ τεός εἰμι . . .

(*Od.* 16.187–88)

[No, I am not a god. Why liken me to the immortals?
But I am your father . . .]

The play on words here (in both θεός εἰμι . . . τεός εἰμι and οὔ τίς) has been noticed by Goldhill.²⁶ He suggests that the recognition by Telemachus is what is needed to restore the continuity of the *oikos* and that the play on words emphasizes Odysseus' status as mortal and his rejection of an immortal life (associated with his rejection of the offer of Calypso). But a quite different point can be made if we continue to identify with the position of the skeptic. The wordplay of θεός/τεός highlights that an acceptance of one's father is a leap of pure faith, in essence no different from recognizing Odysseus as a god.²⁷ Thus, *polytropic* (perfectly persuasive) Odysseus persuades Telemachus of the impossible: that he is really his father and that he is not a god. But in so doing, he himself moves into an impossible position of pure certainty. Let us look again at Telemachus' line of skepticism οὐ γάρ πώ τις ἑὸν γόνον αὐτὸς ἀνέγνω (*Od.* 1.217). There is not only the pun on "no one" but also a double meaning in *gonon* (already commented on), which can signify both "begetter" and "offspring." In persuading Telemachus that he is his father, Odysseus thus assumes the position of superhuman knowledge (the subject who is supposed to know); he becomes this "no one" who alone knows his offspring. There is once more an uneasy conjunction of power and powerlessness. Odysseus can persuade Telemachus that he is correct, but only by moving into a superhuman position of knowledge, which it is his desire to deny: he is, after all, trying to prove that he is merely a man. We can compare this father-son reunion with the situation of the Cyclops, who has no need to doubt that he knows his son. Insofar as he is asocial, not known by other Cyclopes, why should he? There are simply no other candidates for his son's paternity. When Odysseus convinces Telemachus that he is his father, he is moving into the position of certainty associated with the asocial Cyclops: it is either an impossible, asocial certainty or a certainty that depends on the fantasy of an asocial world. This fundamental impasse is significant for the entire poem, which portrays Odysseus as constantly veering between two poles. He seems to be a figure of limitless *metis*, whose omnipotent powers are always able to facilitate his approach to his telos. But because of, not despite, his *metis*, Odysseus seems to lose any possibility of meaningfully fixing his identity.²⁸

Let us return to Polyphemus to explore further the problem of the father. His appeal to Poseidon begins with an identification with the position of son, followed by a reference to Poseidon's claim to be his father: τοῦ γὰρ ἐγὼ πάϊς εἰμί, πατὴρ δ' ἐμὸς εὔχεται εἶναι (*Od.* 9.519). Polyphemus is introduced to doubt because he has lost his eye; he therefore appeals to his father to heal him and thus return him to a doubt-free universe. But this is precisely what Odysseus declares is impossible.

> "αἲ γὰρ δὴ ψυχῆς τε καὶ αἰῶνός σε δυναίμην
> εὖνιν ποιήσας πέμψαι δόμον Ἄϊδος εἴσω,
> ὡς οὐκ ὀφθαλμόν γ' ἰήσεται οὐδ' ἐνοσίχθων."
> Ὣς ἐφάμην· ὁ δ' ἔπειτα Ποσειδάωνι ἄνακτι
> εὔχετο χεῖρ' ὀρέγων εἰς οὐρανὸν ἀστερόεντα·
> "Κλῦθι, Ποσείδαον γαιήοχε, κυανοχαῖτα·
> εἰ ἐτεόν γε σός εἰμι, πατὴρ δ' ἐμὸς εὔχεαι εἶναι . . ."

(*Od.* 9.523–29)

["I only wish it were certain I could make you reft of spirit
and life, and send you to the house of Hades, as it is certain
that not even the Shaker of the Earth will ever heal your eye for you."
So I spoke, but he then called to the lord Poseidon
in prayer, reaching both arms up toward the starry heaven:
"Hear me, Poseidon who circle the earth, dark-haired. If truly
I am your son, and you acknowledge yourself as my father . . ."]

Polyphemus' appeal is an appeal to a figure of authority to heal his wound. In brief, his appeal to his father, his recognition of his father, is a recognition of his entrance into the world of symbols, the Lacanian symbolic, a recognition of the law of the father. For the father is called upon after the destruction of the Cyclops' self-sufficiency. The appeal to the father is an appeal to an outside source to cover up an internal doubt. But the genie of doubt has now irrevocably left its bottle. This is the point of Odysseus' reply, which hands Polyphemus an elementary lesson concerning the consequences of his entry into language. We should emphasize that Odysseus is quite right. Poseidon will certainly not heal his son, for his status as father is dependent on Polyphemus' entrance into a world of symbols, which in turn comes from the recognition of his dependence on others. Odysseus demonstrates that the lack at the heart of the Cyclops is now constitutive, that his ongoing demands will remain unfilfilled. He introduces Polyphemus to his desire that lies beyond his demands. Polyphemus thus emerges as a mortal subject, and this passage from immortality to mortality gives further point to Odysseus' wry reference to Hades; the certainty that Polyphemus' eye will not be healed is already a certainty that sooner or later he will make the trip to Hades.[29] The Cyclops is pulled back from his psychotic refusal of (the language of) society and now must face his mortality.

This position of the Cyclops mirrors the position of Telemachus. Before the blinding, the Cyclops was certain that he was better than Zeus. His blinding leads to an impasse that results in an appeal to a father to make him whole. Only after this appeal to the father does Odysseus intervene to tell him that his desire will never be fulfilled. This suggests that Polyphemus' appeal to his father is already a kind of recognition that he has suffered loss. This acknowledgment suggests that the paternal function is operative. Even if Poseidon were able to heal him, what he cannot undo is the reality that Polyphemus has suffered loss. The Cyclops can doubt the power of his real father (and his father's ability to make up the loss that he has allowed his son to endure) precisely because the Cyclops has accepted that he has been wounded and because he has rejected the self-certainty that went with his belief in his own wholeness. So, too, Telemachus' doubt of the identity of his real father is a sign that the paternal function is operative.

The origin of language among the Cyclopes thus coincides with the emergence of desire; and it is the convergence of language and desire that allows us to return to the difficulties of the name *Polyphemus*. We have already suggested that the episode cannot function as a myth for descriptivism, because the naming of the Cyclops only occurs as a response to the blinding. But insofar as his name, after the primal baptism by the other Cyclopes, seems to stay forever the same in the poetic tradition that followed, do we not have evidence for the antidescriptivist position; that is, do we not have evidence for *Polyphemus* acting as a rigid designator, in antidescriptivist terms? Let us once more turn to Zizek and his criticism of antidescriptivism.

> The basic problem of antidescriptivism is to determine what constitutes the identity of the designated object beyond the ever-changing cluster of descriptive features—what makes an object identical-to-itself even if all its properties have changed; in other words, how to conceive the objective correlative of the "rigid designator," to the name in so far as it denotes the object in all possible worlds, in all counterfactual situations. What is overlooked, at least in the standard version of antidescriptivism, is that this guaranteeing the identity of an object in all counterfactual situations—through a change of all its descriptive features—is *the retroactive effect of naming itself:* it is the name itself, the signifier, which supports the identity of the object.[30]

In the process of naming itself, in the act of baptism, we act as if there was an objective correlative of the rigid designator. What is forgotten is that the act of naming itself creates the illusion of such a self-identical object. What connects a rigid designator to a self-identical object is the desire of the namer for such an object; and in the naming of the Cyclops in *Odyssey* 9, we see the emergence of a rigid designator—the name *Polyphemus*—at the moment desire is introduced to the Cyclopean species. The other Cyclopes see a talkative, blinded, decentered Cyclops; they call him "chatterbox," which is a description of his qualities. But from this moment on, due to their (and our) desire, this is the name that will be grafted onto him, and it will stay the same in all possible worlds. The episode thus stages the moment when a descriptive cluster pertaining to the Cyclops is misrecognized as a "rigid designator" signifying his identity; but this "identity" is constituted by nothing other than the desire of those who name him. Part of the retroactive power of naming is on display in general critical readings of the episode itself. For surely one of the most profound critical assumptions that underpin understanding of the episode is that the person called Polyphemus in *Odyssey* 9 was *always* Polyphemus. But this is only retroactively the case. The naming of the Cyclops by his fellow beings can provide us with the illusion that this Cyclops was always Polyphemus. But this can only blind *us* to the profound changes in the species that the entrance of Odysseus brings about.

The Cyclopean Split

There is a great range of representations of the Cyclopes in Greek literature, and scholars have long tried to explain the divergences.[31] Nevertheless, it is possible to discern a basic split into two major types, a split that can tell us much more about the significance of the Cyclops' blinding. First, there is the idealized picture of the "golden age" Cyclopes. We can see here the roots of the picture of the pastoral, peaceful Cyclops that appears in bucolic poetry, together with its darker side, the myth of the noble savage. In opposition to this is the *homo faber* tradition of the Cyclopes, most obviously evident in the representation in Hesiod, where they forge the thunderbolts of Zeus.[32] From my previous remarks on Polyphemus' entrance into language proper, we can perhaps begin to see the way in which *Odyssey* 9 makes use of this split between *homo faber* and golden age Cyclopes. *Odyssey* 9 stages the mythical moment when the two traditions meet, a time when the golden age Cyclops becomes Polyphemus as *homo faber*. To substantiate this, we need merely emphasize the inquisitiveness of Polyphemus after the blinding. His blindness leads to a wandering, as he frantically searches both for those responsible for his loss and for allies to help him recover this loss.[33] We can now better understand the point of the vivid depiction of the split Cyclopean home: there is the island they actually live on and the smaller island opposite. The latter is perfectly suited for cultivation, but the Cyclopes—in their self-sufficiency—have no need to cultivate. Is it only a matter of time before Polyphemus' newly found curiosity causes him to build a boat, cross the strait, and discover the second island?[34]

Odysseus' picture of the second island certainly holds out a strong temptation. As Norman Austin has argued, the island is repeatedly defined by what it is not. It is not visited by hunters, nor farmed by farmers, not held by flocks: "It would be difficult to find in Homer, or indeed anywhere else in Greek, a passage of comparable lengths so richly sown with negatives as *Od.* 9.106–148."[35] Austin also notes the shift from the indicative mood to the optative within the negative description: "[T]he Cyclopes had no shipwrights *who might have belabored* (to build) ships, *which might have brought to completion* the many things for which men cross the sea in ships. *They would have belabored* the island to make it also a good settlement."[36] To imagine Polyphemus making this voyage is to swallow him up once more in the normative ethics of Odysseus, who projects a certain set of ethical values onto the island's emptiness. Yet though Odysseus' narrative offers this as a possibility, it stops crucially short of actualizing it. Polyphemus is left hanging. We do not know the values that Polyphemus will invent on the second island or even if the Cyclopes will ever get there. Though Polyphemus is on the verge of self-exploration (indeed, self-creation), at this point his self remains empty, unwritten. Odysseus' narration of his interaction with the Cyclops leaves us with the (utopian as well as dangerous) possibility of a quite different world.[37]

2

Phaeacia

The Impossible Choice of Subjectivity

Odysseus' impact on the Cyclops is explicitly acknowledged in the narrative—he boasts about his victory and denies that the Cyclops can ever be healed, even as we know this boast results in his own deferred return. But his impact on the Phaeacians is just as spectacular. Indeed, their punishment at the hands of Poseidon, who is on the verge of burying their civilization under a mountain when the poem abandons them forever, is a notorious interpretative crux within *Odyssey* scholarship. Odysseus does not boast about his success in convincing them to take him home, nor does he ever acknowledge himself as the agent that destroys their society. It also seems true that the Phaeacians suffer more obliquely. They confront only the possibility of obliteration, not an incurable wound. But a closer attention to the peculiar world of the Phaeacians and its similarities to the world of the Cyclopes can help us make sense out of this strange punishment and the significance of Odysseus' role in it. For what is crucial—and cruel—about the punishment is less its content (the obliteration under a mountain) than its form: because the gods do not fully follow through with their threat, they force the Phaeacians to confront their utter ignorance concerning their very survival.

As we are told, the Phaeacians are both close relations of the Cyclopes and yet opposites. Indeed, this status provides the key to what they have in common. Once, the Phaeacians shared a common home on *Hyper*eia (land beyond the horizon, land of excess) with the "more than men" (ὑπερηνορεόντων) Cyclopes,[1] until the Phaeacians fled because of the Cyclopes' strength. Their flight was a complete one. In contrast to the Cyclopean rejection of civilization, the new Phaeacian world is hypercivilized.[2] Whereas the Cyclopes have no need to plant any crops, the Phaeacians have perfect crops, producing perfect yields without the possibility of failure. The Cyclopes reject the norms of *xenia:* (the established aristocratic rituals of guest-friendship); the Phaeacians pass on every single guest (without failure) to his or her destination. The Cyclopes have neither ships nor need for them, while the Phaeacians have perfect ships that always bring their guests to their destination, without the need of a navigator.[3] This endless, steady stream of successful acts of passage can be linked to the particular way the Phaeacians sail their ships. For the ships do not need to be steered but go to their destination without any pause, as if in an automatic response to the thoughts of the Phaeacians. There is no moment of indecision or time when a Phaeacian seaman pauses to reflect where to go.[4] In this regard, we might pause over the significance of the name of their land, Scheria. The name appears related to σχερός, an adjective suggesting a line without limits.[5] The Phaeacians, it seems, live in a land without beginning or end, where all is seen, known, and thus taken for granted.

This produces some unexpected similarities to the Cyclopes. For like the Cyclopes, the Phaeacians do not seem to doubt themselves. Their peculiar relation both to the gods and to language would seem to justify this. While the Cyclopes reject the gods outright, the Phaeacians are somehow too close to them. Alcinous tells us that the gods have always appeared clearly to the Phaeacians and hide nothing from them, and he goes on to mention that this "closeness" to the gods is shared by the Cyclopes.[6] While the Cyclopes do not communicate at all, the Phaeacians communicate too well. The Cyclopes reject language outright and the possibility of deception that goes with it. The Phaeacians have a perfect language, which also precludes the possibility of deception.

But if Phaeacian society is characterized by the perfection of their mode of exchange—their language is transparent, their transportation of guests perfect—it is not just any society. As with the Cyclopes, it is clearly a patriarchal one. This is evident in the obvious suitability of Nausicaa as a possible wife for Odysseus in a fantasized *oikos*. I will discuss the implications for the poem's construction of gender later. For now, note that the system of patriarchal exchange—the flawless passing on of skills from father to father—fits in well with the picture of the rest of Phaeacian society as it is presented by Alcinous.

> ἀλλ' ἄγε νῦν ἐμέθεν ξυνίει ἔπος, ὄφρα καὶ ἄλλωι
> εἴπηις ἡρώων, ὅτε κεν σοῖς ἐν μεγάροισι
> δαινύηι παρὰ σῆι τ' ἀλόχωι καὶ σοῖσι τέκεσσιν,
> ἡμετέρης ἀρετῆς μεμνημένος, οἷα καὶ ἡμῖν
> Ζεὺς ἐπὶ ἔργα τίθησι <u>διαμπερὲς ἐξέτι πατρῶν</u>.
>
> (*Od.* 8.241–45)

> [[C]ome then, attend to what I say, so that you can tell it
> even to some other hero after this, when in your palace
> you sit at the feasting with your own wife and children beside you,
> remembering our excellence and what Zeus has established
> as our activities, through time, from the days of our fathers.]

Alcinous' words come at a particularly sensitive time; Odysseus has just defeated the Phaeacians in the games, and Alcinous is about to reaffirm (somewhat defensively) what he believes to be the essence of Phaeacian superiority: their skill at dancing and at transporting men homeward on their ships. But the superiority in the system of transportation affirmed by Alcinous is parallel to the Phaeacians' skill in communication. The excellence of the Phaeacians has been passed on unchanged from the time of their fathers, from father to father. Alcinous presumes that Odysseus' return will likewise be to an *oikos*. But what will the message passed on by Odysseus to his wife and children be? It will be a message from a father to a wife and son about a world where messages are passed perfectly from father to son. Phaeacian society is in this respect, too, the exact reverse of that of the Cyclopes. Whereas the Cyclopes' society circumvented patriarchal tension of succession between father and son by freezing the *oikos* in time and thus eliminated generational conflict, the Phaeacians circumvent the tension by providing a utopian solution of a perfect transfer of power from father to son. The Cyclopes were fathers without fathers. There was therefore no gap between the real fathers and the symbolic representation of paternal authority, the Name-of-the-Father. On Phaeacia, because of the perfection of the relationship between father and son, each real father does not fall hopelessly short of an idealized symbol of the father but coincides with it. Both societies, for different reasons, lack a gap between a real father and a symbolic father.

Unfriendly Phaeacians

So the society of the Phaeacians is an idealized, impossible version of a patriarchy. However, this perfection seems to have some complications. For alongside the ability of the Phaeacians to pass on every stranger to his destination is their now notorious "unfriendliness" to strangers.[7] The key to their unfriendliness emerges after the games, when Alcinous recounts a tale told by his father, Nausithous, about the anger of Poseidon.

> Tell me your land, your neighborhood and your city,
> so that our ships, straining with their own purpose, can carry you

> there, for there are no steersmen among the Phaiakians, neither
> are there any steering oars for them, such as other ships have,
> but the ships themselves understand men's thoughts and purposes,
> and they know all the cities of men and their fertile
> fields, and with greatest speed they cross the gulf of the salt sea,
> huddled under a mist and cloud, nor is there ever
> any fear that they may suffer damage or come to destruction.
> Yet this I have heard once on a time from my father, Nausithoos
> who said it, and told me how Poseidon would yet be angry
> with us, because we are convoy without hurt to all men.
> He said that one day, as a well-made ship of Phaiakian
> men came back from a convoy on the misty face of the water,
> he would stun it, and pile a great mountain over our city, to hide it.
> So the old man spoke, and the god might either bring it
> to pass, or it might be left undone, as the god's heart pleases.
>
> (*Od.* 8.555–71)

The Phaeacians are perfect hosts. But they also know that, sooner or later, one of their trips will entail the destruction of themselves and their society. Odysseus' arrival is an accident waiting to happen, but because of this it provides the context for the tension on Phaeacia.[8] The Phaeacians are perfectly willing to pass any ordinary man along; indeed, their identity (as perfect hosts) depends on it. Yet they must also be on the lookout for the more-than-man, the out-of-the-ordinary man who will destroy their perfection. This is the key to their strange mixture of suspicion and kindness. The Phaeacians have an impossibly perfect relation to exchange, and they (unconsciously) seem to know that it is impossible; their entire existence as Phaeacians depends on the disavowal of this possibility.[9] This unconscious knowledge appears in their suspicious attitude toward others. It also helps explain their obsession with Odysseus' identity. The Phaeacians try to determine if Odysseus is different from the succession of other guests transferred to their destinations. Phaeacian civilization is characterized by a constant questioning of the identity of the series of men who arrive, but a questioning (springing from the unconscious seed of doubt sown by Nausithous' prediction) that perennially proves that they have no need to doubt their superiority to others. Their identity is based on never having to think twice, on showing an absence of doubt in transporting strangers to their destination. Yet each new arrival makes them compulsively doubt the absence of doubt; and so they are unfriendly.

From the opposing perspective, Odysseus needs to prove to the Phaeacians that he is "just another man," in order to escape Phaeacia and reach his telos at

Ithaca. The persuasive powers that Odysseus uses in the *Apologoi* in order to get home have been carefully explored by Most.[10] Odysseus' rhetoric hints at the need for a safe passage home and persuades the Phaeacians of the merit of this. In an important sense, he fools the Phaeacians. But from the perspective of the Phaeacians, could they not have been fooled?

The "choice" confronting the Phaeacians is rather more complex. It is a forced choice, which can be illustrated quite concisely by returning to Lacan. In *The Four Fundamental Concepts of Psychoanalysis* (1978), Lacan illustrates the paradox involved in the entrance of the human subject into language with the following "choice": "Your money or your life." This choice is deceptive in that it *precludes* choice. One can only choose life—to choose money entails losing both money and life, and thus subjective status is necessarily haunted by loss.[11] This is the sort of choice that faces the Phaeacians. The basis of Phaeacian society, their uniqueness, is their perfection as hosts. To refuse to pass on Odysseus is to refuse to be perfect hosts and thus to give up on the very quality that makes them Phaeacians. They may unconsciously be suspicious of Odysseus, but to refuse to send him home is to allow that suspicion to enter their conscious existence. Self-knowledge would be akin to self-destruction and the recognition that their ideals of themselves were utterly false. If Odysseus is refused passage, can they ever be sure that anyone else deserves safe passage? They eventually do choose to send him on. This results in the loss of a ship and in the ongoing possibility of loss instantiated in the mountain that threatens to bury them. It is thus relatively unimportant whether or not the Phaeacians are able to escape Odysseus' rhetorical trickery. For sooner or later, they must be fooled. Odysseus merely plays out the role already carved out by Nausithous' prediction, and the loss that comes with his trick is their ticket to subjectivity. In what follows, I look more carefully at the Phaeacians' emergence as subjects and at the price to be paid.

The Emergence of a Limit in a Limitless World

The impossible choice of the Phaeacians can help us show what is at stake in the games of book 8. Laodamas and Euryalus invite Odysseus to participate in order to help assuage any doubt that he might be "out of the ordinary." The task for Odysseus is more complex, for to win at the games is to risk self-exposure. Whereas the strength of his polytropic abilities seems to guarantee his eventual arrival at his telos, the situation on Phaeacia is quite different. For here, the exposure of his power is precisely what threatens to dissolve it; by winning the game, he runs the risk of giving the game away. Odysseus' control over the Phaeacians depends on his ability to appear as ordinary, as just another voyager on the way to his destination. Odysseus' ability (and need) to walk this tightrope can help us understand both the latent threat in Laodamas' invitation to compete and Odysseus' reluctance. For in offering the invitation, Laodamas is quick to remind Odysseus that ships are waiting to take him home (*Od.* 8.151–52). This reminder of Phaeacian control over Odysseus' *nostos* hints at the potential cost of his failure to compete, and Odysseus assents only when his failure to compete would arouse even more suspicion. His eventual entrance is devastating.

> Ἦ ῥα καὶ αὐτῶι φάρει ἀναΐξας λάβε δίσκον
> μείζονα καὶ πάχετον, στιβαρώτερον οὐκ ὀλίγον περ
> ἢ οἵωι Φαίηκες ἐδίσκεον ἀλλήοισι.
> τόν ῥα περιστρέψας ἧκε στιβαρῆς ἀπὸ χειρός·
> βόμβησεν δὲ λίθος· κατὰ δ' ἔπτηξαν ποτὶ γαίηι
> Φαίηκες δολιχήρετμοι, ναυσίκλυτοι ἄνδρες,
> λᾶος ὑπὸ ῥιπῆς. ὁ δ' ὑπέρπτατο σήματα πάντων
> ῥίμφα θέων ἀπὸ χειρός. ἔθηκε δὲ τέρματ' Ἀθήνη
> ἀνδρὶ δέμας ἐϊκυῖα, ἔπος τ' ἔφατ' ἔκ τ' ὀνόμαζε·
> "καί κ' ἀλαός τοι, ξεῖνε, διακρίνειε τὸ σῆμα
> ἀμφαφόων, ἐπεὶ οὔ τι μεμιγμένον ἐστὶν ὁμίλωι,
> ἀλλὰ πολὺ πρῶτον. σὺ δὲ θάρσει τόνδε γ' ἄεθλον·
> οὔ τις Φαιήων τόδε γ' ἵξεται οὐδ' ὑπερήσει."

(*Od.* 8.186–98)

[He spoke, and with mantle still on sprang up and laid hold of a
    discus
that was a bigger and thicker one, heavier not by a little
than the one the Phaiakians had used for their sport in throwing.
He spun, and let this fly from his ponderous hand. The stone
hummed in the air, and the Phaiakians, men of long oars
and famed for seafaring, shrank down against the ground, ducking
under the flight of the stone which, speeding from his hand lightly,
overflew the marks of all others, and Athene, likening
herself to a man, marked down the cast and spoke and addressed him:
"Even a blind man, friend, would be able to distinguish your mark
by feeling for it, since it is not mingled with the common
lot, but far before. Have no fear over this contest.
No one of the Phaiakians will come up to this mark or pass it."]

This interchange opens out into a wide variety of themes explored in the poem. For example, Athena's remark that even a blind man could distinguish

Odysseus' *sema* anticipates the inability of the blinded Polyphemus to detect the disguised Odysseus in book 9. It also hints at what is at stake in the signs of another blind man, the songs of the bard Demodocus. These episodes will be commented on in detail later. But let us first focus on the effect of Odysseus' *sema* on his fellow competitors. I earlier suggested that the cohesion of Phaeacian civilization depended on their belief that they were perfect hosts. Every traveler who heretofore arrived in their land has been passed on effortlessly to his destination, becoming (for the Phaeacians) another sign in an indefinite series of signs without limit. We can also presume that each traveler took part in the games; for the Phaeacian invitation to Odysseus to compete seems part of the general ritual involved in welcoming strangers. But if previous guests participated, they surely lost, for Alcinous is quick to boast that the Phaeacians surpass others in the games (περιγιγνόμεθ' ἄλλων, *Od.* 8.102 ff.). Alcinous can only make this claim if the Phaeacians remain undefeated. Herein lies the first indication that Odysseus is different; in the games, his discus goes incomparably beyond those of the Phaeacians: ὁ δ' ὑπέρπτατο σήματα πάντων. This society of excess, where successful communication occurred because of the lack of boundaries limiting their civilization, is itself exceeded. It finds its limit in a discus that goes beyond its terms of reference. For the Phaeacians, Odysseus is not just another link in a chain to be superseded by another link. Instead, he opens up a gap between all the previous *semata* and his own, immeasurable *sema*. For the Phaeacians, Odysseus is not just any fellow competitor but is unbeatable, a figure of omnipotence. This is the point underlined by Athena: οὔ τις Φαιήων τόδε γ' ἵξεται οὐδ' ὑπερήσει. No one among the Phaeacians can exceed this mark. Odysseus' throw has suggested to the Phaeacians the possibility of a game with quite different rules to the one they normally play and has therefore opened up a gap between their society and an unimaginable other. Odysseus seems to be (here as with the Cyclopes) the instigator of this gap.

This problem of the Phaeacian games is another of the poem's impossible test cases. For can there really be games with an outsider if the outsider is destined always to lose? What sort of competition could this possibly be? Just as the Cyclops spoke an impossible language before the loss of his eye, so, too, the Phaeacians will only truly start to compete in games after they recognize the possibility that they might lose. Just as Odysseus inaugurated the beginning of language on the island of the Cyclopes, he inaugurates the beginning of competition on Phaeacia. Before Odysseus, an endless series of competitors arrived and were defeated. But how will the Phaeacians receive the competitor who will arrive after Odysseus? The next set of games on Phaeacia will be different. Odysseus therefore halts the Phaeacian games-without-loss, and this very role is nicely highlighted by Athena before the games begin.

> τῶι δ' ἄρ' Ἀθήνη
> θεσπεσίην κατέχευε χάριν κεφαλῆι τε καὶ ὤμοις,
> καί μιν μακρότερον καὶ πάσσονα θῆκεν ἰδέσθαι,
> ὥς κεν Φαιήκεσσι φίλος πάντεσσι γένοιτο
> δεινός τ' αἰδοῖός τε, καὶ ἐκτελέσειεν ἀέθλους
> πολλούς, τοὺς Φαίηκες ἐπειρήσαντ' Ὀδυσῆος.
>
> (*Od.* 8.18–23)
>
> [[A]nd upon him Athene
> drifted a magical grace about his head and shoulders,
> and made him taller for the eye to behold, and thicker,
> so that he might be loved by all the Phaiakians, and to them
> might be wonderful and respected, and might *bring to an end the
> many contests* by which the Phaiakians tested Odysseus.][12]
>
> (translation modified)

Odysseus will, quite literally, bring an end to the many games at Phaeacia.[13] Before Odysseus arrived, the games were a series without limit, an indefinite string of "many" individual contestants arrived, were defeated, and were sent on their way. But because Odysseus will be the first external victor, the nature of these games (and Phaeacian society) will change.[14] He will end one sort of games but inaugurate a new set of games; the finisher of one sort of Phaeacian society, he is the founder of another. In this regard, it is worth taking a closer look at Alcinous' promise to Odysseus that he will provide him with a ship that will set off on its *first* voyage.

> ἀλλ' ἄγε νῆα μέλαιναν ἐρύσσομεν εἰς ἅλα δῖαν
> πρωτόπλοον...
>
> (*Od.* 8.34–35)
>
> [Come then, let us drag a black ship down to the bright sea,
> one sailing now for the first time...]

This reference to a first voyage only achieves its true meaning retroactively. For after Odysseus has departed and once the mountain hovers over Phaeacia as a reminder of the eternal possibility of loss, the ship that carried Odysseus to his destination and is later turned into stone will indeed be remembered as a first ship, the founder of a new era.[15] Never again will Phaeacian ships travel without a thought from the crew to the destination. From now on, they will always reflect on their decisions. Odysseus' *sema*, far beyond their *semata*, opens up the possibility of another place from where the Phaeacians can look at themselves. The awareness of such a place creates the hitherto disavowed gap between real Phaeacian fathers and a symbolic father. For they are now aware of a hypothetical position outside Phaeacian society.[16] But the existence of this place "outside" is an immediate correlative to a loss that is endemic to themselves: they are no longer perfect.

The Phaeacians are thus left in the same position as Cyclopean society after Polyphemus' blinding, though for different reasons. Both the Cyclopes and the Phaeacians become imperfect at the moment they endure loss. But the Cyclops suffers loss by having something subtracted that can never be healed (his eye), while the Phaeacians are rendered imperfect by the addition of an ideal that they realize they can never attain (suggested by Odysseus' discus throw). The loss suffered by one Cyclops opens a channel of communication to others and destroys their self-sufficiency. The perfect communication between Phaeacians is shattered by Odysseus. The Cyclopes and Phaeacians now each have an external ideal (an ego ideal, in psychoanalytic terms) with which they can measure themselves and that also allows them to bracket their symbolic identities. They are split. Aware of their symbolic identities, they are now also faced with the possible awareness of something outside of themselves, which in turn means they have every reason to doubt themselves. They face a difficult problem. Harmony could be maintained with ease on Phaeacia between Phaeacians with a firm belief in the symbolic authority of fathers. But can such harmony exist when such authority is doubted?

The Language of Certainty

Despite Odysseus' success with the discus, the initial Phaeacian reaction is to continue their disavowal—and their suspicion. Alcinous persists in his quest to find out Odysseus' identity, which leads to Odysseus' *Apologoi*. Here, the reaction of the king to Odysseus' words, together with the manner of the question concerning Odysseus' identity, can tell us a great deal about the language of the Phaeacians.

> ὦ Ὀδυσεῦ, τὸ μὲν οὔ τί σ᾽ ἐΐσκομεν εἰσορόωντες
> ἠπεροπῆά τ᾽ ἔμεν καὶ ἐπίκλοπον, οἷά τε πολλοὺς
> βόσκει γαῖα μέλαινα πολυσπερέας ἀνθρώπους
> ψεύδεά τ᾽ ἀρτύνοντας, ὅθεν κέ τις οὐδὲ ἴδοιτο·

(*Od.* 11.363–66)

[Odysseus, we as we look upon you do not imagine
that you are a deceptive or thievish man, the sort that the black earth

breeds in great numbers, people who wander widely, making up lying stories, *from sources which no one could see for himself.*]¹⁷

(translation modified)

Alcinous' reaction to Odysseus' tales is a strange one. For his belief in Odysseus' stories runs against their obvious implausibility, which has been commented on since antiquity.¹⁸ What can explain Alcinous' belief in Odysseus' truthfulness? It seems that this is another misrecognition of Odysseus, for Alcinous denies that Odysseus is thievish *(epiklopos)*, the very quality that Athena will affirm of him in book 13.¹⁹ Odysseus is defined by his ability to manipulate language, to be someone that tells lies like the truth. Yet this by itself does not explain the misrecognition. For why would a species that mingle openly with the gods misrecognize anyone? The self-confidence betrays a certain naïveté, which we can detect by looking more closely at Alcinous' definition of lying. He begins by suggesting that lying is something that "many" men do, and we can safely presume that the referents of the many men are the long list of voyagers who have passed through Phaeacia on their way to their respective destinations. But he is more specific. Liars are those many men who make claims from a place that eludes verification: ὅθεν κέ τις οὐδὲ ἴδοιτο. Let us ask a simple question. If liars tell stories that cannot be verified, how does Alcinous know that they are liars? In short, why does he not concede the possibility that they may be telling the truth but that it is merely a truth he is unable to verify? A reasonable conclusion is that Alcinous thinks he knows more. Liars are defined by their fantastical construction of events that they have not experienced, "from sources which no one could see"; they are dismissed as liars because Alcinous believes himself to be in the position of the place from where no one might see. This makes good sense; given that Alcinous and the Phaeacians pride themselves on their ability to travel everywhere and that they live in a land without boundaries (Scheria), their reservoir of empirical knowledge in inexhaustible. Because of the confidence that comes with such a position of (supposed) knowledge, Alcinous is fully equipped to divide his visitors into liars and truth-tellers. If their words correspond to his (greater) knowledge, they are truth-tellers; if they do not, they are liars.

Yet if Alcinous sees everything, he does not see that he has a blind spot. For the belief in his own knowledge means that he is quite unable to deal with a man who tells lies like the truth. The aspect of the *Apologoi* overlooked by Alcinous is that Odysseus' tales can be doubted but not automatically disbelieved. Odysseus' story of his encounter with Polyphemus illustrates this nicely. Odysseus' blinding of the Cyclops coincides with the destruction of the former

Cyclopean civilization. This is clarified when Odysseus emphasizes that Polyphemus will never be healed, that his former, monadic society is gone forever. What matters for the narrative, however, is that the loss of the Cyclopean civilization means that Odysseus' tale is impossible to validate.

> σχέτλιε, πῶς κέν τίς σε καὶ ὕστερον ἄλλος ἵκοιτο
> ἀνθρώπων πολέων; ἐπεὶ οὐ κατὰ μοῖραν ἔρεξας.
>
> (*Od.* 9.351–52)

[Cruel, how can any man come and visit
you ever again, now you have done what has no sanction?]

No one else will visit the Cyclopes again. Yet this is not just because of fear of their cannibalism. No one else will visit them because they will no longer exist as Cyclopes. The ruse underlying Odysseus' tale works on several levels. He tells a story about fabulous, superhuman, mythical beings, whose existence a reader would naturally question. We have further reason to doubt their existence because of the lack of any corroborating witness; the companions who supposedly accompanied him on the voyage to the island are all dead.[20] But the content of Odysseus' tale makes matters more complex. For he tells of his blinding of the Cyclops, a blinding that forces the formerly asocial Cyclopes to communicate with each other. So if someone else did come to the island, what would such a person find? Surely it is quite possible that he or she would come upon an ordinary human society, where people are no longer monadic but communicate with each other in the agora; that is, that individual would not discover Cyclopes. The *Apologoi* thus tell a tale that demands doubt but that is constructed in such a way as to make its falsity impossible to demonstrate. For the possibility of verifying the truth of the tale disappears at the moment Odysseus leaves. This explains Alcinous' difficulty. Because he is unable to disprove Odysseus' tale, he makes the (unwarranted) presumption that Odysseus is telling the truth. The only alternative would be consciously to doubt, to assume that Odysseus speaks "from sources which no one could see for himself" [ὅθεν κέ τις οὐδὲ ἴδοιτο], but this option is simply not available in the Phaeacian universe. The *Apologoi* therefore function in a similar manner to the games; both Odysseus' hurling of the discus and his tales are outside the terms of reference (the *semata*) of the Phaeacians. Yet because their civilization is based on a disavowal of this possibility, this aspect of Odysseus is ignored.

We can now understand why Alcinous can recount both the story of Nausithous concerning Poseidon's future destruction of Phaeacian society and also the particular form that destruction takes.

φῆ ποτὲ Φαιήκων ἀνδρῶν εὐεργέα νῆα
ἐκ πομπῆς ἀνιοῦσαν ἐν ἠεροειδέι πόντωι
ῥαισέμεναι, μέγα δ' ἧμιν ὄρος πόλει ἀμφικαλύψειν.
ὣς ἀγόρευ' ὁ γέρων· τὰ δέ κεν θεὸς ἢ τελέσειεν
ἤ κ' ἀτέλεστ' εἴη, ὥς οἱ φίλον ἔπλετο θυμῷ.

(*Od.* 8.567–71)

[He said that one day, as a well-made ship of Phaiakian
men came back from a convoy on the misty face of the water,
he would stun it, and pile a great mountain over our city, to hide it.
So the Old Man spoke, and the god might either bring it
to pass, or it might be left undone, as the god's heart pleases.]

Alcinous thinks that the prophecy will either be completed or not. Yet this is of course not what happens. Alcinous remembers the prophecy of Nausithous and announces that the perfect conveyance of men will stop. The poem abruptly leaves the Phaeacians at the point of divine indecision as they embark on prayers and sacrifice to Poseidon. The story is halted midline, at a point of absolute doubt.

> So he spoke, and they were afraid and made the bulls ready.
> So these leaders of the Phaiakians and men of counsel
> among their people made their prayer to the lord Poseidon,
> standing around the great altar. But now great Odysseus awakened . . .
> (13.184–87)[21]

It is precisely this indeterminacy (a moment when it is unclear what will happen, a moment of crisis) that is inconceivable for Alcinous. His former reaction to Nausithous' prophecy was a deterministic one; the god would either bring it about or not, regardless of Phaeacian efforts. The deterministic outlook is shattered. If Phaeacian society was formerly characterized by the absence of any blind spots (because the Phaeacians believed themselves to be all-seeing),[22] the departure of Odysseus does not announce a simple reversal, the change from a world of light to a world of darkness. Rather, the mountain of Poseidon and Zeus casts a permanent shadow over Phaeacia. In this case, the traumatic impact on the lives of the Phaeacians comes from the uncertainty that the hovering mountain introduces to their world. Critics who have puzzled over what kind of ethical impact this episode should make on the reading of the poem are therefore identifying with the new situation of the Phaeacians. Before, they lived in a world that was as closed as it was "open," precisely because they only ever saw their ethical judgments and worldview endlessly confirmed.

Now they are forced into questioning what the gods want from them and thus what the mountain signifies. It is therefore not so much the utter destruction itself that is traumatic but their utter ignorance about the future—the encounter with the enigma of what the Other wants from them.

We can now finally turn to Alcinous' famous remarks about naming.

εἴπ' ὄνομ', ὅττι σε κεῖθι κάλεον μήτηρ τε πατήρ τε,
ἄλλοι θ' οἳ κατὰ ἄστυ καὶ οἳ περιναιετάουσιν.
οὐ μὲν γάρ τις πάμπαν ἀνώνυμος ἔστ' ἀνθρώπων,
οὐ κακὸς οὐδὲ μὲν ἐσθλός, ἐπὴν τὰ πρῶτα γένηται,
ἀλλ' ἐπὶ πᾶσι τίθενται, ἐπεί κε τέκωσι, τοκῆες.

(*Od.* 8.550–54)

[Tell me the name by which your mother and father called you
in that place, and how the rest who live in the city about you
call you. No one among the peoples, neither base man
nor noble, is altogether nameless, once he has been born,
but always his parents as soon as they bring him forth put upon him a
 name.]

Critics have pounced on Alcinous' words, noting the pun on οὔ τις: "To name oneself 'no one' is not to be without a name, then";[23] "Everyone is born into a social context, named, classified, located in society before one has any say in the matter."[24] In short, no one is nameless. Yet although this maxim is repeated as if it were a universal truth, these critics have too easily overlooked that this position is enunciated by a Phaeacian. In a society that has not experienced doubt, whose communal identity depends on a disavowal of anything beyond its own *semata*, everyone definitely, indubitably has a name. Yet because these are Alcinous' words, we should be less certain. For if everyone is given a name, to what is the name given? There is a subtle gliding over of the (temporally and logically) prior moment when a child is not yet inside language (and ideology). There are, one assumes, no naming ceremonies on Phaeacia, ceremonies that dramatize the terrifying (and utopian) moment when a child is not yet named. In psychoanalytic terms, the Phaeacians seem to be unable to acknowledge the possibility of the utter rejection of language and the possibility that a being might not be incorporated into the world of language by means of a name.[25] In short, they reject the possibility of psychosis. This failure is itself mirrored in the way Phaeacian society is based on its separation from the Cyclopes, a tribe of mad, lawless creatures. But as with the Cyclopes, the Phaeacians are introduced to a figure outside their system of reference. After he leaves, they see a ship turned to stone and wait for the fall of a mountain. Accordingly, both the blinded Polyphemus and the Phaeacians are left hanging at moments of radical doubt. For the Phaeacians must surely realize that there is nothing "natural" about the imposition of names, that it is contingent, insofar as they themselves have created these names. At this point, can any Phaeacian confidently declare that anything has a name?

In the Beginning Was Proteus

Odysseus' encounters with the Phaeacians and Cyclopes are traumatic for both species, and Odysseus is the agent who produces that trauma. A consequence is that both species begin to desire for the first time. Both stories also interrogate the related problems of beginnings and endings—that is, the general problems involved with symbolic systems of classification and their ultimate inadequacy. These themes recur, in a more abstract way, in a too rarely discussed episode of the *Odyssey:* the encounter between Menelaus and Proteus. In the case of the Phaeacians and Cyclopes, the intervention of Odysseus is a turning point in their civilizations; it signifies their emergence as properly human societies that are forced to confront their own finitude. In the story of Proteus—the god who has "first" embedded in his own proper name and yet who seems to be a being without limit, a series of endless *tropoi* or masks—the intervention of Menelaus will also radically change his conception of the universe. There is also the shared theme of deception. Odysseus deceived both the Phaeacians and Cyclopes, even as they both were species who believed themselves to be impervious to deception. In the case of Proteus, too, an infallible truth-teller seems to get deceived. But how?

The story of Proteus' deception in *Odyssey* 4 puts great emphasis on counting.[1] Proteus regularly counts his seals, and he is tricked when his system of counting betrays him: he is quite unable to account for the disguised presence of Menelaus and his three companions. I will soon argue that the trick depends on a specific mode of counting, in particular how Proteus counts from four to five. But before interpreting the manner in which Eidothea tricks this obsessive counter, this "unerrring" old man of the sea, it is worth trying to provide some context for the problems of counting. Within the Homeric poems, what does the sequence 3-4-5 suggest?

Leonard Muellner has provided an answer from an analysis of the *Iliad*. In that poem, he argues, the passage from three to four symbolically defines the difference between man and god. To try and fail to do something three times remains a normal, human pattern of failure; to make a fourth attempt is to move into a shady realm between god and man. Consider the transgressive assault by Patroclus on Troy. Patroclus has attacked the wall of Troy three times and is embarking on his fourth attempt when Apollo forces him back (16.705 ff.). Later, his fourth attack produces his doom.

> Patroklos sprang upon the Trojans with evil intent,
> three times then he sprang upon them, <u>equal to rushing Ares</u>,
> shrieking terribly, and three times he slew nine men.
> But when he was rushing forward that fourth time <u>equal to the *daimon*</u>
> then the end of life rose up before you, Patroklos.
>
> (16.783–87)[2]

Muellner notes that this fourth attempt is taboo and that Patroclus' "final transgression is across the line that Apollo guards between mortals and Ares."[3] The attack is therefore a fundamental challenge to the order that guarantees the separation of men from gods, and Muellner goes on to argue that this transgression is linked to the meaning of *menis*, the anger that is the theme of the *Iliad*. For divine *menis* is appealed to in the course of the poem when this order is threatened, when taboos are violated.

But though this passage from the third to the taboo fourth assault is certainly significant, it is worth lingering over this moment of failed transition. For in punishing the fourth assault, what remains truly taboo (and untouched) is the possibility of a fifth attack. If Patroclus becomes equal to the god on the fourth attempt, he is clearly not yet a god; he temporarily takes a god's place, but this is not yet permanent identity with a god. The narrative establishes an order through a prohibition: no humans are allowed beyond three assaults, and if any should go as far as a fourth, they will be punished. But its prohibition also creates a question even as it stimulates a desire: what would happen if Apollo were not to intervene, if a human could reach five?

If the sequence 3-4-5 is crucial to the key episodes of the *Iliad*, it is equally significant for the narrative structure of the *Odyssey*. For though we might expect the opening books to bring our attention to the twenty-year absence of Odysseus, we find out instead about the courtship of Penelope. Antinous tells

Telemachus that Penelope has been frustrating the desires of the suitors for three years already, and it is soon to be the fourth (*Od.* 2.89–90). When we compare these words to Muellner's analysis of the taboo fourth assault of Patroclus, we can see how Antinous' words have a darker sense to which he remains quite blind. The narrative hints that three years is at the limit of what is permissible and that the fourth year will be a crucial one, either bringing disaster (if they cannot survive it) or ultimate happiness.

This number sequence has already played a role in the book, which opens with a speech of Aegyptius, who asks why an assembly has been called after so many years. We are provided with a brief biography of Aegyptius. He has four sons; two remain at home, one is a suitor, and the fourth went to Troy with Odysseus. An element of tragedy is introduced as we are told that his fourth son has already died, eaten in the cave of the Cyclops. The narrative emphasizes that it is the lost, fourth son that continues to haunt the thoughts of Aegyptius.

> Even so, he could not forget the lost one. He grieved and mourned for him,
> and it was in tears for him, now, that he stood forth and addressed them.
>
> (*Od.* 2.23–24)

It is the fourth son, the one that is missing and out of reach, who motivates his actions. Further, Aegyptius' feelings toward this son are characterized by a nagging uncertainty. For though he is not present, as his other sons are, Aegyptius does not know whether this absence is permanent—that is, whether he has died. His fourth son is, for Aegyptius, uneasily between life and death. The possibility that he might be alive fuels his fantasy of a paternal happiness with all of his sons alive alongside him: this fourth son is the gateway to a world without loss. There is thus once more a parallel with Patroclus, whose desire for a fourth, transgressive assault is also a desire to attain something that is out of reach, and for that very reason, his desire pushes him on further in an effort to attain it. In the *Iliad*, Apollo guards the limit beyond the fourth assault and punishes his desire with his death. In the opening of *Odyssey* 2, the narrator informs us of the ultimate futility of Aegyptius' desire by telling us of his son's death at the hands of the Cyclops. His desire for the complete safety of his children becomes an impossible desire, and Odysseus' journey to the cave of the Cyclops makes it so.

The reference to Aegyptius' son's death in the Cyclops' cave brings further relevant associations. Critics have long been keen to point out parallels between the transgressive behavior of the suitors and the actions of the Cyclops.

Both pervert the laws of *xenia;* both indulge in socially prohibited forms of eating.[4] Both the Cyclops and the suitors seem to believe in the possibility of a limitless indulgence of their desires, an indulgence that fails to respect the fundamental *Iliadic* limit. The Cyclops eats transgressively because he can imagine no one who could regulate his behavior and thus impose a limit on it—he believes the Cyclopes to be better than Zeus. In book 2, Eurymachus not only threatens that the suitors will eat all of Odysseus' possessions; he imagines a permanent deferral of the only thing that could stop them—the marriage of Penelope.

> . . . and his possessions will wretchedly be eaten away, there will not
> be compensation, ever, while she makes the Achaians put off
> marriage with her, while we, awaiting all this, all our days
> quarrel for the sake of her excellence . . .
>
> (*Od.* 2.203–6)

Both the Cyclops and the suitors live in a fantasy world where there are no limits to their ongoing enjoyment. In this context, Odysseus' careful choice of four men to help him blind the Cyclops, while he himself counts as the fifth, might assume greater significance.[5] The narrative, by emphasizing that the taboo fourth time has just arrived for the suitors and the Cyclops, suggests that the end of their indulgences is at hand.

The numerological question of the significance of the sequence 3-4-5 within the poem thus spills into the question of what it means to desire in a human as against a nonhuman way. It has long been recognized that the problem of the economy of desire, of what can and cannot be desired in the controlled economy of the *oikos*, is a central theme of the *Odyssey*. In trying to understand the deception of Proteus, it will prove helpful to keep in mind this problematic economy produced by the creation of limits and their transgression.

Let us briefly recount the Proteus story. Driven off course to Egypt, Menelaus is uncertain about how to continue his *nostos*, until Eidothea suggests that her father, Proteus, will give him directions.[6] The catch is that Menelaus must first capture this polytropic figure. As luck would have it, Eidothea herself has a suggestion as to how he should go about it.

> At the time when the sun has gone up to bestride the middle of
>   heaven,
> then the ever-truthful Old Man of the Sea will come out of the water
> under the blast of the West Wind, circled in a shudder of darkening
> water, and when he comes out he will sleep, under hollow caverns,

> and around him seals, those darlings of the sea's lovely lady,
> sleep in a huddle, after they have emerged from the gray sea,
> giving off the sour smell that comes from the deep salt water.
> There I will take you myself when dawn shows and arrange you
> orderly in your ambush; you must choose from your companions
> those three who are your best beside your strong-benched vessels.
> Now I will tell you all the devious ways of this old man.
> First of all he will go among his seals and count them,
> but after he has reviewed them all and noted their number,
> he will lie down in their midst, like a herdsman among his
>   sheepflocks.
> Next, as soon as you see that he is asleep, that will be
> the time for all of you to use your strength and your vigor,
> and hold him there while he strives and struggles hard to escape you.
>
> (*Od.* 4.400–416)

The tale is thematically charged. It involves not just any deception but one that disrupts the relationship between a single leader and his herd of seals—a motif that will recur in the *Apologoi*, when Odysseus' relationship to his companions, whose numbers come up inexorably through each death-filled encounter, is under the spotlight. Equally intriguing is the parallel between Proteus and the protean Odysseus. For Proteus, like Odysseus, is polytropic; when attacked, he has the ability to alter his appearance in order to scare off his attacker (by turning into an array of wild animals: a lion, a bear, etc.). Yet polytropic Odysseus seems to be the deceiver par excellence, while Proteus is a victim of deceit in *Odyssey* 4. If the similarity of these episodes of trickery invites a comparison between the polytropic characters, we are left with a troubling question: what is it that differentiates Odysseus from Proteus, deceiver from deceived?

Let us look more closely at the trick. Menelaus and his men seem to elude the grasp of Proteus because Eidothea hides them with sealskins, a scheme in turn made possible by the ambrosia she gives them to help mitigate the terrible stench of the animals (*Od.* 4.445 ff.). Proteus would then be fooled because he counts Menelaus and his companions as seals, not humans. However, this conventional interpretation fails to account for the emphasis the story puts not only on numbers but on the manner in which numbers are assigned; for Proteus always counts his seals, and Eidothea is careful to specify that Menelaus choose three companions. This suggests that even if Proteus fails to recognize Menelaus and his men because of their disguises, we still have a more basic difficulty. If Proteus is careful to count his seals as they come out of the water, why does he not notice that there are four extra, the disguised Menelaus and his men? He must be a peculiarly bad counter, which would seem to be a strange attribute of a god who is supposedly infallible. Or is it so strange?

Rather than take Proteus' infallibility for granted, we should perhaps pay more attention to the manner of his arithmetic and to Eidothea's ability to manipulate it. First, we should note that Proteus counts in a very specific way, highlighted by Eidothea.

> φώκας μέν τοι πρῶτον ἀριθμήσει καὶ ἔπεισιν·
> αὐτὰρ ἐπὴν πάσας <u>πεμπάσσεται</u> ἠδὲ ἴδηται,
> λέξεται ἐν μέσσηισι, νομεὺς ὣς πώεσι μήλων.
>
> (*Od.* 4.411–13)

[First of all he will go among his seals and count them,
but after he has reviewed them all and noted their number,
he will lie down in their midst, like a herdsman among his sheepflocks.][7]

Proteus counts in fives (πεμπάσσεται).[8] When he calculates the presence/absence of his group of seals, he does so not by cumulatively calculating their number (nor, despite his persistent counting, do we ever find out how many seals he has) but, rather, by ensuring that they make up a multiple of five. Our brief discussion of the transgression of Patroclus suggests that the form of his counting may have a wider significance: to reach five within the Homeric poems means to reach the realm of the gods, and thus Proteus counts in a perfectly divine manner. But the form of counting also points toward an obvious way to trick Proteus: if five seals are added to his flock (or, indeed, if five are taken away), his form of counting would not help him detect this. If Proteus is infallible, it is because he always thinks he accounts for all his seals. But this is because of the narrowness of his perspective rather than any particular wisdom. He is a scientist and infallible knower who never questions the prejudices that govern his counting inquiries. Yet this is not the whole of the trick Eidothea uses. Indeed, if she did simply take five seals away, Proteus would be none the wiser. Instead, she engineers something that will be much more traumatic for him: she specifies that Menelaus must choose only three other companions to join him.

Let us look at the lines that highlight Proteus' counting of the mixture of seals and disguised seals after Eidothea's addition.

> ἔνδιος δ' ὁ γέρων ἦλθ' ἐξ ἁλός, εὗρε δὲ φώκας
> ζατρεφέας, πάσας, δ' ἄρ' ἐπώιχετο, <u>λέκτο δ' ἀριθμόν</u>·

ἐν δ' ἡμέας πρώτους <u>λέγε</u> κήτεσιν, οὐδέ τι θυμῶι
ὠίσθη δόλον εἶναι· <u>ἔπειτα δὲ λέκτο καὶ αὐτός</u>.

(*Od.* 4.450–53)

[At noon the Old Man came out of the sea and found his well-fed
seals, and went about to them all, and counted their number,
and we were among the first he counted; he had no idea
of any treachery. Then he too lay down among us.]

What is important in these lines is the explicit pun on the Greek verbs for "lying" and "counting," a pun noted by commentators.[9] It is impossible to tell the aorist middle form of λέγω, meaning "count," from the aorist of λέχομαι, meaning "lie down." But what is the significance of the pun? Proteus continues his normal process of counting his seals in groups of five, but this time something important has changed; he now finds out that there are four extra seals. He is now at the liminal point reached by Patroclus in his *aristeia* (his conventional display of martial power)—and emphasized by Muellner— poised between the human and the divine. Proteus, however, reaches this in-between realm from the reverse direction. Patroclus moved from the realm of mortals (three attacks) toward immortality (five attacks) and was killed because of his taboo fourth assault; he never reached the immortal realm of five. By contrast, Proteus "lives," as it were, in the immortal realm of five, where his ability to count correctly is a sign of both his infallibility and, consequently, his divinity. He is only forced to enter the liminal realm of four because of Eidothea's trick.

At this point in the story, as Proteus counts four extra seals, Menelaus, as narrator, intervenes to insist that Proteus suspects nothing. But because Proteus believes himself to be an infallible god, for whom his own deception is inconceivable, he needs to find another explanation for the apparently missing fifth seal. Here, we can make use of the pun on λέχομαι. All translators agree in translating his action after the trick as "he himself lies down." But we can also activate the possibility of understanding λέχομαι as the aorist middle of λέγω: Proteus, forced to confront the missing seal that punctures his perfect world of fives, counts himself (λέκτο καὶ αὐτός). Herein lies the subtlety of Eidothea's trick: she understands in advance that Proteus, faced with the problem of a missing seal, will simply count himself. When confronted with a gap in his universe, Proteus takes himself as (fetish) object to fill up that gap.[10]

This episode is thus much more than a joke on Proteus' poor arithmetic. For what is at stake is how human Homeric subjects are constituted. The story displays a pattern that we have seen occurring in Odysseus' encounters with the Cyclopes and Phaeacians; we witness the moment when an unerring, certain, godlike figure—in this case, Proteus—begins to doubt himself for the first time. The episode starts with Menelaus seeking out help from the all-knowing Proteus; but after the trick, Proteus is the helpless one, captured against his will and utterly ignorant of which of the gods have plotted against him.

We might chart out some consequences of this moment of doubt by looking at the way the episode complicates the relationship between the human subject and the world of objects. First, Proteus treats himself as an object, as something to be counted. Proteus himself is thus uneasily caught between his status as counting subject and that of object of his own counting—a status that formerly belonged to the seals alone. He is thus split, and this split will have important consequences for his relationship to the world structured by his counting—in this episode, signified by the herd of seals. Before the trick, we can presume that the unerring old man of the sea had never given a second thought to either the number of his seals (presuming his counting system to be infallible) or his relations with the seals as a group. But his new status as doubter invites us (and Proteus) to reconsider this relationship. What is the relationship of this doubting Proteus to his construction of the world around him, exemplified by his seals, if he can now locate himself, as object, in the world around him? Here, we can see the outlines of an ideological problem at the heart of much of the Homeric poems. What must occur for a group to be constructed symbolically as a group (say, the Greeks at Troy or the companions of Odysseus), and what happens if the master of that group doubts his mastery?

To clarify Proteus' position and this ideological problematic, we can turn to a theoretical problem within structural linguistics. Though a contemporary problem, it can provide an important tool for helping us to understand the complexities of deception within the *Odyssey*. Since Saussure, the problem of language's construction of meaning has depended on the relation between signifier and signified. How can we ever be sure that any signifier refers to any signified? For if we acknowledge (as we must) that the process of meaning is inexhaustible, that there will always be the possibility of the arrival of another signifier that will retroactively change all that went before, are we not confronted with an endless deferral of sense? A certain structuralism evades the problem by focusing attention on an arbitrarily frozen moment. By concentrating on an idealized moment in time, a closed system of signifiers is created. A signifier can then be linked to a signified precisely insofar as all the other (now finite) signifiers do not refer to it. Yet this solution, flirted with by Saussure, does nothing to evade the crucial problem. Without such a totalizing system, there can be no guarantee that any signifier refers to its signified, yet such a system is by definition impossible; for there can always be another signifier, changing all that went before.[11] In Lacanian terms, the question is one of the limits of the symbolic order. For if the symbolic has no limit, then we would seem to be forced to admit the impossibility of sense. Yet any external limit to the symbolic is equally unsatisfactory, as it denies the obvious: the possibility of another external limit, ad infinitum.

Lacan answers the problem by admitting the impossibility of any external limit to the symbolic; but he nevertheless suggests that an internal limit can be posited. If it is impossible to conceive of an external limit, it is possible (paradoxically) to conceive this very impossibility. Herein lies the internal limit to the symbolic, which provides us with the Lacanian concept of "suturing."

> Suture, in brief, supplies the logic of a paradoxical function whereby a supplementary element is *added* to the series of signifiers in order to mark the *lack* of a signifier that could close the set. The endless slide of signifiers (hence a deferral of sense) is brought to a halt and allowed to function "as if" it were a closed set through the inclusion of an element that acknowledges the impossibility of closure.[12]

This paradoxical function creates the conditions of possibility for what Lacan calls a master signifier. A master signifier (which gives "illegitimate" retroactive sense to the chain of signifiers) is an external element that forcibly grafts signifier onto signified.[13] Yet any master signifier is logically parasitic on this prior lack of such a signifier. This ensures that the master signifier must be an external impostor (its mastery can only work in the mode of "as if"—there is no true "master," only someone playing the role of a master); this in turn preserves the possibility of one more signifier. This logical possibility is precisely what guarantees a constitutive gap between signifier and signified, and it is in the gap between signifier and signified that Lacan locates the subject. This gap creates the breathing space for the subject by providing it with a certain freedom from the signifier. The subject is, for Lacan, that for which no signifier can account. In our Homeric story, too, it is the emergence of something that cannot be accounted for—Proteus' loss of a seal—that will introduce the god to the world of subjectivity. How? The loss of a seal opens up an empty place in the universe for Proteus, into which he is now able to project an alienated version of himself through language—that is, with signifiers. Before such a place existed, there was no possibility of Proteus existing as a subject, because his system of counting went on automatically without any subjective involvement on his part. Without this gap, there was no space available for Proteus to refer to himself: Proteus was nothing more than his infallible system of counting and thus was not a subject at all.

A clarification of Lacan's notion of human alienation in the symbolic can be of help here.

> A metaphor [for the desiring subject] often used by Lacan is that of something *qui manque à sa place*, which is out of place, not where it should be or usually is; in other words, something which is missing. Now for something to be missing, it must first have been present and localized; it must first have had a place. And something only has a place within an ordered system—space-time coordinates or a Dewey decimal book classification, for example—in other words, some sort of symbolic structure.[14]

For Lacan, the subject cannot simply be equated with a symbolic structure (e.g., language), because the symbolic structure is emphatically alien to the subject: the subject exceeds the language that tries to classify it. The symbolic structure, made up of a series of signifiers, thus can try to represent the subject, but it can never completely succeed, because all it can do—in its effort to pin the subject down—is refer to other signifiers. Any notion of something "missing" is necessarily dependent on a symbolic structure, and this is a sign of a fundamental impotence that haunts the structure; when inside the symbolic, there is no way to directly reach the world outside of it. One can only refer to it by means of further signifiers—that is, within the terms of the structure itself. Nevertheless, the subject is inconceivable without such a symbolic structure; only an ordered system allows one to determine what is missing, and this gap in the structure creates a place for the subject. This helps explain Lacan's definition of the subject as that which one signifier represents for another signifier. We can relate this to Proteus; any future counting done by Proteus will occur against the background of this empty place opened up by the loss of one of his seals. His future counting will be part of an attempt to account for this empty place opened up by the loss of the seal. This empty place provides Proteus with the breathing room for self-exploration; it is also a place from which the coherence of the counting system itself can always be questioned.

Before the trick, Proteus, as a god, seems not to have been pinned down by space-time coordinates. His perfect polytropy defied spatial limitation, and his immortality defied temporal limitation. Thus, the effect of the trick played on him is to introduce him to limits—a symbolic system. Before the trick, he lived in a world that was impervious to change, and this itself seems to be suggested by the way Eidothea can predict his behavior. She *knows* he will come out of the sea at midday and count his seals, because he *always* comes out of the sea at midday and counts his seals. Proteus lives in a static universe, where the same thing happens over and over again, and this coincides with his perfect counting system; in his world free of spatiotemporal limits, he proves to himself again and again that he has the same number of seals.

It is perhaps now possible to see why the tale of Proteus opens up a crucial ideological question. What is at stake is the manner in which groups are constituted—in this case, what is at issue is the relationship of the seals to their leader, Proteus. The significant difference lies between a group that is constituted by its allegiance to a real, empirical leader and a group that is constituted by nothing other than the members' self-difference—that is, a group whose center is nothing, a void, the surplus element marking the lack of a signifier. The argument here has important ramifications, for what is at stake is the possibility of the critique of the violence imposed by the arbitrariness of numeration. I have so far concentrated on the counter, Proteus, and what is at stake for him in his counting dilemma; I now shift focus and consider the creatures counted. For humans, any constitution of a group as a group suggests some sort of acceptance (whether conscious or unconscious) of one's inclusion in the group, of being counted, and thus of the legitimacy of the system that counts you. Questioning this legitimacy is a classic first step toward enlightenment. We need go no further for illustration than the ideological dilemma faced by Achilles in the *Iliad*. He not only confronts Agamemnon; in Book 9, he questions the legitimacy of the shared ideological logic that links heroes together, the "heroic code." He thus rejects the group identity that he now believes to have been pushed on him against his will.

In the story of Proteus, counting itself assigns an identity to the seals and makes them a part of a group. Because those counted in this tale are animals, it might seem unnecessary (even absurd) to pose the question of the legitimacy *for them* of the system of Proteus' counting. After all, as animals, they are in no position rationally to question it. But as I have suggested, the narrative already puts under question the well-known structuralist divide between humans and gods by focusing on the moment when a divine being becomes subject to human doubt. Could it not also put into question the divide between humans and animals? If a god can become human by the introduction of doubt, the failure to make use of this doubt can reduce a human to the status of an animal in a herd. By an unthinking acceptance of group status, human subjects would seem to forfeit the quality that defines them as subjects. The parallel between Odysseus and Proteus is therefore deeper. Not only are they polytropic, but the ultimate sign of their cunning is their ability to gather together their subordinates—seals in the first case, human companions in the second. On this reading, the tale of Proteus would be an effort to demystify the relationships between people by redescribing them as a relationship between a god and seals. In Lacanian terms, the relationship of signs to conscious thought is the mystical world of ideology and mistaken meaning. The apparent harmony of the relationship between Proteus and his seals would thus be indicative of the way ideology legitimizes hierarchy and would give us a parallel to the apparent harmony at work between Odysseus and his men. But when we read the tale as illustrating the relationship between signifiers and the subject, we have a glimpse into the underlying structure of this imaginary ideological relationship. Proteus is an idiotic, senseless counter, and the seals are victims of this idiocy. So too Odysseus' men are ultimately attached to the idiocy of Odysseus' authority.[15]

So let us turn to the relationship of Proteus to his seals, exploring it within the terms of reference of structural linguistics already outlined. In the tale, the real, empirical seals function as referents; the concept "seal" functions as the signified; and the numbers allocated to the concept "seal" function as signifiers. The obvious reading of the deception would be to explain it in terms of a confusion of sign (signifier and signified combined) and referent. Thus, Proteus would be fooled because his concept of a seal is disrupted by Menelaus' disguise: he counts as seals people who are not really seals.[16] However, in my interpretation, this disguise functions as a way to reveal that something more basic is at stake: the relation between signifier and signified.[17]

The protean Proteus is evidently a figure who upholds the possibility of one more signified: but insofar as he is perfectly protean, a figure of pure change, Proteus does not recognize the internal limit of the symbolic, which is the only way of ensuring the possibility of meaning. Eidothea's trick stages the moment when his system of counting fails, when a gap emerges between signifier and signified. But how does this trick affect Proteus? The first significant moment arrives when Proteus counts his seals: οὐδέ τι θυμῶι / ὠίσθη δόλον εἶναι· ἔπειτα δὲ λέκτο καὶ αὐτός. When he realizes a seal is missing,[18] when he finds a signifier with no signified corresponding to it, he tries to close up the gap with another signified. But the only signified available is himself; Proteus thus counts himself for the first time.[19]

It is tempting to see this as his first moment of self-consciousness. But the text emphasizes that he remains unaware that this is a trick at all: οὐδέ τι θυμῶι / ὠίσθη δόλον εἶναι. Proteus' belief in his infallibility continues; he goes about with business as usual and lies down among his seals: λέκτο καὶ αὐτός.[20] This is at the conscious level. But unbeknownst to him, behind his back, something has changed. One seal has disappeared, and he himself has moved into the void where that seal once was. Proteus counts himself; but he does not do so consciously. The ambiguity of the signifier λέκτο reflects the splitting of Proteus between what he does consciously and what he does unconsciously; he consciously "lies down," and he unconsciously becomes self-aware, "counts himself." Freud argued that slips of the tongue and punning jokes provide evidence of the workings of "another place" that undermines our conscious universes.[21] In Lacan's rewriting of Freud, the gap between signifier and signified (which in turn opens up the gaps between signifiers) allows us to locate this "other place." Puns and wordplays point toward the unconscious as they continually affirm that we, as conscious subjects, are never fully in control of what we say. For Proteus, this other place is opened up by the loss of a seal, a logical place that guarantees that there is a constitutive gap between signifier and signified. The ambiguity of the signifier λέκτο is evidence for the gap. Proteus' action of "lying down" no longer means what it used to mean, because his subjectivity will now be at stake through his "self-counting." Proteus acts out a pun, and as he does so he becomes a human subject.

Let us now turn to the second significant moment in Proteus' development. For though Proteus continues with business as usual by lying down with his seals, his unreflective existence does not last much longer. There is evidence of his failure of nerve in his struggle with Menelaus. On a simple reading of the tale, we have another puzzling aspect of Eidothea's trick. Just because Menelaus now has access to the sea god, there seems no clear reason why this should help him. For if Proteus remained protean, upholder of a symbolic without limit, representative of an infinite series of masks, there would surely be no need for him ever to give in to Menelaus. Menelaus would merely have been given access to an ever-changing god only to find out that his ever-changing masks were enough to defy capture endlessly. Yet, of course, Proteus does yield. Why?

Rather than see the delay in giving in to Menelaus as a problem, we should perhaps see it as the entire point of the episode. For it is in effect a temporal confirmation of the gap opened up between what happens to Proteus (the traumatic trick, the self-counting) and his ability to register that trick consciously. Proteus belatedly comes to terms with Eidothea's trick (and the pun he unwittingly acted out) and is now in some way aware of the possibility of a world outside his own, which in turn forces him to recognize the limits of his own world. Before the trick with the seals, Proteus would never have thought of giving in, because he had no reason to doubt his own status as perfectly, infinitely polytropic. But conscious doubt has now crept into his universe, in confirmation of the earlier self-counting that occurred unconsciously. Only at this moment does Proteus become self-conscious, insofar as he consciously doubts himself. His self-doubt in the struggle against Menelaus is a belated recognition of the fact that his seals were not naturally assigned numbers, that their enumeration depended on a counter. He knows that signifier is attached to signified because someone—that is, Proteus—made the attachment, and this self-objectification heralds the possibility of Proteus developing an ego—an objectified, definitive version of the self. Before this moment, we must assume that Proteus always counted correctly but had no idea who was doing the counting. The emergence of Proteus as subject is thus correlative to the loss of the seal. The seal causes (for Proteus) a gap to emerge in the universe; his doubt functions as a belated recognition of that gap; his future ability to count seals will depend on a projection of a self into that gap. The tale therefore suggests that self-consciousness arrives late on the scene. Proteus begins to suspect (but too late) what he himself was unconsciously doing all along; he is now conscious of an agency that has undermined his conscious existence and was thus prior to it. His self-consciousness is parasitic on his unconscious, and his objectified self (his ego) can never be the whole story.

In the Beginning Was a First Name

But we have not yet finished with Proteus' problematic relation to language. For the story provides us with a series of puns on Proteus' name. Indeed, the episode is replete with beginnings. Eidothea claims that Proteus will <u>first</u> count his seals (πρῶτον ἀριθμήσει, 4.411) and, later, that he will <u>first</u> count Menelaus' men disguised as seals (πρώτους λέγε, 4.452). She encourages Menelaus to capture him when he <u>first</u> goes to sleep (πρῶτα κατευνηθέντα, 4.414), and Proteus himself will begin his transformations by turning into a lion <u>first</u> (πρώτιστα λέων γένετ', 4.456). What is the significance of this further punning? At the very least, the problem of counting and inclusion is now written into the name of our protagonist. This might alert us to the possibility that the wider narrative pattern, involving a shift from infallible certainty to doubt, might have repercussions for how we conceive of our elementary symbolic link to the world of language: our proper names.

The simplest explanation would involve adhering to the split between human and god as a meaningful framework for this episode, reading the tale as the depiction of Proteus' arrival as a human named subject in *Odyssey* 4. For insofar as he is an infallible god, he is not a creature subject to language and the necessary possibility of deception that language brings with it. His arrival as a mortal would thus coincide with his subjection to language. There is a good deal of circumstantial evidence for this. Proteus' appearance, as a god, from the unknown realms of the sea occurs in the middle of the day (*Od.* 4.400 ff.), the time for epiphany.[22] In this liminal time and space, the realms of the human and divine can encounter one another. If this is a time when gods can be seen, Eidothea's gift of ambrosia, the "immortal" liquid, allows the human companions of Menelaus to enter, temporarily, the realm of the god.[23] These narrative details thus provide hints that Proteus is on display at a moment of vulnerability, when he is on a level footing with mortals who have been artificially strengthened. Eidothea's trick takes advantage of this moment of vulnerability to drag him into the realm of mortals; once he has been tricked and there is a gap in the universe for Proteus, he is no longer a god.

If this is the case, then Proteus' name must have been ironic; to borrow the terms of John Peradotto, it was an example of a significant name "motivated by its contrary or contradictory [meaning]."[24] For if, before the trick, Proteus represented a language without closure, a world without a gap, this must mean the positing of no end or beginning to the signifying chain. Compare Lacan's comment on the way the sense of a sentence is retroactively constructed: "It's quite clear, for example, that if I start a sentence you won't understand its meaning until I've finished it, since it's really quite necessary for me to have spoken the last word of the sentence if you are to understand where its first one was."[25] Before the trick, this retroactive construction of a beginning of a sentence never occurred within Proteus' universe. Proteus indulged in an impossible counting, a counting without a beginning or end; and because the symbolic can only create meaning by imposing limits and boundaries on reality—indeed, what we call "reality" is itself a product of these socially constructed, defined spaces—Proteus had no symbolic existence at all. He was a being of the Lacanian Real, the seamless world prior to language, which has no symbolic limit written upon it and which constantly resists the efforts of the symbolic to categorize it completely. The trick stages the first time that Proteus truly counts. *Odyssey* 4 narrates the moment when Proteus finally lives up to his name by creating a limit, a beginning, to the signifying chain. Proteus now allows the last signifier to determine retroactively the first, and he therefore creates meaning. This interpretation also helps us make more sense of the emphasis the tale places on Proteus' speech. For Eidothea's trick ends (and her victory is complete) the moment her father speaks to Menelaus. It is his words that signify that he has lost.

> And he will try you by taking the form of all creatures that come
>   forth
> and move on the earth; he will be water and magical fire.
> You must hold stiffly on to him and squeeze him the harder.
> But when at last he himself, *speaking in words, questions you,*
> being now in the same form he was when you saw him sleeping,
> then, hero, you must give over your force and let the old man
> go free, and ask him which one of the gods is angry with you,
> and ask him how to make your way home on the sea where the fish
>   swarm.
>
>   (*Od.* 4.417–24)
>   (translation modified)

If we see Proteus as divine prior to the trick, then we can understand these words as his first words, his first proper speech act. This would help us make sense out of another interesting aspect of the tale. For until Menelaus captures him, forcing him to speak, Proteus maintains a total silence within the narrative.[26]

This also suggests a further irony in Proteus' supposed infallibility. Proteus was indeed an unerring, ever truthful prophet; but his ability to maintain such a status depended on his rejection of speech. Eidothea's trick is thus completed when Proteus speaks, because the act of speech itself is enough to guarantee that he can no longer be infallible. To enter language is to admit the possibility that one can be in error or deceived. Eidothea's trick provided Proteus with a truly representational language; it allowed him to continue counting his seals, but this counting is of a fundamentally different sort because it occurs against the background of the loss of a seal. A fundamental Lacanian maxim is that a thing must be lost in order for it to be represented—a maxim that seems to be luridly realized in the *Apologoi,* where it is only by their death that the companions of Odysseus are allowed inclusion in the poem. For Proteus, his number system is no longer equivalent to the seals (as was the case before the trick) but represents them. The loss of the seal now makes sense to Proteus because of the system of counting up to five that determines it as lost. This loss opens up a space for Proteus to come to be as a desiring subject: he desires because there is now a lack within his universe. But this desire means that he no longer has all the answers and therefore is not unerring.

The story ends with one further development, which can help us see the properly traumatic encounter, for Proteus, with the enigma of what the Other wants. For insofar as Proteus himself holds out the hope of a truthful, unerring prophecy (access to the realm of a complete, all-knowing Other of knowledge), his awareness of his own fallibility is also a puncturing of that hope. He himself becomes a living witness to the way the Other lacks. Eidothea's suggestion that Menelaus should hold on to Proteus until he asks him a question also sets up a basic narrative expectation for us. What will be the first question the old man ever articulates in language? Let us turn to the text.

> τίς νύ τοι, Ἀτρέος υἱέ, θεῶν συμφράσσατο βουλάς,
> ὄφρα μ' ἕλοις ἀέκοντα λοχησάμενος; τέο σε χρή;
> ὣς ἔφατ', αὐτὰρ ἐγώ μιν ἀμειβόμενος προσέειπον·
> οἶσθα, γέρον· τί με ταῦτα παρατροπέων ἐρεείνεις;

> ["Which of the gods now, son of Atreus, has been advising you
> to capture me from ambush against my will. What do you want?"
> So he spoke, and I in turn spoke up and made answer:
> "You know, Old Man. Why try to put me off with your answer?"]

> (*Od.* 4.462–65)

The remarkable thing about this question is the way Menelaus refuses to answer it. Menelaus acts as if Proteus is still infallible and therefore impossible to deceive. Though Menelaus was, in some sense, the direct agent of the trick, he appears to misunderstand the significance of the trick completely. He acts as if Proteus is an all-knowing being impervious to deception, when Menelaus' recent ability to pin him down proves the exact reverse: Proteus has just been fooled and wants to know why. In short, Menelaus quite misses the performative dimension of the trick itself, which changes Proteus. If the episode at first seems to end in a successful act of communication because Menelaus obtains the information he needs to get home from Proteus, the failure of Menelaus to answer Proteus' question suggests that there is also a more profound failure of communication. Not only is Proteus' question not answered, but Menelaus' refusal to answer suggests that he does not even trust Proteus' sincerity. Ironically, it is as if Menelaus takes the place of the divine Proteus before the trick, trusting in language's ability simply to describe the world outside of itself, rather than taking some part in constructing the universe of symbols.[27]

We can understand the failure of Proteus' counting system as his first encounter with the Other as a symbolic system. In turn, we can understand his perplexed question to Menelaus as his own first encounter with the Other as a system that is not whole but lacking—with the Other as desire. Proteus has been wrested out of a complacent existence in a coherent, whole universe into a new one he does not yet understand. His question signifies both an effort to find out what has happened to him and a desire to find out what his place in this world will be. To ask, "What do you want?" [τέο σε χρή] (4.463), is also to ask, "What do you want from me?" His encounter with language has resulted in a loss (the lost seal) and thus a desire to heal that loss. He then turns to the first person he encounters in order to find an answer to his desire. He hopes that finding out what Menelaus desires can provide an answer to what he himself desires—a return to a time before desire, when he lacked nothing. The roles of prophet and seeker of prophecy are reversed, even if Menelaus is quite oblivious to this shift. For Proteus' hope is that if he could answer the question of Menelaus' desire, of why he dragged him into the mortal world, the god could plug the gap that generates his own desire. From now on, Proteus will desire through others, gaining access to what he wants through the desires of others. Proteus thus asks the most basic, childlike kind of question to the being he believed produced him. What do you want from me? Why have you brought me into the world?

Let us now turn to a second possible interpretation of Proteus by testing out the possibility that he has been a doubter from the start of the episode, if we had but paid close enough attention; that is, we can read the narrative symptomatically, looking back for the signs of Proteus' infallibility that our interpretation might suggest. This might be more unsettling for us, as it more directly involves *our* desire. As I suggested earlier, the tragedy of Proteus depends on the way we, as readers, can make sense of the signifier *Proteus*. It thus implicates us through our abilities to make sense of language, even as it depicts Proteus' own failure to understand himself. With this in mind, it is worth paying closer attention to what I added to the tale in order to make sense of it.

There is clearly a delay necessary before we can make sense of Proteus' name; the story provides an "etymology" of a name, making retroactive sense of something that appeared senseless. But in trying to make retroactive sense of the tale, I had to forge a connection between the sense of Proteus as "first" and the sea god. This link turned Proteus into a figure not unlike the famed messenger-slave of antiquity who is completely unaware of the tattoo, engraved on his skull, that tells of his impending doom—a story Lacan himself used to illustrate the alien nature of the human unconscious.

> But in Freud it [the unconscious] is a question of something quite different, which is a *savoir*, certainly, but one that involves not the least *connaissance*, in that it is inscribed in a discourse, of which, like the "messenger-slave" of ancient usage, the subject who carries under his hair the codicil that condemns him to death knows neither the meaning nor the text, nor in what language it is written, nor even that it had been tattooed on his shaven scalp as he slept.[28]

The tragedy comes from our belated recognition that this was always an accident waiting to happen to Proteus. There is added irony in that what Proteus remained unaware of—and what necessitated his doom—was not something distant from him, but, rather, something too close to him for him to see: he fails to understand something that promises to constitute his essence, his own proper name as Proteus. This failure to see exactly what constitutes him is correlative to the message engraved on the slave's head.[29]

But here we need pause to doubt. For rather than take his behavior of counting seals at face value, we might use our awareness of his foolishness to ask a question. Why was he counting his seals so obsessively in the first place?[30] We might compare Proteus to the neurotic, who constantly thinks, counts, and recounts. This pseudo intellectual activity functions as a defense against his unconscious desire. If he can convince himself that he is consciously in control at all times, he would be able to forget the way he is ruled by unconscious desires. His constant conscious activity allows him to keep thinking and thus ignore the unconscious thought processes that nevertheless continue to govern him. He engages in a futile effort to deny the way he is split by language. This suggests a different way of understanding Proteus' actions; for surely he, too, in his obsessional devotion to counting his seals endlessly, seems to be much more neurotic than mad. If so, then the gap previously posited between his limitless counting and his name (signifying "first" and thus imposing a limit) is partially bridged. Proteus' incessant counting is an ongoing attempt to postpone something that he unconsciously knows: that he is a finite, living being, defined by language's limits. His name, *Proteus*, rules him in ways he refuses to acknowledge; he is ruled by it because he constantly tries to flee its truth, to avoid the necessary limit of the counting sequence by a constant counting of an indefinite sequence. In Proteus' case, we can now see a different motivation for his constant counting: for why else would he do it unless he was—in some way— aware of the possibility of failure?

Here the tale becomes more disturbing for us. For up until now, it seemed possible to take a certain amount of intellectual pleasure in the way we understand Eidothea's trick while Proteus does not. We make sense of the tale (if my reading of the significance of Proteus' counting is correct) by identifying with Eidothea's cleverness in tricking her father. But the final twist in this tale is that Proteus' ultimate error may be not in counting incorrectly but, rather, in the way he places so much effort on the process of counting, of making sense itself. The tale allows us, for a moment, to occupy a relatively secure position of knowledge in contrast to Proteus; we understand what is happening to him in ways that he fails to understand. But the tale pulls the rug out from under our feet by illustrating how the obsessional attachment to certain knowledge systems may itself prove to be a source of error and denial. Our pleasure in making sense out of the story of the deception of Proteus leaves us with a worry: what are we denying or ignoring as we make sense of the text; and what is at stake in such an obsessive desire to make sense out of the poem, to be caught up in its own obsession with numbers?[31]

From Counter to Counted

Let us now turn to the seals. For Proteus' counting clearly has consequences for the objects of his counting, his herd of seals. Given that the Homeric poems are obsessed with the problems of classification,[32] this topic is worthy of closer attention. Crucial here is the way that groups are formed through their common allegiance to a master, a master who holds the place of a master signifier. A master is someone whose power can only function while it is unchallenged, because the mastery itself is inherently senseless. If the subjectivization of Proteus takes us to the very brink of the logic of the master signifier, this subjectivization has consequences for those who are mastered.

It is perhaps simplest to examine this by comparing the problems with personal identity faced by both Proteus and the seals. Before the trick, Proteus never questioned his identity as master of his seals. If we are told that he is an unerring god, nevertheless his failure to question his own role suggests that he may only be a human fool who thinks he is a god. He is thus foolish in Lacanian terms. For Lacan, a fool is someone who believes that the role he or she plays is an actual property of himself or herself. He uses the example of a king who believes he *is* a king, rather than a contingent individual playing out the socially mandated role of king.[33] Proteus' self-counting allows him to establish a distance between the roles he plays and the subject who plays them. He thus experiences an emptying out of his invulnerable identity as counter of seals and of his identity as their natural master. But what is crucial here is that a similar process can be imagined for the seals.

Let us take as our starting point the way that the narrative questions the border between humans, gods, and animals. What happens if we anthropomorphize the seals?[34] Before the trick, Proteus' seals were grouped together as seals because of the performative nature of Proteus' counting. His counting of the seals coincided with the attribution to them of an identity (the ego identity of being Proteus' seals). But the emptying out of the identity of Proteus also leaves a question mark over the identity of the seals. What will happen to them if their counter, Proteus, no longer counts them? For if Proteus falls "down" from immortality into mortal status (or a more explicit confrontation with his mortal status), is it not possible that these animals too will fall "up" into the status of human mortals? If so, they will do so in and through a confrontation with a choice. They can either confront the contingency of their identity (realize that they are only playing out the role of Proteus' seals—that they are not really his seals but only his seals insofar as he counts them as his) or try to return to the safety of a fixed identity, the (now false) knowledge of being his seals. If Proteus is a human who unsuccessfully fantasizes that he is a god, perhaps the seals are humans who prefer to act as a herd of seals. If we read this tale as an allegory for ideological strategies, we can see it opening up the question of the fear that confronts subjects who realize the contingency of their socially mandated roles. Such roles offer an alternative to doubt in the form of a fixed identity, hoping that this fixed identity is preferable to the abyss of doubt.[35]

From Proteus to Odysseus

We can now tentatively explore how the tale of Proteus raises questions about the *Odyssey* as a whole and, in particular, about its central character, Odysseus.

For the duplicity in Proteus' own name can be related to the notorious riddles concerning the way the narrative fails to speak Odysseus' proper name in the proem. Goldhill has suggested that the lack of a proper name identifying *andra* (and the replacement instead with *polytropon*) functions as a *griphos*.

> The surprising lack of a proper name in the first line(s) of the epic, then, prompts the question not simply of *to whom* does the opening expression refer, but of *what* is (to be) recognized in such a periphrastic reference. Indeed, the withholding of the name invests the proem with the structure of a *griphos*, a riddle, an enigma, where a series of expressions (of which *polutropon* is the first) successively qualifies the term *andra* as the name "Odysseus" is approached.[36]

A crucial problem suggested by the *griphos* is the problem of closure.[37] How can one ever fully define what a "man" is when there is always one more predicate that can be attached to him, retroactively changing any essence? As I have tried to show, this is the crucial problem of language itself, and it is explored in the tale of Proteus. By refusing to name Odysseus, the poem opens up a space where the identity of its major character can be constructed and reconstructed. It allows the hero to experiment with different masks, alternative options for being in the world. The person who is *not* named Odysseus is temporarily free from the constraints and obligations imposed by a social identity; the seductive illusion entertained is that he can be who he wants to be.

The nameless subject of the *Odyssey* thus seems to have a certain freedom within language, a freedom that is correlative to the storyteller's freedom to tell different tales. But the Proteus tale forces us to reevaluate this freedom. Just as Proteus is, at first, a being who is nothing more than an endless series of masks, so, too, the plot of the *Odyssey* is notoriously endless. The anticipated reunion of Penelope and Odysseus, the longed-for *nostos*, does not end the poem; the poem instead points beyond itself to an enigmatic further journey for Odysseus, prophesied by Teiresias. The poem thus seems to perpetuate this fantasy of an endlessly changing and plural self. But the problem with this fantasy is that it runs the risk of destroying any possibility of making sense of the self at all. In psychoanalytic terms, it flirts with psychosis: if there are no limits to the self, then the self seems to run the risk of total dissolution into senselessness. For sense itself depends on the stability and definition that limits provide. Rather than achieving a utopian, plural self, we run the risk of losing the self entirely as it becomes fundamentally ripped up in pieces and dissolved because of its lack of an anchoring point. The Proteus tale suggests that some limit is necessary for language to make any sense at all and that this limit brings with it a necessary loss, a prohibition of whatever is beyond the limit. This sets up parallel questions for the wider narrative of the poem: Are there any limits to Odysseus' polytropy? If so, what is Odysseus' relationship to the loss that created those limits?

We might start to answer these questions by returning to Odysseus' use of *metis* in his encounters with the Cyclops and the Phaeacians. In both cases, his *metis* succeeds. He manages to escape the clutches of the Cyclops, and he also procures his ride home from the Phaeacians. But the success of his trickery has its darker side. Odysseus succeeds, but both the Cyclops and the Phaeacians lose spectacularly. The Cyclops lose his eye; the Phaeacians lose their ability to transport strangers anywhere without a care. It is well known (and much discussed) that Odysseus' success against the Cyclops is dependent on an identification with a paradoxical identity that signifies absence and loss: the identity of "No one."[38] I suggest that this paradoxical identity should also influence how we understand the fate of the Phaeacians and Cyclopes. Proteus moved into a truly human realm when he was forced to recognize the loss of one of his seals. I suggest that Odysseus, in his encounter with the Phaeacians and Cyclopes, performed a similar role to the lost seal. He forces the Phaeacians and Cyclopes to come to terms with the possibility of loss. If this interpretation is correct, then Odysseus' paradoxical identity as "No one" becomes more significant. If human identity is contingent, it can only be so against a background of the loss of belief in any fixed identity. Odysseus' role as *Outis*, "No one," signifies this loss. It is precisely this loss of belief in themselves that Odysseus forces the Cyclopes and Phaeacians to undergo. In turn, this suggests that we need to reevaluate Odysseus' role in the entire poem. He is not simply a human survivor; he is someone who brings the concept of loss to others.[39]

4

From Stones to Statehood

Sublime Objects in the Odyssey

No object can satisfy desire, and this lesson must be learned by the Phaeacians and Cyclopes. But can an object cause it? The origin of desire on Phaeacia coincides with the appearance of two objects that cause wonder in the onlookers. The Phaeacians are left under the shadow of a huge mountain that threatens to destroy them, and we witness their amazement at the sight of one of their ships turned into stone. These stones have counterparts on the island of the Cyclops. Odysseus closes that story with a final image of Polyphemus hurling a pair of huge stones at his ship—but the stones conspicuously miss their target. Can we make anything of this coincidence?

We can sketch an answer by linking the endings of these two stories to other mythic tales of origin where stones play a central role—the story of Deucalion and Pyrrha and the story of the birth of Zeus. As these tales will show, stones are silent objects that produce a sense of wonder and puzzlement in the viewers and thus set the viewer's desire in motion by raising fundamental, unanswerable questions. So the *Odyssey* leaves the Phaeacians at the very moment they begin to ponder what the sudden appearance of stones might mean. But though we need some sort of identification with the Phaeacians in order to see the narrative significance of the appearance of these stones—as they ask the ultimately unknowable question of what these stones mean—we should also recognize that the narrative allows us to keep a certain distance from them. We see them reacting, working through their fascination and wonder, and as we do so, we witness the poem's attempt to show us human society as such being constituted. For the Phaeacians are to be defined by the distance they keep from these strange objects of fascination.

Consider a basic narrative pattern at work in Odysseus' interactions with the Phaeacians. Before Odysseus' entrance, Nausithous' prophecy functioned as a symptom of the impossible nature of Phaeacian society: he told of a guest who would destroy the Phaeacians, but to refuse to accept a guest is to violate the symbolic quality that made them who they were. As such, the prophecy of his appearance could not be properly integrated into the Phaeacian worldview. It was therefore acknowledged but ignored. On Odysseus' departure, this particular enigma is resolved (the moment the prophecy comes true, Alcinous is on hand to remember it and thus explain it). But this does not mean that the land of the Phaeacians becomes a truly open world, dissolving the symptom of their unfriendliness. Rather, the internalized, repressed enigma of Nausithous' prophecy is replaced by an external one: the puzzlement at the meaning of the stones. Indeed, the first stone, as Zeus and Poseidon plan it, is explicitly designed to produce wonder.

> ὁππότε κεν δὴ πάντες ἐλαυνομένην προΐδωνται
> λαοὶ ἀπὸ πτόλιος, θεῖναι λίθον ἐγγύθι γαίης
> νηΐ θοῇ ἴκελον, ἵνα <u>θαυμάζωσιν</u> ἅπαντες
> ἄνθρωποι, μέγα δέ σφιν ὄρος πόλει ἀμφικαλύψαι.
>
> (*Od.* 13.155–58)

[When all the people are watching her from the city
as she comes in, then turn her into a rock that looks like
a fast ship, close off shore, so that all the <u>people may wonder</u>
at her. And hide her city under a great mountain.]

(translation modified)

It is well known that there is a link in archaic poetry, strengthened by etymological play, between a people *(laos)* and stones *(laas)*. The emergence of people from stones—paradigmatically, in the myth of Deucalion and Pyrrha—is an indication of the split between the human world of animate beings and the inhuman world of inanimate rocks. Consider the following apt remarks of Haubold: "Carrying in themselves a memory of their non-existence (the stone), the *laoi* in early Greek hexameter are never far from the state from which they spring. This means, on the one hand, that we are left in close and threatening contact with non-being."[1] One could predict that this confrontation with non-being might be the source of wonder for the Phaeacians as they see their frozen ship. But we can be more precise. For what is interesting about events on Phaeacia is that such a confrontation applies more directly to the second stone: only the emergence of the mountain threatens collective obliteration. With the first stone, by way of contrast, the gods both give and take away. They take away the supreme symbolic quality that had constituted the Phaeacians as Phaeacians: their mobility, linked to the perfection of their communicative chain that guaranteed truthfulness, the perfect passing of Phaeacian identity down through the generations. For though the Phaeacians were never immortal, they did live in a society where no one doubted the immortality of the species, premised upon this communicative power. But the gods also give. For the first stone is not amorphous but, instead, "like a ship." It is not meaningless, insignificant matter but already promises some sort of representational ability. We can tentatively link this first stone to the process of mythmaking that will occur in this society after Odysseus leaves. The stone will become a sign of a golden age, a way of life that has disappeared but continues to be remembered in the people's interpretations of the stone sign. Indeed, the actions of Zeus and Poseidon are complicit in allowing this possibility of mythmaking to the Phaeacians. Further, an imagined link between the shape of the stone and the perfect ship that it replaces might be the first effort to heal the wounds of the communicative impasse that will now characterize Phaeacian society. Their social relations are hampered by doubt, but they may come to hold themselves together by the belief in their former perfection, itself dependent on the possibility that the strangely shaped rock was once really a ship. In connecting shape to lost ship, they stitch together a mythic story about themselves. But the second stone puts this hope under question. For any meaningfulness they choose to construct from the past must now take place against the possibility of a complete destruction of the entire culture.

We are now in a better position to assess the relationship between the wonder that stones produce and their status as signifiers of nonbeing. For the wonder itself is already an attempt not only to recognize this possible symbolic obliteration but also to make sense of it and tame it. So the emergence of stones on Phaeacia sets up a sliding scale between a kind of wonder already mediated by some attempt to give meaning to a culture's existence (the stone "like a ship") and a more terrifying wonder linked to complete nonexistence. To translate these events into human terms, we need to remember that events on Phaeacia happen backwards: they are an inhuman species becoming human, whereas we are already human, engaged in the process of making sense out of a world that resists these efforts. So we need to reverse the order of the stones in order to ponder the significance for mortals: we first confront the stark possibility of utter obliteration (the mountain) and then, by "pathetic fallacies," try to drain away some of the terror provided by this possibility. We find order (the stone is "like a ship") in meaninglessness.[2]

Zeus, First and Last

We can connect the tale of the Phaeacians to another famous stone story, the birth of Zeus as told in the *Theogony*.[3] Kronos is given a prophecy that one of his sons will usurp him. To prevent this, he swallows his own children one by one as Rhea gives birth to them. But the baby Zeus, due to the machinations of Rhea, is spirited into a cave and replaced by a stone. Kronos then swallows the stone, though he will ultimately be unable to digest it. When the grown-up Zeus returns to liberate his siblings, Kronos vomits up this stone. Thus, the object that had been eaten last is thrown up first.[4] It then is set up at Pytho as a *sema*, "a thing of wonder to mortals" [θαῦμα θνητοῖσι βροτοῖσι]. This object of wonder has thus been transferred from inside Kronos' body into the public realm of mortals, where it becomes an external sign of the very thing that Kronos could not digest and that accordingly caused his downfall.

Note the shared pattern between this tale and that of the Phaeacians. First, there is a prophecy that cannot be properly understood. Then, there is an attempt to either ignore or avoid that prophecy: Kronos thinks swallowing children will help him avoid it; the Phaeacian "unfriendliness" is a symptom of the way they believe they can ignore it. This internal *aporia* becomes externalized in the form of a stone. From this point on, the stone itself takes the place of the former prophecy; it is itself enigmatic, senseless, but also thought-provoking.

But the difference between these stories is perhaps more interesting than the similarities. The tale of trickery that produces Zeus' birth is designed to explain how the divine world of Olympus became stabilized and how the generational conflict between the gods came to an end. After he ousts his father, Zeus will rule in perpetuity. In comparison, the story of the destruction of the world of the Phaeacians is a tale of the destabilization of a quasi-divine world and the emergence of a human one. Because of this, what happens to the stones, the signs of wonder, is quite different in each case. In the story of Zeus, the destabilized immortal world, confronted with the stone that overthrew the father of the gods, the sign of the fragility of generational order, does not simply disappear: rather, it is thrust upon mortals. It is as if, unable to deal with the possibility of generational tension, the gods simply download onto the mortal universe the thing that signifies their instability. Mortals will have to deal with this awesome object, but Olympus will be free of it. By way of contrast, the Phaeacians become mortal when they are forced to confront the meaninglessness of stones, the puzzle they provide, and the potentiality of the Phaeacians' ultimate nonbeing that comes with them. If this interpretation is right, are we not left with the strange possibility that the entire universe on Olympus after Zeus comes to power is remarkably like the Phaeacian world before the entrance of Odysseus? The gods and the Phaeacians are both species that exist by ignoring the hidden signs of their own vulnerability—the *sema* at Pytho and the prophecy of Nausithous.

Deucalion and Pyrrha

Let us now compare events on Phaeacia with a more famous tale of stones and people, the story of Deucalion and Pyrrha. Its most significant details are related by Apollodorus; I provide them in my own translation, adding the Greek where relevant. Though Apollodorus provides only a summary of the myth, doubtless collected from a range of sources, there are more than enough details to suggest a series of parallels with the mythic situations of the Phaeacians and Cyclopes. The tale itself revolves around the central etymology of *laos* (people) from *laas* (stone). But the felicity of the pun once more lies in the manner in which it reveals the peculiar mix of sense and senselessness that characterizes human society.

> Zeus by pouring heavy rain from heaven flooded the greater part of Greece, so that all men were destroyed, except a few who fled to the high mountains in the neighborhood (τὰ πλησίον ὑψηλὰ ὄρη). Then the mountains in Thessaly parted (τὰ κατὰ Θεσσαλίαν ὄρη διέστη), so that all the world outside the Isthmus and Peloponnese was overwhelmed. But Deucalion, floating in the chest over the sea for nine days and nights, drifted to Parnassus, and there, when the rain ceased, he landed and sacrificed to Zeus, the god of Escape. Zeus sent Hermes to him and allowed him to choose what he would, and he chose to get men (ὁ δὲ αἱρεῖται ἀνθρώπους αὐτῶι γενέσθαι). And, at the bidding of Zeus, picking up stones, he threw them over his head (ὑπὲρ κεφαλῆς ἔβαλλεν αἴρων λίθους), and the stones which Deucalion threw became men, and the stones which Pyrrha threw became women. Accordingly people were called metaphorically people (λαοί) from λᾶας, "a stone."[5]

It is worth noting immediately some links between this story and the tales of the Cyclopes and Phaeacians in the *Oydssey*. There are two groups of survivors of the flood: those who escaped destruction by living on mountaintops and Deucalion and Pyrrha, who lived because of their ability to construct a sailing vessel. Though the survivors who fled to the mountains are mentioned only to be ignored, it is significant that Apollodorus' tale links sea to mountain in his description of the trip of Deucalion and Pyrrha to Parnassus. The pairing of survivors on mountains and survivors at sea returns us to the impossible civilizations of the seafaring Phaeacians and the mountain-dwelling Cyclopes. The link is strengthened by the curious reference to a cataclysmic destruction in Phaeacian history. Nausithous, the Phaeacian founder who led the Phaeacians' migration away from the Cyclopes, was born to Periboea. But her father, Eurymedon, had somehow destroyed his people.

> Ναυσίθοον μὲν πρῶτα Ποσειδάων ἐνοσίχθων
> γείνατο καὶ Περίβοια, γυναικῶν εἶδος ἀρίστη,
> ὁπλοτάτη θυγάτηρ μεγαλήτορος Εὐρυμέδοντος,
> ὅς ποθ' ὑπερθύμοισι Γιγάντεσσιν βασίλευεν.
> ἀλλ' ὁ μὲν ὤλεσε λαὸν ἀτάσθαλον, ὤλετο δ' αὐτός·
>
> (*Od.* 7.56–60)

[First of all Poseidon, shaker of the earth, and the fairest
in form of women, Periboia, had a son Nausithoos.
She was the youngest daughter of great-hearted Eurymedon,
who in his time had been king over the high-hearted Giants.
But he lost his recklessly daring people and himself perished.]

Part of the genealogical story told about the Phaeacians alludes to a past loss; the Phaeacians are clearly survivors of this loss that is not explained, just as Deucalion and Pyrrha have survived a loss. But it is in the stone throwing that the connection becomes more explicit. For the myth of Deucalion and Pyrrha portrays both a choice and a pact at the origins of humanity. There is a choice for a social world, which comes into being via the emergence of *anthropoi*. But this choice only comes after the enactment of a pact between Deucalion and Pyrrha (ratified by an absent third party, Zeus) to hurl stones. The manner in which they hurl these stones is crucial. First, they must turn their backs to the trajectory of the stones they throw. They create people, but they cannot see what they create; stones become people, and this is, in an important sense, brought about by their throw. Yet they remain blind to how this happens.

What exactly is it that they remain blind to? There are a couple of possible interpretations. We can first pay attention to what literally happens in the myth. For what happens is the emergence of a pun. The word *laos* turns into *laas*. What "causes" people in this myth of origins is nothing more—if we take the myth at face value—than the similarity at the level of the signifier between *laas* and *laos*. In this myth, the suggestion is that people come into being when language begins to function autonomously, behind the backs of subjects. It is tempting to relate this to Lacan's thesis on the "agency of the letter," the crucial argument for his often repeated claim that the unconscious is structured like a language. The argument is not simply that slips of the tongue, puns, and distortions of the texts of our dreams show us that our language is disrupted by unconscious desire. These disturbances of language not only show us that we are thinking unconsciously; they suggest how unconscious thought operates—through manipulations of language at the level of the signifier.[6] Accordingly, in this myth, humans become humans at the moment that a pun is made, when desire begins to slide metonymically between signifiers—stones becoming people and so on. What Deucalion and Pyrrha confront is language working autonomously, behind their backs.

We can also try to interpret the meaning of the pun on *laos* and *laas* at the level of what is signified. What is the significance of describing the origins of humanity as from stones? This tale of origins tries to make sense of the origins of humanity by pointing out that humanity comes into being when we recognize that there is some connection between people and stones. Thus, the pun tries to make sense of an event that Deucalion and Pyrrha, the first humans, are unable to see. The stone is an object that seems to cause the birth of people, but we can never be certain of how this process of causation itself occurred, because we remain blind to it. Nevertheless, the positing of a verbal link between stones and people is a significant, paradigmatic gesture. It is an attempt to use language to make sense out of an inexplicable event, an effort to make sense out of the nonsense of human origins from stones. Stones—mute, senseless objects—disappear, and people emerge in their place. The task of Deucalion and Pyrrha (and also us, their human ancestors) is to try to make sense of this metamorphosis. The link in language between *laos* and *laas* is the first effort at providing an account of their origins. As such, it is parallel to the stone "like a ship" that emerges for the Phaeacians.

This reading would seem to offer a story of progression from nonsense to sense at the origins of humanity, from mute stones to speaking humans. Yet things do not proceed quite so smoothly; for even as the myth depicts the disappearance of stones, the pun itself on *laas* and *laos* suggests that the "senseless" part of our origin as stones remains with us in our language. If we are people who can make sense of the world, the very word we have for ourselves links us to our senseless, stone origins. If this is correct, then the pun functions as a reminder that the choice *for* language is inexplicable *within* language. Language circles around an origin that humans remain blind to; it is a response to that fundamental blindness. Stones function as a reminder of the limits of our ability to make sense of the world. But precisely because of this, they are objects of wonder.

The Colossos as Sublime Object

This particular set of symbolic associations attached to stones in Greek has much in common with Jean-Pierre Vernant's elegant essay on the *colossos*, originally a dark, erect slab of stone, which eventually comes to substitute for corpses at the tombs of the dead during the archaic period. Though the word *colossos* never occurs in Homer, Vernant's imaginative analysis of the symbolism of stones can help us understand the significance of the stones on Phaeacia.

> When a colossos is used as a substitute for the corpse, in the tomb, it is not meant to reproduce the features of the dead man or to create the illusion of his physical presence. What it embodies in permanent form in stone is not the image of the dead man but his life in the beyond, the life that is opposed to that of living men as the world of night is opposed to the world of light. The colossos is not an image; it is a "double," as the dead man himself is a double of the living man.[7]

Neither entirely in the realm of the human, nor yet in the world beyond, the silent stone of the *colossos* functions as a perpetual bridge between the two. As with the stones of Deucalion and Pyrrha, it does this by attempting to represent the unrepresentable; and this, according to Vernant, is the peculiar function of a religious sign.

> The religious sign is not simply a piece of mental equipment. Its purpose is not limited to evoking in men's minds the sacred power to which it refers. Its intention is always to establish a true means of communication with this power and to really introduce its presence into the human world. But while it thus aims, so to speak, to establish a bridge with the divine, it must at the same time emphasize the gap, the immeasurable difference between this sacred power and anything that attempts to manifest it, perforce inadequately, to the eyes of men.[8]

The *colossos* as a religious sign is unable to represent "the world beyond," "night," the realm of the unsignified. But it comes as close as is possible to signifying this, by representing the impossibility in its own form: because it is mute, senseless, and inexplicable, it displays the impossibility of access to the world beyond. Yet this stone is also fascinating and monstrously terrifying. It causes us to wonder about it and thus motivates our desire to pursue pathways to the divine. To relate this to Deucalion and Pyrrha, let us simply emphasize that their social pact (emergence as a *laos*) is set into motion by the effort to explain their origins from senseless stones *(laas)*.

One further detail of the Deucalion and Pyrrha tale is worthy of consideration here. They throw the stones over their heads. Why? This act emphasizes the vulnerability of Deucalion and Pyrrha as they enter the realm of mortals. The stones cause them to duck. Their heads disappear for a second, only to reappear. But their reappearance coincides with an awareness of the prior absence into which the heads move. As Deucalion and Pyrrha throw the stones, they symbolically "lose their heads."[9] This is highly suggestive of what happens to human identity when we become a linguistic species. Deucalion and Pyrrha's entrance to the social world coincides with this loss of the aspect of themselves (their heads) that seems to give the greatest promise of individuality. Their heads are lost, and their efforts to go on with life can only come after a recognition of the possibility of this loss of what signifies the essential self, the missing head.

Let us now return to the specific form of the Phaeacian punishment. We have discussed the petrifaction of the ship and the emergence of the mountain. But it is worth emphasizing that these are merely the climax to a series of highly significant references to stone both in Odysseus' *Apologoi* and during the rest of his stay in Phaeacia. For the action of Zeus and Poseidon in rendering a ship stone should be compared with the former perfect mobility of the Phaeacian ships. It is an imposition of a limit, and this can help us explain the manner in which Poseidon carries out the punishment.

βῆ ῥ' ἴμεν ἐς Σχερίην, ὅθι Φαίηκες γεγάασιν.
ἔνθ' ἔμεν· ἡ δὲ μάλα σχεδὸν ἤλυθε ποντοπόρος νηῦς
ῥίμφα διωκομένη· τῆς δὲ σχεδὸν ἦλθ' ἐνοσίχθων,
ὅς μιν λᾶαν θῆκε καὶ ἐρρίζωσεν ἔνερθε
χειρὶ καταπρηνεῖ ἐλάσας· ὁ δὲ νόσφι βεβήκει.

(*Od.* 13.160–64)

[[H]e went off
striding to Scheria, where the Phaiakians are born and live. There
he waited, and the sea-going ship came close in, lightly
pursuing her way, and the Earthshaker came close up to her,
and turned her into stone and rooted her there to the bottom
with a flat stroke of his hand. And then he went away from her.]

The motion of the Phaeacian ships is highly unusual because they lack helmsmen.[10] This strange quality helps explain Poseidon's gesture. Before this grounding of a ship, the ships of Phaeacia moved, but no human agent caused their movement: they signified pure mobility.[11] Poseidon's gesture halts this mobility, but in making this gesture, he creates the possibility for a true agent of movement. By alerting the Phaeacians to the possibility that any act of moving the ship might fail, he creates the possibility that they can now act in a human way because they will no longer be in complete control of their acts. Poseidon fastens the ship to the ground and then leaves. His simultaneous presence followed by absence—"he was (already) far away"[12]—follows a pattern that is familiar in the *Odyssey*. He opens a gap in the universe of the Phaeacians in much the same manner as the loss of a seal opened up a gap in the universe of Proteus. This constitutive gap heralds the emergence of a "world beyond" the hitherto limitless land of the Phaeacians. It is this "beyond," outside the newly created boundaries of Phaeacia, that the mute stone immediately tries to represent. Just as the Cyclopes are no longer Cyclopes after Odysseus' departure, so the Phaeacians will no longer live in a land without limits (Σχερ-ίη).

Yet Poseidon's behavior here is not unique; for it repeats the logic of Odysseus' arrival and departure, to which it is thematically linked. Only after Odysseus has departed do the Phaeacians come to understand his symbolic role: he is the man who was destined to fulfill the prophecy of Nausithous. The last in the series of former voyagers passed on effortlessly to their destination, he is also the first in the new series.[13] This understanding involves a fundamental shift in the way the Phaeacians now think about their identity. If before Odysseus' intervention, they always directly knew who they were as Phaeacians, any further access to themselves will now be temporally based; they have to look back to the past or forward to the future for the answers to identity questions. They discover retroactively, when they understood the prophecy, what was always the case: that Odysseus was the man who would destroy them and that they were thus always vulnerable. They construe themselves as victims of Odysseus, acknowledging the justice of the claim of Nausithous that they had hitherto ignored. Their knowledge of themselves is a reaction to the events themselves and is thus too late to provide unmediated self-knowledge. Self-knowledge comes at a price: they certainly know who they were, but not who they are. The incident of the hanging mountain involves a necessary projection of their identities. They can anticipate (through guesswork) how the mountain's fall (or failure to fall) might change them, but they do not know what will happen. Precisely this gap between knowledge and identity was missing before Odysseus arrived. We can never gain direct access to who we are; we need to either take a detour through the past (knowledge of who we were) or project ideas of what we want to be into the future. In either case, any diachronic knowledge (of past, of future) must pass through an alienating symbolic synchronic structure.[14]

People Who Live on Phaeacia Should Not Throw Stones

Poseidon's gesture of "grounding" Phaeacian society makes more sense when seen against the background of the ships' mobility. But it is also previewed in Odysseus' earlier interactions with the Phaeacians during the games. For there, too, a stone appeared.

> Ἦ ῥα καὶ αὐτῶι φάρει ἀναΐξας λάβε δίσκον
> μείζονα καὶ πάχετον, στιβαρώτερον οὐκ ὀλίγον περ
> ἢ οἴωι Φαίηκες ἐδίσκεον ἀλλήλοισι.
> τόν ῥα περιστρέψας ἧκε στιβαρῆς ἀπὸ χειρός·
> βόμβησεν δὲ <u>λίθος</u>· κατὰ δ' ἔπτηξαν ποτὶ γαίηι
> Φαίηκες δολιχήρετμοι, ναυσίκλυτοι ἄνδρες,
> <u>λᾶος ὑπὸ ῥιπῆς</u>. ὁ δ' ὑπέρπτατο σήματα πάντων
> ῥίμφα θέων ἀπὸ χειρός. ἔθηκε δὲ τέρματ' Ἀθήνη
> ἀνδρὶ δέμας ἐϊκυῖα, ἔπος τ' ἔφατ' ἔκ τ' ὀνόμαζε·
> "καί κ' ἀλαός τοι, ξεῖνε, διακρίνειε τὸ σῆμα
> ἀμφαφόων, ἐπεὶ οὔ τι μεμιγμένον ἐστὶν ὁμίλωι,
> ἀλλὰ πολὺ πρῶτον. σὺ δὲ θάρσει τόνδε γ' ἄεθλον·
> οὔ τις Φαιήων τόδε γ' ἵξεται οὐδ' ὑπερήσει."
>
> (*Od.* 8.186–98)

[He spoke, and with mantle still on sprang up and laid hold of a discus
that was a bigger and thicker one, heavier not by a little
than the one the Phaiakians had used for their sport in throwing.
He spun, and let this fly from his ponderous hand. The stone
hummed in the air, and the Phaiakians, men of long oars
and famed for seafaring, shrank down against the ground, ducking
under the flight of the stone which, speeding from his hand lightly,
overflew the marks of all others, and Athene, likening
herself to a man, marked down the cast and spoke and addressed him:
"Even a blind man, friend, would be able to distinguish your mark
by feeling for it, since it is not mingled with the common
lot, but far before. Have no fear over this contest.
No one of the Phaiakians will come up to this mark or pass it."]

Poseidon turns the ship into stone with a downward gesture of his hand.[15] In so doing, he fixes the Phaeacian ship to the ground and thus provides a point of solidity, a foundation, for Phaeacian society as a whole. Odysseus hurls a stone with his hand, which causes the Phaeacians to cower in fear under the flight of the stone. We should note not only the further association of λίθος and λαός[16] but the way the Phaeacians are forced to turn toward the ground (ποτὶ γαίηι). As the Phaeacians duck under Odysseus' stone, they are given a preview of Poseidon's later rooting of their society to the ground. The ducking mirrors the ducking of Deucalion and Pyrrha. The discus whirs over their heads, making the Phaeacians aware of the vulnerability of their heads. Odysseus' discus throw is a symbolic decapitation, introducing them to the possibility of a real decapitation. At the moment they confront their first loss in their games, they are confronted with the possibility of loss of life.[17] This is an important context for Athena's remark that Odysseus' throw will be forever out of the reach of the Phaeacians. It is the narrative's equivalent of Odysseus' remark to the Cyclops that his eye will never be healed. In both cases, the remarks emphasize the introduction of desire to the species, though in quite different ways. Athena makes the Phaeacians aware of an external limit, a point that they cannot reach, which suggests that they are internally lacking; they do not have the ability they once thought they had. Odysseus' blinding of the Cyclops causes him to reach outside of himself for an answer to his internal lack.

On Phaeacia, Odysseus reacts to Athena's words in the following way.

> Again he spoke to the Phaiakians, in language more blithe:
> "Now reach me that mark, young men, and then I will make another
> throw, as great as this, I think, or one even better."
>
> (*Od.* 8.201–3)

Odysseus hurls one discus and then goes on to threaten the Phaeacians with a much greater throw. This remains at the level of threat, however, because Alcinous later intervenes to appease him. But the threat of a great throw of a stone is surely significant. For, after Odysseus leaves, Poseidon comes even closer to carrying out exactly what Odysseus promises to achieve. Poseidon's first act, the turning of a ship into stone, destroys the Phaeacian identity as bringers of guests to their destination without a thought; his second act, the threat of hurling a mountain upon them, puts their entire civilization in danger. The first threat by itself leaves open the possibility that their change of status as agents may not radically alter their civilization. It allows them to continue in a mode of disavowal: they may have lost one ship, but that does not mean that their civilization itself has altered in any fundamental way; they could go on with business as usual on Phaeacia. The second threat removes this possibility by forcing them to recognize the possibility of a complete symbolic destruction of all that is Phaeacia. This double threat of Poseidon allows us to understand, retroactively, Odysseus' threat of a second throw. The Phaeacians ignore the possibility that Odysseus might be telling the truth about such a throw, and thus they ignore its significance for their civilization. By ignoring it, the Phaeacians continue to buy themselves more time to take comfort in their illusory identity.

Let us now turn to the end of Odysseus' narrative of his adventure with the Cyclops. For there, too, the tale ends with two prominent acts of stone throwing. I have argued that the presence of stones on Phaeacia is symbolically significant, suggesting the new presence of a point of solidity in a society that had previously been all flux. The civilization of the Cyclopes has the opposite problem. It is a society with no movement, and this can help us explain the quite different change in the significance of stones there. There are two major rocks that have narrative prominence. The first is the massive boulder that guards the entrance to the Cyclops' cave. The second is the mountaintop that Polyphemus breaks off to hurl at Odysseus. But rather than stones emerging in this static society, two stones disappear from it. The episode ends with the Cyclops hurling two stones that emphatically miss their target.

> ἧκε δ' ἀπορρήξας κορυφὴν <u>ὄρεος μεγάλοιο</u>,
> κὰδ δ' ἔβαλε προπάροιθε νεὸς κυανοπρώιροιο
> τυτθόν . . .
>
> (*Od.* 9.481–83)

[He broke away the peak of a great mountain and let it
fly, and threw it in front of the dark-prowed ship
by only a little . . .]

> αὐτὰρ ὅ γ' ἐξαῦτις πολὺ μείζονα λᾶαν ἀείρας
> ἧκ' ἐπιδινήσας, ἐπέρεισε δὲ ἶν' ἀπέλεθρον·
> κὰδ δ' ἔβαλε προπάροιθε νεὸς κυανοπρώιροιο
> τυτθόν . . .
>
> (*Od.* 9.537–40)

[Then for the second time lifting a stone far greater
he whirled it and threw, leaning into his cast his strength beyond
    measure,
and the stone fell behind the dark-prowed ship by only
    a little . . .]

The manner of the departure of these two stones is once more significant. The importance of the head of the mountain already seems clear from our previous discussion of the vulnerability of heads. Polyphemus, having already lost his self-sufficiency because of the blinding, now adds to that loss the image of a headless, wounded mountain—as if to function as a stone sign of what he has forever lost.[18] The loss of the mountaintop is also the loss of the Cyclopean home: Polyphemus will no longer be able to return to his isolated, mountaintop home, because he destroys that home as he attempts revenge on Odysseus. What he does, in response to what he wants, is incompatible with who he has always been. His status as monad is gone forever as he is forced toward the agora, the place of human assembly that the Cyclopes previously lacked. The Cyclops' act as desiring and vengeful being thus changes the geographical landscape around him that was central to his monadic status: once he has made a trip to the agora, it is as if the narrative signposts the impossibility of returning to a life alone on the mountaintops. But what is the significance of the "much bigger" stone he hurls?

As I have suggested, one other stone plays an important role in Odysseus' interaction with the Cyclops. It is the rock that closes off the Cyclops' cave from the outside world.

> αὐτὰρ ἔπειτ' ἐπέθηκε θυρεὸν μέγαν ὑψόσ' ἀείρας,
> ὄβριμον· οὐκ ἂν τόν γε δύω καὶ εἴκοσ' ἄμαξαι
> ἐσθλαὶ τετράκυκλοι ἀπ' οὔδεος ὀχλίσσειαν·
> τόσσην ἠλίβατον πέτρην ἐπέθηκε θύρῃσιν.
>
> (9.240–43)

[Next thing, he heaved up and set into position the huge door stop,
a massive thing; no twenty-two of the best four-wheeled
wagons could have taken that weight off the ground and carried it,
such a piece of sky-towering cliff that was he set over his gateway.]

This stone later prevents Odysseus from killing Polyphemus on the spot, as he realizes that neither he nor his companions could push it away. This could well be the *lithos* that Polyphemus will later remove from his doorway (ἀπὸ μὲν λίθον εἷλε θυράων, 9.416). The removal of the stone from the doorway of the cave suggests that his closed, isolated home will now be opened up to wider Cyclopean society. The Cyclopes become a people the moment they open up their homes to the outside world. The stone is raised from the doorway for the final time, never to be placed back at the entrance. We can also describe the effect of this stone throwing in the terms used by Vernant in his analysis of the *colossos*. For the psychotic Cyclopes lived in the world beyond the human realm, the realm of darkness, of the unsignified, which the religious sign of the *colossos* pointed toward.

The case of the Cyclops' two failed throws suggests further symmetry between events on Phaeacia and the island of the Cyclopes. The final image of the Cyclops is of an impotent thrower; he hurls away rocks that miss their target, and this emphasizes that his former belief in his own strength can no longer be taken for granted. He is no longer a being of supreme power but one who cannot hit what he aims at. Is this not an image that is a fitting conclusion to the discus contest on Phaeacia? The final view we have of the Cyclops is a preview of the new view the Phaeacians must have of themselves as discus throwers after Odysseus' victory has deprived them of any belief in their omnipotence; compared to Odysseus, the Phaeacians are as impotent at throwing as the Cyclops. This Cyclopean impotence is hinted at in Athena's remarks.[19] But this also works in reverse; for by hurling the stones into the sea, the Cyclops looks out, for the first time, toward the universe beyond his island. The gaze toward the water, in a futile effort to attack Odysseus in revenge for his own lost eye, suggests that the Cyclops, too, is about to look beyond his isolated realm to the risks and hazards of the sea, spurred on by his efforts to find his lost eye. Like the Phaeacians, he is about to become a sailor who has no idea where he is going.

The Two Faces of the Father

I have up to now outlined the symbolic differences that separate the Phaeacians and the Cyclopes, differences that the *Odyssey* itself—through the way it emphasizes their former unity—suggests we pursue. Their split was into "inhuman" realms where language operated either perfectly (Phaeacia) or not at all (the Cyclopes). The narrative suggests that these two societies become unified as *human* subjects when they are forced to accept language as an imperfect system. They also receive what they lack from the other: Phaeacians are provided with a limit to their limitless land, a point of senseless solidity in their world of sense; the Cyclopes, by losing a complete solidity, gain a doorway into a world beyond their enclosed worlds. But this transformation can also be explained by their changing relationship to another figure central to both their civilizations, their father-god, Poseidon.[20]

On Phaeacia, Poseidon is the patron god, responsible for their key symbolic quality, their seamanship.[21] On the island of the Cyclopes, Polyphemus appeals to Poseidon as a father-curer who holds out the hope of an end to his pain. In both cases, we are provided with a picture of the god as a kindly father figure who offers protection. But this is in stark contrast to the apparent viciousness of his punishment of the Phaeacians. For in what possible sense can the Phaeacians, who have treated Odysseus with respect and performed their allotted duty in transporting him home, deserve the petrifaction of their ship?[22] There is a further parallel between, on the one hand, the pain Poseidon senselessly inflicts on the Phaeacians at the end of the Phaeacian story and, on the other, the finale of Odysseus' encounter with Polyphemus. For in the latter, Polyphemus suffers a blinding that his father was quite powerless to prevent. On Phaeacia, Poseidon acts as a cruel, senseless, punishing father. On the island of the Cyclopes, Polyphemus believes his father will heal him, but Odysseus intervenes to emphasize that any such paternal promise is illusory: his father will never be such an agent of healing. What can we make of this connection?

To provide an answer, we can return to the fantasized nature of both societies. I have suggested that Phaeacia is an imagined world where paternal authority is unchallenged and benign. By contrast, the Cyclopes were a species of fathers who rejected paternal law and whose authority was accordingly senseless. This split in the figure of the father (between sense and senselessness) is central to Lacan's understanding of the enigma of paternity.

> [T]he non-coincidence of symbolic and real father means precisely that some "non-father" (maternal uncle, the supposed common ancestor, totem, spirit—ultimately the *signifier* "father" itself) is "more father" than the (real) father. It is for this reason that Lacan designates the Name-of-the-Father, this ideal agency that regulates legal, symbolic exchange, as the "paternal metaphor": the symbolic father is a metaphor, a metaphoric substitute, a sublation [*Aufhebung*] of the real father in its Name which is "more father than father himself," whereas the "non-sublated" part of the father appears as the obscene, cruel and oddly impotent agency of the superego.[23]

The fantasized universes of the Cyclopes and Phaeacians isolate a single dimension of paternal authority. The Phaeacians—split off from their "mad" neighbors, the Cyclopes, in the mythical past—live as if they are unaware of the obscene aspect of paternal authority, as if the nonsublated aspect of the father (which signifies the limit of his rule) does not exist. The Cyclopes reject the law in its entirety and thus are entirely free from any sublation. With this as background, we can understand how the actions of Poseidon introduce the Cyclopes and Phaeacians to the dimensions of the father that they lack. Polyphemus' loss of an eye introduces him into the symbolic, and this coincides with an appeal to Poseidon as benign father, a father who promises to be the ideal agent who regulates symbolic exchange. In stark contrast, it is precisely the "obscene" dimension of the father that is missing on Phaeacia. For the Phaeacians act as if there is no limit to paternal authority. Poseidon's petrifaction of the ship creates a limit at the same time as he appears as the mad, senseless, punishing father who lurks beneath the surface benevolence of paternal authority.

We are now in a position to understand—and accept—the motivation for the senseless punishment of the Phaeacians provided by Poseidon himself; he claims he is angry at them for allowing Odysseus, the blinder of his son, to return home.

> Father Zeus, no longer among the gods immortal
> shall I be honoured, when there are mortals who do me no honor,
> the Phaiakians, and yet those are of my own blood. See now,
> I had said to myself Odysseus would come home only after
> much suffering.
>
> (*Od.* 13.128–32)

Poseidon seeks to punish the Phaeacians even as he recognizes that he is their ancestor. They are punished for helping Odysseus, whom Poseidon despises because he blinded his son Polyphemus. But what is interesting about Poseidon's words is that this is the first time a blood connection between him and the Phaeacians is alluded to within the poem. At the moment he punishes them, Poseidon recognizes himself as their father. This looks back to Odysseus' forceful proclamation that Polyphemus' wound could not be healed that in turn demonstrated the impotence of Poseidon as a father. Is it not this awareness of his impotence that motivates Poseidon's senseless, vindictive attack? Poseidon's wrath toward Odysseus, which rebounds on his Phaeacian children, is the reactive anger of a father who is forced to witness the wounding of his son and yet is unable to help. His delayed reaction to the failure of his symbolic authority returns in the madness of vengeance. Poseidon is angry because of his impotence. He thus replays a quite common Homeric motif, which we might call the motif of the angry (but impotent) father. As examples, we need only consider the reaction of Priam to the death of Hector in the final book of the *Iliad;* not only is he mad with grief at the loss of his son, but his anger rebounds on his other sons.[24]

There is also a marked similarity in the situations that the Phaeacians and Cyclopes are left to confront. Polyphemus is left hoping (against hope) for a father to cure his wound. The Phaeacians are left hoping (against hope) that Poseidon will temper his anger and that their sacrifices will suffice to prevent the mountain from obliterating their civilization. Both appeal to the authority of the Name-of-the-Father, but both are also aware—for the first time—that this authority provides no guarantees.

5

Metis and Monstrosity

Odysseus' and Demodocus' Battle of Wits

Odysseus brings to Phaeacia not just loss but the concept of loss. It is perfectly possible that the Phaeacians will survive as a species, but it will be a species that must confront the possibility of their utter obliteration. This means that Odysseus' deception of them is a particularly interesting example of the workings of the well-known Odyssean theme of *metis* (cunning). We do not simply watch the Phaeacians being deceived by Odysseus. We see them learning a theoretical point about the nature of trickery: its success is never guaranteed; it can always misfire. Indeed, *metis* only gains consistency as a concept through the possibility of its failure. For a cunning that always succeeded would be something much more sinister—the workings of a nondesiring, all-powerful species, and so one who has no identity or self at all. This, of course, is not to deny that there is something intriguing about these mythical species, just as there is something fascinating about the way Odysseus deceives them. It is, however, to underline the dark side of *metis*, its links to destruction and loss.

Michael Lynn-George has forcefully articulated the danger of the scholarly fascination with *metis*. For Lynn-George, it betrays an unwarranted optimism in the ability of *metis* to deceive and a certain unacknowledged critical arrogance. Fascination with *metis* is complicit with scholarly desire to see such cleverness, which in turn masks the enjoyment that structures critical pleasure in seeing *metis*. Here is Lynn-George's summary of the scholarly consensus.

> *Metis* is construed as mastery of metamorphosis, the ability to assume every kind of form without being imprisoned within any; elusive, encircling but never encircled, the master of *metis* achieves mastery through metamorphosis. It is *the art of seeing without being seen*. Closed in on itself, the subject

defined by *metis* nevertheless prefers to see itself as a limitless circular form: it no longer has a beginning or an end, it can seize anything and yet can be seized by nothing. Turning through rings "without limit," *metis* would embrace the unlimited. *Metis* has not only become a form of the ideal, untouchable critic; it contains the promise of infinite knowledge.[1]

In contrast to this lure of infinite knowledge, Lynn-George emphasizes that there is no such unlimited success and that every theft is necessarily open to the possibility of detection. We can make use of this insight to come to grips with the Homeric poems. For the *Odyssey* signals its awareness of this distinction by showcasing two impossible worlds where this is not the case. Not only do the worlds of the Cyclopes' island and Scheria contain this "promise of infinite knowledge," but they are inhabited by species that believe in their own infinite knowledge—until Odysseus changes them. So Odysseus forces them to live in a world where the possibility of theft exists, one in which it is always open to the possibility of detection. The stones that appear at the end of the tales signify exactly this.

In what follows, I want to push the limits of what is at stake in Odysseus' deception and also examine its relationship to loss. We find out, retroactively, that the Phaeacians have been deceived: Odysseus was never quite who they thought he was. But what are the mechanisms of this deceit? For it is not simply the deceiver who believes himself to be untouchable; rather, the deceiver manipulates the desires of those whom he deceives, desires that are ultimately tied to certain images they have of themselves, certain notions of identity. The Phaeacians trust Odysseus because they have something at stake in believing in their omnipotence, and so they ignore his threat. Odysseus is thus persuasive because he offers up, in his words, the image of themselves they already have. In this sense, we can say that Odysseus is certainly unseen, but only from the perspective of the Phaeacians, who ignore any aspect of Odysseus that does not coincide with what they want to see. Of course, this self-delusion is exactly what they will be forced to come to terms with. They will be introduced into an unreliable world of symbols, where any story could be a lie or where any sign of emotion might be a ruse. But the force of this should in turn cause us to question our emotional attachments to any identification we have with the poem's characters. The Phaeacians believe Odysseus and identify with his stories. But they do not recognize the destruction he will leave in his wake. Do we not do the same? In what follows, I will at least try to complicate the generally accepted humanist picture of the sorry, forlorn hero seeking his *nostos,* and I will emphasize instead the destabilizing aspects of Odysseus as trickster, the potential unreliability of him at the very moments we may be tempted to believe him.

The Phaeacians are already lost the moment Odysseus arrives. Were they to refuse to send him home and thus avoid the wrath of Poseidon, they would just as surely destroy their identity as perfect hosts. But the outcome of events on Phaeacia is still crucial for Odysseus. For what is at stake is nothing less than his *nostos*. The Phaeacians are both his potential ticket home and a possible obstacle to his journey home (should they decide not to transport him to Ithaca). Should Odysseus be revealed as the agent of Phaeacian destruction alluded to by Nausithous, he would have no guarantee that his trip home would not be lost. He therefore needs the Phaeacians to perform one last function in their role as seamen, even as he destroys their identity as seamen. Consequently, the logic of the narrative demands that the Phaeacians be fooled into thinking that he is harmless. Odysseus' rhetoric, which appeals to the unique excellence of the Phaeacians even as his actions undermine it, manages to accomplish this.

In outlining this situation on Phaeacia, I am following the lead of John Peradotto, who has pointed out that the punishment meted out to the Phaeacians invites a retroactive reading of Odysseus' interactions with the Phaeacians in book 8.

> The relationship between the Phaeacian audience and Odysseus's narrative is interesting, for it touches their lives in a profound and serious sense that transcends mere "entertainment." Demodocus's narrative of Odysseus was, for them, "entertainment," distanced as their lives were from its subject. But Odysseus's story of Poseidon's enmity puts in a whole new light the Phaeacian decision to escort him home. Now their own future safety is implicated in that decision.[2]

In principle, we need not question Odysseus' sincerity in his tale to the Phaeacians. He might be no more than a weary, troubled character on his way home, and the Phaeacians might just be victim to a senseless act of violence that resists attempts to explain it by reference to the narrative situation in the *Odyssey*. But, nevertheless, the link made between the punishment itself and Odysseus' departure, together with the infamous problem of Phaeacian unfriendliness, surely signals to us that it is worth at least reconsidering the way Odysseus presents himself to the Phaeacians. To do this, we need only to continue our identification with the Phaeacian position after Odysseus leaves and retroactively to question the merits of trusting him. Regardless of Odysseus' intentions in the matter, the Phaeacians have been objectively deceived; Odysseus was not who they thought he was. If we identify with the deceived Phaeacians and retrace events in this paranoid way, distrusting the actions of Odysseus retroactively, we can explain a great deal of the curious interactions between

Odysseus and the Phaeacians in book 8 and, in particular, his encounter with the bard Demodocus.[3]

There are wider issues at stake in the deception. If Odysseus' tales about himself are the crucial means by which he deceives his listeners, then this seems to betray distrust in the function of song. In *Odyssey* 8, after all, the actions and words of Odysseus run parallel to the songs of the bard Demodocus, to which they are implicitly compared, and Odysseus' affinity with bards is a motif of the entire poem.[4] But in the songs of Demodocus, we can see a different side to poetry. For if Odysseus' words and actions deceive the Phaeacians, the songs of Demodocus can be read as an antidote to this deception; they are a series of attempts to warn the Phaeacians of the danger posed by Odysseus. The interchange between Odysseus and Demodocus functions as a staged competition between poets, a competition that also outlines two possible uses for song; if poetry can mystify, it can also enlighten.[5] I suggest that to view Homeric poetry as internally and irremediably split between possible deception and enlightenment is as significant as the more common generic split between "praise poetry" and "blame poetry."[6] Odysseus' rhetoric mystifies by providing the picture of a suffering, helpless hero, a picture that is attractive to the Phaeacians because they want to believe that Odysseus poses no threat to them. His helplessness also reinforces their own belief in their infallibility. Demodocus' songs provide other, more disquieting alternatives to this picture of the hapless hero—alternatives that the Phaeacians cannot understand, precisely because they refuse to read allegorically, to see the songs as meaning something else. Reading the songs allegorically is not to reduce them to those other meanings. It is, however, to zero in on the possibility of other meanings, the moment of openness before the songs have come to mean something else, and the limitations of a knowing audience that refuses to allow such moments. It is to see the poem as interrogating different modes of reading as it shows us the modes of reading of its characters. For the Phaeacians refuse to read allegorically because their own reading of the words of Demodocus and Odysseus are used to reinforce the image they have of themselves.

Demodocus' First Song: πήματος ἀρχή

Demodocus first tells a tale of origins, the quarrel between Achilles and Odysseus that brought about the "beginning of woe" [πήματος ἀρχή].[7] The traditional importance of such a quarrel has been elucidated by Nagy.[8] The quarrel between Achilles and Odysseus is caught up in the tension between *bie* and *metis* (force and cunning), with Odysseus the representative of *metis*,

Achilles the representative of *bie*. The traditional importance of this tension between the two heroes of the major poems allows us to see it as a latent narrative that lies behind much of the tension on display throughout books 8–13. I will return to it. Yet, rather than follow the path of scholars who seek a specific mythic occasion for this original quarrel, this "beginning of woe" that leads to the Trojan War,[9] we should stress instead its appropriateness to the general theme of origins in the first half of the *Odyssey*. Demodocus sings of a beginning that coincides with a quarrel; this scission in the realm of the social is described in terms of a conflict between Odysseus and Achilles, *metis* and *bie*. In the (mythical) beginning, there is an *eris* (a primal strife), and the conflation of *eris* with origins in Demodocus' song make it particularly relevant to Phaeacian society. Before the arrival of Odysseus, Phaeacia is an impossibly harmonious society, a society without *eris*.[10] Yet within moments of the completion of Demodocus' song about an original *neikos* (quarrel) between Odysseus and Achilles (*Od.* 8.75), a *neikos* occurs on Phaeacia. Odysseus is asked by Laodamas and Euryalus to take part in the games and refuses. This leads to taunting from Euryalus: νείκεσέ τ' ἄντην [he quarreled with him].[11] Odysseus' eventual decision to take part in the games, together with the particular form of his interaction with the Phaeacian men, seems to be a belated attempt to impose damage control onto the effects of the *neikos* he has caused. Demodocus' song of an original *neikos* is thus prophetic: it tells of one "beginning of woe" while suggesting that he knows all too well that Odysseus is the figure who introduces the "beginning of woe" to Phaeacia.[12]

We have a familiar mythic situation: a blind figure with insight is ignored by a metaphorically blind audience. In this case, we can provide a clear explanation for the failure of communication. Demodocus' song demands to be read carefully (it is emphatically not mere entertainment) and understood allegorically: it appears to be about another place but is already about Phaeacia itself. But the peculiar relationship to language of the Phaeacians means that reading allegorically is precisely what is not available to them. They believe that they are immune to language's powers of deception and that the meaning of poetry (and all language) is self-evident because it coincides with what they believe poetry means.

Demodocus' song produces a peculiar reaction on the part of Odysseus. He cries but also covers his head. His reaction is elaborately described: the moment Demodocus begins his song, Odysseus' head disappears behind his mantle. This significant act by Odysseus is commonly understood as a spontaneous emotional reaction to the reference to the Trojan War. But the importance of Odysseus' strategy of self-occlusion on Phaeacia might cause us to rethink this interpretation. Suspicion is increased when we compare this description of the veiling of the head with another tale of a hidden head, the tale in which Odysseus later describes the attempts of Sisyphus to push his rock to the top of the hill. I here juxtapose the episodes.

τότε γὰρ ῥα κυλίνδετο πήματος ἀρχὴ
Τρωσί τε καὶ Δαναοῖσι Διὸς μεγάλου διὰ βουλάς.
ταῦτ᾽ ἄρ᾽ ἀοιδὸς ἄειδε περικλυτός· αὐτὰρ Ὀδυσσεὺς
πορφύρεον μέγα φᾶρος ἑλὼν χερσὶ στιβαρῇσι
κὰκ κεφαλῆς εἴρυσσε, κάλυψε δὲ καλὰ πρόσωπα·
αἴδετο γὰρ Φαίηκας ὑπ᾽ ὀφρύσι δάκρυα λείβων.
ἦ τοι ὅτε λήξειεν ἀείδων θεῖος ἀοιδός,
δάκρυ᾽ ὀμορξάμενος κεφαλῆς ἄπο φᾶρος ἕλεσκε
καὶ δέπας ἀμφικύπελλον ἑλὼν σπείσασκε θεοῖσιν·
αὐτὰρ ὅτ᾽ ἂψ ἄρχοιτο καὶ ὀτρύνειαν ἀείδειν
Φαιήκων οἱ ἄριστοι, ἐπεὶ τέρποντ᾽ ἐπέεσσιν,
ἂψ Ὀδυσεὺς κατὰ κρᾶτα καλυψάμενος γοάασκεν.

(*Od.* 8.81–92)

[[F]or now the beginning of the evil rolled on, descending
on Trojans, and on Danaans, through the designs of great Zeus.
    These things the famous singer sang for them, but Odysseus,
taking in his ponderous hands the great mantle dyed in
sea-purple, drew it over his head and veiled his fine features,
shamed for tears running down his face before the Phaiakians;
and every time the divine singer would pause in his singing,
he would take the mantle away from his head, and wipe the tears off,
and taking up a two-handled goblet would pour a libation
to the gods, but every time he began again, and the greatest
of the Phaiakians would urge him to sing, since they joyed in his
    stories,
Odysseus would cover his head again, and make lamentation.]

Καὶ μὴν Σίσυφον εἰσεῖδον κρατέρ᾽ ἄλγε᾽ ἔχοντα,
λᾶαν βαστάζοντα πελώριον ἀμφοτέρῃσιν.
ἦ τοι ὁ μὲν σκηριπτόμενος χερσίν τε ποσίν τε
λᾶαν ἄνω ὤθεσκε ποτὶ λόφον· ἀλλ᾽ ὅτε μέλλοι
ἄκρον ὑπερβαλέειν, τότ᾽ ἀποστρέψασκε κραταιίς·
αὖτις ἔπειτα πέδονδε κυλίνδετο λᾶας ἀναιδής.
αὐτὰρ ὅ γ᾽ ἂψ ὤσασκε τιταινόμενος, κατὰ δ᾽ ἱδρὼς
ἔρρεεν ἐκ μελέων. κονίη δ᾽ ἐκ κρατὸς ὀρώρει.

(*Od.* 11.593–600)

> [Also I saw Sisyphos. He was suffering strong pains,
> and with both arms embracing the monstrous stone, struggling
> with hands and feet alike, he would try to push the stone upward
> to the crest of the hill, but when it was on the point of going
> over the top, the force of gravity turned it backward,
> and the pitiless stone rolled back down to the level. He then
> tried once more to push it up, straining hard, and sweat ran
> all down his body, and over his head a cloud of dust rose.]

The rolling out of evil is echoed in the rolling of the rock. Odysseus' suffering, which is on display as Demodocus recounts his tale, mirrors the suffering of Sisyphus. But most intriguingly, the persistent efforts of Sisyphus in pushing the rock have the effect of generating a cloud of dust that clouds his head. Odysseus also constantly struggles to cover his head with his robe in response to the song.

Let us now turn to the suggestive connection between Odysseus and Sisyphus made by John Peradotto at the end of his book on the *Odyssey*. For Peradotto, the persistent efforts of Sisyphus mirror Odysseus as a "degree-zero" figure, from which new stories can always be generated.

> To what does the name "Odysseus" refer? in the final analysis, it refers in a sense to no one, to nothing, but nothing in the rich sense of the zero-degree, which signifies not simply nonbeing, but potentiality, what it means for the empty subject of narrative to take on any predication or attribute, for Athena to simulate anyone (13.313), for dormant Proteus to become anything that is, for Outis to become *polytropos*. It is the point where Sisyphus, true progenitor of Odysseus, unlike his immobilized companions Tityrus and Tantalus, rebounds against failure, forever resilient even in the realm of death to face Krataiïs, the ruthless power of necessity. It is the zero-point where every story ends, rich with the possibility of another beginning.[13]

We can reverse the terms of Peradotto's optimistic picture. For though Sisyphus is indeed a relentless toiler against necessity's hard rock, the existence of the rock provides the conditions of possibility necessary for Sisyphus' attempts to master it. It is the necessary point of failure for every attempt at trickery: it can only be temporarily—never permanently—effaced. We return once more to the relationship between rocks and the social. The rock functions as the constitutive limit of the social. The rock Sisyphus pushes is exactly the kind of rock that the Phaeacians lack.[14] Odysseus' story of Sisyphus is a further preview of the shadow of the mountain that is soon to introduce the Phaeacians to mortal society. For as they begin to sacrifice to Zeus, in order to keep the mountain from falling on them, they have embarked on a Sisyphean labor, a labor that not only will prove perennial but will be without any possibility of ultimate success.

But more significant for my present purpose is the self-occlusion engineered by Sisyphus. Through the insistence of his efforts and by the dust that arises from them, his head becomes clouded over: κονίη δ' ἐκ κρατὸς ὀρώρει. To return to Peradotto's reading of the pushing of the stone as metaphor for the workings of narrative, Odysseus' "stories" are indeed told and retold; but in the process of the telling, the agent of the telling seems to disappear. The tale of Sisyphus is not just a story told, followed by a return to a new beginning. The telling of the tale itself seems to have the ability to efface the identity of the teller, as if to provide the illusion that the tale is innocent. The interaction between Demodocus and Odysseus seems to reverse the process; as Odysseus tries to hide his role as creator of *eris*, the song of Demodocus attempts to make this role public knowledge. In response, Odysseus continues to try to shield himself. It is as if the simultaneous appearance of Odysseus' head with the words of Demodocus would make it easier for the Phaeacians to make a connection between the two. Odysseus hides because he tries to evade the truth of Demodocus' song.[15]

The reaction of the Phaeacians to Demodocus' song is itself interesting and comes close to replaying the narrative pattern traced in the story of Achilles' quarrel with Odysseus. The Phaeacians first rejoice in his words (τέρποντ' ἐπέεσσιν, *Od.* 8.91), but this joy is later tempered as King Alcinous sees that all is not well with Odysseus.[16] However, he makes no effort to find out what Odysseus hides; instead, he is bewitched by what he sees on the surface, the tears of Odysseus. Alcinous is clearly moved by Odysseus' apparent sufferings. This not only prevents Alcinous from considering what Odysseus hides; it also leads to the cessation of Demodocus' song, as the herald takes him away (*Od.* 8.105 ff.). If Alcinous is a bad interpreter of the actions of Odysseus as well as a bad interpreter of Demodocus' song, it is interesting that Demodocus' tale itself also hints at Agamemnon's poor interpretation of the quarrel between Odysseus and Achilles.

> Μοῦσ᾽ ἄρ᾽ ἀοιδὸν ἀνῆκεν ἀειδέμεναι κλέα ἀνδρῶν,
> οἴμης τῆς τότ᾽ ἄρα κλέος οὐρανὸν εὐρὺν ἵκανε,
> νεῖκος Ὀδυσσῆος καὶ Πηλεΐδεω Ἀχιλῆος,
> ὥς ποτε δηρίσαντο θεῶν ἐν δαιτὶ θαλείῃ
> ἐκπάγλοις ἐπέεσσιν, ἄναξ δ᾽ ἀνδρῶν Ἀγαμέμνων
> χαῖρε νόῳ ὅ τ᾽ ἄριστοι Ἀχαιῶν δηριόωντο.

ὣς γάρ οἱ χρείων μυθήσατο Φοῖβος Ἀπόλλων
Πυθοῖ ἐν ἠγαθέῃ, ὅθ᾽ ὑπέρβη λάϊνον οὐδὸν
χρησόμενος. τότε γάρ ῥα κυλίνδετο πήματος ἀρχή . . .

(*Od.* 8.73–81)

[[T]he Muse stirred the singer to sing the famous actions
of men on that venture, whose fame goes up into the wide heaven,
the quarrel between Odysseus and Peleus' son, Achilleus,
how these once contended, at the gods' generous festival,
with words of violence, so that the lord of men, Agamemnon,
was happy in his heart that the best of the Achaians were quarreling;
for so in prophecy Phoibos Apollo had spoken to him
in sacred Pytho, when he had stepped across the stone doorstep
to consult; for now the beginning of evil rolled on . . .]

There is a marked contrast between the joy felt by Agamemnon in reaction to the prophecy and the description of the toil that will ensue. Because of this, G. M. Calhoun argued long ago that Demodocus' tale is a "story based on the motif of the misunderstood oracle."[17] Calhoun argues that the oracle referred to the quarrel between Agamemnon and Achilles (with which the *Iliad* begins), not the quarrel between Odysseus and Achilles. Agamemnon is thus fooled, feeling joy at an event that predicts massive suffering. We can strengthen Calhoun's argument by noting its significance for the Phaeacians. For a misunderstanding of this kind defines the situation on Phaecia. The story of the Trojan War can be read as an allegory for the problem of the relationship of deceit to utter destruction. As such, it has special significance for Alcinous. For here, too, the initial joy at the song will soon turn to grief, when Phaeacian civilization faces destruction. Here, too, is a naive king, whose pity for Odysseus blocks the possibility of an understanding of the impending disaster.

The Victory of Metis: *Demodocus' Second Song*

Alcinous halts the song of Demodocus and suggests the Phaeacians turn to the pleasure of the games. Euryalus immediately invites Odysseus to take part, which forces him to walk a rhetorical tightrope: he must display enough prowess to end the Phaeacian taunts, but not so much that he destroys Phaeacian belief in their identity as perfect transporters of guests, which would destroy his *nostos*. He boasts of excellence in all sports but tempers these claims by professing modesty with regard to the speed of his feet. This modesty allows Alcinous, after a humiliating Phaeacian defeat in the discus throw, triumphantly to proclaim that the real Phaeacian virtues are those that involve the feet, including swift transportation and, later, dancing.

> οὐ γὰρ πυγμάχοι εἰμὲν ἀμύμονες οὐδὲ παλαισταί,
> ἀλλὰ ποσὶ κραιπνῶς θέομεν καὶ νηυσὶν ἄριστοι·
>
> (*Od.* 8.246–47)
>
> [For we are not perfect in our boxing, nor yet as wrestlers,
> but we do run lightly on our feet, and are excellent seamen . . .]

Alcinous' words betray him here, for they are a clear contradiction of his earlier statement before the games commenced that the Phaeacians surpass others both in their speed of foot and in boxing and wrestling (˜ὅσον περιγιγνόμεθ' ἄλλων / <u>πύξ τε παλαισμοσύνηι</u>, *Od.* 8.102–3). Alcinous takes the scraps offered by Odysseus, retreating to an affirmation of what he believes to be the crucial quality that distinguishes the Phaeacians from others. It is this Phaeacian feature that Poseidon will later destroy. Because Odysseus does not utterly destroy their belief in their identity, he buys himself the time to escape. Yet by a series of hints, the narrative suggests that the modesty shown by Odysseus is far from genuine, and Demodocus' second song reinforces this. Let us consider some possible reasons to doubt his sincerity.

Odysseus first claims that he is vulnerable in the footrace, then goes on to suggest that Philoctetes is a superior archer to him. The first claim seems to receive backing from the *Iliad*. In book 23 Odysseus actually runs in a footrace against Antilochus and Ajax. There, the narrator makes it quite clear that Odysseus is up against superior performers: Antilochus is the best of the youth (νέους ποσὶ πάντας ἐνίκα [he was superior to all the youths in his speed of foot], *Il.* 23.756), while Ajax leads the way up until the race's end. But here a complication occurs: Odysseus prays to Athena for help; she upsets Ajax' balance, causing him to slip and fall into the cow dung. The fastest man in the footrace loses out to Odysseus because of a trick. The lesson of the footrace in book 23 of the *Iliad* seems to be that Odysseus is quite capable of winning a footrace despite the greater foot speed of others.[18] This in itself might be enough to suggest that Odysseus' words in book 8 point toward the other epic tradition. But there is an even more marked resemblance. After Odysseus' success, Antilochus claims that he is from an earlier generation.

> εἰδόσιν ὕμμ' ἐρέω πᾶσιν, φίλοι, ὡς ἔτι καὶ νῦν
> ἀθάνατοι τιμῶσι παλαιοτέρους ἀνθρώπους.
> Αἴας μὲν γὰρ ἐμεῖ' ὀλίγον προγενέστερός ἐστιν,
> <u>οὗτος δὲ προτέρης γενεῆς προτέρων τ' ἀνθρώπων</u>·

ὠμογέροντα δέ μίν φασ' ἔμμεναι· ἀργαλέον δὲ
ποσσὶν ἐριδήσασθαι Ἀχαιοῖς, εἰ μὴ Ἀχιλλεῖ.

(*Il.* 23.787–92)

[Friends, you all know well what I tell you, that still the immortals
continue to favour the elder men. For see now, Aias
is elder than I, if only by a little, but this man
is out of another age than ours and one of the ancients.
But his, they say, is a green old age. It would be a hard thing
for any Achaian to match his speed. Except for Achilleus'.]

Antilochus' remarks thus contradict those of the Odysseus of *Odyssey* 8, who explicitly refused to compare his own exploits to those of earlier generations.

τῶν δ' ἄλλων ἐμὲ φημι πολὺ προφερέστερον εἶναι,
ὅσσοι νῦν βροτοί εἰσιν ἐπὶ χθονὶ σῖτον ἔδοντες.
ἀνδράσι δὲ προτέροισιν ἐριζέμεν οὐκ ἐθελήσω . . .

(*Od.* 8.221–23)

[But I will say that I stand far out ahead of all others
such as are living mortals now and feed on the earth. Only
I will not set myself against men of the generations before . . .]

The remarks to the Phaeacians are belied by the remarks made about him in the *Iliad*. Not only is he perfectly capable of winning a footrace despite his inferior ability, but his presumed humility, compared to earlier generations, is undermined by the words of Antilochus. He emphasizes that Odysseus is not a stranger to those generations but someone who can eerily transcend time: he is both older and yet somehow evergreen.

Whether Odysseus really is a member of the earlier generation or not is only a part of what is at stake here. For that could only be determined by reference to the statements of the epic tradition itself, and Antilochus' words about Odysseus in *Iliad* 23 are clearly a part of that tradition and contradict Odysseus' claim about himself in *Odyssey* 8. What is much more significant is that Odysseus' ability in athletics makes him appear as if he is one of the older generation, and this ability prompts Antilochus' remarks. When Odysseus claims he is not one of the older generation in *Odyssey* 8, he is not simply stating a fact but making a claim about his athletic abilities. When we turn to the most obvious part of the epic tradition that we might expect to back up his claim—the funeral games of the *Iliad*—we find a statement that completely contradicts his claim about his lack of ability in comparison to the previous generation. We can make two points about this. First, we should note that what we could call epic self-consciousness, the awareness of itself as traditional poetry, its ability to refer to other stories within the epic tradition, is also a consciousness of its own inadequacy.[19] Its claims to truth are self-contradictory, insufficient. But correlatively, epic generates a hero—Odysseus—who becomes a kind of monster of *metis*, a quasi-human figure whose cunning can seem to evade the boundaries that constitute mortal human life.

Let us now turn to his modesty regarding archery.[20] Philoctetes' ability at archery was of course necessary for the fall of Troy. But if this effort is an event that makes Troy's sack inevitable, it is also one of a series of such events that are ultimately facilitated by Odysseus.[21] Philoctetes is only brought to Troy through the intervention of Odysseus, who recovers him from Lemnos. Philoctetes is the "best" archer, but Odysseus' intervention in bringing him to Troy clarifies that Odysseus is in control of whether Philoctetes is allowed to exhibit that prowess. In all three cases of Odysseus' alleged inferiority produced in book 8, we thus find alternate stories that suggest he is already one step ahead. Though he refuses comparison to earlier generations, he is miraculously already one of them; though an incompetent runner destined to lose, he nevertheless can still win; though he is inferior in archery to Philoctetes, without his intervention Philoctetes' potential for archery would never have been realized. The narrative therefore hints at a string of reasons why Odysseus should be doubted, even as the Phaeacians want to believe him—a belief that allows them to cling to their own belief that they are "best" at transportation. Once more, the point is not so much that Odysseus is lying but, rather, that his words point to a kind of impasse in the tradition itself, which contradicts them: the Phaeacians can properly neither believe nor disbelieve him.

Demodocus' second song can be read as a commentary on the dangers of Odysseus' rhetoric. In response to Odysseus' dubious protestations of vulnerability because of his slowness of foot, Demodocus tells the story of how the lame Hephaestus tricked the faster Ares.

> οὐκ ἀρετᾶι κακὰ ἔργα· κιχάνει τοι βραδὺς ὠκύν,
> ὡς καὶ νῦν Ἥφαιστος ἐὼν βραδὺς εἷλεν Ἄρηα,
> ὠκύτατόν περ ἐόντα θεῶν οἳ Ὄλυμπον ἔχουσιν,
> χωλὸς ἐὼν τέχνηισι· τὸ καὶ μοιχάγρι' ὀφέλλει.
>
> (*Od.* 8.329–32)

[No virtue in bad dealings. See, the slow one has overtaken
the swift, as now slow Hephaistos has overtaken
Ares, swiftest of all the gods on Olympos, by artifice,
though he was lame, and Ares must pay the adulterer's damage.]

The tale of guile defeating speed looks back to Odysseus' actions in defeating Ajax in *Iliad* 23. Demodocus may know very well that Odysseus' slowness of foot is no obstacle to him defeating the Phaeacians with his *metis* and that the last vestige of their self-confidence is about to be destroyed. But this song also returns to the theme of conflict between *bie* and *metis* opened up in his first song. The quarrel between Odysseus and Achilles is followed by a tale of victory of (Odyssean) guile over (Achillean) speed. We can identify Odysseus with the guile of Hephaestus, Achilles with the swift of foot Ares. If Demodocus' song is a veiled warning to the Phaeacians, it also pays a backhanded compliment to Odysseus; he seems to know that Odysseus' *metis* can overcome the *bie* of Achilles.[22]

Yet this far from exhausts its thematic significance. Hephaestus finds out about the adultery of Aphrodite and Ares, but he finds out too late, after the act is completed. What is of special interest is that the adultery is both "hidden" and occurs "at first."

> Αὐτὰρ ὁ φορμίζων ἀνεβάλλετο καλὸν ἀείδειν
> ἀμφ' Ἄρεος φιλότητος ἐϋστεφάνου τ' Ἀφροδίτης,
> ὡς τὰ πρῶτα μίγησαν ἐν Ἡφαίστοιο δόμοισι
> λάθρηι· πολλὰ δ' ἔδωκε, λέχος δ' ἤισχυνε καὶ εὐνὴν
> Ἡφαίστοιο ἄνακτος·
>
> (*Od.* 8.266–70)
>
> [Demodokos struck the lyre and began singing well the story
> about the love of Ares and sweet-garlanded Aphrodite,
> how they first lay together in the house of Hephaistos
> secretly; she gave him many things and fouled the marriage
> and bed of the lord Hephaistos.]
>
> (translation modified)

Hephaestus' naive faith in Aphrodite is broken. But it is broken "in secret," and this emotional wound dealt to Hephaestus occurs "at first." This sin that shatters Hephaestus' unreflective belief in his wife's fidelity is an original sin, the puncturing of a primal innocence on his part.

Hephaestus' reaction to this loss replays a common Odyssean theme.

> βῆ ῥ' ἴμεν ἐς χαλκεῶνα, κακὰ φρεσὶ βυσσοδομεύων·
> ἐν δ' ἔθετ' ἀκμοθέτωι μέγαν ἄκμονα, κόπτε δὲ δεσμοὺς
> ἀρρήκτους ἀλύτους, ὄφρ' ἔμπεδον αὖθι μένοιεν.
> αὐτὰρ ἐπεὶ δὴ τεῦξε δόλον κεχολωμένος Ἄρει,

βῆ ῥ᾽ ἴμεν ἐς θάλαμον, ὅθι οἱ φίλα δέμνι᾽ ἔκειτο,
ἀμφὶ δ᾽ ἄρ᾽ ἑρμῖσιν χέε δέσματα κύκλωι ἁπάντηι·
πολλὰ δὲ καὶ καθύπερθε μελαθρόφιν ἐξεκέχυντο,
ἠΰτ᾽ ἀράχνια λεπτά, τά γ᾽ οὔ κέ τις οὐδὲ ἴδοιτο,
οὐδὲ θεῶν μακάρων· πέρι γὰρ δολόεντα τέτυκτο.

(*Od.* 8.273–81)

[[H]e went on his way to his smithy, heart turbulent with hard
  sorrows,
and set the great anvil upon its stand, and hammered out fastenings
that could not be slipped or broken, to hold them fixed in position.
Now when, in his anger against Ares, he had made this treacherous
snare, he went to his chamber where his own dear bed lay,
and spun his fastenings around the posts *in a perfect circle*,[23]
while many more were suspended overhead, from the roof beams,
thin, like spider webs, which not even one of the blessed
gods could see. He had fashioned it to be very deceptive.]

(translation modified)

In reaction to the wound caused by Aphrodite's adultery, Hephaestus turns to technology, and his trickery ensues from his technological skill. The sequence is reminiscent of Odysseus' later tale of his interaction with the Cyclopes; there, too, the Cyclops turns to (the trickery of) language in an attempt to heal the wound caused by Odysseus' blinding. But the apparent perfection of Hephaestus' trick returns us to the question of the limits of *metis* in ensuring ideological control. At first, the perfection of Hephaestus' craft suggests that his guile might have the near omnipotent ability to check the transgressive desire of Ares and Aphrodite. Not only do the bindings bear no trace of their creator (not even the gods can see them), but Ares and Aphrodite are enclosed in a perfect circle: ἀμφὶ δ᾽ ἄρ᾽ <u>ἑρμῖσιν</u> χέε δέσματα <u>κύκλωι ἁπάντηι</u> [[he] spun his fastenings around the posts in a perfect circle]. The workings of guile appear invincible, creating a symbolically important circle ensnaring the transgressors.[24] Yet the particular words used to describe this apparently perfect closing of a circle betray its later failure. For the encirclement of the bedposts (<u>ἑρμῖσιν</u>) previews the later twist in Demodocus' tale as the god Hermes (<u>Ἑρμείας</u>) declares that he would still be willing to sleep with Aphrodite despite Hephaestus' punishment.[25] The apparent success of the trick in forming a perfect circle in no way halts the desire for the sin that preceded the circle: perfect punishment makes the sin all the more desirable, not less.

Demodocus' Final Song

Demodocus closes his trio of songs by telling the tale of the wooden horse. This forms a fitting climax to the series of tales on the theme of *bie* and *metis*, for despite Achilles' martial prowess, this trick of Odysseus will eventually destroy Troy.[26] But the tale is of particular significance for the situation on Phaeacia, as Demodocus' song is again prophetic. The city of Troy "covers over" the horse (ἀμφικαλύψῃ, *Od.* 8.511), as the land of the Phaeacians will soon be covered over by the shadow of the Cyclopean mountain.[27] The disaster on Troy foreshadows the coming disaster on Phaeacia. But there is a more significant parallel between the quandary of the Trojans with regard to the wooden horse and the quandary of the Phaeacians with regard to Odysseus. Odysseus' stay on Phaeacia is characterized by persistent attempts by his hosts to discover who he is. In continually seeking the identity of their temporary visitor, the Phaeacians hope to assure themselves that he is not the agent of their destruction. Their quest soon comes to a halt when Odysseus tells them his name at the start of the *Apologoi*, a label of identity they believe far too easily. But it is in the persistence of these attempts that they replay the key aspect of the story of the Trojan horse; the Trojans also need to find out what is inside the Trojan horse in order to save their city, and they ultimately fail to do this. Both the horse and Odysseus are objects of enchantment; both captivate the desire of their beholders; both bring a disastrous end to the civilizations they pierce.

But despite the similarities, there is an equally interesting difference. In the either-or world of Phaeacia, where there is no place for ambiguity, the Phaeacians believe that there is no puzzle, no trick, that cannot be rationally explained. Odysseus' trick fools the Phaeacians for the first time and thus makes them aware of their vulnerability; but there is more to the trick than this. For even when they later discover that Odysseus is indeed the agent of their destruction, they still have no rational way of explaining why he tricked them.[28] This gives added significance to a further aspect of Odysseus' rhetoric of modesty.

> ξεῖνος γάρ μοι ὅδ' ἐστί· τίς ἂν φιλέοντι μάχοιτο;
> ἄφρων δὴ κεῖνος γε καὶ οὐτιδανὸς πέλει ἀνήρ,
> ὅς τις ξεινοδόκωι ἔριδα προφέρηται ἀέθλων
> δήμωι ἐν ἀλλοδαπῶι· ἕο δ' αὐτοῦ πάντα κολούει.
>
> (*Od.* 8.208–11)

[[F]or he is my host; who would fight with his friend? Surely any man can be called insensate and a nobody,

who in an alien community offers to challenge
his friend and host in the games. He damages what is his.]

Because the Phaeacians live in a world where everyone is a friend and where their status as hosts is not challenged, Odysseus has no trouble persuading them that only a madman would choose to bring an *eris* to society. But his words also trace the limits of Phaeacian society. For precisely the possibility of the act of a madman has been disavowed as the founding gesture of Phaeacian society: in the beginning, they fled the force of the violent Cyclopes. Odysseus also suggests that such a man would be a "no one," a pun that will play such an important role in the trick of the Cyclops.[29] But as he rejects such a man, Odysseus also describes the effect that his own arrival will later be understood to have had on the Phaeacians. The Phaeacians believe they understand Odysseus' motivations when he tells them his name: he is Odysseus, and his identity centers on his desire to return home. But after they transport him home and find that he was the agent of their destruction all along, they will be forced to reconsider this interpretation. His identity will then become a puzzle, an unanswered question: why on earth did he bring an *eris* to their land? For the Phaeacians, he will indeed function as a "no one," a pure question mark; they can no longer believe his innocent stories, yet they have no way of finding out enough about him to explain what he has done to them. The appearance of the stones on Phaeacia is just a substantiation (for the Phaeacians) of this pure ignorance, an object signifying their incomprehension, reminding them of the puzzle of Odysseus' lack of identity.[30]

Odysseus' role as agent of destruction allows us to see a darker aspect to his reaction to the last song of Demodocus. In response to the tale of the Trojan horse, he pines away with grief and is then likened (in a famous "reverse simile") to a woman about to be dragged off to slavery.

> ταῦτ' ἄρ' ἀοιδὸς ἄειδε περικλυτός· αὐτὰρ Ὀδυσσεὺς
> τήκετο, δάκρυ δ' ἔδευεν ὑπὸ βλεφάροισι παρειάς.
> ὡς δὲ γυνὴ κλαίῃσι φίλον πόσιν ἀμφιπεσοῦσα,
> ὅς τε ἑῆς πρόσθεν πόλιος λαῶν τε πέσῃσιν,
> ἄστεϊ καὶ τεκέεσσιν ἀμύνων νηλεὲς ἦμαρ·
> ἡ μὲν τὸν θνήσκοντα καὶ ἀσπαίροντα ἰδοῦσα
> ἀμφ' αὐτῷ χυμένη λίγα κωκύει· οἱ δέ τ' ὄπισθε
> κόπτοντες δούρεσσι μετάφρενον ἠδὲ καὶ ὤμους
> εἴρερον εἰσανάγουσι, πόνον τ' ἐχέμεν καὶ ὀϊζύν·
> τῆς δ' ἐλεεινοτάτῳ ἄχεϊ φθινύθουσι παρειαί·
> ὣς Ὀδυσεὺς ἐλεεινὸν ὑπ' ὀφρύσι δάκρυον εἶβεν.

(*Od.* 8.521–31)

[So the famous singer sang his tale, but Odysseus
melted, and from under his eyes the tears ran down, drenching
his cheeks. As a woman weeps, lying over the body
of her dear husband, who fell fighting for her city and people
as he tried to beat off the pitiless day from city and children;
she sees him dying and grasping for breath, and winding her body
about him she cries high and shrill, while the men behind her,
hitting her with their spear butts on the back and the shoulders,
force her up and lead her away into slavery, to have
hard work and sorrow, and her cheeks are wracked with pitiful
    weeping.
Such were the pitiful tears Odysseus shed from under his brows.]

Usual critical reaction has involved recognizing the breadth of poetic vision employed in the identification with the loser, the quiet articulation of the destructive, nonheroic aspect of war.[31] Odysseus (now believed to be a genuine sufferer) is identified with a victim in the sacking of the city that, more than any other, earned him his epithet "city-sacker" *(ptoliporthos)*. Yet such a reading is in danger of obscuring both the relevance of the image of a destroyed city for the Phaeacians and the particular effect of Odysseus' tears. Odysseus has to be believed to be an ordinary, mortal man in order to gain his *nostos*. The Phaeacians trust the sincerity of his emotional reaction and accordingly identify with him as a mortal man, a figure of suffering, but in doing so, they misrecognize him as agent of Nausithous' prediction.

For the Phaeacians, a belief in Odysseus' status as an "ordinary mortal" obscures the reality of his status as agent of the destruction that hurls them into the realm of mortals. He is a bringer of loss to them, which reduces them to a properly human, mortal status. We have once more arrived at two contradictory aspects of Odysseus. He seems to use tricks for his own survival—a human end. But his success brings utter disaster to his victims. This is no ordinary disaster but is intimately linked with death. The suffering that Odysseus exhibits to the Phaeacians veils his status as bringer of their deaths. This brings to the fore the disquieting aspects of Odysseus as human trickster. In a poem where deception is rife, where every "natural" human quality is persistently questioned, the "natural" emotions that promise to strengthen social bonds between people are all bonds to be played upon by the trickster. To experience natural emotion, to take anything for granted, is to fall prey to the possibility of being fooled. But the results of his tricks for the fantasized societies of the Cyclopes and Phaeacians suggest more than this: his success as a trickster makes him an agent of destruction, a grim reaper.

While Odysseus is conventionally regarded as a figure who endures suffering, we need to remember that he is also a figure who deliberately inflicts suffering on himself to fool others. The blows inflicted on the woman by her captors recalls Helen's description of an Odyssean spying raid into Troy, where part of his disguise as a beggar depended on his self-flagellation.

>αὐτόν μιν πληγῇσιν ἀεικελίῃσι δαμάσσας,
>σπεῖρα κάκ' ἀμφ' ὤμοισι βαλών, οἰκῆϊ ἐοικώς,
>ἀνδρῶν δυσμενέων κατέδυ πόλιν εὐρυάγυιαν.
>
>(*Od.* 4.244–46)

[He flagellated himself with degrading strokes, then threw on
a worthless sheet about his shoulders. He looked like a servant.
So he crept into the wide-wayed city of the men he was fighting.]

The suffering he self-inflicts is done to inflict further suffering on the Trojans. Helen's description here previews Odysseus' fight with the suitors, where his disguise as a beggar is so crucial. But the Phaeacians, too, are beguiled by the harmlessness of Odysseus' appearance as a hapless victim of war. Because they pity him, they cast aside the warning of the destruction of the city alluded to in Demodocus' final song.

6

The Limits of Heroism

Complete destruction, the possibility that confronts the Phaeacians after Odysseus' departure, is a topic more usually associated with the *Iliad*. Consider the following episode: on the verge of sending Patroclus back into the midst of the battle, Achilles fantasizes about the possibility of the mass destruction of Greeks and Trojans.

> αἲ γὰρ Ζεῦ τε πάτερ καὶ Ἀθηναίη καὶ Ἄπολλον,
> μήτέ τις οὖν Τρώων θάνατον φύγοι ὅσσοι ἔασι,
> μήτέ τις Ἀργείων, νῶϊν δ' ἐκδῦμεν ὄλεθρον,
> ὄφρ' οἶοι Τροίης ἱερὰ κρήδεμνα λύωμεν.
>
> (*Il.* 16.97–100)
>
> [Father Zeus, Athene and Apollo, if only
> not one of all the Trojans could escape destruction, not one
> of the Argives, but you and I could emerge from the slaughter
> so that we two alone could break Troy's hallowed coronal.]

Achilles' fantasy articulates a certain truth of this poem of war. It is a fantasy that pursues what Adkins has termed the "competitive virtues," exhibited in their ultimate form in warfare, to their logical conclusion.[1] The *Iliad* showcases a zero-sum world of fighting, where the death of the opponent is exchanged for fame, through the traditional medium of song. Achilles thus articulates a perverted best-case scenario; as a warrior, he dreams of maximizing the glory from others' deaths (he has destroyed *them all*), yet he retains a minimal audience to whom the tale can be recounted. The power of this fantasy allows us to reread much of the earlier narrative. Consider the famous scene of *Iliad* 9, as the members of the embassy arrive at Achilles' tent and find Achilles singing to Patroclus alone.

> τὸν δ' εὗρον φρένα τερπόμενον φόρμιγγι λιγείῃ
> καλῇ δαιδαλέῃ, ἐπὶ δ' ἀργύρεον ζυγὸν ἦεν,
> τὴν ἄρετ' ἐξ ἐνάρων πόλιν Ἠετίωνος ὀλέσσας·
> τῇ ὅ γε θυμὸν ἔτερπεν, ἄειδε δ' ἄρα κλέα ἀνδρῶν.
> Πάτροκλος δέ οἱ οἶος ἐναντίος ἧστο σιωπῇ,
> δέγμενος Αἰακίδην ὁπότε λήξειεν ἀείδων . . .
>
> (*Il.* 9.186–91)

[And they found Achilleus delighting his heart in a lyre, clear-sounding,
splendid and carefully wrought, with a bridge of silver upon it,
which he won out of the spoils when he ruined Eëtion's city.
With this he was pleasuring his heart, and singing of men's fame,
as Patroklos was sitting over against him, alone, in silence,
watching Aiakides and the time he would leave off singing.]

After the starker vision of book 16, it now seems as if the embassy is intruding on something. Achilles and Patroclus seem to be in the process of learning or acting out the kind of dyadic self-sufficiency that will have such powerful effects in the second half of the poem. What they potentially intrude on, as the passage from book 16 clarifies, is an idealized reciprocity of communication: Patroclus listens as audience, waiting until he can take his turn, with Achilles as audience. But at this point in the poem, Patroclus' act of waiting is itself overdetermined. He is one, alone, yet he metaphorically stands in for all the Greeks, who are likewise awaiting the end of Achilles as singer and the beginning of him as actor in battle. Achilles' song takes its place in the space where the fellow Greeks suffer, signifying less what he says (we never find out what these "glories of men" are) than what he refuses to do as he sings. The arrival of the embassy halts this kind of singing, only to replace it with different kinds of vacillation from Achilles. But it also pulls Patroclus away from his status as substitute for all the Greeks and into a metonymic relation to them: he becomes but one of the Greeks, alongside Ajax, Odysseus, and Phoenix, partial links in a chain to the whole host who suffer. Patroclus is thus pulled in two different directions: toward a closer dyadic unity with Achilles, but also toward the Greek host with which he identifies. Much of the rest of the plot will revolve around how this tension plays out. But in their dyadic singing, in what they are doing, playing out their performance of song as the embassy interrupts them, we can trace the logical, if impossible, parameters of the heroic economy of song. At one end, a hero tells of his utter absence of heroic deeds to the whole world as audience. At the other, the hero tells of the destruction of the entire world to no one. These parameters are the "limits of heroism," and Achilles' fantasy would be one answer to them.[2]

This human fantasy also evokes a theme that recurs throughout the *Iliad:* the motif of natural disaster. Scodel has demonstrated that the narrative of the *Iliad* shows an awareness of traditional myths of destruction, while reworking them for its own purpose.[3] Scodel argues that passages of the *Iliad* allude to a range of disaster myths (including that of the flood). But of particular interest to me are the parallels she draws between, on the one hand, the massive loss of life forecast in the proem of the *Iliad* due to the anger of Achilles and, on the other, the explanation for the Trojan War suggested in Hesiod's *Ehoeae*. The *Ehoeae* seems to explain the war as a cataclysmic event planned by Zeus to separate gods from men; but it does so in a way that uncannily recalls aspects of the *Iliad*. Here is the relevant passage listed by Scodel, juxtaposed to the relevant lines of the *Iliad*'s proem.

> Μῆνιν ἄειδε, θεά, Πηληϊάδεω Ἀχιλῆος
> οὐλομένην, ἣ μυρί' Ἀχαιοῖς ἄλγε' ἔθηκε,
> <u>πολλὰς δ' ἰφθίμους ψυχὰς</u> Ἄϊδι προίαψεν
> ἡρώων...
>
> *(Il.* 1.1–4)

[Sing, goddess, the accursed wrath of Peleus' son Achilleus
and its devastation, which put pains thousandfold upon the Achaians,
and hurled forth many strong souls of heroes to Hades ...]

> π]ολλὰς Ἄιδηι κεφαλὰς ἀπὸ χαλκὸν ἰαψ[ει]ν
> ἀν]δρῶν ἡρώων ἐν δηιοτῆτι πεσόντων.
>
> *(Eh.* fr. 204, 118–19 M-W)

[[Zeus intended] to send with bronze many heads of
heroic men who had fallen in the turmoil to Hades.]

Scodel notes that a related formula at *Iliad* 11.53–55 is also suggestive of mass destruction.

> Κρονίδης, κατὰ δ' ὑψόθεν ἧκεν ἐέρσας
> αἵματι μυδαλέας ἐξ αἰθέρος, οὕνεκ' ἔμελλε
> <u>πολλὰς ἰφθίμους κεφαλὰς</u> Ἄιδι προιάψειν.

[And the son of Kronos ... from aloft cast
down dews dripping blood from the sky, since he was minded
to hurl down many heads to the house of Hades.]

The parallels can be attributed to a common tradition on which the *Iliad* draws, rather than simply to later imitation of the *Iliad*'s proem. The *Iliad* thus creatively reworks a story of cosmological disaster into one of human loss; the series of references to the cosmological tradition becomes a means of establishing the gravity of the destruction of life in the Trojan War. But there remains a key difference between natural destruction and the war: "A war, no matter how long and how bitter, does not seem calamitous enough to have been an original form of the myth of destruction; it is, moreover, a normally human and local activity, to be explained historically, rather than a divine visitation."[4] Nature is replaced by culture as historical narratives of the Trojan War commence. But Achilles' fantasy of a union with Patroclus in a world bereft of humans seems to blur this distinction. Achilles' fantasy suggests an act that is certainly not natural—if the fantasized mass destruction is beyond human power, the desire for it is clearly human, within the realm of culture. Yet because of the scale of the loss, it is hard to locate in the realm of sense. Though articulated all too lucidly, it has a thoroughly irrational feel. He fantasizes that he is in the exact situation that faced Deucalion and Pyrrha after the flood, in an asocial, isolated, frozen universe—a universe reminiscent of the isolated *oikoi* of the Cyclopes. It is an inhuman fantasy for destruction on a cosmological scale, for destruction of the human.[5] This chapter will be a sustained attempt to come to terms with this complex, shady realm between "sense" and "nature" and to ponder its effects for the question of an ideology of the Homeric poems.

We can begin by turning to John Peradotto's understanding of the depiction of a "free" self within the *Odyssey*, precisely because it misses out on this aspect of the self.

> In the self-consciousness of his art, the story-teller creates a subject at once *polytropos* and *outis*, a secret base for open predication, rather than a determinate sum of predicates, and thus presents a paradigm of the self as capable, dynamic, free, rather than fixed, fated, defined.[6]

Peradotto assimilates Odysseus' role as "no one" in his encounter with the Cyclops to the "degree zero," the zero point from which all narratives begin. This optimistic moment of pure possibility, suggested by the total absence of an identity, forms a crucial part in Peradotto's Bakhtinian reading of the poem as a conflict between the realms of freedom and necessity. "Freedom" (centrifugal aspects of the narrative, fleeing order) is equated with the struggle to resist the realm of necessity (centripetal aspects, enforcing order). But how are we to relate Peradotto's "dynamic self" to Achilles' fantasy? For surely this fantasy is in no obvious way part of Homeric ideology. In the willful destructiveness of this Achillean wish, we can detect an aspect of a free self that seems to be missing from Peradotto's optimistic picture. Peradotto remarks, "[I]ndividuation escapes predication, and can only be signified by the negative judgment implicit in *Outis*" (Peradotto 1990, 153). He then concludes (from this reading of Odysseus as Outis) that the *Odyssey* depicts a self that is "capable, dynamic, free." But what is lost (in Peradotto's translation) are the destructive possibilities open to this "capable, dynamic" self. Achilles' fantasy certainly transgresses the realm of public law—the series of regulations, spoken and unspoken, that gives heroic behavior a logic and consistency and that is commonly termed the "heroic code." For is not this shocking, unpalatable desire the desire (within Peradotto's own terms) of a "capable," "free" self? Achilles' fantasy and the slaughter leading to the death of Hector, which he later indulges in, are clearly not any simple obedience to social dictates, precisely because they are transgressive. So are we forced to conclude that here, too, Achilles is "free" and "dynamic"? I argue not quite.

Peradotto is right to note a split in the subject between its predicates and a certain "nothing" that evades them. Freedom becomes, for Peradotto, that which escapes the dictates of social discourse and which, accordingly, can only be negatively defined. But to come to terms with the destructive fury rendered explicit in Achilles' fantasy, we need to consider a consequence of this failure of the law to account for social subjects. For this failure of social discourses (which I will call the "public law") means that there is also a failure at the level of predication itself—that is, the public law itself is incomplete. The negative subject that escapes predication brings with it, as a necessary correlate, the knowledge that the law itself is not all-powerful; it, too, is haunted by lack, signified by its inability to account for the subject.[7] This failure at the level of the law opens up more than the possibility of transgression in the name of a liberating freedom. Peradotto's complex, insightful analysis seems to miss the possibility of transgression of the law as the ultimate identification with the law itself.

> As has been shown by numerous analyses from Bakhtin onwards, periodic transgressions are inherent to the social order, they function as a condition of the latter's stability. (The mistake of Bakhtin—or, rather, of some of his followers—was to present an idealized image of these "transgressions," i.e. to pass in silence over lynching parties and the like as the crucial form of the "carnivalesque suspension of social hierarchy"). The deepest identification

which "holds together" a community is not so much identification with the Law which regulates its "normal" everyday circuit, as rather *identification with the specific form of transgression of the Law, of its suspension* (in psychoanalytic terms, the specific form of *enjoyment*).[8]

The law (in the psychoanalytic terms of Zizek) is split into an "ego ideal"—the "normal," everyday realm of the pacifying, civilizing law of the symbolic order—and a hidden, transgressive reverse. The psychoanalytic name for this dark side is *superego*. The realm of the superego involves "enjoyment" because it is not constrained in the dead system of rules that characterizes the public law. Achilles' violence can be understood both as a transgression of the public law and also as a simultaneous identification with its necessary support, its superegoic reverse. More to the point, the Freudian superego is not simply an agency that guarantees the stability of a social order. It is also experienced as a traumatic voice; this enunciation of the law itself—experienced as a voice that commands a law—exceeds the law. It commands obedience, but for no particular reason. Behind the ego ideal, the system of ideal neutral laws that guarantee order, is a traumatic voice that compels us to yield to the sense of these laws but that is itself senseless.[9]

This distinction can help clarify the complexity of the position of Achilles: his sadistic fantasy appears wantonly destructive, yet it is not a simple break with heroic ideology. Instead, it speaks that ideology's hidden truth, its unpalatable dark side. His initial rejection of Agamemnon suspends the workings of the public law, and much of the poem continues with this (utopian) question mark hanging over the heroic ethos. But Achilles' partial awareness of the incompleteness of the law turns into a superegoic fury—as suggested by the fantasy in book 16. Before the quarrel in book 1, the Greek *aristoi* were united as a community around the authority of Agamemnon, a symbolic father. An equal renunciation was imposed on each warrior to establish a stable community.[10] Accordingly, the everyday, public battles continued within the structured parameters of an ethos epitomized by Agamemnon. In the quarrel, Agamemnon's symbolic authority is demolished in the eyes of Achilles, which leads to the latter's *menis*. This does indeed open up a moment when the law is suspended in its inadequacy. But Achilles' recognition of the failure of the warrior code does not lead him, after his withdrawal from battle, to a rejection of it or to a centrifugal resistance to it. Instead, Achilles' fantasy involves an open identification with the law's superegoic dark side. With the point of symbolic authority gone, Achilles dreams of making the law complete, of being faithful to it in a way that is unthinkable for Agamemnon.

What should not be missed is that this very transgressiveness exposes the hidden, renounced enjoyment that structures the world of epic. The heroic ethos always depended on this unspoken/unspeakable superegoic fantasy of total destruction.[11] Herein lies the major reason why the Homeric poems gain a distance from the heroic ideology they put on display. The Homeric poems do more than present a world where heroic ideology functions, is rationally challenged, and is ultimately restored. For the poems demonstrate not only that Homeric ideology is not fully coherent but that it depends on destructive, transgressive fantasies to make up for its weakness. Homer puts on display the senseless enjoyment lurking behind ideology, an enjoyment that law itself pretends to restrain but can hardly avoid bringing into being. Achilles, unlike the other Greek warriors, is someone who goes all the way.

I will later suggest that this split in the law, far from being irrelevant to the *Odyssey*, is fundamental for our understanding of the two separate mass deaths depicted in the poem, those of Odysseus' Ithacan companions and the suitors. The former die because of their ongoing attachment to the principles of the civilizing, symbolic law: though they persistently doubt their allegiance to Odysseus, his *metis* always manages to persuade them of his qualities as leader. The manner of their deaths is appropriate to the hesitant manner of their questioning of his authority; as their number dwindles with each passing disaster, the troops intermittently doubt Odysseus' leadership but are always won over by his persuasive powers. In marked contrast, the mass killing of the suitors bears the hallmark of open enjoyment of the killing. But before turning to the *Odyssey* in the next chapter, I want to look at two interventions of Odysseus in the *Iliad* that can help illustrate the complexities of this splitting of the law (and Odysseus' complex relationship to it in the Homeric poems).

The Splitting of the Law in Iliad 2 and 10

After the humiliations Agamemnon suffered at the hands of Achilles in books 1 and 9, order is twice restored. However, on both occasions, Odysseus, not Agamemnon himself, engineers the restoration. The structural links between *Iliad* 2 and 10 have been analyzed by Haft: "[the Doloneia] bears the same relationship to Book 9 as *Iliad* 2 does to its preceding book: the Embassy and *Iliad* 1 focus upon Achilles; in his absence, the Doloneia and *Iliad* 2 thrust his 'rival' Odysseus into prominence."[12] Haft also points out that books 2 and 10 highlight the power of Odysseus' *metis*, and she convincingly argues that both books foreshadow Odysseus' eventual sack of Troy.[13] There is an explicit narrative connection.[14] Both books begin with Agamemnon in bed. In book 2, Agamemnon is asleep and receives a dream from Zeus that sets in motion the action of the book. In book 10, we again begin by Agamemnon's bedside, though this time his concern for his troops keeps him awake and leads him to set in motion the series of events that make up the Doloneia. But if these are similarities, what will most concern us here is the different manner in which the symbolic authority of Agamemnon is supplanted in books 2 and 10.

In *Iliad* 2, Odysseus' intervention remains at the level of reinforcement—via his persuasive powers—of the public law. As the army begins to flee, Athena appears to Odysseus and commands him to "address each man" [φῶτα ἕκαστον] (2.180), in order to persuade him to return. Consequently, Odysseus addresses "whomever" of the kings is skulking (<u>Ὅν τινα</u> μὲν βασιλῆα καὶ ἔξοχον ἄνδρα κιχείη, 2.188) and then whomever of the men of the people he saw (<u>Ὅν δ' αὖ δήμου τ' ἄνδρα</u> ἴδοι βοόωντα τ' ἐφεύροι, 2.198). The emphasis is on Odysseus' rhetorical power: he has the ability to manipulate his speech to satisfy each individual in the army. But this power is used on behalf of Agamemnon's weakened symbolic authority. This is suggested by Odysseus' appropriation of Agamemnon's scepter, the emblem of symbolic power par excellence (*Il.* 2.188–6)[15], which in turn leads to his marshaling of the troops in the name of the king's right to lead.

"οὐ μέν πως πάντες βασιλεύσομεν ἐνθάδ' Ἀχαιοί·
οὐκ ἀγαθὸν <u>πολυκοιρανίη</u>· <u>εἷς κοίρανος</u> ἔστω,
<u>εἷς βασιλεύς</u>, ὧι δῶκε Κρόνου πάϊς ἀγκυλομήτεω
σκῆπτρόν τ' ἠδὲ θέμιστας, ἵνα σφίσι βουλεύηισι."
Ὣς ὅ γε <u>κοιρανέων</u> δίεπε στρατόν·

(*Il.* 2.203–7)

["Not in any way will all we Achaeans be king here;
A multitude of lords is not a good thing: let there be one lord,
one king, to whom the crooked-counseling son of Kronos
has give the sceptre and judgments, so that he may advise them."
So he ranged through the host, lording it over them.]

(translation modified)

The term πολυκοιρανίη—in particular the contrast with the "one king"—hints at the symptomatic polytropic ability of Odysseus; his persuasive powers allow him to mediate between the one (Agamemnon) and the many (his subjects). Yet what is extraordinary is that Odysseus' verbal deference to Agamemnon is performatively contradicted by his actions. While championing the right of "one king" to lead the troops, Odysseus himself, not Agamemnon, plays the role of that king; though he claims that Agamemnon has the sole right to wield the scepter, Odysseus himself wields it.[16] Odysseus functions as the figure of perfect symbolic authority Agamemnon can only ever dream of being—as Agamemnon's ego ideal. He restores confidence in the realm of public law after Achilles' desertion, but in such a way as to demonstrate the inadequacy of the king. This inadequacy is demonstrated by the implicit comparison to what a "good king" would be.

The only one of the Greek warriors who remains impervious to Odysseus' persuasive powers is Thersites. For my present purposes, it is not necessary to examine his complex interaction with Odysseus. Yet it is worth making some brief remarks. Odysseus sends him howling out of the assembly with the aid of the scepter and thus reinforces its symbolic power. This helps cement the consent to authority on the part of the troops, who claim that this is the best of acts.

νῦν δὲ τόδε μέγ' ἄριστον ἐν Ἀργείοισιν ἔρεξεν.
(*Il.* 2.274)

[Now this is by far the best thing he has done among the Argives.]
(translation mine)

The poem opens with a rhetorical battle between Agamemnon and Achilles over precisely who is the "best" of the Achaeans. Odysseus then salvages the whole expedition by persuading every member of the host to stay. Accordingly, the use of ἄριστον here is suggestive; Odysseus acts out what it would mean for a leader to be *aristos*, at the same time he proclaims his deference to the leader. The possibility of a centrifugal reading of this episode rests in the elaboration of this "acting out." Agamemnon, as leader, is always engaged in a performance, an attempt to live up to an impossible ideal—an ideal acted out in this case by Odysseus. Odysseus' actions open up the manner in which the person of the king himself is contingent. He merely tries to represent a series of interconnected symbolic qualities, qualities that in principle could be located in the person of anyone but that can be fully represented in no one. The short-term consequence of Odysseus' actions is clear; the challenge to the symbolic authority that cemented the Greek warriors is overcome, by reinforcing their belief in the symbolic strengths of an ideal king.

The Doloneia: The Unspeakable Realm of the Trickster

The reinforcement of Agamemnon's symbolic authority in book 2 can be contrasted with the Doloneia. Agamemnon's situation is now more desperate. The embassy to Achilles has failed, and the war continues to go badly. A shadow continues to hang over his leadership. The gravity of the challenge to his symbolic authority explains the marked vocabulary linking "the one" and "the many" in the opening lines of book 10. These lines are worth quoting at length.

> Ἄλλοι μὲν παρὰ νηυσὶν ἀριστῆες Παναχαιῶν
> εὗδον παννύχιοι μαλακῷ δεδμημένοι ὕπνῳ·
> ἀλλ' οὐκ Ἀτρεΐδην Ἀγαμέμνονα, ποιμένα λαῶν,
> ὕπνος ἔχε γλυκερὸς πολλὰ φρεσὶν ὁρμαίνοντα.
> ὡς δ' ὅτ' ἂν ἀστράπτῃ πόσις Ἥρης ἠϋκόμοιο,
> τεύχων ἢ πολὺν ὄμβρον ἀθέσφατον ἠὲ χάλαζαν
> ἢ νιφετόν, ὅτε πέρ τε χιὼν ἐπάλυνεν ἀρούρας,
> ἠέ ποθι πτολέμοιο μέγα στόμα πευκεδανοῖο,
> ὣς πυκίν' ἐν στήθεσσιν ἀνεστενάχιζ' Ἀγαμέμνων
> νειόθεν ἐκ κραδίης, τρομέοντο δέ οἱ φρένες ἐντός.
> ἤτοι ὅτ' ἐς πεδίον τὸ Τρωϊκὸν ἀθρήσειε,
> θαύμαζεν πυρὰ πολλὰ τὰ καίετο Ἰλιόθι πρό,
> αὐλῶν συρίγγων τ' ἐνοπὴν ὅμαδόν τ' ἀνθρώπων.
> αὐτὰρ ὅτ' ἐς νῆάς τε ἴδοι καὶ λαὸν Ἀχαιῶν,
> πολλὰς ἐκ κεφαλῆς προθελύμνους ἕλκετο χαίτας
> ὑψόθ' ἐόντι Διΐ, μέγα δ' ἔστενε κυδάλιμον κῆρ.
>
> (*Il.* 10.1–16)

[Now all beside their ships the other great men of the Achaians
slept night long, with the soft bondage of slumber upon them;
but the son of Atreus, Agamemnon, shepherd of the people,
was held by no sweet sleep as he pondered deeply within him.
As when the lord of Hera the lovely-haired flashes his lightning
as he brings on a great rainstorm, or a hail incessant,
or a blizzard, at such time when the snowfall scatters on ploughlands
or drives on somewhere on earth the huge edge of tearing battle,
such was Agamemnon, with the beating turmoil in his bosom
from the deep heart, and all his wits were shaken within him.
Now he would gaze across the plain to the Trojan camp, wondering
at the number of their fires that were burning in front of Ilion,
toward the high calls of their flutes and pipes, the murmur of people.
Now as he would look again to the ships and the Achaian
people, he would drag the hair from its roots from his head, looking
toward Zeus on high, and his proud heart was stricken with
    lamentation.]

Agamemnon is the only leader awake, while the rest of the army sleeps. As the only one awake, he ponders many things in his heart. He notices the many fires of the Trojans, hinting that he is troubled by the pressures not only of his own soldiers but of the masses of the enemy as well (10.12 ff.). He is a leader whose command of the *aristoi* is under the microscope—especially after the humiliating rejection of his gifts by Achilles. This "one/many" theme even provides symbolic weight to his action of pulling the many hairs from his head (*Il.* 10.15).

At this crucial juncture, we can see the splitting that Zizek has argued is inherent to the law.

> Where does this splitting of the law into the written public Law and its "unwritten" obscene reverse come from? From the incomplete, "non-all," character of the public Law: explicit, public rules do not suffice, so they have to be supplemented by the clandestine "unwritten" code aimed at those who, although they do not violate any public rules, maintain a kind of inner distance and are not truly identified with the "community spirit."[17]

In contrast to book 2, where Odysseus' actions were all performed in public, in the Doloneia Agamemnon opts for a spying mission at night. At the time when his open-air, daytime authority is under the closest scrutiny, a solution is sought from trickery *(metis)*. Such a nighttime mission is already a subversion of heroic, *Iliadic* warfare; it functions as an attempt to shore up Greek confidence in both their situation and leader at a time when conventional strategies of warfare are clearly insufficient. Yet if this is Agamemnon's strategy, he himself is unable to carry it out. The narrative draws attention to his helplessness in the hours of night. To wake the troops, he sends out his brother, Menelaus, who then asks what is to be done when he has completed this task: should he return to Agamemnon to tell him of this? Agamemnon responds:

> αὖθι μένειν, μή πως ἀβροτάξομεν ἀλλήλοιιν
> ἐρχομένω· πολλαὶ γὰρ ἀνὰ στρατόν εἰσι κέλευθοι.
>
> (*Il.* 10.65–66)

> [Better wait here, so there will be no way we can miss one another
> as we come and go. There are many paths up and down the
>   encampment.]

Much of the significance of the Doloneia lies in Agamemnon's recognition of the possibility of this failed encounter. Agamemnon's fallibility in locating his brother under the cover of night previews the later, successful meeting between Dolon and Odysseus. Odysseus and Dolon, too, will have problems recognizing each other, as they meet in the no-man's-land between the Greek and Trojan camps on their respective spying missions. But Agamemnon's marked inability to see through the darkness contrasts with the powers of perception of Odysseus. It is well known that though Odysseus appears to be a hero second to Diomedes in the Doloneia, Odysseus' powers of perception trigger the success of the pair. Odysseus first becomes aware of the presence of Dolon, and this recognition is necessary for the continuation of the episode.[18] Odysseus alone is able to give direction to the nighttime wanderings. But there is something ominous in the contrast between Agamemnon's inability to see and the powers of Odysseus in the darkness. For, as I will shortly explore, a *katabasis* motif runs throughout the Doloneia. Agamemnon's failure is a sign of his mortal fallibility, a fallibility that will soon be supplanted by the uncanny abilities of the trickster Odysseus—who can somehow traverse the barrier that separates life from death. Agamemnon realizes that, as a mortal, he might miss an encounter under the cover of darkness; but this contrast points toward an important question in our understanding of Odysseus: what sort of figure is it who never misses an encounter?[19]

There is a further perversion of ruling ideology in the Doloneia. In response to Nestor's request for a spy, Diomedes immediately volunteers. Diomedes suggests that two might perform the mission with greater success, and he expresses a desire for a companion. If this is all quite predictable, Agamemnon's next intervention is not.

> μηδὲ σύ γ' αἰδόμενος σῇσι φρεσὶ τὸν μὲν ἀρείω
> καλλείπειν, σὺ δὲ χείρον' ὀπάσσεαι αἰδοῖ εἴκων,
> ἐς γενεὴν ὁρόων, μηδ' εἰ βασιλεύτερός ἐστιν.
>
> (*Il.* 10.237–39)

[You must not, for the awe that you feel in your heart, pass over the better man and take the worse, giving way to modesty and looking to his degree—not even if he be kinglier.]

The leader of the *aristoi* gives Diomedes a free choice of his spying companion. The prevailing aristocratic, genealogical privileges, which would normally shackle choice, are suspended by the leader, whose own authority is genealogically based. The king asks for a judgment of merit and then immediately recognizes that this might undermine someone who is "kinglier." A hidden, nighttime expedition of deceit is undertaken in order to allow the open, regulated warfare of the daytime to continue; a king's nighttime suspension of the hierarchy of genealogical authority occurs in order for the hierarchy to survive during the day. At a time when the pacifying, civilizing law of the symbolic order (represented by Agamemnon) is under threat, an underground, illicit plan is put into operation to compensate for its visible weakness. A marked turnaround differentiates this episode from book 2. There, Odysseus shored up Agamemnon's authority by helping create a public identification with the king's symbolic strengths; here, the action suggests a common identification around the king's points of weakness. Because Agamemnon is weak and the ethos holding the Greeks together is tenuous, there is a sense of the need to do anything (even the antiheroic ambush of a trickster) to restore the fragile workings of heroic ideology. The message of *Iliad* 2 seems to be: "Obey your leader, his symbolic powers remain in place despite Achilles' histrionics." But the message of the Doloneia seems to be quite different: "Now is the time to show your ultimate solidarity with your leader, at the time he seems to have lost any right to rule." Why should such a strategy work?

It all hinges on the manner in which the nighttime events of the Doloneia already provide a phantasmic support for the ideology of the daytime. Consider Odysseus' strange response when Diomedes chooses him as companion.

"τούτου γε σπομένοιο καὶ ἐκ πυρὸς αἰθομένοιο
ἄμφω νοστήσαιμεν, ἐπεὶ περίοιδε νοῆσαι."
τὸν δ' αὖτε προσέειπε πολύτλας δῖος Ὀδυσσεύς·
"Τυδεΐδη, μήτ' ἄρ με μάλ' αἴνεε μήτε τι νείκει·
εἰδόσι γάρ τοι ταῦτα μετ' Ἀργείοις ἀγορεύεις."

(*Il.* 10.246–50)

["Were he to go with me, both of us could come back from the blazing
of fire itself, since his mind is best at devices."
Then in turn long-suffering brilliant Odysseus answered him:
"Son of Tydeus, do not praise me so, nor yet blame me.
These are the Argives, who know well all these matters you speak
of."]

The importance of the specific form of Diomedes' praise, with its suggestion of the uncanny abilities of the trickster Odysseus (περίοιδε νοῆσαι) to return "from the blazing of fire," will be dealt with later. For my present purpose, let us focus on the response of Odysseus to Diomedes' praise. He censors Diomedes, halting his effort at listing his qualities. How can we explain this silencing?[20] What "everyone knows" but no one mentions is that the only way the hidden, nighttime operations of the Doloneia can succeed in their purpose of shoring up the deficiencies in public law is if they remain hidden.[21] Diomedes comes close to speaking aloud the hidden, shared guilt of the Greeks. This guilt provides a phantasmic support for the heroic ideology of the daytime. Everybody knows that such actions as occur in the Doloneia go on throughout the war. However, they cannot be publicly acknowledged; the "civilized" ground rules of the game of heroic conflict (the pacifying law, law of the ego ideal) are there to cover over the destructive stupidity involved in the winning of the conflict.

Odysseus' censorship is a reminder that the actions of the Doloneia itself are quintessentially unheroic and therefore not to be publicly articulated. There is nothing heroic about the deliberate lying to Dolon to gain information or about the manner in which Diomedes enjoys the killing of the unarmed, sleeping Thracians.[22] The episode puts on display the sordid underside of the day-to-day activities of the heroic world. The no-man's-land between Greeks and Trojans is a sea of corpses: Diomedes and Odysseus hide among the corpses to capture Dolon (*Il.* 10.349); the Greek leaders manage to find a spot free of corpses for the council that leads to the spying expedition (*Il.* 10.199–200). These images are a far cry from the ideology of "a beautiful death" provocatively explored in the work of Vernant. Indeed, it is its exact reverse.[23] It is not difficult to understand why this must remain hidden, unacknowledged in everyday life: recognition of the merit of choices based outside genealogical boundaries or acceptance of the workings of deceit in open battle would subvert beyond repair the ideology of the heroic ethos. Yet it is the ultimate wager of Odysseus that because everyone (consciously or unconsciously) knows of this "unheroic" dark side of the conflict, a certain solidarity in guilt will prevail. Odysseus' actions as trickster can be neither praised (openly subverting the public law) nor blamed (undermining the phantasmic support of the public law).[24]

We are now in a position to reevaluate the relationship between Odysseus' trickery, his *metis*, and the open, aristocratic form of warfare that characterizes the daytime battles of the poem. This warfare is often assimilated to the realm of *bie*, individual fights performed to establish the respective strength of the warriors. The first thing to notice is that the split in the law between books 2 and 10 suggests a split in the functioning of *metis*. In *Iliad* 2, *metis* acts at the level of persuasion or mystification. The troops are cunningly persuaded by Odysseus to obey their betters; *metis* is exercised on behalf of symbolic values. In the Doloneia, the uncanny powers of Odyssean *metis* are exercised for their own sake, producing a success that is simultaneously exhilarating and unsavory. Killing is normally performed in the name of the law and in a manner faithful to it. But Odysseus' *metis* in the Doloneia complicates the picture: it guarantees a desperately needed success to the faltering authority of Agamemnon, but in an action that transgresses the public code in which that authority speaks. Odysseus (and the Doloneia) implicitly asks the Greeks the following question: how far are you willing to go to be faithful to the law? This suggests that *metis* is not a later ethos that overcomes and replaces an earlier heroic ideal—as the nostalgia of Sophocles' *Ajax* would have it. It is the hidden, phantasmic support of the heroic ethos itself, capitalizing on its followers' solidarity in guilt.

But there is further significance here. If this *metis* is not a later perversion of heroic ideology, it is equally misleading to dismiss it as "primitive" behavior, depending on the rhetoric of evolution. Consider the following passage from Peradotto, which tries to chart the relationship between the "civilized" Odysseus of the *Odyssey* and Odysseus as trickster.

> [I]t is at least as reasonable to assume that the *Odyssey* had the effect of stabilizing a tradition characterized by inconsistency and plurality, of stabilizing, in effect, a multiplicity in the denotation of Odysseus's name, the way a historian's work might stabilize the multiplicity in the interpretations of a particular figure or event, or the way Hesiod appears to be trying to stabilize a polymorphous and inconsistent theogonic tradition, in which divergent narratives vie for something like canonical ideological dominance. Herodotus seems to be reading his mythic narrative tradition in this light when he attributes the character and form of the Greek pantheon largely to the work of Homer and Hesiod. We are encouraged in this view by the *Odyssey*'s deliberate silence (if suppression is not a better word) when it comes to those of Odysseus's unflattering characteristics and acts which, though they surface more conspicuously later in Greek literary evidence, are more at home in more primitive tales of a trickster-type out of which Homer's urbane and civilized Odysseus can readily be inferred to have developed.[25]

The difficulty lies in the conflation of a vocabulary of evolution (the civilized Odysseus develops from an uncivilized trickster) and one of repression (the deliberate silence about the trickster). Is the realm of the trickster an archaic one that the civilized present renders obsolete, or does it act instead as the constitutive dark side of the civilized? There seems to be much at stake in the refusal to speak this aspect of Odysseus out loud and in the eerie silence that ensues. For if it was merely an irrelevant archaism, why would there be such anxiety? Odysseus' words of censorship to Diomedes in the Doloneia cannot help but draw attention to this silence in the realm of the civilized, marking its function as concealer of something repressed. This silence casts a shadow over the evolutionary narrative of development from trickster to civilzation. The rhetoric of evolution participates in the denial of this dark side of the public law—a denial that ultimately is complicit in strenghtening its inherent weakness.

We can now return to the destructive fantasy of Achilles with which I began this chapter. Achilles' fantasy is ultimately the fantasy that Odysseus acts out in the Doloneia. After Patroclus' death, Achilles will fight in such a way as to render obsolete any heroic rules of warfare: he will not receive ransoms for suppliants; he refuses to return the body of Hector for burial[26]—that is, he will replay the "hidden" activities of the Doloneia in broad daylight. The underground act that was performed to solidify the weakening public authority of the king will, with Achilles, no longer remain hidden. Achilles falls victim to the superegoic aspect of the law, while remaining oblivious to any of its pacifying, symbolic aspects.

All this is not to deny an egalitarian aspect to Odysseus. This already seems apparent in the monetary suspension of the public law, the bracketing of the power of genealogical identity. There is much here to remind us of Peradotto's centrifugal figure of the negative; but further exploration of this will require a closer look at Odysseus' spying mission and his meeting with Dolon.

The Doloneia as a Drama of Desire

Lynn-George's analysis of *Iliad* 9 as a "drama of desire" focuses on the ambiguity of the word χρέω, "need." Achilles expresses a "need," yet it is notoriously difficult to specify exactly what Achilles needs. Lynn-George suggests that this need is not for any object but is intersubjective. Achilles needs others to need him; his striving for autonomy from the social is a striving for social recognition. This broader argument frames the following suggestive remark on the Doloneia.

> Agamemnon's very first word in the following book is that which was never to be found in his discourse rejected in book IX, *khreo* (x.43), a word which then reverberates throughout that book in the disturbed wandering about the camp at night (cf. x.85, 118, 142, 172). In one respect it would seem that the approach constructed by Agamemnon in IX is found wanting by Achilles precisely in the inadequacy of its articulation of want.[27]

Agamemnon's "articulation of want" occurs under the cover of night; the weakness of his symbolic authority, weakness rendered visible by Achilles, is supplanted through the nighttime actions of the trickster. When Nestor awakens Odysseus in the Doloneia, he immediately echoes Agamemnon's "need," asking, "What great need has come upon you" [τι δὴ χρειὼ τόσον ἵκει] (10.142). Yet the relationship of the trickster to this "drama of desire" is complex and can provide insight into the situation of Achilles. Let us first return to the words that escaped from Diomedes' lips before Odysseus' censorship intervened.

τούτου γε σπομένοιο καὶ ἐκ πυρὸς αἰθομένοιο
ἄμφω νοστήσαιμεν, ἐπεὶ περίοιδε νοῆσαι.

(*Il.* 10.246–47)

[Were he to go with me, both of us could come back from the blazing of fire itself, since his mind is best at devices.]

Diomedes' remarks on Odysseus' ability to return "from the blazing of fire" evoke the theme of descent to Hades and the "quest for immortality" in the Doloneia, as Wathelet has argued.[28] Wathelet shows that the capture of the brilliant chariot of Rhesus hints at other mythic tales of descent into darkness to locate the chariot of the Sun, which also descends from the sky into the realm of darkness at day's end.[29] The trip seeks to plummet into the depths of darkness to find this burning light and thus to bridge the gap between the world of mortals and the unknown beyond. It is in this sense a "quest for immortality," an attempt to master the mystery of an eternal beyond. Diomedes' suggestion is that the trickster Odysseus is the only person able to achieve this impossible act. His *noos* allows a return "from the blazing of fire."[30] He can defy death, an ability that is the equivalent of the brightest, most impossible of mortal desires: the desire to avoid death.

Yet if Odysseus as trickster appears able to overcome the limit separating life and death and thus to render an impossible desire possible, this ability has its dark side. For the uniqueness of this ability guarantees that the gap is constitutive; so far as Odysseus himself embodies an impossible desire, he emphasizes both his separation from the realm of mortals and the impossibility of that desire for them. To encounter Odysseus with illusions about one's own mortality is to encounter a figure that will destroy those illusions by forcing you to face him as a figure of death. This becomes clear in the killing of Rhesus. Later sources tell us that Rhesus himself would have become invincible had he but survived his first night at Troy and fought for one day.[31] Odysseus' intervention thus forcibly keeps the mortal Rhesus from reaching immortality and preserves the limit between mortals and what remains beyond the scope of mortals. As a figure who protects the absolute status of this limit for others, he takes on the role of a figure without limits: the trickster who crosses every boundary is the person who preserves the sanctity of those boundaries for others. Odysseus functions as a virtual double of the god Hermes—a crosser of boundaries, but also guardian of the liminal.[32] Within the Homeric poems, Hermes is most prominent in his role as *psychopompos*, crosser (and preserver) of the limit between life and death.

The death of the near-invincible Rhesus casts a shadow over the optimistic words of Diomedes, who spoke of a return (ἄμφω νοστήσαμεν) from blazing fire with Odysseus. If Odysseus is viewed as a savior, he is a paradoxical savior whose ability to cheat death only ends up guaranteeing its ultimate sovereignty. The return to life *(nostos)* from Hades is a temporary one, only delaying the inevitable journey back to Hades. So, too, the successful capture of the blazing horses of Rhesus (which provided the allure of the satisfaction of an ultimate desire) is limited by the words of Odysseus as he drives them back into the Greek camp. There, Nestor greets him and praises their extraordinary brightness (they "shine terribly like the rays of the sun," *Il.* 10.547). Here is Odysseus' response.

> ὦ Νέστορ Νηληϊάδη μέγα κῦδος Ἀχαιῶν
> ῥεῖα θεός γ' ἐθέλων καὶ ἀμείνονας ἠέ περ οἵδε
> ἵππους δωρήσαιτ', ἐπεὶ ἦ πολὺ φέρτεροί εἰσιν.
>
> (10.555–57)

[Son of Neleus, Nestor, great glory of the Achaians:
lightly a god, if he wished, could give us horses even better[33]
than these, seeing that the gods are far better than we are.]

These words have far-reaching significance. We can consider them an answer to the problem of desire that has dominated the book and that sets the machinations of the Doloneia in motion. Diomedes believed in Odysseus' ability to satisfy the ultimate desire. The capture of these horses, which evoke the horses of the sun god, seems to fulfill that. Yet Odysseus' words have the effect of deflating the earlier spirit of optimism. The specific task of the Doloneia has been accomplished, but this is not any ultimate satisfaction of the Greek's "want"; there are "even better" horses.[34] These words provide a twist to the events in book 10 (and book 9), and with these words we reach the centrifugal aspect of the narrative. There will always be something beyond the classifiable wants of the Greeks; superegoic attempts to fulfill those needs are destined to remain helpless and, ultimately, self-defeating.[35]

Odysseus' affirmation of the manner in which desire lies beyond every effort to fulfill it provides the parameters for understanding Odysseus' encounter with Dolon. Wathelet has perceptively noticed that Dolon resembles the god Hermes. Dolon has much wealth (he has "much gold, much bronze"), he is ugly, and he involves himself in a nonheroic form of warfare (*Il.* 10.315 ff.). So, too, Hermes is a god associated with commerce and, in particular, the riches of the earth; he is a trickster figure in contrast to the ideal of the heroic warrior.[36] Yet, as I have already suggested, the resemblance to Hermes is also shared by Odysseus. Dolon is a near double of Odysseus. The epithets πολύχρυσος and πολύχαλκος recall the *poly-* epithets shared by Hermes and Odysseus, most notably *polytropos*. But the most significant parallel is their mutual association with the figure of the "lone wolf." Dolon wears a wolf-skin and a cap of marten's hide. Significant attention is drawn to the caps worn by Diomedes and Odysseus. But while Diomedes' helmet is a conventional skullcap, Odysseus' helmet emphasizes his links to the realm of the trickster.

> Meriones gave Odysseus a bow and a quiver
> and a sword; and he too put over his head a helmet
> fashioned of leather; on the inside the cap was cross-strung firmly
> with thongs of leather, and on the outer side the white teeth
> of a tusk-shining boar were close sewn one after another
> with craftsmanship and skill; and a felt was set in the centre.
> Autolykos, breaking into the close-built house, had stolen it
> from Amyntor, the son of Ormenos, out of Eleon,
> and gave it to Kytherian Amphidamas, at Skandeia;
> Amphidamas gave it in turn to Molos, a gift of guest-friendship,
> and Molos gave it to his son Meriones to carry.
> But at this time it was worn to cover the head of Odysseus.
> (*Il.* 10.260–71)

The symbolism of the "lone wolf" in the Doloneia has been explored by Gernet and Davidson.[37] Davidson notes the double characteristics of the wolf—"tour à tour vainqueur et vaincu," victor and victim.[38] She points out that the "lone wolf" is the figure who "strays off alone" and is consequently an outlaw (the old German word *friedlos* means both outlaw and wolf). As such, the wolf clothing is relevant to the wider theme on display in book 10, of trickery outside the boundaries of the law. Dolon's disguise as a wolf is complemented by the evocation of Odysseus' Autolycan background in the description of his cap; Autolycus, "self-wolf," is the enemy of society par excellence, and is also the figure who has the closest relationship to the trickster-god Hermes.[39]

Davidson has also drawn attention to a similarity between the appearance of the wolf motif in the Doloneia and its occurrence in Arcadian myth and in the rites of the cult of Zeus Lykaios. In Arcadian myth, too, the emphasis is on the figure of the wolf at the fringes of the social.

In the myth, Lykaon sacrifices a child and is punished for it by being turned into a wolf. What he does as a wolf is re-enacted in the cult of Zeus Lykaios, which can be considered as a rite of separation for an initiation. The participant in the initiation, having made a sacrifice, leaves human society and takes up the life of a wolf. He *hangs his clothes up on a tree*, crosses a lake, and after a period of separation while he lives like a wolf, finally becomes initiated.[40]

The importance of this initiation rite lies in the striking parallel to the behavior of Odysseus in the Doloneia; for he, too, strips Dolon of his wolf-skin and hangs it up on a tree after Diomedes has killed him.

> ὣς ἄρ' ἐφώνησεν, καὶ ἀπὸ ἕθεν ὑψόσ' ἀείρας
> θῆκεν ἀνὰ μυρίκην· δέελον δ' ἐπὶ σῆμά τ' ἔθηκεν,
> συμμάρψας δόνακας μυρίκης τ' ἐριθηλέας ὄζους,
> μὴ λάθοι αὖτις ἰόντε θοὴν διὰ νύκτα μέλαιναν.
>
> (10.465–68)

[So he spoke, and lifting the spoils high from him he placed them
upon a tamarisk bush, and piled a clear landmark beside them,
pulling reeds together and the long branches of tamarisk
that they might not miss them on their way back through the
running black night.]

Yet despite the parallel, Davidson confesses to a certain difficulty in "fitting this lore into the context of *Iliad X*." She concludes that "we may see Dolon as a *friedlos* figure whom Diomedes and Odysseus have the freedom to kill, masked in their animal skins." Yet this does not explain the success of Odysseus. Why is Dolon not equally free to kill Odysseus? If both are "lone wolves," what differentiates the successful Odysseus from the loser Dolon? There is also a striking difference between the actions of the initiation rite and those of Odysseus. In the ritual, one becomes a wolf when one is divested of one's clothing: Dolon, however, is stripped of his clothing after he has been killed. If we are to follow the logic of the initiation fully, we are left with the paradoxical conclusion that Dolon seems only truly to become a wolf, an outcast, when he is divorced—separated in death—from the trappings of wolfness. How can this be explained?

An answer might lie in Odysseus and Dolon's differing relationship to desire. I have already discussed the importance of Odysseus' words to Nestor, suggesting the constitutive unfulfillability of the *khreo* (need) of the Greeks; this provides us with an opportunity for retroactively understanding the vulnerability of Dolon. He agrees to the spying mission. But he does so only on the condition that Hector will provide him with the horses of Achilles should he be successful (*Il.* 10.321). The epithets πολύχρυσος and πολύχαλκος emphasize that he has no need of material wealth; instead, he yearns for pure prestige, to earn the elusive title of *aristos*. His desire is thus thoroughly reflective—in Lacanian terms, it exemplifies how desire is always mediated, how desire is always "desire of the Other." Dolon desires not simply an object but the object he believes others desire. His desire remains at the level of envy. Because his actions are performed to gain prestige (the recognition of his symbolic community), he is not truly a *friedlos,* an enemy of society. The trappings of wolfness are only a tactical disguise, worn to win prestige. They are not the marks of a true outsider. Because of this, Dolon is vulnerable: he is ultimately dependent on the society he seems to reject. By contrast, Odysseus' role in the episode demonstrates the ultimate futility of Dolon's pursuit and of the quest for prestige in general: he therefore lies beyond every determinate need. He is a pure trickster, not a tactical one. He is not vulnerable to death, because, as a pure trickster and double of Hermes, he functions as the limit itself between life and death.

Of course, this interpretation depends on an acknowledgment that the figure of Odysseus is far more complex than any reading that treats him as an ordinary, human trickster will allow. He is first of all such a trickster, but part of his success is his lack of attachment to the prestige that causes the downfall of Dolon. Odysseus succeeds because he has no aspect of his identity at stake. But this success and the corresponding erasure of any ties to the human world suggest that he can be read allegorically as a figure who is not victim to boundaries, even as he patrols them—and within the divine world, this corresponds to the god Hermes. To imagine a perfect trickster is to imagine a person without any identity, without any vulnerability. To imagine someone without the burden of human life that is a social identity is to imagine the antithesis of human life—a figure of death itself. Odysseus is complex (and fascinating) because of the way he glides between these possibilities. We might explain this by returning to Lynn-George's emphasis on the manner in which any human trick is open to the possibility of detection. Odysseus proves this to be the case by providing us with an image of what an infallible trickster might look like. Part of his makeup as a no one is as a figure whose success is terrifyingly destructive.

We can now turn to Odysseus' erection of the spoils of Dolon as a *sema*. In Wathelet's discussion of the *katabasis* motif, Dolon's death is the act that marks the descent of Diomedes and Odysseus into Hades. But of what are these spoils a sign? They first signify the death of Dolon and thus function as a replacement of his tomb. That the spoils of Dolon should be described as a *sema* is thus quite appropriate: Diomedes and Odysseus follow the soul of Dolon into an unknowable beyond, just as the *sema* of a tombstone represents a place beyond representation. But the particular aspect of this *sema*, which involves the external trappings of Dolon, is also appropriate as a marker of the world to which Diomedes and Odysseus return. They descend into a realm of death, but this realm, because it is outside the reach of the public law, allows the protagonists to indulge in a disgusting enjoyment, a superegoic carnage more "alive" than anything that occurs in the highly regulated warfare of the daytime. The spoils of Dolon, his outer trappings, his shell, indicate a return to the classifying arena of the public law, of the clashing of external identities already determined by the ideological parameters that govern the world of heroes.

Nagy has persuasively argued for a semantic connection between *sema* and *noos*.[41] A *sema* is meaningless unless read, noticed. The ability to make sense out of the differential realm of *semata* is what characterizes a person who has *noos*. Nagy also notes the etymological link between *nostos* and *noos*, explored at length in the work of Douglas Frame.[42] *Noos* helps guarantee a *nostos*. The theme occurs in Diomedes' words about Odysseus: he knows how to use his *noos* (περίοιδε νοῆσαι, 10.247) and thus can guarantee a return from the expedition of *Iliad* 10. Later, Odysseus will mark the boundary between the no-man's-land of the Doloneia and the camp of the Greeks by the *sema* of the trappings of Dolon's body, which cut off the world of the dead from that of the living. The powers of the trickster here seem to exceed any human abilities; he not only can read the differential realm of signs but is able to look into the "beyond" of the other world, to where the souls of the dead depart.

We can now begin to understand the specific manner in which the Doloneia perverts the initiation rite of Zeus Lykaios. The rite involves a temporary, symbolic loss of identity (the hanging up of one's external trappings on a tree) to gain eventual entrance to society. A temporary loss of identity is eventually recuperated by the acceptance into society, the attainment of a social identity. The Doloneia suggests a much more radical loss of identity, for which there is nothing in return. Dolon has his clothes "hung up" by Odysseus as he is severed from his symbolic trappings in death. It is as if the logic of the rite makes the same mistake as Dolon; his temporary, "tactical" adoption of the guise of wolf is ultimately a hoax, performed for a determinate desire, a social affirmation. Dolon's death highlights the danger of this optimism.

"Obscurest of All" Is What Achilles Wants

I have so far traced Dolon's similarity to (and difference from) Odysseus; we should also note his marked similarity to Achilles. Dolon's complex relationship to his desire replays the "drama of desire"[43] of *Iliad* 9. Dolon was rich in bronze, rich in gold, yet fought on for prestige. So, too, Achilles vehemently rejects Agamemnon's offers of material goods (bronze, gold), seeking instead the pure prestige that only Agamemnon's "articulation of want" might provide.[44] Yet Odysseus' actions in the Doloneia provide us with the possibility of a retroactive reading of the drama of *Iliad* 9. Achilles' desire, like Dolon's, is certainly for something excessive within the terms of heroic ideology. Ajax' blunt response to his rejection of the embassy is more than enough to confirm this.[45] Yet before his language suggests a shift to a desire for prestige, before his fury after the death of Patroclus, there remains the utopian moment when the public law is laid bare in its inadequacy.

> ληϊστοὶ μὲν γάρ τε βόες καὶ ἴφια μῆλα,
> κτητοὶ δὲ τρίποδές τε καὶ ἵππων ξανθὰ κάρηνα,
> ἀνδρὸς δὲ ψυχὴ πάλιν ἐλθεῖν οὔτε λεϊστὴ
> οὔθ' ἑλετή, ἐπεὶ ἄρ κεν ἀμείψεται ἕρκος ὀδόντων.
>
> (*Il.* 9.406–9)
>
> [Of possessions
> cattle and fat sheep are things to be had for the lifting,
> and tripods can be won, and the tawny heads of horses,
> but a man's life cannot come back again, it cannot be lifted
> nor captured again by force, once it has crossed the teeth's barrier.]

The uselessness of the winning of the heads of horses previews the Doloneia, which costs Dolon his life. He desired horses, risked his life, and lost it. For the briefest of moments, Achilles seems to flirt with Odysseus' answer in the Doloneia to the question of desire—that there will always be better horses to be won. If Achilles' later threat of a return home, modified by a series of vacillations, can be seen as astute self-positioning in his fight for prestige, this earlier, utopian, Odyssean moment remains. It is a moment when Achilles has demolished unquestioned acceptance of the public law but has not yet been taken over by anger at the loss of his friend. The fury remained at the level of fantasy at the beginning of *Iliad* 16, but after the death of Patroclus, Achilles' return to warfare is an attempt to realize the fantasy. He returns to battle, but he no longer has time for the conventions of warfare. He no longer respects the appeals of suppliants, as he did before, and he refuses to return the corpse of Hector. In short, does not Achilles' obscene enjoyment of the slaughter he performs after he returns to the battle drag the nighttime enjoyment of the killing of the Doloneia into the daytime?[46] The Doloneia is a narrative enactment of the dark side of heroic warfare. But Achilles' fury turns the heroic world upside down, bringing about the sort of carnage earlier witnessed in the killing of the sleeping Rhesus and the Thracians: as Diomedes killed sleeping men, so Achilles kills men who are helpless in comparison to him.

Lacan characterized the superego by its "malevolent neutrality"; it is neutral because it encourages an identification with the law itself once its public, symbolic support has failed. Instead of believing in the law because of its morality, its beneficial social consequences, one fanatically believes in it *because it is the law*. This neutrality allows us to chart the key development of Achilles' thinking in the *Iliad*. Achilles' famous speech in response to Odysseus in *Iliad* 9 acts as the final nail in the coffin of the public law and of Agamemnon as the symbolic father who guarantees it.

> Fate is the same for man who holds back, the same if he fights hard.
> We are all held in a single honour, the brave with the weaklings.
> A man dies still if he has done nothing, as one who has done much.
> (*Il.* 9.319–21)

Any symbolic difference between the *esthlos* (noble) and the *kakos* (cowardly) is eradicated as Achilles contemplates his mortality. Attempts to distinguish them will no longer work; attempts to articulate a rationale for war based on the difference between "good" and "bad" no longer make sense. The shattering of confidence in Agamemnon, the symbolic head of the community of Greeks, coincides with a lack of faith in the public law. Yet there is no sign as yet of any superegoic dimension to the rejection of the public law. In sharp contrast, Achilles' words to the supplicating Lycaon in book 21 recall the rhetoric of radical leveling from book 9. Here, the words are no longer part of a challenge, a questioning of authority, but exult instead in the certainty of an answer.

> In the time before Patroklos came to the day of his destiny
> then it was the way of my heart's choice to be sparing
> of the Trojans, and many I took alive and disposed of them.
> Now there is not one who can escape death, if the gods send
> him against my hands in front of Ilion, not one
> of all the Trojans and beyond others the children of Priam.
> So, friend, you die also. Why all this clamour about it?
> Patroklos also is dead, who was better by far than you are.
> Do you not see what a man I am, how huge, how splendid
> and born of a great father, and the mother who bore me immortal?
> Yet even I have also my death and my strong destiny . . .
> (*Il.* 21.100–110)

Achilles' encounter with Lycaon has received significant critical attention.[47] For now, I merely want to show how the encounter suggests the manner in which the law is split. First note that the poem portrays the death of Lycaon as a second death. Achilles had captured him once before and sold him into slavery. When Achilles sees him, he complains that Trojans are returning from death to fight a second time.[48] The second killing of Lycaon promises to be final. These "two deaths" suggest the two realms of the law. Lycaon was first killed at the time when Achilles still obeyed the public law. But because the public law is deficient, inadequate, he has returned. His second death is at the hands of a superegoic Achilles, a figure who wants to follow through the logic of war all the way, in an attempt to make up for its symbolic inadequacies. Any desire for *kleos*—the prestige of intersubjective recognition that binds the community—is gone. This is now the context for the radical leveling of social rank apparent in his words to Lycaon: with any symbolic system that separates humans into *esthlos* and *kakos* gone, Lycaon is just another mortal hastened on the path to death.[49] There is a crucial difference between this leveling of social rank and that of the Achilles of *Iliad* 9. His former rhetoric in *Iliad* 9 suspends the working of the symbolic law and lingers over the utopian possibility of a return home. His logic there can be roughly summarized as follows: "The public law is a sham; its attempts to differentiate the good from the bad are futile: so let us all go home." His words to Lycaon, after the intervening death of Patroclus, take the logic of the argument a crucial step further: "The public law is a sham, incomplete. Its rhetoric of differentiating the good from the bad has done nothing to protect men held to be 'good' in its own terms. Even Patroclus has died. Therefore, I must do everything in our power to render the law complete, to pursue warfare with an indifference to the code regulating its performance." Achilles obeys the dictates of the superego.

We now can contrast this neutral, superegoic aspect of Achilles in the open air with Odysseus' remarks to Diomedes. For Odysseus, too, asks to be neither praised nor blamed; that is, there is the suggestion that his actions as a trickster cannot be registered "bad" or "good" at the level of the symbolic law. Why? Odysseus' actions obey the spirit, not the letter, of the law. As such, he is merely fulfilling by night the (unspoken/unspeakable) desire of the Achaeans. His actions are thus neutral; he just follows (silently understood) orders, orders that form a superegoic injunction. But this superegoic aspect must be contrasted with Odysseus' final lesson—that such superegoic attempts to render the law whole are ultimately futile. There will always be "better horses"; desire will remain unfulfillable; the (public) law will remain incomplete. The actions of the Doloneia thus "traverse"—that is, work through for us, the readers—a fantasy that will later be acted out on a much larger scale when Achilles returns to battle. Achilles, not privy to the lessons of the Doloneia, does not understand that his mass slaughter will provide no answer to the problem of loss itself and that his fury is futile.

7

The *Odyssey* from the Perspective of Its Victims

Pucci has provided the following influential summary of the differences between the *Iliad* and the *Odyssey:* "The *Iliad* is the poem of total expenditure of life and the *Odyssey* is the poem of a controlled economy of life."[1] Though this judgment is helpful in many ways, there is the danger that it glosses over the deeply troubling aspects of the mass of deaths of the *Odyssey*. An all too common reaction to these deaths is to explain them as justified by the particular social ideology the poem supposedly promotes—for example, to argue that the suitors pay a just price for their challenge to the values of order and civilization.[2] Part of my goal here is to force a reevaluation of such a position. But if we set aside Pucci's judgment on the difference between the poems, the contrast between a "controlled economy" and "total expenditure" is helpful for understanding the gulf separating the Odysseus of books 2 and 10 of the *Iliad*. These books highlight two possible ways of killing and being killed. At the level of public law, the Greeks maintained allegiance to a symbolic master, Agamemnon. They played the game of war by the rules he represented, and they died by those rules. At the level of the superegoic reverse of the law, all symbolic restrictions are lifted; a "cowardly" killing ensues, which is unheroic, destructive, and evocative of the hidden, dark form of warfare associated with the trickster.

These forms of killing and being killed are not antithetical; rather, the latter is an open acknowledgment of the hidden truth of the former. If the former is a "controlled economy" of death, the latter is an instance of "total expenditure." The different manners of death produce corresponding changes in Odysseus' *metis*. It changes from a *metis* exercised on behalf of public law (Odysseus' ability to persuade each of the troops to stay at Troy to complete their mission under the mandate of Agamemnon) to a more disturbing *metis* that seems to transgress the public law even as it shores it up. The uncanny success of this *metis* is both terrifying and enlightening. Odysseus participates in a slaughter that suggests the inevitability of death, but he also underlines the impossibility of fulfilling desire. His (perfectly) successful execution of the law goes hand in hand with a demonstration of the possibility (for us, as readers) of a reflective distance from the violence performed in its name.

These separate forms of death recur in the two separate spheres of death in the *Odyssey:* the deaths of Odysseus' crew and the deaths of the suitors. Nagler has claimed that the death of the suitors is a "grim inversion" of the deaths of Odysseus' crew, that while the proem of the *Odyssey* emphasizes the hero's efforts to save his men, "his 'effort,' his *aethlos* is precisely the *slaughter* of the suitors, the exact equivalent of the companions in the domestic world." According to Nagler, the "passive loss" of the crew is contrasted with the "active destruction" of the suitors.[3] Nagler eloquently argues for a deep ethical anxiety present in Odysseus' killing of his own social group; the energy properly directed toward outsiders is targeted inward. But instead of Nagler's contrast between "active" and "passive," I suggest a distinction between a "controlled economy" of death (for the companions) and "total expenditure," between a death at the level of public law and a superegoic death. Further, rather than affirming the separation, the latter death announces the truth of the former—as in the case of *Iliad* 10 and 2. The obscene enjoyment on show in the killing of the suitors clarifies the manner in which Odysseus' interactions with his companions was structured around a hidden fantasy of his total control of them—a control ultimately dependent on his ability (and repressed desire) to kill them.[4] The death inflicted on the suitors lurks as a hidden threat behind the symbolic authority of Odysseus as leader of his troops. The companions die because of their allegiance to Odysseus and because of his ability (through trickery and mystification) to persuade them of the benevolence of his leadership.

Metis *and the Many*

The problem that Odysseus continually confronts as he plots to kill the suitors is a simple one, yet in its simplicity it raises themes that are central to any leader's ability to exert ideological control. How can one overcome many?[5] The suitors' de facto rebellion against Odysseus' authority as head of the central *oikos* at Ithaca forces Odysseus to confront this problem openly. But if Odysseus faced no similar question in his interactions with his companions, this is only because his control of them is largely taken for granted. Odysseus does not openly think of the need for new measures to control his companions, because his symbolic authority remains effective: the companions' challenge to him (as we shall see) never quite reaches the point of open defiance. Faced with the suitors, however, Odysseus seems to doubt his ability to defeat them. But at the moment his doubt is at its most acute, Athena intervenes to assure his success. She does so in a manner that links the defeat of the suitors to the key successes in Odysseus' *Apologoi*.

> σχέτλιε, καὶ μέν τίς τε χερείονι πείθεθ' ἑταίρῳ,
> ὅς περ θνητός τ' ἐστὶ καὶ οὐ τόσα μήδεα οἶδεν·
> αὐτὰρ ἐγὼ θεός εἰμι, διαμπερὲς ἥ σε φυλάσσω
> ἐν πάντεσσι πόνοισ'. ἐρέω δέ τοι ἐξαναφανδόν·
> εἴ περ πεντήκοντα λόχοι μερόπων ἀνθρώπων
> νῶϊ περισταῖεν, κτεῖναι μεμαῶτες Ἄρηϊ,
> καί κεν τῶν ἐλάσαιο βόας καὶ ἴφια μῆλα.
>
> (*Od.* 20.45–51)

[Stubborn man! Anyone trusts even a lesser companion
than I, who is mortal, and does not have so many ideas.
But I am a god, and through it all I keep watch over you
in every endeavor of yours. And now I tell you this plainly:
even though there were fifty battalions of mortal people
standing around us, furious to kill in the spirit of battle,
even so you could drive away their cattle and fat sheep.]

Athena describes Odysseus' ability to defeat the suitors as if it was just another *aethlos* (heroic contest). The goal is to "drive away their cattle and fat sheep," and the stealing (and consumption) of livestock is the crucial theme in two of the most important tales of the *Apologoi*, the tricking of the Cyclops and the consumption of the cattle of Helios on Thrinacia. But the abruptness of Athena's response is disconcerting. Odysseus' former tales of his *metis* in the *Apologoi* lingered over his tricks and took delight in their ingenuity. Athena confronts him with the inevitability of victory. In contrast to the tricks of *metis*, which classically remain hidden, Athena tells him openly of a perfect success. Though Odysseus is a hero of cunning, a victor in an ongoing series of encounters—encounters he might lose at any time—he is here confronted with the inevitability of victory in all his trials.

Athena's pronouncements suggest a very different *metis* from the one normally associated with Odysseus. Her words signal the split between the two forms of *metis* suggested in my analysis of *Iliad* 2 and 10. If *metis* is performed with specific goals in mind (in the *Odyssey*, the stealing of "cattle and fat sheep"), there is nevertheless a certain delight in the stratagem itself, in the means used to procure the end. The effect of *metis* seems to be bound up not merely in its successful pursuit of a goal but in the manner in which such a goal is attained. As an example, we need look no further than the subtlety of the wordplay in Odysseus' interaction with the Cyclops. Athena's *metis*, however, seems to short-circuit the workings of *metis* by going straight to the goal. The result within the *Odyssey* is perturbing enough: the grisly death of the suitors who stand in the way of the "cattle and fat sheep," even as they will be herded up for their death as if they were cattle or sheep. But Athena's rhetoric suggests the ability to dispose of even greater numbers of men if necessary, "fifty battalions." This ability of *metis* to send masses to their death returns us to the fantasies of mass destruction with which I began the last chapter and that are so much a part of the Homeric tradition. But if there is indeed a contrast between Athena's harsh picture of *metis* and a kinder, gentler one, I want to stress once again that the two are linked. Odysseus' destruction of the suitors renders explicit what was already implicit in Odysseus' interactions with his companions. In both cases, *metis* leads to death.

In what follows, I trace this doubled structure of *metis:* the "public" aspect of trickery and mystification (expounded on at length by Vernant and Detienne)[6] together with its superegoic reverse. The companions, caught in the dead structures of the symbolic law, fall victim to the mystifying powers of Odysseus' *metis*. The suitors suffer a superegoic destruction—previewed in Athena's words already quoted—in exchange for their own superegoic enjoyment on show as they consume the goods of the *oikos*. But though this division is a useful and helpful one, the complexity of the narrative lies in the manner in which the law and its reverse overlap. The companions, who for the most part remain loyal to Odysseus, are not completely alien to enjoyment, nor are the suitors entirely able to divorce themselves from the public law. I will soon trace some of these complexities. But first, we should pause over the deadly aspects of both forms of *metis* and over the predominance of the theme of death in the *Odyssey* as a whole.

Death in the Poem of Life

In the *Iliad*, Achilles' vision of mass destruction is never quite carried out (though there will be plenty of his victims). Many men do survive the war, and his vision of life alone with Patroclus does not materialize. But the fantasy makes us ponder the quite different level of destruction depicted in the *Odyssey*, in particular with regard to the adult males. For whereas some of the adult male population survive the Trojan War, none of the young adult men on Ithaca will survive: the "many strong heads" destroyed in the *Iliad* (πολλὰς ἰφθίμους κεφαλὰς) are replaced by the young men of the Cephallenians. Not one of the crew or suitors will escape destruction: the troops die on the way home; the suitors are killed to a man. This unpleasant truth is too easily overlooked by the advocates of the *Odyssey* as a poem of life.[7] Yet it has a fundamental importance for the reading of the poem. For we can add two highly significant passages from the *Odyssey* to the passages that link the *Iliad*'s proem to disaster motifs.

The first is the introduction to the second Nekuia, which reads as a bitter roll call of the πολλὰς δ' ἰφθίμους ψυχὰς whose death was anticipated in the proem of the *Iliad*. Hermes leads the suitors' mass of *psychai* to Hades, but on arrival they meet a series of *psychai* (souls) who died in the Trojan War.

> Ἑρμῆς δὲ ψυχὰς Κυλλήνιος ἐξεκαλεῖτο
> ἀνδρῶν μνηστήρων· ἔχε δὲ ῥάβδον μετὰ χερσὶ
> καλὴν χρυσείην, τῆι τ' ἀνδρῶν ὄμματα θέλγει
> ὧν ἐθέλει, τοὺς δ' αὖτε καὶ ὑπνώοντας ἐγείρει·
> . . . .
>   αἶψα δ' ἵκοντο κατ' ἀσφοδελὸν λειμῶνα,
> ἔνθα τε ναίουσι ψυχαί, εἴδωλα καμόντων.
> Εὗρον δὲ ψυχὴν Πηληϊάδεω Ἀχιλῆος
> καὶ Πατροκλῆος καὶ ἀμύμονος Ἀντιλόχοιο
> Αἴαντος θ', ὃς ἄριστος ἔην εἶδος τε δέμας τε
> τῶν ἄλλων Δαναῶν μετ' ἀμύμονα Πηλείωνα.
>
>   (*Od.* 24.1–4, 13–18)

[Hermes of Kyllene summoned the souls of the suitors
to come forth, and in his hands he was holding the beautiful
golden staff, with which he mazes the eyes of those mortals
whose eyes he would maze, or wakes again the sleepers.
. . . .
  [They] presently arrived in the meadow of asphodel.
This is the dwelling place of souls, images of dead men.
There they found the soul of Achilleus, the son of Peleus,
the soul of Patroklos, and the soul of stately Antilochus,
and the soul of Aias, who for beauty and stature was the greatest
of all the Danaans, next to the blameless son of Peleus.]

Any narrative of return to a "controlled economy of life" on Ithaca is put on hold, and we are provided instead with a catalog of death. The recent

Cephallenian victims of Odysseus join the most illustrious victims of the Trojan War. But if this "abruptly transfers the scene of the action" away from events in Ithaca, it provides a grim conclusion to the proleptic tale of death begun in the proem of the *Iliad*.⁸ There is a strange solidarity between Odysseus and Hermes. Hermes, the guardian of the liminal, takes on the role of ψυχοπόμπος, the god who accompanies mortals on their final journey to the underworld. He thus completes the earlier toil of Odysseus as a killer. It is a link that was already apparent in the *Odyssey*'s proem.

> Ἄνδρα μοι ἔννεπε, Μοῦσα, πολύτροπον, ὃς μάλα πολλὰ
> πλάγχθη, ἐπεὶ Τροίης ἱερὸν πτολίεθρον ἔπερσε·
> πολλῶν δ' ἀνθρώπων ἴδεν ἄστεα καὶ νόον ἔγνω,
> πολλὰ δ' ὅ γ' ἐν πόντωι πάθεν ἄλγεα ὃν κατὰ θυμόν,
> ἀρνύμενος ἥν τε ψυχὴν καὶ νόστον ἑταίρων.
> ἀλλ' οὐδ' ὣς ἑτάρους ἐρρύσατο, ἱέμενός περ·
>
> (*Od*. 1.1–6)

[Tell me, Muse, of the man of many ways, who was driven
far journeys, after he had sacked Troy's sacred citadel.
Many were they whose cities he saw, whose minds he learned of,
many the pains he suffered in his spirit on the wide sea,
struggling for his own life and the homecoming of his companions.
Even so he could not save back his companions, hard though
he strove to;]

Hermes and Odysseus are linked by the epithet πολύτροπος, which they alone share. The ease of Odysseus' movement across lands and seas suggests an affinity with the boundary-crosser Hermes and underlines the appropriateness of the epithet.⁹ But Hermes' appearance as *psychopompos* in book 24 suggests the possibility of a darker reading of a proem that is already suffused with a spirit of ethical anxiety because of Ithacan deaths.¹⁰ For the completeness of the destruction of the young men of Ithaca links Odysseus as agent of destruction to Hermes as transporter of souls to Hades.

There is a further suggestion of death in the proem's evocation of the many *tropoi* that encircle an unnamed subject. For *poly-* epithets are associated with Hades. The god of death is both πολυδέγμων, the host of many as he receives the souls of mortals one by one, and πολυώνυμος, the person of "many names."¹¹ The many names are euphemisms, repeatedly conjured up to avoid mention of his "unmentionable" essence as the bringer of death, a paradoxical essence that coincides with the nothingness of an unknowable beyond. The failure to name here is appropriate: because this "beyond" is unknowable, it is radically inassimilable to sense, to language. A similar process is at work in the proem of the *Odyssey*; the marked vocabulary of "the many" avoids the classifying name *Odysseus*, but it also fails to mention the hero's most famous *tropos*, Odysseus as Outis. *Outis* is as close as language can get to signifying the unsignified; it signifies only the lack of descriptive features. It is therefore much more than one more descriptive term categorizing the hero; it signifies the realm of the unspeakable that the many *tropoi* of language encircle without quite reaching. The failure to name Odysseus hints at that which resists classification in the hero, which returns us to the senseless realm of death. In a proem that already strains to emphasize the innocence of its hero with regard to the destruction of his men, mention of the hero as a figure of the negative is conspicuously avoided. The proem constantly equates the hero with death in its ongoing, euphemistic failure to equate them.

The structure of taboo allows us to reformulate what Michael Nagler has called the "effort/contest" theme in the proem of the *Odyssey*.[12] Nagler points to a marked vocabulary of conflict that will characterize the ensuing narrative. I quote the proem once more, underlining the words highlighting the "effort/contest" theme noted by Nagler.

> Ἄνδρα μοι ἔννεπε, Μοῦσα, πολύτροπον, <u>ὃς μάλα πολλὰ πλάγχθη</u>, ἐπεὶ Τροίης ἱερὸν πτολίεθρον ἔπερσε·
> πολλῶν δ' ἀνθρώπων ἴδεν ἄστεα καὶ νόον ἔγνω,
> πολλὰ δ' ὅ γ' ἐν πόντωι <u>πάθεν ἄλγεα</u> ὃν κατὰ θυμόν,
> <u>ἀρνύμενος</u> ἥν τε ψυχὴν καὶ νόστον ἑταίρων.
> ἀλλ' οὐδ' ὣς ἑτάρους ἐρρύσατο, <u>ἱέμενός περ</u>·
> αὐτῶν γὰρ <u>σφετέρηισιν ἀτασθαλίηισιν</u> ὄλοντο,
> <u>νήπιοι</u> οἳ κατὰ βοῦς Ὑπερίονος Ἡελίοιο . . .
>
> (*Od.* 1.1–8)

[Tell me, Muse, of the man of many ways, who was driven
far journeys, after he had sacked Troy's sacred citadel.
Many were they whose cities he saw, whose minds he learned of,
many the pains he suffered in his spirit on the wide sea,
struggling for his own life and the homecoming of his companions.
Even so he could not save back his companions, hard though
he strove to; they were destroyed by their own wild recklessness,
fools, who devoured the oxen of Helios, the sun god . . .]

Nagler notes that this theme is replayed on Phaeacia and, later, in the "contest" of the bow that destroys the suitors. For Nagler, the contrast lies between the regulated contests and the perverse effort of destruction involved in killing the suitors. But in light of my reading of the contests on Phaeacia, Nagler's split (between suitors and crew, between "normal" and "perverse" games) is complicated by the universality of the theme of loss. Odysseus' victory in the games on Phaeacia introduced the Phaeacians to the possibility of loss, to the notion of a game that could not be won. This unwinnable game forces the civilization of the Phaeacians to reflect on loss and thus introduces them to their mortality. A society without limits, where every voyage could be made to every destination without risk, without loss, is destroyed by the introduction of an absolute limit. All struggles, all efforts, can only be understood against the backdrop of this mortal limit.

This reading of Odysseus' interaction with the Phaeacians can help us with a further problem of the proem. It is well known that the pointed references to voyages to cities of many men and to the knowledge of their *noos* (πολλῶν δ' ἀνθρώπων ἴδεν ἄστεα καὶ νόον ἔγνω) seem curiously inappropriate because these journeys do not seem to occur in the narrative of the *Odyssey* itself.[13] But effortless traveling to a plurality of destinations perfectly characterizes the Phaeacians before the arrival of Odysseus. There is something grimly foreboding about the ultimate success of Phaeacian transportation: each mortal traveler arrives on Phaeacia and is passed on to his ultimate destination, his telos, by a society that remains unaware of the concept of limit. The inevitability of this arrival at a destination hints at the inevitability of that final voyage—the voyage that involves the accompaniment of Hermes *psychopompos*.[14] Phaeacia, a society where the idea of a boundary in itself is unthinkable within its own terms of reference, duplicates the qualities of the god who performs the same function: Hermes travels everywhere and is a figure for whom boundaries are irrelevant. But though a boundless figure, he preserves the notion of limits (as guardian of thresholds) for the mortal world, limits that are in turn dependent on his guardianship of the ultimate limit keeping mortals from knowing anything of the "life beyond." In book 8, Odysseus takes over this function; he relegates the Phaeacians to the level of mortals as he replaces them as limitless guardian of the limit. Once more, we need to supplement the insights of Peradotto into *Outis:* if it signals "individuality," that which escapes predication, this notion also refers to a realm free of boundaries, the "beyond" of the *sema*, which is death.

Let us now return to the third line of the poem. What can it mean to "know" men's minds (νόον ἔγνω)? The arrival of Odysseus introduced doubt to the minds of the Phaeacians. This doubt coincided with an emergence of freedom, with the ability to act as a moral agent. But his freedom came at a price—the necessary acknowledgment of loss, of mortality. Once more, Nagy's insight into the semantic relationship between *sema* and *noos* is helpful. Before the arrival of Odysseus, the Phaeacians had a perfect *noos*, suggested in the name of their king, Alci*nous*. Every sign was understood, there was no doubt in their universe. Defeat at the hands of Odysseus introduces doubt via the realization of an unwinnable game, a constitutive beyond which is the unknowable. The limit imposed on their ability to read signs signifies their mortality. But it also testifies to a newly discovered Phaeacian freedom. Once they experience self-reflection and doubt, the Phaeacians are able to make free choices. Thus, to know the minds of mortals (νόον ἔγνω) means to be unable to know fully the minds of mortals. Because there is something unclassifiable about mortals, their actions cannot be predicted; they, as subjects, exceed their predications. Herein lies the possibility of a "free self" suggested by Peradotto. But this failure to know the minds of mortals is also to know that the prospect of mortality, the basis for this failure in classification, haunts their conscious existence.

What can we make of the wanderings through cities? Odysseus' defeat of the Phaeacians suggests that he has taken over their role as a sender of humans on to their telos. The proem's conflation of Odysseus with Hermes *psychopompos* (and the unmentioned, unmentionable Hades) suggests the universality of death, a universal wanderer, who descends into the multitude of cities, picking off mortals one by one. If Odysseus here seems to be in dark company, it is perhaps worth recalling first the death, one by one, of his companions and then the all-at-once slaughter of the suitors. The proem mentions the sacking of Troy before listing a series of other cities to be visited, suggesting the vulnerability of every city to the fate meted out to Troy. The *Iliad* reflects on this theme in a dark interchange between Hera and Zeus. Hera demands the sack of Troy but concedes Zeus' right to take other cities.

> Of all cities there are three that are dearest to my own heart:
> Argos and Sparta and Mykenai of the wide ways. All these,
> whenever they become hateful to your heart, sack utterly.
> I will not stand up for these against you, nor yet begrudge you.
> Yet if even so I bear malice and would not have you destroy them,
> in malice I will accomplish nothing, since you are far stronger.
>
> (*Il.* 4.51–56)

Troy takes its place as one in a series of cities to be sacked. Odysseus' role as "city-sacker," suggested in the reference to the sack of Troy in the poem's second line, goes with him as he visits "many" other cities. The universal explorer brings death in his wake.

Homeless Journeys

The *Odyssey* begins where the *Iliad* ended, with Hermes *psychopompos*. In the proem of the *Odyssey*, the epithet *polytropos* links Odysseus to Hermes, the figure whose universal voyages coincide with the journey all of us must make into death. At the end of the *Iliad*, Hermes accompanies Priam to the tent of Achilles "as if he went to his death" (24.328). He returns to Troy with a corpse, a poetic rendering of what Michael Lynn-George has called a "homeless journey."

> While this homeless suppliant achieves his goal, the *Iliad* accentuates the final homelessness of this journey. Unlike in the *Odyssey*, this will be the homecoming of the dead—for the dead a homeless return, the reception one of lamentation and enduring farewell.[15]

With the phrase "Unlike in the *Odyssey*," Lynn-George joins the chorus of those who see only life in the *Odyssey*, who focus on the (supposedly) successful *nostos* of Odysseus and ignore the massive weight of death that haunts the proem and darkly reappears in the second Nekuia.[16] While there is something utopian about Odysseus as a survivor, his survival is dependent (in complex, still be explored ways) on the failure of others to survive. The "homeless journey" Lynn-George describes is the rule, not the exception, for this poem; the "naturalness" of the universality of deaths swallowed in myths of disaster is replayed in a "historical" narrative whose consequences are universal enough to have halted most critical efforts at explaining them.

The unnamed subject of the proem struggles for his *psyche* and for the *nostos* of his companions.

> ... ἀρνύμενος ἥν τε ψυχὴν καὶ νόστον ἑταίρων.
> ἀλλ' οὐδ' ὣς ἑτάρους ἐρρύσατο, ἱέμενός περ.
>
> (*Od.* 1.5–6)
>
> [... struggling for his *psyche* and the *nostos* of his companions.
> Even so he could not save his companions, hard though he strove
> to ...]

The problem of this phrase is greater than any irony implied by a contrast between the *nostos* won by Odysseus and a *nostos* so conspicuously missing for his comrades. It is, rather, the question of the unspoken reverse of this *nostos:* the return to light and safety is premised on the wider backdrop of death, of a journey to Hades. In the Doloneia, Odysseus' abilities as a trickster crossed the boundary between life and death, but in such a way as to emphasize its inevitability. The second Nekuia portrays the different journey of the suitors, who are now *psychai* on a "homeless journey." Even the apparent innocence of the emphasis on Odysseus' "companionship" of his men has a somber connotation, returning us to the identifying description of the god who "loves" to accompany men.

> Ἑρμεία, σοὶ γάρ τε μάλιστά γε φίλτατόν ἐστιν
> ἀνδρὶ <u>ἑταιρίσσαι</u>...
>
> *(Il.* 24.334–35)
>
> [Hermes, for to you beyond all other gods it is dearest
> to be man's companion . . .]

Is Odysseus a dear companion to his men? The ultimate effect of the companionship between Odysseus and his men will be their descent on a final journey to Hades, the obverse of the return to light. The fight to win his own *psyche*, conventionally attributed to Odysseus' fight for life, is a fight for life against the background of death, of the multitude of souls that belong to Hermes/Hades. Hades, the god of death, wins every soul in an endless, indeterminate succession. Hermes guides them to this final destination.

Achilles and the Cyclops

In what follows, I will look in detail at the interactions between Odysseus and his companions as described in selected passages from the *Apologoi*. I want to begin by returning to Odysseus' encounter with the Cyclops, but with a different aim in mind. I earlier described the event from the perspective of the asocial Cyclops; Odysseus' blinding of him introduced him to the social and to the paradoxes of paternal power. Now I shift perspective and try to find out what the tricking of the Cyclops can tell us about Odysseus and his companions. I will concentrate on two aspects of book 9. First, I will consider the words of the psychotic Cyclops before he has been blinded. Because the Cyclops has no concern for the law, his language collapses the distinction between the public and superegoic aspects of the law that structure the workings of ideology in the poem. His rhetoric, in effect, challenges the workings of the law as a whole; because of this, the language of the Cyclops has much in common with the language of Achilles in *Iliad* 9—a parallel I will explore. Because the Cyclops collapses the distinction between the public, civilizing aspects of the law and the superegoic fantasy that structures it, his words call into question the motivations of Odysseus as leader of his companions. A close look at a second aspect of book 9, the trick engineered by Odysseus that allows the companions to escape from the Cyclops' cave, can help us explore this; rather than a simple case of a heroic act of rescue, the trick exemplifies the symbolic control Odysseus has over the companions. The immediate consequence of Odysseus' ability to maintain the allegiance of his companions throughout the *Apologoi* is their destruction.

In the asocial behavior of the Cyclops, it is easy to detect much of the kernel of the plot of the *Iliad*. The profoundly asocial character of the Cyclopes recalls Achilles' rejection of the society of his Greek companions at the start of the *Iliad* and his prayer for their destruction. When Ajax, part of the embassy in book 9, accuses Achilles of savagery, he uses words that come close to repeating the language of Odysseus against the Cyclops.

> αὐτὰρ Ἀχιλλεὺς
> ἄγριον[17] ἐν στήθεσσι θέτο μεγαλήτορα θυμόν.
> σχέτλιος, οὐδὲ μετατρέπεται φιλότητος ἑταίρων
> τῆς ᾗ μιν παρὰ νηυσὶν ἐτίομεν ἔξοχον ἄλλων
> νηλής·
>
> (*Il.* 9.628–32)

[[S]eeing that Achilleus has made savage the proud-hearted spirit
    within his body.
He is hard, and does not remember that friends' affection
wherein we honoured him by the ships, far beyond others.
Pitiless.]

The cannibalism of the Cyclops is reflected in the fantasy of cannibalism revealed by Achilles over the corpse of Hector.[18] The Cyclops' rejection of the realm of the gods with regard to his own "betterness" (*Od.* 9.275–76) recalls Achilles' rejection of authority and self-affirmation in the opening book of the *Iliad* and the fight with Agamemnon over who is "better" (φέρτερος). But most striking of all is the manner in which Odysseus' taunt to Polyphemus after the loss of his eye (a taunt affirming that his lost eye cannot be recovered and thus heralding his entrance to the social) recalls a warning made by Odysseus to Achilles in the ninth book of the *Iliad*.

> ἀλλ᾽ ἄνα εἰ μέμονάς γε καὶ ὀψέ περ υἷας Ἀχαιῶν
> τειρομένους ἐρύεσθαι ὑπὸ Τρώων ὀρυμαγδοῦ.
> αὐτῷ τοι μετόπισθ᾽ ἄχος ἔσσεται, οὐδέ τι μῆχος
> ῥεχθέντος κακοῦ ἔστ᾽ ἄκος εὑρεῖν· ἀλλὰ πολὺ πρὶν
> φράζευ ὅπως Δαναοῖσιν ἀλεξήσεις κακὸν ἦμαρ.
>
> (*Il.* 9.247–51)

[Up, then! if you are minded, late though it be, to rescue
the afflicted sons of the Achaeans from the Trojan onslaught.
It will be an affliction to you hereafter, there will be no remedy
found to heal the evil thing when it has been done. No, beforehand
take thought to beat the evil day aside from the Danaans.]

Odysseus' words are typically prescient. Achilles' fevered attempts to gain sufficient recompense for loss will lead only to further loss—the incurable loss of Patroclus. The indeterminacy of the language of Achilles in *Iliad* 9, his desire for something more than anything Agamemnon can provide, is—as Lynn-George has described—a confrontation with the lack that is the correlative of language: Achilles knows not what he wants but merely that he wants. From a humdrum heroic existence on the playing field of *kleos*, Achilles confronts the problems of his desire. But, as with the Cyclops, he is far from learning the Odyssean lesson, which is emphasized in a significant pun: there is no cure, ἄκος, for grief, ἄχος.[19]

Cedric Whitman has elegantly summed up the substance of Achilles' impossible desire: "Personal integrity in Achilles achieves the form and authority of immanent divinity, with its inviolable, lonely singleness, half repellent because of its almost inhuman austerity, but irresistible in its passion and perfected selfhood. Yet the scale is not weighted in favor of this gleaming vision."[20] "Integrity," "perfected selfhood" mixed with "almost inhuman austerity"—this is a dream for a self without loss, an impossible longing for a world where entrance to the social does not involve loss. In short, Achilles seeks to be a Cyclops—a perfect, whole being. His is a paradoxical desire to be a being without desire, an asocial, monadic one. His desire for a perfect autonomy coincides with the loss of the possibility of freedom, the loss of desire—which is based on lack.

There are deeper similarities between Achilles and the Cyclops. Achilles' speech in *Iliad* 9 was suffused with a rhetoric of radical leveling. With the credibility of the public law (in the person of the king, Agamemnon) suspended, the speech demolished the social codes that differentiated people into categories of noble and evil, *esthlos* and *kakos*. We should pay particular attention to the position of enunciation of the speech. Achilles' reflection on his mortality leads him to speak, for a moment, from an imaginary position outside the heroic world. So, too, the first words of the Cyclops to Odysseus are made by a figure who is outside human society.

ὦ ξεῖνοι, τίνες ἐστέ; πόθεν πλεῖθ' ὑγρὰ κέλευθα;
ἤ τι κατὰ πρῆξιν ἢ μαψιδίως ἀλάλησθε

οἷά τε ληϊστῆρες ὑπεὶρ ἅλα, τοὶ τ᾽ ἀλόωνται
ψυχὰς παρθέμενοι, κακὸν ἀλλοδαποῖσι φέροντες;

(*Od.* 9.252–55)

[Strangers, who are you? From where do you come sailing over the watery
ways? Is it on some business, or are you recklessly roving
as pirates do, when they sail on the salt sea and venture
their lives as they wander, bringing evil to alien people?]

The Cyclops addresses the men as *xeinoi*. He will soon declare that he cares nothing for Zeus or his laws, so what can such a word mean from the lips of a Cyclops? It can only be a mocking rejection of the entire system of *xenia*. He continues by drawing a distinction between wandering pirates and those who travel with a purpose; but again, an important distinction within human society is meaningless to a Cyclops, who rejects such distinctions. The commonsense aspect of the good/bad distinction between piracy and civilized law, between what is *esthlos* and *kakos*, is leveled in the eye of a figure of pure lawlessness. The words of the Cyclops are earlier used by Nestor as he greets Telemachus (*Od.* 3.71–74). But if this seems to be a conventional use of the formula by a law-abiding hero, Nestor's later account of his return home once more complicates the distinction between piracy and civilization.

ὦ φίλ᾽, ἐπεί μ᾽ ἔμνησας ὀϊζύος, ἣν ἐν ἐκείνῳ
δήμῳ ἀνέτλημεν μένος ἄσχετοι υἷες Ἀχαιῶν,
ἠμὲν ὅσα ξὺν νηυσὶν ἐπ᾽ ἠεροειδέα πόντον
πλαζόμενοι κατὰ ληΐδ᾽, ὅπῃ ἄρξειεν Ἀχιλλεύς,
ἠδ᾽ ὅσα καὶ περὶ ἄστυ μέγα Πριάμοιο ἄνακτος
μαρνάμεθ᾽· ἔνθα δ᾽ ἔπειτα κατέκταθεν ὅσσοι ἄριστοι·

(*Od.* 3.103–8)

[Dear friend, since you remind me of sorrows which in that country
we endured, we sons of the Achaians valiant forever,
or all we endured in our ships on the misty face of the water
cruising after plunder wherever Achilleus led us,
or all we endured about the great city of the Lord Priam
fighting; and all who were our best were killed in that place.]

The journey described by Nestor is not performed with a purpose; it is a wandering without any ultimate direction, a series of random piratical expeditions. It also mirrors the actions of Odysseus in approaching the island of the Cyclopes: for within the narrative of return, this is an unmotivated encounter.[21] We can now ponder the significance of the mocking words of the

Cyclops. They not only blur the distinction between law and transgression of the law; they point toward the violence inherent in the public law, toward the manner in which the law itself is a form of piracy.[22] Let us continue the parallel between the Cyclops and Achilles as figures of *bie* (strength). The words of the Cyclops reverse the commonsense opposition between crude violence and pacifying law. The ultimate violence is not in "force" but in the symbolic system that is the backdrop for every act of force, not in the transgression of law implied by "piracy" but in the actions performed in the name of the law. It is not enough to point out that the psychotic Cyclops "mocks" social codes. The codes are suspended and then laid bare in the randomness of the violence they cause. We can thus read the Cyclops' words to Odysseus as an insightful commentary on the incoherence of the ideology Odysseus seems to represent: Odysseus seems to be both civilizer and marauder, a figure who subverts the law as he carries it out.[23]

The language of the Cyclops points toward a hidden truth structuring the travels of Odysseus. From a land of darkness, an immortal night, he sees. But the actions of the episode itself also epitomize the entire *Apologoi*. Odysseus' leadership of his troops comes under the closest scrutiny. They show a deep distrust of him but are unable to break with his authority. The selected men who accompany him to the cave of the Cyclops die one by one, just as the wider narrative of the journey home will portray the death, one by one, of the crew. With this in mind, let us look in closer detail at some more significant words of the Cyclops. In response to the revelation of the name *Outis*, the Cyclops promises Odysseus a reward.

Οὖτιν ἐγὼ πύματον ἔδομαι μετὰ οἷσ' ἑτάροισι
τοὺς δ' ἄλλους πρόσθεν· τὸ δέ τοι ξεινήϊον ἔσται.

(*Od.* 9.369–70)

[Then I will eat Nobody after his friends, and the others
I will eat first, and that shall be my guest present to you.]

In return for the gift of the name, the Cyclops offers his gift—the leader will be eaten last. But underneath the humor lies a grimmer reality. For Odysseus will indeed be the last and only survivor of the voyage after his companions have all perished. The words recall the proem, where the lost *nostos* of the *hetairoi* contrasted with the uneasy ability of Odysseus to escape death. His is a death rite deferred; the final welcome at the gates of Hades is postponed for him but not for his companions. The somber connection between Odysseus and the gods associated with death, Hades and Hermes, provides a strange connection between Odysseus and the Cyclops' word. For, as a figure representing the limit between life and death, he is indeed the last figure left over after the deaths, one by one, of the many. If the Cyclops functions as a figure of death, symbolically consuming humans one at a time, there is also a certain affinity to Odysseus. The joke of the Cyclops is prophetic.

There is another sense in which this prophetic remark is substantiated. For after the Cyclops speaks these words, he will not consume any other of the companions. The next thing the Cyclops will be forced to "consume," to take inside of him, is the sharp stake that is driven into his eye.[24] The effect of this blinding, as argued, is to drag the psychotic, godlike Cyclopes into the mortal realm of the social. The "eating of Outis" signifies precisely this; after the blinding, the Cyclops is no longer a "one" but a being in language (*Poly-phemus*) who has incurred an irrecoverable loss, a "nothing" driven into the oneness of his being that renders him mortal. In the exchange between Odysseus and Polyphemus, Odysseus brings mortality to the Cyclops by appropriating the destructive role of the Cyclops as a bringer of death.

The Cyclops' "gift" to Odysseus splits him from his companions: they will die first; he will die last. It is a split that recurs throughout *Odyssey* 9 and, indeed, the entire *Apologoi*.[25] It occurs later in the peculiar, dual nature of Polyphemus' curse after he believes he has discovered Odysseus' identity. He first prays that Odysseus will not reach home, but then he amends the curse: if this is not fated, at least Odysseus should lose his companions and find troubles at home (9.529–35). Of course, only the amendation to the curse will be completed. But the significance of the split between the many troops and their leader is attached to the wider issue of ideological control the episode raises. Odysseus begins his first speech to the Cyclops by identifying himself as just one of the host of Achaeans.

ἡμεῖς τοι Τροίηθεν ἀποπλαγχθέντες Ἀχαιοὶ
παντοίοις ἀνέμοισιν ὑπὲρ μέγα λαῖτμα θαλάσσης,
οἴκαδε ἱέμενοι, ἄλλην ὁδὸν ἄλλα κέλευθα
ἤλθομεν· οὕτω που Ζεὺς ἤθελε μητίσασθαι.
λαοὶ δ' Ἀτρεΐδεω Ἀγαμέμνονος εὐχόμεθ' εἶναι,
τοῦ δὴ νῦν γε μέγιστον ὑπουράνιον κλέος ἐστί·

(*Od.* 9.259–64)

[We are Achaeans coming from Troy, beaten off our true course
by winds from every direction across the great gulf of the open
sea, making for home, by the wrong way, on the wrong courses.
So we have come. So it has pleased Zeus to arrange it.
We claim we are of the following of the son of Atreus,
Agamemnon, whose fame now is the greatest thing under heaven.]

It has been noted that this refusal to name himself as leader is a necessary part of the deception of the Cyclops, of the Outis trick.[26] But it is also another instance of Odysseus' "modesty." In the Doloneia, he refused to take any credit for his action. But more relevant for the supposed deference to Agamemnon shown here are his actions in *Iliad* 2, where he supplanted the symbolic authority of Agamemnon as he subverted it. Here, the attribution of glory to Agamemnon for the sacking of Troy is opposed by his own status as "city-sacker," in particular through the stratagem of the wooden horse. But it is the ideological effect of this melding into the people that is crucial. The ability of a leader to control his many followers depends on his ability to let the masses identify with the ego ideal he represents; he must not be viewed as an outsider with his own interests, using power for his own personal ends. Rather, the ability to control the many occurs when there is a short circuit between the qualities displayed by the leader and the qualities the troops believe to be their own. Should this happen, the leader then becomes "one of them (or us)." The weakness of Agamemnon in *Iliad* 2 comes from the general feeling that he acts not on behalf of the community but for his own narrower wants (the abduction of the wife of Menelaus, a family matter). Because of this perception, he is no longer primus inter pares—an *aristos* leading a community of *aristoi*—but a selfish outsider. Odysseus' intervention returns the troops to an identification with broader symbolic goals. The disappearances (and appearances) of Odysseus as leader in book 9 are important for the workings of power. If he were to appear as leader at all (rather than as a person embodying the interests of those he leads), it would evidence a weakening of his authority.

The clearest instance of the symbolic control exercised by Odysseus over his men comes at a time when they are dependent on him; during their escape from the cave, when they are attached to the sheep of the Cyclops. The episode has much in common with the tricking of Proteus, and we can use the earlier trick to help us understand this one. As I argued earlier, the trick used against Proteus opened the question of the relationship of the one to the many. Before Proteus' deception, his seals had been constituted as a group by his counting. But as Proteus doubts for the first time, the naturalness of that relationship is questioned (as a gap is opened between signifier and signified). The seals will no longer simply be a group centered around a leader but will (or will not) be made a group by the performative action of the counter. The seals become a group of seals because Proteus counts them as a group. He imposes an end and a beginning to the numerical sequence. In *Odyssey* 9, Odysseus' trick reveals the manner in which his *metis* controls the constitution of Odysseus' crew as Odysseus' crew.

As with the Proteus trick, the crucial aspect of the trick used against the

Cyclops lies not at the level of sign and referent but at the level of signifier and signified. The conventional reading of Polyphemus' deception rests on the assumption that he is fooled by the disguise of Odysseus and his men, hidden beneath the rams (just as the conventional reading of the Proteus deception seems to depend on the disguise of sealskins). Yet this does nothing to explain the different disguises used by Odysseus (attached to one ram) and his men (each tied between three). The description of the split between a ram that is "by far the best" [ὄχ' ἄριστος] (9.432) and an array of other rams that are excellent but of a clearly inferior order duplicates the difference between a man who is "by far the best"—thus a leader of men—and a community of *aristoi*. Polyphemus misses the general disguise of the rams, but his failure to make a distinction between the group and their leader is ultimately far more important.

> τὸ δὲ νήπιος οὐκ ἐνόησεν,
> ὥς οἱ ὑπ' εἰροπόκων ὀίων στέρνοισι δέδεντο.
> ὕστατος ἀρνειὸς μήλων ἔστειχε θύραζε,
> λάχνῳ στεινόμενος καὶ ἐμοὶ πυκινὰ φρονέοντι.
> τὸν δ' ἐπιμασσάμενος προσέφη κρατερὸς Πολύφημος·
> "κριὲ πέπον, τί μοι ὧδε διὰ σπέος ἔσσυο μήλων
> ὕστατος; οὔ τι πάρος γε λελειμμένος ἔρχεαι οἰῶν,
> ἀλλὰ πολὺ πρῶτος νέμεαι τέρεν' ἄνθεα ποίης
> μακρὰ βιβάς, πρῶτος δὲ ῥοὰς ποταμῶν ἀφικάνεις,
> πρῶτος δὲ σταθμόνδε λιλαίεαι ἀπονέεσθαι
> ἑσπέριος, νῦν αὖτε πανύστατος. ἦ σύ γ' ἄνακτος
> ὀφθαλμὸν ποθέεις; τὸν ἀνὴρ κακὸς ἐξαλάωσε
> σὺν λυγροῖς ἑτάροισι, δαμασσάμενος φρένας οἴνῳ,
> Οὖτις, ὃν οὔ πώ φημι πεφυγμένον ἔμμεν ὄλεθρον.
> εἰ δὴ ὁμοφρονέοις ποτιφωνήεις τε γένοιο
> εἰπεῖν, ὅππη κεῖνος ἐμὸν μένος ἠλασκάζει·
> τῷ κέ οἱ ἐγκέφαλός γε διὰ σπέος ἄλλυδις ἄλλῃ
> θεινομένου ῥαίοιτο πρὸς οὔδεϊ, κὰδ δέ τ' ἐμὸν κῆρ
> λωφήσειε κακῶν, τά μοι οὐτιδανὸς πόρεν Οὖτις."
> ὣς εἰπὼν τὸν κριὸν ἀπὸ ἕο πέμπε θύραζε.
> ἐλθόντες δ' ἠβαιὸν ἀπὸ σπείους τε καὶ αὐλῆς
> πρῶτος ὑπ' ἀρνειοῦ λυόμην, ὑπέλυσα δ' ἑταίρους.
> καρπαλίμως δὲ τὰ μῆλα ταναύποδα, πίονα δημῷ,
> πολλὰ περιτροπέοντες ἐλαύνομεν, ὄφρ' ἐπὶ νῆα
> ἱκόμεθ'· ἀσπάσιοι δὲ φίλοις ἑτάροισι φάνημεν,
> οἳ φύγομεν θάνατον· τοὺς δὲ στενάχοντο γοῶντες.

(*Od.* 9.442–67)

[... in his guilelessness [he] did not notice
how my men were fastened under the breasts of his fleecy
sheep. Last of all the flock the ram went out of the doorway,
loaded with his own fleece, and with me, and my close counsels.
Then, feeling him, powerful Polyphemus spoke a word to him:
"My dear old ram, why are you thus leaving the cave last of
the sheep? Never in the old days were you left behind by
the flock, but long-striding, far ahead of the rest would pasture
on the tender bloom of the grass, be first at running rivers,
and be eager always to lead the way first back to the sheepfold
at evening. Now you are last of all. Perhaps you are grieving
for your master's eye, which a bad man with his wicked companions
put out, after he had made my brain helpless with wine, this
Nobody, who I think has not yet got clear of destruction.
If only you could think like us and only be given
a voice, to tell me where he is skulking away from my anger,
then surely he would be smashed against the floor and his brains go
splattering all over the cave to make my heart lighter
from the burden of all the evils this niddering Nobody gave me."
  So he spoke, and sent the ram along from him, outdoors,
and when we had got a little way from the yard and the cavern,
first I got myself loose from my ram, then set my companions
free, and rapidly then, and rounding them up, we
drove the long-striding sheep, rich with fat, until we reached
our ship, and the sight of us who had escaped death was welcome
to our companions, but they began to mourn for the others.]
(translation modified)

The tricking of Polyphemus recalls a number of motifs already commented on. He notices that the rams leave the cave in an unusual order. In particular, his favorite ram sticks out. Normally he is the first to leave and first to return home, but now he is the last of all to leave. The escape from the cave is traditionally viewed as an escape from death for Odysseus' crew, but the manner of the escape has somber overtones; for Odysseus is the last to emerge from the cave, just as he alone will survive the journey to Ithaca. The manner in which the crew are sent out "first" also reflects much of the structure of the *Apologoi;* in a series of other adventures, Odysseus sends out a series of men to find out about the situation, treating them as virtual guinea pigs. As the men discover an assortment of evils, Odysseus then intervenes to save a part of them (it is the reluctance to be treated as an animal that motivates the resistance of Eurylochus).

The form of the trick also illustrates the complete dependence of the crew on the leader. Odysseus, attached to the ram who is "by far the best," is the last to leave the cave; but after the escape, he is the first to untie himself and is then responsible for untying his companions. The crew, a group attached to sheep, are encircled by the actions of Odysseus. They are caught up between Odysseus as "first" and Odysseus as "last." For this reason, this "counting" of the men as sheep is a significant step beyond the counting of Proteus. Proteus was introduced to the concept of limits, of wrapping up a sequence by introducing a beginning and end to the chain of numbers. But the narrative left the relationship between Proteus and his seals open. Here, the "sheep" of Polyphemus (Odysseus' men) are encircled by Odysseus' form of counting.

It is worth lingering over this contrast. We can start by emphasizing the numerous parallels in this scene to the deception of Proteus. We should note not only the persistent vocabulary of firstness (underlined in the passage just quoted) but also the parallel between Proteus' loss of a seal and Polyphemus' loss of a ram. In both cases, the unquestioned ability of a shepherd to protect the animals under his care is punctured by a loss. Through a manipulation of his counting system, Eidothea causes Proteus to lose a seal; Odysseus escapes under Polyphemus' ram and will eventually sacrifice him. However, Polyphemus himself is partly responsible for the loss of the ram, as he sends him away out of the cave (τὸν κριὸν ἀπὸ ἕο πέμπε θύραζ). It is tempting to see the story of the Cyclops and his ram as retroactively suggesting another meaning in the verb used for the counting system of Proteus, πεμπάσσεται (*Od.* 4.412). If we see the root of the verb πέμπω in πεμπάσσομαι, then the middle aspect of the verb may become significant. John Peradotto has already discussed the peculiar status of the middle use of the verb, suggesting the importance for concepts of agency of a middle voice, uneasily situated between active and passive meanings.[27] In Proteus' case, the middle verb may suggest a counting system that remains so bound up with the counter that neither the usual active nor the passive aspects of agency apply. Because Proteus is not self-conscious before Eidothea's trick, he is neither an active agent (he never considers himself an agent) nor a passive victim (which would require some sort of fallibility). When Polyphemus actively sends away a ram (a ram that will never return), he does something Proteus never does, because the latter's peculiar form of counting, based on the middle form of πέμπω, means that he will never let go of a seal. This all changes with Eidothea's trick.[28]

Let us now consider the major difference between the episodes of Proteus and the Cyclops. In the escape from the cave, men are added to the sheep. The question of control of a flock becomes merged with the control of people, as people are physically attached to that flock. Once more, the second narrative episode (Polyphemus and the sheep) is not simply "different" from the first narrative (Proteus and his seals) but invites a retroactive, allegorical reading of it as always about the relationship of the one to the many, a reading that poses a general ideological problem. In turn, both these episodes invite us to the central narrative question of the poem, the relationship of Odysseus to his men.

This circling of the men by Odysseus also recalls other stories within the *Odyssey*. Through the trickery of Hephaestus in the second song of Demodocus, the spiders' webs wrapped up Ares and Aphrodite in a perfect circle (χέε δέσματα κύκλωι ἁπάντηι). The circle is perfect and yet imperfect, for it remains a circle constructed by Hephaestus, an agent external to the circle as such, which allows us to detect him. Odysseus' trick saves his companions, but at the same time, he demonstrates an ideological control over them. This theme is not only found in the *Odyssey*. For Odysseus' persuasive tactics in *Iliad* 2 repeat the gesture. At the time when the men are on the verge of returning home, he looks back in time to the beginning of the expedition to Troy; he then recalls a prophecy of Calchas that Troy would be taken in the tenth year. His memory and prediction (which take over the role of the prophet) restore the faith of the Greeks in the mission; but they also are an instance of controlling them. Odysseus allows the troops to identify with a certain story told about the Trojan War—a story of a beginning and end, a story that he himself constructs. When the troops identify with this story, they then play their (scripted) parts as loyal soldiers in it.

The irony of the disguise of the men as sheep is that it is utterly appropriate to the behavior of the men. Odysseus' men behave like sheep, following their leader through thick and thin. They look like sheep, act like sheep, and so on. The disguise of livestock, as the companions are hidden under the Cyclops' sheep by Odysseus, depends on a distinction between humans and livestock: otherwise it would not be a disguise. But this hides the ways in which the companions are being treated as livestock by Odysseus. It is a kind of Odyssean joke. How best can you fool an ideological dupe, a sheep, into thinking he is not a sheep? By disguising him as one!

The parallel between the sheep and men is neatly indicated by the description of the rounding up of the sheep after the men are released: πολλὰ περιτροπέοντες. We can follow Stanford in taking the verb as transitive, meaning "round up" the many sheep.[29] But in this rounding up we should note a pun on the most famous epithet of Odysseus, *polytropos*. The sheep are encircled by the "many turns" of the men, just as the men themselves were earlier encircled by the man of many turns, Odysseus. This is the context for the later remarks of the crew, when they rebuke Odysseus for endangering their lives (*Od.*

9.498 ff.). His taunting of Polyphemus does indeed put all of their lives at risk, but only insofar as they collectively pledge allegiance to him.

To return to Hephaestus, his trickery was successful, but it was not the trick of an invincible trickster. It was in response to an act of adultery he was helpless to prevent. As soon as the circle of the web is complete, Hermes suggests a desire to transgress it, to break its bonds. A trickster ultimately relies on his ability to disguise himself as the agent of the trick. This allows us to explain the conclusion of the trick of the sheep—the consumption of the ram.

> [W]e ourselves stepped out onto the break of the sea beach,
> and from the hollow ships bringing out the flocks of the Cyclops
> we shared them out so none might go cheated of his proper
> portion; but for me alone my strong-greaved companions
> excepted the ram when the sheep were shared, and I sacrificed him
> on the sands to Zeus . . .
>
> (*Od.* 9.547–52)

Burkert has confessed a certain unease at Odysseus' sacrifice of the "good ram to whom he owes his life."[30] He overcomes his queasiness by reminding himself that the entire purpose of the "quest" was to find food. However, the theme of the relationship between the leader and his troops adds a further significance to the consumption of the ram. The companions are happy to give the ram, "by far the best" of the flock, to Odysseus. It is thus a recognition of his status as "by far the best." But this sign of his superiority is immediately consumed. At the end of the trick, the leader disappears with the flock into nothingness, and Odysseus merges back into the midst of his men, the position in which he had located himself at the beginning of the episode by denying any special role for himself in the sacking of Troy. The death of the sheep is also grimly foreboding. Odysseus' men will also die, soon enough.

One further aspect of the tricking of Polyphemus is worthy of note. Polyphemus fails to notice the significance of the "best" ram being out of place, last instead of first. Through the blinding, he is fooled because he expects someone big and strong and only encounters "No one"; the situation is now reversed. He does notice the single big ram that sticks out from the rest, but his awareness of this fact is of no help to him because he fails to note its significance. The reason for this failure is of special interest. Polyphemus is fooled because of a certain emotional vulnerability: he believes the ram to have come out last out of a sense of solidarity with his blinded master. The moment Polyphemus presumes an emotional bond between himself and his beloved ram coincides with the moment he is fooled. The initial wound signaled his dependence on others; he now discovers that dependence opens up the possibility for self-deception.

This is a particularly human form of self-deception. We can certainly accuse him of anthropomorphism, of the pathetic fallacy. For he appears to make the cardinal error of treating a nonhuman creature as if it was a human. We could explain this as a kind of children's category mistake. Recently introduced to language and the suffering that goes with it, Polyphemus presumes that sentient beings are victim to the emotional needs of speaking beings.[31] He reads his own needs into the behavior of the ram. Once more, there is a more important truth lurking here. Anthropomorphism can never offer a sure means of avoiding deception, because the possibility that the ram really is mirroring his own affection back to him is a real one. This is a direct effect of the domestication of animals. In short, if Polyphemus makes an error, it is based on the failed identification of the desire of another. Precisely this possibility of misidentification makes him human.

The Cattle of the Sun

It is a common critical story that the companions of Odysseus deserve to die: they choose to eat the cattle of the Sun, for which they are morally culpable.[32] This view coincides with the apparent judgment of the proem: αὐτῶν γὰρ σφετέρῃσιν ἀτασθαλίῃσιν ὄλοντο (*Od.* 1.7) [They were destroyed by their own wild recklessness]. But the ability of Odysseus to control his men makes the matter more complex. For what can it mean to speak of the moral errors of a group of men who are always identified with their leader? It is highly significant that when Eurylochus produces the only open challenge to Odysseus' leadership, he does so in words that echo the proem. He claims that the victims of the Cyclops died because of Odysseus.

> τούτου γὰρ καὶ κεῖνοι ἀτασθαλίῃσιν ὄλοντο.
>
> (*Od.* 10.437)

[[F]or it was by this man's recklessness that these too perished.]

Eurylochus' position is quite clear. He does not hold Odysseus and the companions mutually responsible for the disasters that befall them. He presumes that the men themselves, insofar as they follow the leader's orders, are at the mercy of the leader's judgments. This might seem irrelevant for the responsibility of the crew in eating the cattle of the Sun. In this specific case, Odysseus' men disobey his command: he tells them not to eat the cattle, and they eat the cattle behind his back as he sleeps. This returns us to the surface reading of the proem; Odysseus could not save his men, sorely though he tried. But we have already seen that Odysseus' rhetoric of modesty about his failures is not above suspicion; it might point toward the subtler ruses of Odyssean power. For if it is true that the companions are subject to Odysseus' control, might not the most convincing display of that power involve having them perform tasks of his choosing at the time they believe they are acting autonomously? I want to suggest that the narrative signposts this possibility. For the story of the cattle of the Sun has much in common with the other *aethloi* of Odysseus.

The narrative pointer comes at the beginning of the episode. When Odysseus tells his men of the warning of Circe to avoid the island of Helios, he is countered by Eurylochus, who, tired by wandering, asks for the opportunity to have supper on the island. Here is Odysseus' reply.

> ὣς ἔφατ' Εὐρύλοχος, ἐπὶ δ' ᾔνεον ἄλλοι ἑταῖροι.
> καὶ τότε δὴ γίνωσκον ὃ δὴ κακὰ μήδετο δαίμων,
> καί μιν φωνήσας ἔπεα πτερόεντα προσηύδων·
> "Εὐρύλοχ', ἦ μάλα δή με βιάζετε μοῦνον ἐόντα.
> ἀλλ' ἄγε νῦν μοι πάντες ὀμόσσατε καρτερὸν ὅρκον·
> εἴ κέ τιν' ἠὲ βοῶν ἀγέλην ἢ πῶϋ μέγ' οἰῶν
> εὕρωμεν, μή πού τις ἀτασθαλίῃσι κακῇσιν
> ἢ βοῦν ἠέ τι μῆλον ἀποκτάνῃ· ἀλλὰ ἕκηλοι
> ἐσθίετε βρώμην, τὴν ἀθανάτη πόρε Κίρκη."

(*Od.* 12.294–302)

> [So spoke Eurylochus, and my other companions assented.
> I saw then what evil the divinity had in mind for us,
> and so I spoke aloud to him and addressed him in winged words:
> "Eurylochus, I am only one man. You force me to it.
> But come then all of you, swear a strong oath to me, that if
> we come upon some herd of cattle or on some great flock
> of sheep, no one of you in evil and reckless action
> will slaughter any ox or sheep. No, rather than this, eat
> at your pleasure of the food immortal Circe provided."]

Odysseus gives in to the argument of Eurylochus, even as he is careful to point out that he knew this would guarantee an evil outcome (καὶ τότε δὴ γίνωσκον). Most figures of Greek myth could utter this speech and be persuasive, but there is something perplexing about Odysseus uttering it. The hero of trickery, who has spent most of his time on Phaeacia exhibiting the ability of his *metis* to overcome any *bie*, now claims to be subject to the "force" of Eurylochus. This force, which must refer to the ability of the many companions to overcome him, has its own roots in the persuasive powers of Eurylochus: it is *bie* once more dependent on a previous act of *metis*. It is not a simple act of force at all. The alleged force exerted on Odysseus also echoes the poem's most famous lines exemplifying his *metis*. I here juxtapose the relevant lines.

> ἦ μάλα δή με βιάζετε μοῦνον ἐόντα.
>
> (*Od.* 12.297)

[Eurylochus, I am only one man. You force me to it.]

> εἰ μὲν δὴ μή τίς σε βιάζεται οἶον ἐόντα,
> νοῦσόν γ' οὔ πως ἔστι Διὸς μεγάλου ἀλέασθαι·
>
> (*Od.* 9.410–11)

[If alone as you are no one uses violence on you, why, there is no avoiding the sickness sent by great Zeus;]

The Cyclops believed himself to be blinded by someone called "No one." In the encounter with the cattle of the Sun, this named figure of anonymity is replaced by an anonymous *daimon* who is plotting evil behind the scenes (κακὰ μήδετο δαίμων).[33] Odysseus, the master of *metis*, hints at the workings of a hidden *metis* even as he professes helplessness and claims he is the victim of force. With this in mind, Odysseus' own reference to the *atasthalia* that will lead to the companions' destruction becomes less straightforward. It is as if he refuses to exercise his *metis* at the time it is most necessary for a caring leader to do so, and thus he gives them every opportunity to show their infamous *atasthalia*. The refusal to show *metis* begins to look like another ruse of *metis*. How can this interpretation be of help in understanding the episode?

Rather than viewing the episode as one of pure impiety, explaining the loss of the crew, we could view the episode as another one of the tricks performed by the ultimate trickster, which reworks many of the themes of *metis* already considered. Douglas Frame has explored the connections between the stealing of the cattle of the Sun and the theft of the flocks of the Cyclops; he argues that the adventures of the *Apologoi* share features of solar mythology and that both are linked to the hero's evasion of death. The cave and flock of the Cyclops are common features of solar mythology, as the Sun also owns cattle and sheep located within a cave. The most likely etymology of the name of the Cyclops points to his status as a sun god: "The Cyclops, as 'circle-eyed,' would originally have symbolized the sun itself."[34] Let us lay out the parallels: in both episodes, there are herds of animals who are privileged possession of divine figures characterized by their powers of sight; in both episodes, the herds are stolen and then consumed. The consequence in both cases is a demand for a similar recompense by the aggrieved parties—the death of the crew of Odysseus.

The comparison runs deeper. In both cases, there is a deception of a supposedly omnipotent being. The contempt of the Cyclops for Odysseus is matched by the "all-seeing" nature of the Sun.

> These are the cattle and fat sheep of a dreaded
> God, Helios, who sees all things and listens to all things.
>
> (*Od.* 12.322–33)

What is extraordinary about the episode is that this god who sees and hears all will not witness the actions of the companions of Odysseus. He finds out about it when it is too late, from a message from Lampetia (*Od.* 12.374 ff.).[35] The theme of knowledge arriving "too late" is common in the *Odyssey*. Hephaestus discovered the crime of Ares and Aphrodite too late; the Sun saw the crime, but he could not prevent it. The Cyclops did not remember the prophecy of Telemus until after his circular eye had been punctured. Because the companions are able to consume the cattle, their action in and of itself suggests a symbolic blinding of the Sun; the trick reveals that the Sun, along with the Cyclops, has a blind spot. Far from an all-seeing being, he is a vulnerable one. But what is intriguing is that this temporary blindness of Helios coincides with a temporary blindness of Odysseus. He claims he is lulled to sleep by the gods. When he wakes up, it is "too late."

> καὶ τότε μοι βλεφάρων ἐξέσσυτο νήδυμος ὕπνος·
> βῆν δ' ἰέναι ἐπὶ νῆα θοὴν καὶ θῖνα θαλάσσης.
> ἀλλ' ὅτε δὴ σχεδὸν ἦα κιὼν νεὸς ἀμφιελίσσης,
> καὶ τότε με κνίσης ἀμφήλυθεν ἡδὺς ἀϋτμή·
> οἰμώξας δὲ θεοῖσι μετ' ἀθανάτοισι γεγώνευν·
> "Ζεῦ πάτερ ἠδ' ἄλλοι μάκαρες θεοὶ αἰὲν ἐόντες,
> ἦ με μάλ' εἰς ἄτην κοιμήσατε νηλέϊ ὕπνῳ,
> οἱ δ' ἕταροι <u>μέγα ἔργον ἐμητίσαντο</u> μένοντες."
>
> (*Od.* 12.366–73)

[At that time the quiet sleep was lost from my eyelids,
and I went back down to my fast ship and the sand of the seashore,
but on my way, as I was close to the oar-swept vessel,
the pleasant savor of cooking meat came drifting around me,
and I cried out my grief aloud to the gods immortal:
"Father Zeus, and you other everlasting and blessed
gods, with a pitiless sleep you lulled me, to my confusion,
and my companions staying here *contrived a great deed*."][36]

This coincidence of moments of blindness between Odysseus and the Sun suggests a near identification. The cattle are eaten because neither Odysseus nor the Sun sees. The obvious suggestion is that the episode portrays the limits of Odysseus' *metis*. But can we be so sure? There are once more reasons for doubt. *Metis* returns in the action of the companions, who "contrive a great deed." Odysseus' ability to perform acts of *metis* is transferred for this one and only time to the companions, who both perform the deed and pay for their status as direct agents of this act of *metis*. The companions are also allowed to venture on ahead to meet their doom, a scenario that is repeated throughout the *Apologoi*.[37] But most intriguing is the parallel with the Cyclops, where the *metis* of Odysseus involved his *noos*, his ability to outwit the pseudo-omnipotence of the Cyclops. The result was the consumption of the sheep. In the encounter with Helios, the result is the same: the acute powers of perception of the divine being are unable to prevent the consumption of his livestock. The only difference is that the loss of the cattle occurs because of Odysseus' failure to see. Odysseus' ultimate *metis* perhaps lies in his ability to turn a blind eye to the events he knows his companions will perform; as a result, he escapes the revenge of the aggrieved victim, who focuses his wrath on the immediate agents of the *mega ergon*.

Significant other details can help us clarify the complexity of the situation. In response to the eating of the cattle, Helios threatens to shine in the realm of Hades.

> Unless these are made to give me just recompense for my cattle,
> I will go down to Hades' and give my light to the dead men.
> (*Od.* 12.382–83)

The consumption of the cattle threatens to collapse the boundary between day and night, between the realm of life and light and that of darkness and death. The guarantee of the death of the companions given to Helios preserves this limit. This preservation of a limit recalls the actions of Odysseus in the Doloneia. The successful capture of the blazing horses of Rhesus is an act of *metis* that promises (but only promises) to be the ultimate act of trickery satisfying every desire. But as soon as the horses are captured, they already point toward something better beyond them. The perfection of Odysseus' *metis* functioned to highlight the constitutive aspect of human desire. Any attempt to achieve the impossible goal of capturing the Sun fails, for as soon as the impossible goal is achieved, it is no longer impossible. It points toward a further impossible goal beyond the one achieved. The Doloneia suggested a necessary built-in failure in every human attempt at achieving one's desire; the events of *Odyssey*

12 suggest that this human failing is built into the divine world. To capture the chariot of the Sun is to be identified with an "all-seeing" being. But the Sun's loss of his cattle, together with his agreement not to shine in Hades, suggests that this "all-seeing" god does not see everything. Hades is left untouched by light; it is a region beyond Helios' ken and continues to function as a blind spot. Even the Sun can be fooled, because of the darkness that lies outside of his realm. The power of the Sun to see everything has a limit.

The agreement between Zeus and Helios is symbolically significant. In exchange for the death of mortals, Helios agrees to his own fallibility. Indeed, he has no choice in this matter. For if he shone in Hades, the limit separating the realm of the mortals and immortals would be smashed, and thus the crew of Odysseus could not be punished with death. To satisfy his desire, he must recognize a limit to his powers. The recognition of this blind spot (associated with the darkness of Hades and thus with death) provides the conditions of possibility for *metis* to function. It introduces an irreducible element of doubt into human affairs. The lesson of the eating of the cattle of the Sun is that no one sees everything, not even all-seeing gods. The functioning of *metis* is parasitic on this blind spot. But there is a further implication. *Metis* cannot be reduced to powers of perception. It is instead related to an ability to manipulate powers of perception (to turn or not to turn a blind eye). It is dependent on the uncertainty as to which is which. An act of apparent stupidity can be *metis* at its most cunning, just as the most self-evidently rational act can be the action of a fool.

The similarity between the tricking of the Cyclops and the tricking of Helios stages this uncertainty. If the tricking of the Cyclops is a straightforward case of powers of perception defeating a counterpart, the Helios episode hints that apparent blindness can itself be feigned. Any simple attempt to distinguish the acts of a "good," all-seeing Odysseus who cares for his men from the blunder of a leader who provides them with the rope to hang themselves is complicated by the same outcome that both events guarantee: the death of the companions. We can ask which is more harmful to his men, his perception or the failure of that perception? But if this must remain a question without answer (it is left open to doubt), it is worth pondering a final connection between the two episodes. After the companions consume the cattle, Odysseus tells of the consequences.

αὐτὰρ ἐπεί ῥ' ἐπὶ νῆα κατήλυθον ἠδὲ θάλασσαν,
νείκεον ἄλλοθεν ἄλλον ἐπισταδόν, οὐδέ τι μῆχος
εὑρέμεναι δυνάμεσθα· βόες δ' ἀποτέθνασαν ἤδη.

(*Od.* 12.391–94)

[But when I came back again to the ship and the seashore,
they all stood about and blamed each other, but we were not able
to find any remedy, for the oxen were already dead.]

The impossibility of finding a "cure" (μῆχος) for the deed that has been completed recalls the words of Odysseus to the Cyclops after his blinding. There, the appeal to the father was a recognition of the son's dependence on others. The prayer looked to a separate figure of authority to cure the loss of the eye that had made the Cyclops a social being. Odysseus' reply had reminded the Cyclops that no appeal to a father could help him. In *Odyssey* 12, the impossibility of a finding a cure signals the imminent deaths of the companions. It seems to suggest the failure of Odysseus as a father figure for his men. It is as if the men themselves remained oblivious to the lesson about fathers Odysseus himself had acted out in the blinding of the Cyclops.

There is a connection to another episode. There is a quarrel, a νεῖκος, among the crew. *Odyssey* 8 staged the first νεῖκος on Phaeacia, which in turn heralded the entrance of that civilization to the social as a contested space. The first "quarrel" among the companions of Odysseus divides them into a group of individuals with competing beliefs. No longer followers of orders, they now stage a *neikos* in order to come to terms with their situation. Previously, they had always acted as a collective, obeying the orders of Odysseus. There is one exception. They ate the cattle of the Sun of their own volition. But regardless of the role of Odysseus' *metis* in this event, it is notable that they still acted as a collective persuaded by a leader. The quarrel in response to the consumption of the cattle is the first time the companions of Odysseus have involved themselves in the struggles of the social world; at this point, they can no longer be defined by their allegiance to Odysseus. But the irony is that this occurs too late. This provides a special significance to Odysseus' words confirming the death of the cattle: βόες δ' ἀποτέθνασαν ἤδη. The obvious referent is the cattle of Helios. But the companions are also in an important sense "already dead." They are already dead because, until it was too late, they had always acted like livestock, cattle (or sheep) following their master.

The Magic of Circe, the Magic of Odysseus

Though it is possible to trace the tension between Odysseus and his men throughout the *Apologoi*, I shall finish my discussion by considering the moment of greatest crisis, when the companions are closest to rebellion. When

Odysseus finds out from Eurylochus about the disappearance of the group of men who entered the house of Circe, he decides to try to rescue them. Once he has succeeded, he is ordered by Circe to return to the other companions and bring them to her home. At this point, he encounters the resistance of Eurylochus. Eurylochus tries to persuade the companions not to return with Odysseus to the house of Circe, warning them that they will be turned into wolves or lions (*Od.* 10.431 ff.). There is a well-known inconsistency in the narrative here. Earlier, Odysseus had informed us that Eurylochus had no idea what had happened to the men. Eurylochus followed the companions into the house of Circe, but because he suspected treachery, he decided not to enter. He waited patiently outside for them, but they never reappeared (*Od.* 10.251 ff.). How can Eurylochus know that there is a danger of metamorphosis into animals if he has no idea of the fate of his companions or of the powers of Circe?

Heubeck has suggested that the inconsistency can be explained away by Eurylochus' intuition of what happened to other victims of Circe: when they had earlier approached the house of Circe, a crowd of animals had approached them.[38] Yet once again the apparent narrative inconsistency should make us look for wider significance in the episode. Here is the description of Circe's victims.

> In the forest glen they came on the house of Circe. It was
> in an open place, and put together from stones, well-polished,
> and all about it there were lions, and wolves of the mountains,
> whom the goddess had given evil drugs and enchanted,
> and these made no attack on the men, but came up thronging
> about them, waving their long tails and fawning, in the way
> that dogs go fawning about their master, when he comes home
> from dining out, for he always brings back something to please
>   them . . .
>
> (*Od.* 10.210–17)

The wild animals are compared to dogs fawning. Any individual strength is gone and is replaced by pathetic attempts to please a master. A similar simile occurs later in book 10, when the rest of the companions greet Odysseus as he returns from Circe's house.

> And as, in the country, the calves around the cows returning
> from pasture back to the dung of the farmyard, well filled with
>   grazing,
> come gamboling together to meet them, and the pens no longer
> can hold them in, but lowing incessantly they come running
> around their mothers, so these men, once their eyes saw me,

came streaming around me, in tears, and the spirit in them made them
feel as if they were back in their own country, the very
city of rugged Ithaka, where they were born and raised up.

(*Od.* 10.410–17)

Odysseus' relationship with his companions is likened to the dependence of calves on their mother. But the simile does not stop there; not only is Odysseus likened to the mother of the companions, but he is also identified with their fatherland. The identity of the companions as members of a fatherland, Ithaca, is parallel to their obedience to and dependence on Odysseus as a father figure, the leader of the community on Ithaca.[39] The companions are revealed as being utterly at the whim of Odysseus as their master, and this situation recalls the earlier appearance of Circe's victims, fawning dogs who are controlled by the scraps from the table of the master (*Od.* 10.242 ff.). As it happens, feasting plays a prominent role in Odysseus' interactions with Circe. He had refused to dine with Circe until the companions who were victims of Circe had been changed back into their human form.

> Oh, Circe, how could any man right in his mind ever
> endure to taste of the food and drink that are set before him,
> until with his eyes he saw his companions set free? So then,
> if you are sincerely telling me to eat and drink, set them
> free, so my eyes can again behold my eager companions.

(*Od.* 10.383–87)

One set of the companions is freed in order to be able to take part in the feast. Once they are freed, Circe encourages Odysseus to gather the rest of the companions, who are (excessively) overjoyed to see him and who are compared to dependent farmyard animals. This is the context for the challenge of Eurylochus.

> Εὐρύλοχος δέ μοι οἶος ἐρύκακε πάντας ἑταίρους
> καὶ σφεας φωνήσας ἔπεα πτερόεντα προσηύδα·
> "ἆ δειλοί, πόσ' ἴμεν; τί κακῶν ἱμείρετε τούτων;
> Κίρκης ἐς μέγαρον καταβήμεναι, ἥ κεν ἅπαντας
> ἢ οὖς ἠὲ λύκους ποιήσεται ἠὲ λέοντας,
> οἵ κέν οἱ μέγα δῶμα φυλάσσοιμεν καὶ ἀνάγκῃ,
> ὥς περ Κύκλωψ ἔρξ', ὅτε οἱ μέσσαυλον ἵκοντο
> ἡμέτεροι ἕταροι, σὺν δ' ὁ θρασὺς εἵπετ' Ὀδυσσεύς·
> τούτου γὰρ καὶ κεῖνοι ἀτασθαλίῃσιν ὄλοντο."

(*Od.* 10.429–37)

[Only Eurylochus was trying to hold back all my other
companions, and he spoke to them and addressed them in winged
    words:
"Ah, poor wretches. Where are we going? Why do you long for
the evils of going down into Circe's palace, for she will
transform the lot of us into pigs or wolves or lions,
and so we shall guard her great house for her, under compulsion.
So too it happened with the Cyclops, when our companions
went into his yard, and the bold Odysseus was of their company;
for it was by this man's recklessness that these too perished."]

Eurylochus addresses the companions, not Odysseus. He argues that a descent into the house of Circe will turn them into the fawning animals witnessed earlier. His rhetoric is extremely interesting. He compares the act of the collective descending into this house with the earlier entrance into the cave of the Cyclops. Prevalent in both examples is the rhetoric of encirclement. The companions entered the μέσσαυλος of the Cyclops, the place that is normally associated with the pen in which cattle are enclosed at night for their greater safety.[40] That encirclement led not to safety but to death, and it was performed by the "circle-eyed" Cyclops, who penned them in.[41] But Eurylochus makes it clear that Odysseus was not a part of this encircled crowd of men and is responsible for the deaths. Odysseus entered together with them, but Eurylochus' emphasis on this suggests that Odysseus was separate from the men (σὺν δ' ὁ θρασὺς εἵπετ' Ὀδυσσεύς) and responsible for the entrance. The underlying argument of Eurylochus is, I think, that in entering the cattle enclosure of the Cyclops, the men themselves are acting as cattle, beholden to a master. The same motif of encirclement occurs in the Circe episode. Frame has already suggested that Circe's name may be etymologically linked to *krikos*, the Greek word for "ring."[42] At any rate, the pattern described by Eurylochus is the same. An entire group of men descend into a house as a collective under the leadership of Odysseus; there, they will be encircled by a quasi-divine being whose name signifies the encirclement. Consequently, can we not see an irony in the metamorphosis described by Eurylochus? The companions will be turned into the fawning animals seen earlier, the victims of Circe's magic. But in the act of entering this house as a group, under the leadership of Odysseus, they are already acting as livestock. The irony of the metamorphosis is that in its depiction of the fantastic, it displays the underlying truth of the relationship between Odysseus and his men.

If we pay attention to the details of Circe's magic, we can read the episode as a competitive one, but not in the usual sense. We should not be distracted by the antidote given by Hermes to Odysseus, which lets him save himself and his men from her magic. For Circe's magic was, if we pay attention to its detailed description, curiously limited from the very beginning. It consists of two different kinds of metamorphoses, each of which has a counterpart in the ideological powers of Odysseus. First, there is the physical transformation of the first set of companions into pigs. Their outside appearance is altered, but their inner nature remains the same; they are humans with the appearance of animals. So what seems to be a strength of Circe's is also a weakness: she changes only their physical appearance, while "the minds within them stayed as they had been before."[43] Odysseus, in contrast, does not change his companions' outward appearance (his men look exactly the same when he returns safe to them from Circe's house), but their mental essence, their *noos* within, is definitely not the same as before. They behave and act as dogs.

This split might cause us to pay more attention to the first sign we are offered of Circe's magic. As the first set of companions approach her abode, they see a monstrous sight (αἰνὰ πέλωρα, 10.219): there are creatures that have the appearance of lions and wolves, but rather than attacking the men who approach the threshold of Circe's domain, they fawn. Once more, we have a disjunction between the inside and outside of a creature: the behavior (*noos*) does not match the appearance, and it is surely this that is "monstrous," challenging the expected order of the world. Of course, it is impossible to tell what Circe has done to these creatures: are they men who have been turned into wolves, or are they wolves that have been domesticated? Regardless of this, a perplexing detail still sticks out. If they are wild animals who have been domesticated, it is appropriate that they appear at the threshold, the place where dogs, trained by masters, preserve the inside of the *oikos* from the attack of strangers. Such dogs are fierce to outsiders, gentle to insiders, always in response to the orders of the master. This comparison lets us see a curious gap in Circe's powers. The tamed wolves fail as guard dogs, because they are too tame: the split between appearance and internal *noos* is set in stone.[44]

Compare the rigidity of these guardians of the thresholds with the interaction between Odysseus and Eurylochus. For does not Odysseus set up Eurylochus as a substitute guardian of half his men? Further, when Eurylochus challenges Odysseus' authority, he acts as a subordinate who loses sense of his role and thus challenges his master; he is fierce at the very time he should fawn. His verbal attack on Odysseus' leadership is an attempt to break the circle of Odysseus' authority. He refuses to follow the first group of companions into the house of Circe, then he refuses to accompany Odysseus back to eat the (scraps of the) feast. He accordingly challenges the position of Odysseus as leader. Moreover, in his failure to fall in with his joyful Cephallenian companions who greet Odysseus "as if they were back in their own country," Eurylochus questions Odysseus' identity as a Cephallenian. The challenge to Odysseus' authority produces the following reaction from Odysseus.

> So he spoke, and I considered in my mind whether
> to draw out the long-edged sword from beside my big thigh,
> and cut off his head and throw it on the ground, even though
> he was nearly related to me by marriage.
>
> (*Od.* 10.438–41)

Odysseus provides us with apparent biographical information about Eurylochus; he is a very close relative. This affirmation of closeness is a pointer toward the symbolic closeness of Eurylochus to Odysseus. He rebels against Odyssean authority and challenges it. He also has much in common with another antagonist of Odysseus, Dolon. Eurylochus' name signifies ability in the activity for which the trickster Odysseus is famous, just as Dolon's name signifies trickery. Eurylochus also came to the brink of losing his head for this challenge, as Dolon lost his head. Odysseus' threat against Eurylochus clarifies what is at stake in the encounter. Only Odysseus has the ultimate right to impose order on his troops. Eurylochus utters words suggesting that he is not a man who will silently follow his leader. But when Eurylochus shows disobedience, Odysseus does not need to use force to put down the minor uprising; the threat of force itself is sufficient. In the end, Odysseus' symbolic authority (witnessed by the manner in which the rest of the companions fall in behind his leadership, with Eurylochus himself eventually following) is sufficient to keep the companions together. By his threat of violence to Eurylochus, Odysseus "tames" him. He thus shows the flexibility at manipulating the boundaries between behavior and external appearance. This was the very thing that was absent in the "monstrously" tame wild animals of Circe.

The Suitorial Superego

Let us now turn to our second set of deaths, to Odysseus' active killing of the suitors. The obliviousness of the suitors to the social conventions structuring the life of the *oikos* has received a great deal of critical attention.[45] Though much of this criticism has overlooked the perturbing, transgressive manner in which the suitors are killed and thus (implicitly or explicitly) has justified the murder of them, the disturbing aspects of their death have been well brought out by Nagler. However, there is much truth in both positions: the suitors do violate social conventions, yet there is something unsavory about their deaths at the hands of Odysseus. I suggest (with Nagler) that there is a close connection between the form of the suitors' transgressions and the form the revenge of Odysseus eventually takes. A comparison with the authority Odysseus exercises over the companions can be of help here.

The suitors have no concern for the public law, the symbolic authority of the father. If the workings of paternal law depend on its status as an unused threat, a signifier alone, the situation on Ithaca provides one scenario of what can happen when this symbolic authority ceases to function. Odysseus accuses the suitors of lacking *aidos*, the sense of shame that structures a community (*Od.* 20.171). *Aidos* functions as the recognition of the impossibility of pure enjoyment, of having it all; one's place in the social is determined by a sacrifice, and *aidos*—the "shame" felt before others—reminds each social individual of the sacrifice that is constitutive of the social. It functions as an injunction of restraint.[46] When Odysseus accuses the suitors of a lack of *aidos*, he accuses them of losing such a sense of restraint. On Ithaca, Odysseus' departure coincides with the loss of the person who can ensure the renunciation of enjoyment. Further significant commentary on the situation of the suitors comes from Penelope, as she talks to the disguised Odysseus.

> οὔτ' Ὀδυσεὺς ἔτι οἶκον ἐλεύσεται, οὔτε σὺ πομπῆς
> τεύξῃ, ἐπεὶ οὐ τοῖοι σημάντορές εἰσ' ἐνὶ οἴκῳ,
> οἷος Ὀδυσσεὺς ἔσκε μετ' ἀνδράσιν, εἴ ποτ' ἔην γε,
> ξείνους αἰδοίους ἀποπεμπέμεν ἠδὲ δέχεσθαι.
>
> (*Od.* 19.313–16)

[Odysseus will never come home again, nor will you be given
conveyance, for there are none to give orders left in the household
such as Odysseus was among men—if he ever existed—
for receiving respected strangers and sending them off on their
   journeys.]

There are no leaders, σημάντορες, "givers of signs," left in the house, and thus there is no one who can regulate patterns of exchange. What is missing from Ithaca is not Odysseus the man but, instead, the symbolic role Odysseus had formerly played. Ithaca misses not his person but his "word."[47] Ithaca lacks the *semata* (uttered by Odysseus) around which the community was formerly structured.[48] The failure of Odysseus' symbolic authority over the suitors sharply differentiates them from the companions; with the latter, words ran the show. This helps us understand other key differences. Whereas the companions acted as if they were livestock—meekly following a master—the suitors consume the livestock of the absent master. The companions' obedience to Odysseus involved a constant deferral of enjoyment. Enjoyment is what they expected to receive at the end of their journey, an end that is forever postponed. The death, one by one, of the companions corresponds to what can be understood as a series of sacrifices in the name of an ever receding enjoyment: it is as if Odysseus is telling them, "Obey me one more time, and through your sacrifices I will finally bring you what you desire!" The suitors' behavior is the exact opposite of this. They simply enjoy. They have no concern for an economy of renunciation. But this is not a complete rejection of the law in and of itself, for they remain attached to what Odysseus' symbolic authority demanded that they renounce. Odysseus is gone, and the workings of the public law are put on hold; as a consequence, the suitors are stuck in a seemingly indefinite period of consumption. They indulge themselves in the fantasy of consumption that is the ultimate support of the public law regulating the *oikos*.

Thus, though Odysseus is gone, the suitors are not free from the law but, rather, cling to the transgression of the law as a collective; this shared enjoyment of what the law prohibits reveals the law's superegoic dimension. This makes ethical evaluation of the behavior of the suitors more complicated than critics have generally noted. The suitors have been condemned as immoral because of their perversion of the economy of the feast and their disregard for the public laws that govern a community. This goes hand in hand with a black-and-white moralizing narrative. Bad suitors are killed because of their evil, by the good Odysseus, who restores order. But the suitors are not condemned by Odysseus within the terms of the public law. They are condemned for ignoring it. Here is Odysseus' summary on the suitors' behavior after their death.

> τούσδε δὲ μοῖρ' ἐδάμασσε θεῶν καὶ σχέτλια ἔργα·
> οὔ τινα γὰρ τίεσκον ἐπιχθονίων ἀνθρώπων,
> οὐ κακὸν οὐδὲ μὲν ἐσθλόν, ὅτίς σφεας εἰσαφίκοιτο·
> τῶ καὶ ἀτασθαλίῃσιν ἀεικέα πότμον ἐπέσπον.
>
> (*Od.* 22.413–16)

[These were destroyed by the doom of the gods and their own hard
    actions,
for these men paid no attention at all to any man on earth
who came their way, no matter if he were base or noble.
So by their own recklessness they have found a shameful death.]

The suitors are not classifiable within the terms of the public discourse. If their actions are in some sense evil, *kakos*, this is not the crucial question. The suitors suspend the workings of the law as such. If the public law (under Odysseus, before he left) categorized behavior into noble and base, the suitors render such a distinction meaningless: they do not care if anyone is noble or base, *esthlos* or *kakos*. The situation is similar to the one on the island of the Cyclops; to dismiss the Cyclops as evil within the system of ethics imparted to his adversary misses the crucial point. It implies a set of rules by which both protagonists play when one of the pair rejects those rules outright. We can also draw a parallel to Odysseus' remark in the Doloneia that Diomedes should neither praise nor blame him (*Il.* 10.259–60). In the *Iliad*, praise or blame was irrelevant to the actions of the trickster, because his actions revealed the "spirit" of the law, the fantasy of winning at all costs that is hidden in the daytime *ethos* of the heroic code. The heroic code is a series of open, everyday laws that regulate renunciation; but such regulations are suspended in the enjoyment of the unregulated killing that takes place in the Doloneia.[49] So, too, the suitors merely do what the "spirit" of the law demands. The public law proclaims the need for renunciation, but it does so in the name of a deferred enjoyment: it is as if it exhorts to the people, "Preserve the livestock and property of the *oikos* to guarantee a fair share for all!" The suitors, in the absence of a father to regulate renunciation, consume. Accordingly, they render inoperative the symbolic values (*esthlos* or *kakos*) that are ultimately nothing other than terms used to regulate this renunciation.

We can now turn to the manner of the suitors' death. The companions fell victim to their attachment to the symbolic values Odysseus represented, and they died passively. Odysseus never had to use force against them but, instead, remained a figure of reason, of persuasion. Obedience to the public law brings death at its hands. The suitors identify with the superegoic imperative to enjoy, and they consequently arouse the superegoic dimensions of Odysseus' authority. Rather than a kindly, pacifying father, his murder of the suitors bears witness to the obscene, terrifying father that always acted as a support to the public image. The suitors are killed en masse at a feast in the hall; they die as they consume. They are also encircled by the actions of Odysseus, just as the companions were encircled. Odysseus enters the hall first and ensures that the doors behind him will be closed.[50] The significance of the encirclement in the hall is flagged in the text by the warning given to the suitors by Theoclymenus.

ἆ δειλοί, τί κακὸν τόδε πάσχετε; νυκτὶ μὲν ὑμέων
εἰλύαται κεφαλαί τε πρόσωπά τε νέρθε τε γοῦνα,
οἰμωγὴ δὲ δέδηε, δεδάκρυνται δὲ παρειαί,
αἵματι δ' ἐρράδαται τοῖχοι καλαί τε μεσόδμαι·
εἰδώλων δὲ πλέον πρόθυρον, πλείη δὲ καὶ αὐλή,

ἱεμένων Ἐρεβόσδε ὑπὸ ζόφον· ἥλιος δὲ
οὐρανοῦ ἐξαπόλωλε, κακὴ δ' ἐπιδέδρομεν ἀχλύς.

(*Od.* 20.351–57)

[Poor wretches, what evil has come on you? Your head and faces
and the knees underneath you are shrouded in night and darkness;
a sound of wailing has blazed out, your cheeks are covered
with tears, and the walls bleed, and the fine supporting pillars.
All the forecourt is huddled with ghosts, the yard is full of them
as they flock down to the underworld and the darkness. The sun
has perished out of the sky, and a foul mist has come over.]

(translation modified)

Theoclymenus' words are particularly vivid. They prophesy the deaths of the suitors and preview the second Nekuia. But they also recall the death of the companions. The "hall" [αὐλή] is full of the *eidola* (the ghosts) of the suitors, who exist in a strange world between day and night; it should be day, yet the sun has disappeared from the sky, suggesting an eclipse.[51] Many of the companions died in the *messaulos* of the Cyclops; the last of them died because of the eating of the cattle of the Sun (an episode, as we have seen, closely associated with the tricking of the Cyclops) at a time when the Sun did not see them. Let me emphasize two points. First, in both series of deaths, the victims are encircled because of their common point of identification: the companions identify with Odysseus as symbolic father, the suitors with the enjoyment this father prohibited. This identification leads to their collective deaths. But it is of particular interest that Theoclymenus' description of the suitors' coming death is a picture saturated with uncanny forms of life. Not only are "animate" beings depicted with the shadow of death hanging over them, but inanimate objects come to life. In the absence of the sun, the walls and pillars begin to bleed, as if they have miraculously come to life. The metaphor used of their wailing reinforces this: their wailing "blazes," as if the darkness and death of the scene is lit up by the blazing life of the men who are pictured in it.[52] It is no coincidence that the closest parallel to this vocabulary mixing life and death occurs in book 12, as the cattle eaten by the companions miraculously refuse to die.

> The next thing was that the gods began to show forth portents before
> us.
> The skins crawled, and the meat that was stuck on the spits bellowed,
> both roast and raw, and the noise was like the lowing of cattle.

(*Od.* 12.394–96)

The picture is horrific and vivid. The supernatural portents are generally explained in terms of the threat they pose to the moral order of the mortal world. Though this interpretation is far from in error, I think a more complete explanation can be given by analyzing these events through their relation to the two forms of paternal authority so far considered. Both the crying of the cattle who refuse to die and the life-in-death of the suitors and the banquet hall suggest the insufficiency of symbolic authority.

> [T]he father *qua* Name of the Father, reduced to a figure of symbolic authority, is "dead" (also) in the sense that *he does not know anything about enjoyment*, about life substance: the symbolic order (the big Other) and enjoyment are radically incompatible. Which is why the famous Freudian dream of a son who appears to his father and reproaches him with "Father, can't you see I'm burning?" could simply be translated into *"Father, can't you see I'm enjoying?"*—can't you see I'm alive, burning with enjoyment? Father cannot see it since he is dead, whereby the possibility is open to me to enjoy not only *outside* his knowledge, i.e., unbeknownst to him, but also *in his very ignorance*.[53]

The consumption of the cattle of the Sun goes on outside the knowledge of two fathers, both Odysseus and the Sun itself. In particular, the vulnerability of the Sun (the all-seeing "big Other" of the *Odyssey*, privileged representative of the symbolic order) testifies to the weakness of the symbolic order. I suggested earlier that this gap in the Sun's authority was necessary for *metis* to function. I can now suggest a second reading. Behind the backs of Odysseus and the Sun, the narrative stages an uncanny episode of enjoyment. If it is customary to evoke the sense of death that the consumption of the cattle evokes, we also need to emphasize that this is the one episode of the *Apologoi* where the companions are really alive. They are not constrained by the dead authority of the symbolic law. This can also help us understand the suitors. Theoclymenus merely articulates a truth that has always characterized them. Though "death" enshrouds them, they nevertheless are "alive" in this death; they are not mortified in the realm of the symbolic.

The consumption of livestock is the point where companions and suitors merge in their enjoyment; the companions appear to give the slip to symbolic authority by way of an act that recalls the most significant aspect of the suitors' behavior. Yet I have suggested that the death of the companions is more complex. The difficulty lies in ascertaining the relationship between Odysseus and the companions at the moment of their death. Does he turn a blind eye? It remains unclear (indeed, undecidable) if the moment of enjoyment is not the most subtle form of symbolic control. A similar complexity lingers over the final actions of the suitors. The suitors seem to be characterized throughout the *Odyssey* by a complete disregard for symbolic authority. They ignore rhetorical appeals to the figure of the absent Odysseus. More importantly, at the time when Telemachus is approaching the moment of manhood and thus threatens to replace Odysseus as head of the *oikos*, they plot to murder him because of the threat he poses to their enjoyment. But things are not so simple. For though the murder of Telemachus seems to suggest the ultimate failure of symbolic authority, the suitors show ongoing hesitations, both in their attempt to murder him and in their attitude toward his growing symbolic authority. Indeed, they eventually call off their attempted ambush of him.

> ὣς οἱ μὲν τοιαῦτα πρὸς ἀλλήλους ἀγόρευον·
> μνηστῆρες δ' ἄρα Τηλεμάχῳ θάνατόν τε μόρον τε
> ἤρτυον· αὐτὰρ ὁ τοῖσιν ἀριστερὸς ἤλυθεν ὄρνις,
> αἰετὸς ὑψιπέτης, ἔχε δὲ τρήρωνα πέλειαν.
> τοῖσιν δ' Ἀμφίνομος ἀγορήσατο καὶ μετέειπεν·
> "ὦ φίλοι, οὐχ ἥμιν συνθεύσεται ἥδε γε βουλή,
> Τηλεμάχοιο φόνος· ἀλλὰ μνησώμεθα δαιτός."
>
> (*Od.* 20.240–46)

> [Now, as these men were conversing thus with each other,
> the suitors were compacting their plan of death and destruction
> for Telemachos, and a bird flew over them on the left side.
> This was a high-flown eagle, and carried a tremulous pigeon.
> Now it was Amphinomos who spoke forth and addressed them:
> "O friends, this plan of ours to murder Telemachos will not
> ever be brought to completion; so let us think of our feasting."]

That the prophecy is interpreted as having a meaning in and of itself shows a failure of nerve on the pattern of the suitors. The heed Amphinomos pays to this bird-sign is in marked contrast with the famous skeptical rejection of bird-signs espoused by Eurymachus in book 2 in response to Halitherses' prophecy of the return of Odysseus.

> ὦ γέρον, εἰ δ' ἄγε δὴ μαντεύεο σοῖσι τέκεσσιν
> οἴκαδ' ἰών, μή πού τι κακὸν πάσχωσιν ὀπίσσω·
> ταῦτα δ' ἐγὼ σέο πολλὸν ἀμείνων μαντεύεσθαι.
> ὄρνιθες δέ τε πολλοὶ ὑπ' αὐγὰς ἠελίοιο
> φοιτῶσ', οὐδέ τε πάντες ἐναίσιμοι· αὐτὰρ Ὀδυσσεὺς
> ὤλετο τῆλ', ὡς καὶ σὺ καταφθίσθαι σὺν ἐκείνῳ
> ὤφελες· οὐκ ἂν τόσσα θεοπροπέων ἀγόρευες,

οὐδέ κε Τηλέμαχον κεχολωμένον ὧδ' ἀνείης,
σῷ οἴκῳ δῶρον ποτιδέγμενος, αἴ κε πόρῃσιν.

(*Od.* 2.178–86)

[Old sir, better go home and prophesy to your children,
for fear they may suffer some evil to come. In these things
I can give a much better interpretation than you can.
Many are the birds who under the sun's rays wander
the sky; not all of them mean anything; Odysseus
is dead, far away, and how I wish that you had died with him
also. Then you would not be announcing all these predictions,
nor would you so stir up Telemachos, who is now angry,
looking for the gift for your own household, which he might give
   you.]

Penelope later complains of the lack of σημάντορες (givers of signs) in the household. The failure of signs from a father figure corresponds to the failure of the cosmic realm of the sky and gods to provide clear signs (the failure of the Lacanian "big Other"). Halitherses' prophecy is an attempt to restore the Other, to validate the rule of the father over the suitors. It is this that is rejected: Halitherses' paternalism is to be exercised over his own children alone, and he is not to treat others as children. But it should also be noted that with the realm of the big Other suspended, every action of agents around the suitors that is performed in the name of the public good is transformed into a vulgar pursuit of personal gain. Halitherses' real agenda, suggests Amphinomos, is to procure gain for himself (a gift for his household), through the eventual success that will come of stirring up Telemachus; in short, the suitors merely do openly what Halitherses (and others, when the public law functions) do behind the veneer of symbolic authority. The later acceptance of the bird-sign in book 20 announces a return in the faith of the functioning of the Other. Amphinomos interprets the bird-sign, and the interpretation itself is of secondary importance to the fact that Amphinomos believes that there is a need for interpretation. The sign is, in a sense, interpreted before the actual interpretation occurs. The specific interpretation of the interplay between the pigeon and eagle merely plays out what one would have already expected from the implicit restoration of the Other as guarantor of meaning. Amphinomos suggests that the attempt to kill Telemachus, the emerging replacement to Odysseus, must be given up.

The appearance of a meaningful *sema* coincides with the suitors' abandonment of their plan to kill the figure who is about to become a new *semantor*—this is the veiled purpose of Halitherses' prophecy of encouragement, as

Eurymachus realizes. Herein lies the failure of nerve of the suitors. At a crucial point, the suitors equivocate about the power of the public law. Their enjoyment is tempered by a gnawing doubt—a doubt that can be traced from the wonder they experienced at the first "fatherly" speech of Telemachus in the assembly of book 2 to their consent to Telemachus' command to allow the disguised Odysseus to take part in the contest of the bow. The companions die at the moment when a question mark hangs over their obedience to the symbolic authority of Odysseus. The death of the suitors occurs when their apparent rejection of this authority—signified by the manner in which they eat up his household goods—is punctured by the emergence of doubt. It is as if in the topsy-turvy world of the suitors, the everyday relationship between public law and its superego dark side is reversed: their enjoyment is sustained by an unconscious, unspoken belief in the symbolic power of the father.

We can now provide some brief remarks about Odysseus' slaughter of the suitors. Nagler is surely correct in suggesting that Odysseus' transference of the bow out of the contest and against the suitors is highly significant.

> Clearly the boundary Odysseus is about to cross with his next bowshot will not only precipitate outright fighting but the killing of one's own retainers, the most illegitimate kind of violence, brought right into the *oikos* from the outer world, where it is problematic enough. This moment is a kind of Rubicon, by crossing which the hero simultaneously declares his identity and brings "Iliadic" combat back into the epic, and his household.[54]

The reference to the Iliadic aspect of the killing is quite conventional and returns us to the contrast suggested by Pucci between the *Iliad* as a poem of the "total expenditure" of war and the *Odyssey* as a poem of the economy of life.[55] We need to be more precise. The killing of the suitors does not evoke the everyday battle scenes of the *Iliad*, the "controlled economy" of death; it recalls the superegoic aspects of them, the "total expenditure" of death. In particular, in a few hundred lines, it retells the story of the *menis* of Achilles. Let us look in detail at the offer of recompense by Eurymachus (*Od.* 22.45–67) and the supplications of Leodes and Phemius (*Od.* 22.310–25, 343 ff.)

As Odysseus embarks on the slaughter, Eurymachus tries to prevent him, first by suggesting that Antinous was the major figure responsible for the looting, then by offering to compensate Odysseus in full for all the suitors' expenditures.

"οὐ δὲ φείδεο λαῶν
σῶν· ἀτὰρ ἄμμες ὄπισθεν ἀρεσσάμενοι κατὰ δῆμον,

ὅσσα τοι ἐκπέποται καὶ ἐδήδοται ἐν μεγάροισι,
τιμὴν ἀμφὶς ἄγοντες ἐεικοσάβοιον ἕκαστος,
χαλκόν τε χρυσόν τ' ἀποδώσομεν, εἰς ὅ κε σὸν κῆρ
ἰανθῇ· πρὶν δ' οὔ τι νεμεσσητὸν κεχολῶσθαι."
  τὸν δ' ἄρ' ὑπόδρα ἰδὼν προσέφη πολύμητις Ὀδυσσεύς·
"Εὐρύμαχ', οὐδ' εἴ μοι πατρώϊα πάντ' ἀποδοῖτε,
ὅσσα τε νῦν ὕμμ' ἐστὶ καὶ εἴ ποθεν ἄλλ' ἐπιθεῖτε,
οὐδέ κεν ὣς ἔτι χεῖρας ἐμὰς λήξαιμι φόνοιο,
πρὶν πᾶσαν μνηστῆρας ὑπερβασίην ἀποτῖσαι.
νῦν ὑμῖν παράκειται ἐναντίον ἠὲ μάχεσθαι
ἢ φεύγειν, ὅς κεν θάνατον καὶ κῆρας ἀμύξῃ·
ἀλλά τιν' οὐ φεύξεσθαι ὀΐομαι αἰπὺν ὄλεθρον."

(*Od.* 22.54–67)

["Then spare your own
people, and afterward we will make public reparation
for all that has been eaten and drunk in your halls, setting
each upon himself an assessment of twenty oxen.
We will pay it back in bronze and gold to you, until your heart
is softened. Till then, we cannot blame you for being angry."
Then looking darkly at him resourceful Odysseus answered:
"Eurymachus, if you gave me all your father's possessions,
all that you have now, and what you could add from elsewhere,
even so, I would not stay my hands from the slaughter,
until I had taken revenge for all the suitors' transgression.
Now the choice has been set before you, either to fight me
or run, if any of you can escape from death and its spirits.
But I think not one man will escape from sheer destruction."]

Eurymachus' offer of fair and fitting recompense recalls the offers of Agamemnon to Achilles in *Iliad* 9. Eurymachus offers gold and bronze, as Agamemnon famously did, an offer in turn spurned by Achilles.[56] Odysseus rejects the fair bargain of Eurymachus in the name of something more. This returns us to the vexed problem of what Achilles wants. The wording of each rejection is strikingly similar.[57]

<u>οὐδέ κεν ὣς ἔτι</u> θυμὸν ἐμὸν πείσει' Ἀγαμέμνων
<u>πρίν γ' ἀπὸ πᾶσαν</u> ἐμοὶ δόμεναι θυμαλγέα λώβην.

(*Il.* 9.386–87)

[Not even so would Agamemnon have his way with my spirit
until he had made good to me all this heartrending insolence.]

<u>οὐδέ κεν ὣς</u> ἔτι χεῖρας ἐμὰς λήξαιμι φόνοιο,
<u>πρὶν πᾶσαν</u> μνηστῆρας ὑπερβασίην ἀποτεῖσαι.

(*Od.* 22.63–64)

[even so, I would not stay my hands from the slaughter,
until I had taken revenge for all the suitors' transgressions.]

For all the talk of the restoration of "economy" to the *oikos* at Ithaca, Odysseus here acts like the Achilles of *Iliad* 9; Odysseus is convinced of the insufficiency of material goods to grant him the intersubjective recognition that he needs, the realm of pure prestige. His action also demonstrates how a return to the regime of the public law—the essence of Eurymachus' proposal—is somehow not enough, just as Achilles' *menis* had wounded beyond repair the symbolic authority of Agamemnon. Odysseus' next words to Eurymachus are just as striking. The ultimatum to fight or flee, followed by a prophecy of death for all regardless of the choice, echoes the choice between two deaths articulated by Achilles in *Iliad* 9 (a long life but "social" death in Phthia or death and *kleos* at Troy).⁵⁸ The possibility of this choice to fight or flee is then played out on a larger scale in the choice that confronts the Greek host in books 2 and 10. But Odysseus' quick decision for an all-embracing death for the suitors moves us swiftly away from the indeterminacy of the embassy scene of *Iliad* 9, into the kind of *menis* that drives Achilles in the later books.

With this in mind, let us now look at the supplication of Leodes. Achilles ignores the appeals of suppliants in the frenzied killing of books 20–22; any appeal made to him in the name of the public law is rejected. So, too, Leodes is represented as an exception to the general recklessness of the suitors; he never violated the women of the house, and he made every effort to halt the actions of the suitors (*Od.* 22.313 ff.). His appeal falls on deaf ears, as Odysseus kills him along with the others. Here are the last words of Leodes.

ἀλλά μοι οὐ πείθοντο κακῶν ἄπο χεῖρας ἔχεσθαι·
τῷ καὶ ἀτασθαλίῃσιν ἀεικέα πότμον ἐπέσπον.
αὐτὰρ ἐγὼ μετὰ τοῖσι θυοσκόος οὐδὲν ἐοργὼς
κείσομαι, ὡς οὐκ ἔστι χάρις μετόπισθ' εὐεργέων.

(*Od.* 22.316–19)

[But they would not listen to me and keep their hands off evil.
So by their own recklessness they have found a shameful
death, but I was their diviner, and I did nothing;
but I must fall, since there is no gratitude for past favors.]

Leodes speaks the language of *charis*, which is the language of supplication, an aspect of the public law. Dolon's supplication in *Iliad* 10 involves the claim that his father will render *charis* to Diomedes and Odysseus if he is spared.[59] The failure to render proper *charis* is also the reason proferred by Achilles for his quarrel with Agamemnon: he received no *charis* from the Greeks, despite his incessant fighting on their behalf (*Il.* 9.317–18). The failure of *charis* drives Achilles to turn to a rhetoric that eradicates difference: the indifference of death to the goodness or evil of a man (9.319–21). Leodes speaks the language of exchange across time, of the need to repay debts incurred for good services; this is rejected by the kind of Odysseus who comes close to the blind fury of Achilles. But the words of Leodes take on further significance when considered alongside the later, successful supplication of the bard Phemius. Phemius will also ask for Odysseus' pity, but once more in a particular manner.

> αὐτῷ τοι μετόπισθ' ἄχος ἔσσεται, εἴ κεν ἀοιδὸν
> πέφνῃς ...
>
> (*Od.* 22.345–46)

[You will be sorry in time to come, if you kill the singer of songs ...]

Phemius' reference to the grief soon to come to Odysseus repeats the prophetic warning Odysseus himself had given to Achilles during the embassy.

> αὐτῷ τοι μετόπισθ' ἄχος ἔσσεται, οὐδέ τι μῆχος
> ῥεχθέντος κακοῦ ἔστ' ἄκος εὑρεῖν·
>
> (*Il.* 9.249–50)

[It will be an affliction to you hereafter, there will be no remedy found to heal the evil thing when it has been done.]

It is as if the bard has access to the poetic tradition about Odysseus that has momentarily escaped the notice of the protagonist himself, who is lost in his fury. As the slaughter of the suitors approaches, Odysseus repeatedly refers to the harm inflicted on him by their consumption; he refers to this harm in terms of an ἄχος—the pain involved in the affront to public law that is the driving force behind Achilles' rejection of the public law.[60] He acts as if he is unaware of his own lesson to Achilles: he embarks on a hopeless, superegoic quest to make up for the grief he suffered, forgetting that there can be no sufficient cure (ἄκος) for this. With his symbolic authority revealed to be insufficient, Odysseus launches a destructive attempt to make up for its self-evident failure. We can perhaps now see a hint of the futility of Odysseus' fury in the earlier words of Leodes: οὐκ ἔστι χάρις <u>μετόπισθ'</u> εὐεργέων. Phemius' intervention thus has something of the feel of damage control. Odysseus is on the brink of turning into an Achilles, as he acts out the same errors he so brilliantly diagnosed for Achilles during the embassy.

With this aspect of Odysseus in the foreground, it is worth looking more closely at his remarks to Eurycleia after the slaughter is complete.

> ἐν θυμῷ, γρηῦ, χαῖρε καὶ ἴσχεο μηδ' ὀλόλυζε·
> οὐχ ὁσίη κταμένοισιν ἐπ' ἀνδράσιν εὐχετάασθαι.
> τούσδε δὲ μοῖρ' ἐδάμασσε θεῶν καὶ σχέτλια ἔργα·
> οὔ τινα γὰρ τίεσκον ἐπιχθονίων ἀνθρώπων,
> οὐ κακὸν οὐδὲ μὲν ἐσθλόν, ὅτίς σφεας εἰσαφίκοιτο·
> τῶ καὶ ἀτασθαλίῃσιν ἀεικέα πότμον ἐπέσπον.
>
> (*Od.* 22.411–16)

[Keep your joy in your heart, old dame; stop, do not raise up
the cry. It is not piety to glory so over slain men.
These were destroyed by the doom of the gods and their own hard
    actions,
for these men paid no attention at all to any man on earth
who came their way, no matter if he were base or noble.
So by their own recklessness they have found a shameful death.]

These lines have been conventionally understood as being "human and compassionate" and therefore "out of tune with the archaic ferocity of the rest of the Book"[61]—wise Odysseus prevents overzealous Eurycleia from indulging a hubristic desire to gloat over dead enemies. But rather than see this as a typical gesture of restraint from a *sophron* Odysseus,[62] we can read a darker meaning. The crucial parallel to this warning to Eurycleia is the words to Diomedes in the Doloneia; just as those acts were outside the realm of the public law and therefore to be neither praised nor blamed, so, too, was the killing of the suitors. Odysseus' silence is not a mark of his humanity as much as it is an attempt to cover up the transgression of his obscene act. The killing of the suitors, together with the killing of the Thracians in the Doloneia, must remain unspoken if the realm of public law is to continue to function. Accordingly, Odysseus tries to write himself as agent out of the story. The suitors, themselves participants in a regime of enjoyment that cared nothing for the difference between *esthlos* and *kakos*, die in a similar manner. Odysseus acts as if their deaths, inexplicable within the terms of public law (articulated in the speech of Eurylochus), are almost a natural occurrence, brought about by no one.[63]

Let me end this discussion by appending some comments to Nagler's excellent discussion of Odysseus' vital remarks that end the contest of the bow and begin the slaughter of the suitors.

> "οὗτος μὲν δὴ ἄεθλος ἀάατος ἐκτετέλεσται·
> νῦν αὖτε σκοπὸν ἄλλον, ὃν οὔ πώ τις βάλεν ἀνήρ,
> εἴσομαι, αἴ κε τύχωμι, πόρῃ δέ μοι εὖχος Ἀπόλλων."
>
> (*Od.* 22.5–7)
>
> [Here is a task that has been achieved *aaatos*.
> Now I shall shoot at another mark, one that no man yet
> has struck, if I can hit it and Apollo grants met the glory.]

Though the meaning of *aaatos* is uncertain, Nagler persuasively argues that it should be taken as a negative prefix attached to the stem *ate*. For Nagler, the phrase suggests a distinction between the contest of the bow as a peaceful method of conflict resolution and the chaotic fight with the suitors "under the influence of destructive passion." Though I agree with this, I think this reading can be improved by understanding the situation of the suitors (and companions) in terms of the social orders of the Cyclopes and Phaeacians. I have argued that the public law functioned perfectly within Phaeacian society. Because of the perfect working of the law, Phaeacia was a society without enjoyment. By contrast, the Cyclopes were obvious to the Name-of-the-Father: they did nothing but enjoy (epitomized in their cannibalism), oblivious to any social renunciation. We can therefore be quite precise about the effect of Odysseus' discus throw on Phaeacia, which brings an end to those games. But the introduction of a limit also renders the public law on Phaeacia incomplete and necessitates a phantasmic support for it. The place occupied by Odysseus' discus is the place where the Phaeacians will structure their enjoyment as a support for their law. As soon as Odysseus leaves, the public law, the workings of the Name-of-the-Father and the words required to sustain it, will be incomplete; behind it will lurk an obscene father, representing a superegoic imperative to enjoy—a Cyclops. Of course, the enjoyment of the Cyclopes will now be regulated by a collective renunciation of enjoyment imposed by way of the necessary loss that is the price of entrance to a social world. What is the importance of this for the suitors and companions?

At first glance, the companions resemble the Phaeacians, the suitors the Cyclopes. The former inhabit a world without enjoyment, the latter a world of Cyclopean enjoyment. But the elaborate description of the staging of the contest of the bow lingers on the moment when these two disparate aspects of the law meet. Odysseus, the winner of games, upholder of the symbolic control of his men through the public, "civilized" aspects of *metis*, now embarks on a superegoic revenge: the "contest" he now begins will be one that lacks any social niceties and instead proceeds straight to the death of the adversaries. The contest with *ate* is a contest where Odysseus enjoys. We see here the moment when the threat of force on which his symbolic authority depends explodes into an orgy of violence. From the perspective of the suitors, the staging of the contest of the bow indicates the manner in which their enjoyment never broke with the law. They enjoyed in an indefinite, interim period when Odysseus was absent, for as long as Penelope lingered over the choice of a replacement and Telemachus had not yet reached manhood. The worlds of the Phaeacians and Cyclopes were fantasy worlds, illustrating two impossible relations to the law. Yet the clarity of these fantasies provides a matrix with which we can understand the two sets of deaths around which the poem is structured.

8

What Does a Phaeacian Woman Want?

Odysseus brings the concept of lack, correlative to the emergence of desire, to the Cyclopes and Phaeacians, through the metaphor of an irremediable loss. From this point on, the illusion that these peoples may get what they want can only be sustained by the belief in stories—that is, myths—that tell of a time when they still had the part of themselves that is now missing. The Phaeacians and the Cyclopes become humans who tell each other mythic tales about their nostalgic past—as a way of gentrifying the problem of lack itself. The narrative of the *Odyssey*, split between the fairy-tale world of Phaeacia and the *Apologoi*, on the one hand, and the realism of the events on Ithaca, on the other, also presents a split in the figure of Odysseus. In his encounter with the Phaeacians and Cyclopes, the power of his *metis* causes him to function as a quasi-omnipotent being who forces them to deal with the problem of lack. In his return to Ithaca, this power is put to work in a human context, with eerie and destructive consequences.

But what can this interrogation of the problem of loss tell us about gender in the *Odyssey*? It has been a common critical tactic to make use of the fantasized world of gendered relations on Phaeacia, in particular Odysseus' interactions with Nausicaa and Arete, to frame readings of Odysseus' return to Ithaca.[1] I want to build on these readings in the next two chapters, but by emphasizing that the impossibility of the fantasized society of the Phaeacians needs to be part of any analysis. For the world of the Phaeacians is not only a make-believe world but a world that we see coming to an end. So, too, the view of gender harmony on Phaeacia is not simply idealized—though undoubtedly it is—but an impossible idealization. It is a fantasy of gender that stands in opposition to or denial of the mechanisms of desire. So when Odysseus, on his return to Ithaca, tries to impose the fantasy of gender harmony at work on Phaeacia onto the chaotic disorder of his own *oikos,* he is engaged in an impossible project. On this reading, Odysseus' encounter with Penelope and the *oikos* lets us see Odysseus fall victim to a gender ideology that has been demonstrated to be an impossible fantasy.

We can begin this reading by contrasting Odysseus' encounters with Nausicaa and Penelope. In Phaeacia, he primarily functions as the object of Nausicaa's desire. In recent years, the usual question has been, what is wrong with Nausicaa as love object for Odysseus?[2] But this misses an equally pertinent question: what is right about Odysseus as love object for Nausicaa? Paradoxically, what is right about him, qua object of desire, is that he is unattainable. He simply causes her desire, without providing any hope of satisfaction. Thus, the old critical unease with the episode—that it leaves Nausicaa unpleasantly in the lurch—is fully justified: "Who does not feel that there is something hard and unsatisfying in this ending of her first passion?"[3] If there is something "unsatisfying," it is for the simple reason that the story dramatizes and centers upon the emergence of this lack of satisfaction. For Nausicaa—and metonymically for Phaeacian society as a whole—Odysseus plays the role of an idealized male other that she will never be able to have, and this role radically changes the world of the Phaeacians. By contrast, at Ithaca, Penelope is not so much the woman he gets as the impossible love-object that Odysseus must recognize he can never properly have. Odysseus, object of desire on Phaeacia, must confront the complications of his own desire as he confronts Penelope. Thus, the emergence of the question of what Nausicaa wants will allow us to revisit, in the next chapter, the vexed problem of what Penelope wants.

But before turning to Nausicaa's desire, I will consider briefly the role of gender in other mythic narratives of the origins of humanity, to assess the implications for Phaeacia. I will return to the myth of Deucalion and Pyrrha, but I will also consider the myth of the origins of justice in Plato's *Protagoras* and, finally, Hesiod's tale of Pandora. The point of introducing these myths, which occur in works of literature from very different periods and have different functions in each work, is to focus on what they have in common: the traumatic emergence of sexual difference for human societies. When the shared motifs of these stories have been allowed to emerge, I hope to further specify the situation on Phaeacia. For it, too, can be read as not only a myth of the origin of humanity but a myth telling of the emergence of human, sexual desire.

Deucalion and Pyrrha

In the tale of Deucalion and Pyrrha, the origin of human society coincides with an emergence of a radical doubt. Deucalion and Pyrrha create human beings, but they remain ignorant of how humans come into being. The "trouble" with gender identity is intimately related to this ignorance.[4] The different stones hurled by Deucalion and Pyrrha turn into men and women, but Deucalion and Pyrrha are unable to see how this split occurs, since they throw the stones behind their backs. This is made particularly clear in Ovid's version of the tale.

> descendunt: velantque caput tunicasque recingunt
> et iussos lapides sua post vestigia mittunt.
> saxa (quis hoc credat, nisi sit pro teste vetustas?)
> ponere duritiem coepere suumque rigorem
> mollirique mora mollitaque ducere formam.
>
> (*Met.* 1.398–402)

[They descend: they veil their heads and loosen their robes
and throw the stones behind their back, as ordered.
The stones (who would believe this, unless ancient tradition was the witness)
began to put aside their hardness and stiffness,
to become slowly soft and take on form when softened.]

After the flood, humanity is reborn as a species split in two by gender. But no explanation for this split is available. For we should read this tale from the perspective of the perplexed protagonists. The split into men and women could be related to the stones they throw: Deucalion and Pyrrha do throw separate stones. But nothing guarantees this. Indeed, the problem of belief is doubled. We cannot simply believe that men are men and women are women because we trust tradition, the *vetustas* of the tale that tells us of the split. For the implausibility of the tradition is written into the tale itself, which showcases its own implausibility. This becomes clear later, as we see humans emerge.

> inque brevi spatio superorum numine saxa
> missa viri manibus faciem traxere virorum
> et de femineo reparata est femina iactu.
>
> (*Met.* 1.411–13)

[And in a short time, by the divine spirit of those above, the stones
thrown by the hands of the man took on the face of men,
and from the female throw, woman was made.]

Even if we trust that Ovid is telling the truth, that he is the latest purveyor of the information in store in the ancient tradition, from what source does that truth ultimately come? The only available humans are Deucalion and Pyrrha, but they look the other way. So doubt is always already there.

One of the things it is perfectly reasonable to doubt is the link between the throw of the original woman or man and the species of woman or man. We could be skeptical and see this "link" as already a fantasy of Deucalion and Pyrrha (though nothing guarantees this either), who simply cannot know the truth but already have the desire to apportion the new universe of gender in a symmetrical way. At any rate, a gendered species is created from nothing, and the species drags the obscurity of its origins into existence with it. So the myth grants the possibility of the ongoing existence of the human species, carried out through sexual reproduction, but it takes away any possibility of ultimately explaining gendered identities—at least for the being themselves. To the essentialist questions "Am I really a woman?" or "Am I really man?" the only answer is to trust the myths of other beings that have believed themselves to be men or women. Here, then, we have a myth about a constitutive "gender trouble." But there is more at stake. For any ultimate cause of men and women as men and women is taken away. Gender is not simply an attribute of the human subject. It is its lack of cause and also the traumatic perplexity caused by that lack of cause.

Plato's Protagoras

In the myth of the origins of human justice, told by Protagoras to Socrates in Plato's *Protagoras*, similar problems of gender linger beneath the surface. Protagoras relates his myth of the origins of human society to Socrates to explain why all in a community must take a share in justice.[5] In the beginning, humans were equipped by Prometheus with fire that allowed them to survive the elements. However, when they later tried to live together in cities, they were unable to interact peacefully with each other; they lacked any sense of justice and self-restraint (*aidos*). Because Zeus feared the utter destruction of humanity in these fights, he decided that he had to endow humans with justice in order to facilitate civilized interaction between them. But he instructs Hermes to distribute justice in a particular manner.

Now Hermes asked Zeus about the manner in which he was to give conscience [*aidos*] and justice to men: "Shall I distribute these in the same way as the practical crafts? These are distributed thus: one doctor is sufficient for many laymen, and so with the other experts. Shall I give justice and conscience to men in that way too, or distribute them to all?" "To all," said Zeus, "and let all share in them; for cities could not come into being, if only a few shared in them as in the other crafts. And lay down on my authority a law that he who cannot share in conscience and justice is to be killed as a plague on the city."[6]

The distribution of justice to all seems to guarantee social harmony. But there is a curious limit to this harmony. For despite Zeus' gift, the possibility remains that someone will reject a share in this justice. Zeus demands that this person be banished from society. Protagoras will later suggest that the community view any man who does not partake of justice as an utter madman.[7] The possibility of the existence of the madman seems to suggest a certain weakness of justice. Though it is given to all, the madman is a person who is an exception to its universal rule; for the community, it matters little whether he rejects this justice or simply was never allocated it in the first place. This is of particular interest to the events on Phaeacia: the community of the Phaeacians was set up at the moment they fled the Cyclopes—creatures who were brutish, of extraordinary strength, and heedless of the constraints imposed by justice.[8] They thus have much in common with Protagoras' madman, who seems to provoke a key question: what is the relationship between madness and the rule of law?

The community of law is founded on the prohibition of a desire, an exception to its functioning. Let us turn once more to Lacan's play on words in the phrase "Nom (Non) du père." The rule of the father (the reign of his symbolic control) is dependent on a shared renunciation, an acceptance of his "No." The madman refuses this "No"; he is a living reminder of the possibility of an utter rejection of symbolic codes. But what is relevant for my present purposes is the relationship of women to this political community. It is clear in Protagoras' tale that the public sphere of politics rendered possible by the distribution of justice is a male space. The attitude of men to justice depends on their belief that they have received something in exchange for the initial renunciation (the political power at work in the agora, the realm of justice). The madman must be expelled from the community to preserve the workings of justice. But because women gain less from the renunciation, their relationship to the community of justice would seem to be markedly different. They have less reason to be anxious about the expulsion of a madman, because they have less to lose from the collapse of the workings of justice. If the madman who cares nothing for renunciation poses an external threat to the community, women, insofar as they have less reason to observe the spirit of renunciation on which the law depends, are an internal threat; they are a potentially disruptive element in the heart of the community.[9] As an internal reminder that male rule depends on an arbitrary renunciation of desire, women also hint, by their existence outside the community of justice, that the rule of law is an imposture—this renunciation of desire itself cannot be justified in rational terms. The person who refuses to acknowledge the law simply must be expelled in order for the community to function.

It is worth outlining the importance of this for the situation on Phaeacia, by sketching my argument in advance. Odysseus' entrance on Phaeacia signals the return to Phaeacia of an awareness of the possibility of madness (a possibility banished when the Phaeacians fled the Cyclopes). But the return of a madman to Phaeacian society is engineered by two women, Nausicaa and Arete. When the naked and terrifying Odysseus appears to Nausicaa and her maids in *Odyssey* 6, she alone is unafraid of him. Later it will be Arete who guarantees his trip home. The horror of a figure who utterly rejects society, as embodied in the species of the Cyclopes, who the Phaeacians previously fled, returns to Phaeacian society through the person of Odysseus. For he will, in the imagination of those who see him, first appear as a bestial, lawless figure, only to be shepherded into Phaeacian society by the agency of Nausicaa and Arete. Not only does Odysseus' appearance signal a Phaeacian awareness of a "madness" that cares nothing for the rule of justice, but it also coincides with the emergence of Nausicaa as an internal challenger to the rule of paternal law. The external and internal threat to order combine. Woman comes into being as a dangerous mediator between the apparent "sense" of male law and its disavowed senselessness.

Hesiod's Pandora

Hesiod's tale of Pandora's creation—and so, too, of the creation of gender—can provide the final key for our analysis of events on Phaeacia. I have already suggested that a belief in a natural, gendered identity is a privileged manner in which a subject can avoid the problem of lack. Let us call this ideology of gender a belief in *sexual symmetry:* man and woman are viewed as determinate identities that complement each other.[10] Woman complements man insofar as she is believed to make up for man's incompleteness, and vice versa: together, man and woman make a whole. But this is not the only way of thinking about gender in the archaic period. Loraux has drawn attention to something unexpected in Hesiod's tale of the origin of women. The myth of Pandora in the *Theogony* (570–612) seems unconcerned with women's role as producer of children. Indeed, the theme of fertility is notably absent, and there is no effort to elucidate any determinate characteristics of a feminine identity. Further, women and men are not portrayed as constituent parts of the greater whole, of "humankind." Pandora is not a complementary partner to "man" within the more general category of *anthropoi*. Instead, the appearance of Pandora shatters the previous unity of the human species. This is an *asymmetrical* theory of gender. Though I will shortly examine Loraux' analysis in greater detail, it is worth pointing out at the outset a major point of disagreement—a disagreement that is central to the claims of this chapter. Loraux contrasts an asymmetrical theory of gender in Hesiod with a symmetrical theory of gender said to prevail in the Homeric poems: "In Homer . . . everything is simpler," and there is a "relationship of happy complementarity between the two sexes: the *philotes*, or sexual love, that unites men and women."[11] Prima facie, this claim is reasonable. The *Iliad* and the *Odyssey* seem relatively unconcerned with the origins of women, and an alleged *philotes* between Penelope and Odysseus continues to be the basis for criticism of the later books of the epic. Loraux' judgment certainly has been followed by the vast majority of feminist criticism of the *Odyssey*, which has for the most part accepted that a theory of gender symmetry lies behind the poem. In sharp contrast, my first claim is that Odysseus' interaction with Nausicaa is a similar tale of the origin of gender and that it leads to a separation of the "race of women" from men. As such, this tale repeats, in significant ways, much of the asymmetry that forms the basis for Loraux' elegant reading of the myth of Pandora.

Let us now go to the heart of Loraux' argument about gender in the *Theogony*, by considering her commentary on the following lines.

> ἐκ τῆς γὰρ γένος ἐστὶ γυναικῶν θηλυτεράων,
> τῆς γὰρ ὀλοίιόν ἐστι γένος καὶ φῦλα γυναικῶν
>
> (*Theog.* 590–91)
>
> [The race of women and all femininity come from her (the first woman)
> From her comes that cursed race, the tribes of women.][12]

Loraux makes the following, apt remark on these lines: "[W]omen are descended from womankind alone, produced originally as Pandora, a solitary sample, in contrast to the collectivity that is already an established principle of mankind." Pandora is mother not of humanity, as might be expected in such a myth of origins, but of women: "The tradition is born in heterodoxy, and the founding text situates the race of women in an original state of separation." Before the arrival of Pandora, it was not "men," *andres*, who existed, but *anthropoi*, humanity. It was not just humanity, however, but "men and gods," whose happy partnership is shattered by the arrival of the *genos gunaikon*: "As the instrument of this rift, woman separates men from gods. Better yet, she separates them from themselves, since she introduces sexuality, that asymmetry of self and other."[13] Loraux here concurs with Pucci, who sees in the ambiguity of the first woman, a *kalon kakon*, the sign of humanity's fall.[14] But if woman is a sign of the fall of humanity, of its separation from a happier time when it was closer to the gods, this does not make woman the *cause* of that fall—at least not the efficient cause. If, in Hesiod's tale of origins, it is easy to conflate the two, it is nevertheless important to note that woman arrives on the scene too late to function as cause. The rift between men and gods has already happened (through Prometheus' tricking of Zeus), and she is no more than the figure that represents that rift. This misrecognition of sign as cause is the source of much of Greek misogyny; it is the patriarchal error par excellence, and it will be important for my later analysis of the *Odyssey*'s most famous misogynist, Agamemnon. For now, let us continue to follow Loraux.

If Pandora separates humans from the gods, she does so by an association with artifice and culture. Zeus creates her, but her birth is also due to the craft of Hephaestus and Athena, the goddess of *metis*.

> γαίης γὰρ σύμπλασσε περικλυτὸς Ἀμφιγυήεις
> παρθένῳ αἰδοίῃ ἴκελον Κρονίδεω διὰ βουλάς·
> ζῶσε δὲ καὶ κόσμησε θεὰ γλαυκῶπις Ἀθήνη
> ἀργυφέῃ ἐσθῆτι· κατὰ κρῆθεν δὲ καλύπτρην
> δαιδαλέην χείρεσσι κατέσχεθε, θαῦμα ἰδέσθαι·
> [ἀμφὶ δέ οἱ στεφάνους νεοθηλέας, ἄνθεα ποίης,
> ἱμερτοὺς περίθηκε καρήατι Παλλὰς Ἀθήνη·]
> ἀμφὶ δέ οἱ στεφάνην χρυσέην κεφαλῆφιν ἔθηκε,
> τὴν αὐτὸς ποίησε περικλυτὸς Ἀμφιγυήεις
> ἀσκήσας παλάμῃσι, χαριζόμενος Διὶ πατρί.
>
> (*Theog.* 571–80)

[The very famous limping god fashioned from earth
the likeness of a shy maiden, in accordance with the will of Cronos'
 son.
The bright-eyed goddess Athena girded and beautified her
with shining clothing; she spread down from her head an

embroidered veil, a wonder to look at.
And Pallas Athena put around her head lovely garlands,
flowers of newly grown herbs.
She also put on her head a golden crown
which the limping god himself made
working it with his own hands, doing favor to father Zeus.]

(translation modified)[15]

The trappings of Pandora suggest a figure of deception. But, as Loraux argues, we cannot quite dismiss the "evil" of woman as the consequence of a "trap of simple appearances," as if "woman" persistently and deceptively hid a secret of woman. We need first to pose a further question.

> Is woman, then, a trap of simple appearances? I suspect that such a reading of the text might lead us to dismiss an important question: indeed, what makes the woman into a wholly exterior being in the first place? Certainly the notion of disguise is an essential part of the veil, and likewise a part of the word *kalyptre* (the word for veil, from the verb "to conceal"). Yet, unlike the "veiled woman" from the Indo-European myths so dear to Georges Dumezil, the creature in the *Theogony* is no hidden form beneath deceitful disguise. Her veil does not conceal anything other than a woman: not a god, a demon, or a man. It hides nothing, because the woman has no interior to conceal. In short, in the *Theogony*, the first woman *is* her adornments—she has no body.

Much of Loraux' later analysis follows from this shrewd observation. Pandora, as a *parthenos*, is in no way a fixed identity: rather, because she is a mask without an original, she signifies the failure of every identity. She stages determinate identities, but she does not do so in the name of any determinate identity—she has no fixed interior to conceal. This disturbing aspect of the *parthenos* effectively undermines any discourse about gender that would seek to anchor the representation of woman in the natural world. This provides an important twist to the importance attached within Greek culture to the passage from unwedded virgin to wife, from *parthenos* to *gyne*.[16] Within the Greek discourse that seeks to impose a natural identity on women, the shift from *parthenos* to *gyne* signals the shift between two fixed identities: a single, virginal girl becomes a *gyne* through marriage. But the depiction of the *parthenos* as a challenge to every identity means that this process is undermined—there is always the possibility that any natural identity of woman is no more than the mask of the *parthenos*. The distinctness of the *gyne* is potentially challenged. It is this ambiguity that, Loraux suggests, is created by Zeus' fabrication of Pandora.[17]

πρῶτος γὰρ ῥα Διὸς πλαστὴν ὑπέδεκτο γυναῖκα
παρθένον.

(*Theog.* 513–14)

[He [Epimetheus] first received the *parthenos gyne* from Zeus.]

Epimetheus receives Pandora; but he receives her as a woman who is both a *gyne* and a *parthenos*. Any separation of the two into "natural" roles is a denial of the ambiguity that is present from the moment of her creation. Phaeacia is a fantasized society where communication is perfect and there is no deceit. In terms of gender, it can hardly countenance the kind of radical ambiguity of social roles posed by the figure of the *parthenos*. Indeed, the perfect, unquestioned, gendered identities that seem to be on display on Phaeacia are a symptom of the absence of the *parthenos*. Odysseus' arrival, as we shall see, changes this. But we might also note the link between the story of Pandora and the other myths of origin described earlier. For Pandora is an actualization of the potential problem set up in the myth of Deucalion and Pyrrha. The blindness to sexual origins has, as its logical correlate, a woman who is pure seeming, who bears masks of identity with nothing to guarantee them. We might even read Protagoras' tale as exhibiting a horror at the collapse of masks, the removal of the gap between inside and outside that the *parthenos* represents.

Arete as Gyne

Now let us turn to the women on Phaeacia. I argued in chapter 5 that Demodocus' tale of the originary *neikos* between Achilles and Odysseus looked forward to the *neikos* between Odysseus and Euryalus that lured Odysseus into the games on Phaeacia. Odysseus' victory introduced the Phaeacians to loss; before his arrival, every traveler had been defeated and passed on to his destination, preserving the internal solidarity of Phaeacian society. Odysseus destroys the Phaeacians' feeling of omnipotence. The quarrel with Odysseus leads to a scission in Phaeacian society, which is ultimately made permanent by the mountain that is left hovering over the Phaeacian's island. Yet it is not accurate to say that there was never a *neikos* before Odysseus' arrival. There were plenty of quarrels, but they had a fleeting existence, disappearing the moment they came into being, resolved by Arete, the idealized wife of Alcinous. Here is the disguised Athena's description of her.

. . . Ἀρήτην· τὴν δ' Ἀλκίνοος ποιήσατ' ἄκοιτιν
καί μιν ἔτισ' ὡς οὔ τις ἐπὶ χθονὶ τίεται ἄλλη,

> ὅσσαι νῦν γε γυναῖκες ὑπ' ἀνδράσιν οἶκον ἔχουσιν.
> ὣς κείνη περὶ κῆρι τετίμηταί τε καὶ ἔστιν
> ἔκ τε φίλων παίδων ἔκ τ' αὐτοῦ Ἀλκινόοιο
> καὶ λαῶν, οἵ μίν ῥα θεὸν ὣς εἰσορόωντες
> δειδέχαται μύθοισιν, ὅτε στείχῃσ' ἀνὰ ἄστυ.
> οὐ μὲν γάρ τι νόου γε καὶ αὐτὴ δεύεται ἐσθλοῦ,
> οἷσί τ' ἐΰ φρονέῃσι, καὶ ἀνδράσι νείκεα λύει.
>
> (Od. 7.66–74)

> [... Arete, and Alkinoos made her his wife, and gave her
> such pride of place as no other woman on earth is given
> of such women as are now alive and keep house for husbands.
> So she was held high in the heart and still she is so,
> by her beloved children, by Alkinoos himself, and by
> the people, who look toward her as to a god when they see her,
> and speak in salutation as she walks about in her city.
> For there is no good intelligence that she herself lacks.
> She dissolves quarrels, even among men, when she favors them.]

Arete is the perfect idealized *gyne*. She keeps house for her husband but remains subservient to him. In return for this, she is honored. Her abilities are clearly exceptional. But it is worth asking what these abilities mean for Phaeacian society as a whole. What is the significance of her dissolution of quarrels "even among men" and what sort of quarrels between men might these be? Here, we might look outside of Phaeacia to the major quarrels between men that dominate the poem—the constant tension between Odysseus and the suitors over who will win over Penelope. Indeed, tension between the suitors themselves quickly erupts during the bow contest after a series of them fail to string it. Antinous responds to this tension by refusing to try to string the bow. When the disguised Odysseus begs for permission to string it himself, Antinous reminds Odysseus—and the other suitors—of a previous gathering where fighting broke out.

> The honeyed wine has hurt you, as it has distracted
> others as well, who gulp it down without drinking in season.
> It was wine also that drove the Centaur, famous Eurytion,
> distracted in the palace of great-hearted Peirithoös
> when he visited the Lapiths. His brain went wild with drinking,
> and in his fury he did much harm in the house of Peirithoös.
>
> (Od. 21.293–98)

Antinous only mentions the quarrel between men. He tactfully leaves unsaid that this quarrel between the Lapiths and the Centaurs is a quarrel over a woman (for, drunk with wine, Eurytion tried to carry off Peirothoös' bride, Hippodameia). By seeking to postpone the contest of the bow, Antinous tries to maintain the atmosphere of the feast and resolve the tension produced when intramale competition seems to be on the verge of disrupting that enjoyment. Of course, he fails. But in his near success, we can appreciate the sort of skill Arete appears to have. Her ability to resolve quarrels between men over women maintains a certain sort of gender harmony on Phaeacia. Accordingly, we can relate the exceptional abilities of Arete to the wider, idealized picture of gender politics on Phaeacia. There is a perfect division of sexual roles: just as Phaeacian men are skilled in sailing ships, so the women are "skilled in weaving and dowered with wisdom bestowed by Athene, to be expert in beautiful work, to have good character" (*Od.* 7.109–10). Because Phaeacian women epitomize a certain ideal of womanhood, there is no reason for Phaeacian men to doubt them. Both sexes know who they are. The neatness of this identity split is guaranteed by Arete herself, who resolves the quarrels that potentially could disrupt it. In the terms of Loraux, the dangers represented by the *parthenos* are nowhere to be found. Arete is only ever the solution to problems, never the troubling sign of them.

Let us consider this role of Arete with regard to the general competitive atmosphere on Phaeacia. There is clearly a system of competition on Phaeacia, as exemplified in the games. Yet these are games the Phaeacians never lose to outsiders. Their constant victories over outsiders preserve an internal solidarity. But what is the source of the quarrels between Phaeacians? Quarrels occur because of jostling for positions within a hierarchy; one member of the society seeks to win regardless of the cost for social cohesion. Precisely such asocial figures, the Cyclopes, have been successfully banished from Phaeacian society. The Cyclops care nothing for *aidos*, the spirit of collective renunciation that structures the social. This banishing of figures who want to win at all costs might suggest that there would be no desire at all for competition on Phaeacia, yet the Phaeacians continue to play their painless series of games. How can they do this? Any quarrel that might arise from the playing of the games is immediately ironed out by the tension-resolving qualities of Arete. The Phaeacians try to have it both ways: they wish to banish the destructive aspects of competition (which undermine the harmony of social life), but they still want to continue to play the game. Arete appears as a symptom of this indecision—a symptom in the precise Freudian sense of a compromise formation.[18] She allows the Phaeacian men to play the games without the destructive aspects of quarrels that result from games. She helps preserve the illusion that games can be played without any of the destructive social consequences normally associated with loss.

It is worth lingering over this picture of Phaeacia. If we view Phaeacia as an imaginary, idealized society that has never experienced loss, then the "quarrels" resolved by Arete cannot be real quarrels, because the knowledge of the destructive nature of such quarrels (should they not be resolved) is simply not yet available to the Phaeacians. They are fundamentally innocent. But, of course, we could see the Phaeacians as an embryonic human society that represses this possibility of loss. Their belief in their own omnipotence can only occur if they repress the unconscious knowledge of their own infallibility. But the repressed returns in a pair of symptoms: the Phaeacians' notorious "unfriendliness" and the peculiar person of Arete.[19]

Arete's status as compromise formation is also evident in her quasi-divine status. She is honored "like a god" (*Od.* 7.71). Indeed, her status helps clarify the strange relationship the Phaeacians have with the gods. For though the Phaeacians sacrifice to the gods, it is unclear why. Sacrifice, as a particular mode of communication between humans and gods, depends, in human society, on the possibility of its failure. The gods inhabit a world exterior to the human one, yet one that is believed to have a relation to it. Sacrifice attempts to bridge the gap. Yet the Phaeacians interact openly with the gods; there is no mystery in these interactions, no unknown world beyond that of Phaeacia. But the Phaeacians themselves are not gods. They live in a halfway house between humans (who are split off from gods) and gods (who are not subject to human life cycles). Arete allows them to preserve this position. They worship her as if she was a god. She has a paradoxical presence in the world of Phaeacia: though part of the Phaeacian *genos*, she nevertheless is worshiped as if she was superior to it. Though "one of them," her qualities are nevertheless incomprehensible, godlike.[20] If the Phaeacians have a godlike existence, it is the skills of Arete that allow them to maintain it.

Zizek has provided the following definition of a symptom: a symptom is "a formation whose very consistency implies a certain non-knowledge on the part of the subject: the subject can 'enjoy his symptom' only insofar as its logic escapes him."[21] To interpret the symptom correctly is to dissolve it. On Phaeacia, the existence of Arete as idealized woman (resolver of quarrels) is correlative to Phaeacian nonknowledge concerning the possibility of loss (represented by their ongoing success in the games). Her status as quasi-divine is correlative to Phaeacian nonknowledge concerning the inscrutability of the world of the gods, their separation from mortals. All the myths of origin I have considered in this chapter focus on an original gap of utter loss that opens up as a human society emerges; Arete is a figure who masks that very gap.

From Parthenos to Gyne

If there is no trace of the untrustworthiness of the *parthenos* on Phaeacia, there are certainly virgin maidens. For the episode on Phaeacia lingers over the status of Nausicaa, a young girl on the verge of marriage. But what is significant about this coming-of-age of Nausicaa is the knowingness of the protagonists, Alcinous and Nausicaa herself. In human society, this rite of passage is fraught with difficulty and danger, a danger that the mask-wearing *parthenos* highlights. But the lack of worry exhibited by Alcinous for Nausicaa at this crucial stage for the continuation of a species' social identity suggests that we need to imagine a world in which the transfer from *parthenos* to *gyne* passes without a hitch. For it seems to create no obvious anxiety on the part of the ruling men. It is precisely such an idealized succession from virginity to womanhood that the *Odyssey* begins to depict for Nausicaa—until the arrival of Odysseus complicates matters. For he explodes the harmony that had previously characterized her relationship to her parents.

At the beginning of book 6, Nausicaa is approached by Athena in disguise. Athena suggests that Nausicaa should do the Phaeacian washing, but in such a manner as to emphasize the status of Nausicaa as *parthenos:* she will not stay unmarried long and is being courted by the best of the Phaeacians (*Od.* 6.34–36). When Nausicaa relays the message of Athena to her father, she does so in euphemistic terms that tell us much about the situation on Phaeacia.

> ὣς ἔφατ'· αἴδετο γὰρ θαλερὸν γάμον ἐξονομῆναι
> πατρὶ φίλῳ· ὁ δὲ πάντα νόει καὶ ἀμείβετο μύθῳ·
> "οὔτε τοι ἡμιόνων φθονέω, τέκος, οὔτε τευ ἄλλου."
>
> (*Od.* 6.66–68)

> [So she spoke, but she was ashamed to speak of her joyful
> marriage to her dear father, but he understood all and answered:
> "I do not begrudge you the mules, child, nor anything
> else."]

Nausicaa's actions and words are governed by *aidos,* shame. She does not speak openly about her desire for marriage. But her silence is immediately recognized by her father. There is nothing unexpected or deceitful in the desire of this virgin maiden. The father, Alcinous, whose name itself indicates the strength of his *noos,* understands everything: πάντα νόει.[22] This ability to understand everything undermines the possibility of any "feminine" deceit on Phaeacia: the reason the passage from *parthenos* to *gyne* is unproblematic is because it is regulated under the all-knowing *noos* of the father. This infallible paternal power should cause us to pause over the *aidos* shown by Nausicaa, for it has the effect of emptying out the significance normally associated with the concept. *Aidos* is a reflective behavior that lingers on the necessity of the recognition of a common loss in order to preserve the social. It depends on a shared renunciation. This renunciation opens up the possibility of a satisfaction of desire outside of the realm of the social: it is thus an indication of the limit of paternal authority (which only polices the realm of the social), not part of the limitlessness of paternal authority.

In Nausicaa's case, what she seems to desire is immediately revealed by Alcinous' remarks. Her desire is already understood by her father, even though it is not articulated. We can explain this further by contrasting this desire with what psychoanalysis suggests is properly human desire.[23] For psychoanalysis, there is no desire without a prohibition. The prohibition sets up a limit, and desire comes into being as a desire to transgress this limit. On Phaeacia, Nausicaa's desire is in no way transgressive; for her father already knows what she wants and is quite happy to go along with it.[24] Nausicaa renounces nothing. Alcinous wants to help bring to fulfillment the desire that she does not speak but that he nevertheless knows. In Lacan's terms, "desire" is what is left over after every need enunciated in a demand has been satisfied. For Nausicaa, no such leftover exists: it is immediately short-circuited, rerouted into the reservoir of knowingness of her father. Her demand for a husband is understood by her father and will be satisfied. Nothing remains, which suggests that her desire is not a true, human desire. Her feeling of *aidos* is equally paradoxical; insofar as she is aware of nothing outside the parameters of paternal law, it is an unreflective "shame"—that is, not shame at all.[25]

Enter Pandora

Let us now turn to the encounter between Nausicaa and Odysseus. Their meeting is elaborately prepared within the narrative. Odysseus is asleep, and the Phaeacian maidens are playing catch with a ball. At this point, Athena intervenes with a stratagem.

> ἔνθ' αὖτ' ἄλλ' ἐνόησε θεὰ γλαυκῶπις Ἀθήνη,
> ὡς Ὀδυσεὺς ἔγροιτο, ἴδοι τ' εὐώπιδα κούρην,
> ἥ οἱ Φαιήκων ἀνδρῶν πόλιν ἡγήσαιτο.
> σφαῖραν ἔπειτ' ἔρριψε μετ' ἀμφίπολον βασίλεια·
> ἀμφιπόλου μὲν ἅμαρτε, βαθείῃ δ' ἔμβαλε δίνῃ.
> αἱ δ' ἐπὶ μακρὸν ἄϋσαν· ὁ δ' ἔγρετο δῖος Ὀδυσσεύς.

(*Od.* 6.112–17)

[[T]hen the grey-eyed goddess Athene thought what to do next;
how Odysseus should awake, and see the well-favored young girl,
and she should be his guide to the city of the Phaiakians.
Now the princess threw the ball toward one handmaiden,
and missed the girl, and the ball went into the swirling water,
and they all cried out aloud, and noble Odysseus wakened.]

Is this a simple narrative maneuver to begin the episode, or does it have more symbolic significance? We will find out later in the poem that one of the Phaeacian skills that is unsurpassed (and, as they believe, unsurpassable) is dancing. In book 8, after their defeat in the games, Odysseus marvels at the Phaeacian dancers, who also play catch with a ball, a *sphaira*.

οἱ δ' ἐπεὶ οὖν σφαῖραν καλὴν μετὰ χερσὶν ἕλοντο,
πορφυρέην, τήν σφιν Πόλυβος ποίησε δαΐφρων,
τὴν ἕτερος ῥίπτασκε ποτὶ νέφεα σκιόεντα
ἰδνωθεὶς ὀπίσω· ὁ δ' ἀπὸ χθονὸς ὑψόσ' ἀερθεὶς
ῥηϊδίως μεθέλεσκε, πάρος ποσὶν οὖδας ἱκέσθαι.

(*Od.* 8.372–76)

[These two, after they had taken up in their hands the ball, a beautiful thing, red, which Polybos the skilled craftsmen had made them, one of them, bending far back, would throw it up to the shadowy clouds, and the other, going high off the ground, would easily catch it again, before his feet came back to the ground.]

The Phaeacians are perfect dancers who never drop the ball.[26] Yet Odysseus' arrival on Phaeacia coincides with a Phaeacian game of catch in which a ball is dropped. But it is dropped in a particular manner. Nausicaa's throw misses its target, and the ball disappears into the sea, out of her reach.[27] The ball escapes from the limits of Phaeacian society and points toward a realm beyond their boundaries, out of reach of Nausicaa. This not only contrasts with the perfection of the later throws during the Phaeacian dance; it also parallels Odysseus' discus throw. In the games with the Phaeacian men, he, too, makes a throw that travels to a point beyond the frame of reference of the Phaeacian competitors. That throw opened up the possibility of loss to the Phaeacians, as does the missed throw of Nausicaa. The loss of the ball makes Nausicaa aware of a limit on Phaeacia, and this awareness coincides with the appearance of Odysseus.

If the missed throw opens a wound in Phaeacian society, signaling its limitations and the possibility of something different beyond that limit, this wound is immediately covered by Odysseus. He moves into the gap opened up beyond the island of Phaeacia by the lost ball. The loss of the ball promises to introduce Nausicaa to her desire, because she is on the verge of experiencing loss: the lost ball might cause her to seek something "out of reach," unattainable.[28] But this confrontation is postponed, because Odysseus immediately moves into the realm of the "beyond" opened up by the loss of the ball. Odysseus' later success in the discus can be seen as a confirmation of the effects of the dropped ball of Nausicaa. Before his appearance on Phaeacia, there had only been a string of heroes who competed with the Phaeacians, and all were defeated.[29] Odysseus proves himself to be an outsider who is better than the *aristoi* on Phaeacia, and consequently Nausicaa desires him as the first outsider who is better than the representatives of her own *genos*. Because the earlier arrivals had been inferior to the Phaeacians, there was no reason for Nausicaa to desire them. The throw of the ball into the unknowable beyond opens up a space for Nausicaa's fantasies, a place from where Phaeacia, as a complete society, can be judged.[30] Odysseus is the first to move into that space, promising to heal the wound opened up by the loss of the ball. Odysseus will of course leave, but the society of the Phaeacians is transformed by this departure. Nausicaa no longer unreflectively desires the men of her *genos*. She will always want something more than they have to offer. In short, she becomes a true *parthenos*. If she is later to play the role of *gyne*, professing allegiance to a single adult male on Phaeacia, the male will constantly appreciate that her allegiance to him is undermined by the unspoken desire for something more—a desire that he will be utterly unable to fathom. Despite all future protestations of her fidelity, there will now always be the danger of a breach of that fidelity; Phaeacia will have lost its innocence.

We can also explain this change on Phaeacia in terms of Nausicaa's relationship to shame. Before Odysseus' entrance, Nausicaa's shame was hollow, part of a social game that was always already understood and thus not real. Her ignorance of the possibility of transgressing paternal law meant that she had nothing to be ashamed of. Odysseus' entrance provides her with the desire for something prohibited, in the figure of the superior Odysseus. Nausicaa is then on the verge of becoming a liminal figure, less bound by the limits of Phaeacian society, precisely because she is aware of something beyond those limits. She therefore desires more than Phaeacian males have to offer. For Freud, the disquieting reality of the sexual instinct lay in the way it resisted satisfaction: "We must reckon with the possibility that something in the nature of the sexual instinct itself is unfavourable to the realization of complete satisfaction."[31] The entrance and disappearance of Odysseus forces Nausicaa to confront an unsatisfied desire. Because her desire exceeds the boundaries of Phaeacia, she provides a profound threat to any stable sense of identity (male or female) within Phaeacian society.

The fall of the Phaeacians, their entrance to the realm of mortality, is thus intimately associated with the emergence of Nausicaa's desire. For as soon as the Phaeacians become aware of the limits of their society, they are immediately torn asunder from their happy, open relationship with the gods. With this in mind, let us look more closely at Nausicaa's initial trip to the shore to wash clothes. The time and place of the encounter of the Phaeacian maidens is elaborately described. Though they initially appear to be going to a river, it later becomes clear that it must be the mouth of a river by the seashore.[32] When Odysseus later recounts the tale to Arete in the following book, we discover that he fails to mention the maidens' screams; instead, he claims to have been awoken by the rays of the midday sun.[33] These features in themselves duplicate the scenario in which Eidothea tricked Proteus; he emerged from the sea onto the shore at midday, the liminal mythic time that blurs the boundaries between humans and gods. In *Odyssey* 6, we find ourselves once more in a situation that evokes epiphany, an in-between time that facilitates the merging of the human and divine worlds but that also renders nonreflective immortals vulnerable. The tricking of Proteus dragged the immortal god into the reflective realm of mortals; so, too, Nausicaa will lose her unreflective innocence and enter the mortal world of desire. The vulnerability of the Phaeacian maidens (though they themselves are blissfully unaware of this vulnerability) is highlighted in the manner of their dance; before it begins, they remove their veils. If this helps create a mood of eroticism, there is also the darker motif of a possible rape.[34] The general atmosphere of vulnerability is enhanced by the striking similarity, long noted by commentators, between the careful packing of the wagon and mules with the paraphernalia required for the washing and another famous epic journey: Priam's descent on his wagon into the tent of Achilles in *Iliad* 24.[35] The *katabasis* motif is replayed here, as Nausicaa and the maidens enter a zone between the mortal and immortal worlds. What follows will definitively split them off from their unreflective, carefree universes.

But perhaps most interesting of all is the manner in which the arrival of Odysseus replays the moment of the original split that separated the Phaeacians from the Cyclopes. When Odysseus arrives, his appearance horrifies the Phaeacian maidens. This is quite understandable, as the narrative emphasizes his bestiality, in an important simile.

ὣς εἰπὼν θάμνων ὑπεδύσετο δῖος Ὀδυσσεύς,
ἐκ πυκινῆς δ' ὕλης πτόρθον κλάσε χειρὶ παχείῃ
φύλλων, ὡς ῥύσαιτο περὶ χροῒ μήδεα φωτός.
βῆ δ' ἴμεν ὥς τε λέων ὀρεσίτροφος, ἀλκὶ πεποιθώς,

ὅς τ' εἶσ' ὑόμενος καὶ ἀήμενος, ἐν δέ οἱ ὄσσε
δαίεται· αὐτὰρ ὁ βουσὶ μετέρχεται ἢ ὀΐεσσιν
ἠὲ μετ' ἀγροτέρας ἐλάφους· κέλεται δέ ἑ γαστὴρ
μήλων πειρήσοντα καὶ ἐς πυκινὸν δόμον ἐλθεῖν·
ὣς Ὀδυσεὺς κούρῃσιν ἐϋπλοκάμοισιν ἔμελλε
μείξεσθαι, γυμνός περ ἐών· χρειὼ γὰρ ἵκανε.
σμερδαλέος δ' αὐτῇσι φάνη κεκακωμένος ἅλμῃ,
τρέσσαν δ' ἄλλυδις ἄλλη ἐπ' ἠϊόνας προὐχούσας.
οἴη δ' Ἀλκινόου θυγάτηρ μένε· τῇ γὰρ Ἀθήνη
θάρσος ἐνὶ φρεσὶ θῆκε καὶ ἐκ δέος εἵλετο γυίων.

(*Od.* 6.127–40)

[So speaking, great Odysseus came from under his thicket,
and from the dense foliage with his heavy hand he broke off
a leafy branch to cover his body and hide the male parts,
and went in the confidence of his strength, like some hill-kept lion,
who advances, though he is rained on and blown by the wind, and both
eyes kindle; he goes out after cattle or sheep, or it may be
deer in the wilderness, and his belly is urgent upon him
to get inside of a close steading and go for the sheepflocks.
So Odysseus was ready to face young girls with well-ordered
hair, naked though he was, for the need was on him; and yet,
he appeared terrifying to them, all crusted with dry spray,
and they scattered one way and another down the jutting beaches.
Only the daughter of Alkinoos stood fast, for Athene
put courage into her heart, and took the fear from her body.]

Except for Nausicaa, the maidens all flee, believing something bestial, inhuman, has arrived on Phaeacia. The peace now prevalent on Phaeacia was instituted when Nausithous fled the monstrous Cyclopes, who had harmed them with their might (*Od.* 6.55 ff.). The surprise and terror of the maidens can be explained by the success of the former split. Since Nausithous led the Phaeacians away from Hyperia and the Cyclopes, no such monstrous man has appeared on Scheria. Yet on this occasion, the flight is not total; Athena intervenes to take away the fear from Nausicaa, who alone refuses to flee (*Od.* 6.139–40). Nausicaa then tries to persuade the other girls not to flee, but in a significant way. She argues, in effect, that the original splitting off from the Cyclopes holds good and that it is inconceivable for a violent man to intrude into Phaeacian society.

στῆτέ μοι ἀμφίπολοι· πόσε φεύγετε φῶτα ἰδοῦσαι;
ἦ μή πού τινα δυσμενέων φάσθ' ἔμμεναι ἀνδρῶν;
οὐκ ἔσθ' οὗτος ἀνὴρ διερὸς βροτὸς οὐδὲ γένηται,
ὅς κεν Φαιήκων ἀνδρῶν ἐς γαῖαν ἵκηται
δηϊοτῆτα φέρων· μάλα γὰρ φίλοι ἀθανάτοισιν.
οἰκέομεν δ' ἀπάνευθε πολυκλύστῳ ἐνὶ πόντῳ,
ἔσχατοι, οὐδέ τις ἄμμι βροτῶν ἐπιμίσγεται ἄλλος.

(*Od.* 6.199–205)

[Stand fast, girls. Where are you flying, just because you have looked on
a man? Do you think this is some enemy coming against us?
There is no such man living nor can there ever be one
who can come into the land of the Phaiakians bringing
warlike attack; we are so very dear to the immortals,
and we live far apart by ourselves in the wash of the great sea
at the utter end, nor do any other people mix with us.]

Nausicaa's words seem persuasive. After all, Odysseus, the civilized hero of the poem, is certainly not a Cyclops. But he does function as one for the Phaeacians—that is, he plays the role of a Cyclops to perfection. The Cyclops had earlier been described as creatures with far greater *bie* than the Phaeacians and as a species who were hostile to them. Odysseus' discus throw will soon show that he is far greater in *bie*, and his presence is destined to destroy Phaeacian society.[36] The result of the total flight from the Cyclopes was the creation of an enclosed, endogamous society, where paternal law functioned perfectly because everyone was subject to it and where external visitors were always inferior to the Phaeacians. Nausicaa argues as if this situation was destined to continue forever. But the dropping of the ball and the entrance of Odysseus into her fantasy frame have already changed this.[37]

To explain this event, I borrow the terms used in the story of origins of Protagoras. In that story, the perfection of the social world is created by the renunciation of all (adult, male) citizens, rendering anyone who refuses the renunciation a madman. Here, the encounter between Odysseus and Nausicaa heralds the return of the (banished) madman to the world of Phaeacia. Nausicaa will never be content with the attentions of Phaeacian men again but will always want something more, something beyond the limits of Phaeacian civilization. From the perspective of Phaeacian men (caught within the constraints of paternal law), this desire will seem inexplicable: they are confronted with the traumatic, unanswerable question, what does a woman want? The return of Odysseus thus functions as the return of a Cyclops, a reappearance of that which had been disavowed in the founding gesture of Phaeacian civilization.

This provides a very different context for Odysseus' words of praise to Nausicaa, words that Loraux provided as evidence for the "conventional" depiction of complementary gender identities in the Odyssey.[38] Odysseus first compares her to a god but then lists her human attributes.

> εἰ δέ τίς ἐσσι βροτῶν, οἳ ἐπὶ χθονὶ ναιετάουσι,
> τρισμάκαρες μὲν σοί γε πατὴρ καὶ πότνια μήτηρ,
> τρισμάκαρες δὲ κασίγνητοι· μάλα πού σφισι θυμὸς
> αἰὲν ἐϋφροσύνῃσιν ἰαίνεται εἵνεκα σεῖο,
> λευσσόντων τοιόνδε θάλος χορὸν εἰσοιχνεῦσαν.
> κεῖνος δ' αὖ περὶ κῆρι μακάρτατος ἔξοχον ἄλλων,
> ὅς κέ σ' ἐέδνοισι βρίσας οἶκόνδ' ἀγάγηται.
> οὐ γάρ πω τοιοῦτον ἐγὼ ἴδον ὀφθαλμοῖσιν,
> οὔτ' ἄνδρ' οὔτε γυναῖκα· σέβας μ' ἔχει εἰσορόωντα.
>
> (*Od.* 6.153–61)

[But if you are one among those mortals who live in this country,
three times blessed are your father and the lady your mother,
and three times blessed your brothers too, and I know their spirits
are warmed forever with happiness at the thought of you, seeing
such a slip of beauty taking her place in the chorus of dancers;
but blessed at the heart, even beyond these others, is that one
who, after loading you down with gifts, leads you as his bride
home. I have never with these eyes seen anything like you,
neither man nor woman. Wonder takes me as I look on you.]

Odysseus describes Nausicaa as a woman of extraordinary beauty, but in the quiet reference to a competition between males for her hand in marriage, there is, I think, an inevitable comparison to Helen. We can compare this description of Nausicaa with the later description of Arete. If Arete dissolves the quarrels between men, Nausicaa looks suspiciously like a woman whose excessive beauty, at least as noticed by Odysseus, could create those quarrels. Odysseus describes her as if she was more than a simple virgin; rather, she now embodies the darker characteristics of a *parthenos*. This might account for Odysseus' strange praise of her as surpassing any man *or* woman he has seen. The crucial feature of the *parthenos* is that she challenges the identity of woman; she is neither unproblematically a virgin maiden nor a *gyne* but plays the role of both. To return to Loraux, the *parthenos* is a series of representations hiding nothing, providing a challenge to every identity, but (necessarily) on behalf of no particular identity. Before Odysseus' entrance to Phaeacia, gender roles there had been perfectly distributed: it was a world where everyone's gendered identity was fixed. On Phaeacia, gender was not the sign of a fall from an original state of grace. Nausicaa changes this, because she begins to desire, which in turn casts a shadow over the perfection of Phaeacian society. She will no longer be content with the Phaeacian man apportioned to her as husband, which will in turn destroy any easy parity between the sexes. Her desire introduces sexual asymmetry. Rather than "equal," symmetrical gendered identities of man and woman, who play complementary roles, the situation becomes different; men will continue to play games amongst themselves on Phaeacia, and these male games will be part of a fight to prove themselves worthy for women. But a new worry now haunts these games: will the women ever be satisfied with their efforts? Before Nausicaa's emergence as *parthenos*, the Phaeacian women, epitomized by Arete, were both the motivators of the games and those who helped resolve the destructive aspect of the competitions. After, they lose their trustworthiness as arbitrators, because there is the constant danger of their dissatisfaction with Phaeacian society. Their previous gendered identities have been radically undermined; they are about to embark on a world where those identities, no longer certain, will be constantly contested.

Aidos *as Reflection*

I have already suggested the importance of the reflective nature of *aidos* and the problem of Nausicaa's initial shame before her father, which he immediately sees through. But things become more complicated after the meeting with Odysseus. When Odysseus tells Alcinous of his encounter with Nausicaa, he suggests that Nausicaa was at fault for not bringing the suppliant straight to him. In response, Odysseus notoriously lies on Nausicaa's behalf.

> "ξεῖν', ἦ τοι μὲν τοῦτό γ' ἐναίσιμον οὐκ ἐνόησε
> παῖς ἐμή, οὕνεκά σ' οὔ τι μετ' ἀμφιπόλοισι γυναιξὶν
> ἦγεν ἐς ἡμετέρου· σὺ δ' ἄρα πρώτην ἱκέτευσας."
>   τὸν δ' ἀπαμειβόμενος προσέφη πολύμητις Ὀδυσσεύς·
> "ἥρως, μή μοι τοὔνεκ' ἀμύμονα νείκεε κούρην·
> ἡ μὲν γάρ μ' ἐκέλευε σὺν ἀμφιπόλοισιν ἕπεσθαι,
> ἀλλ' ἐγὼ οὐκ ἔθελον δείσας αἰσχυνόμενός τε,
> μή πως καὶ σοὶ θυμὸς ἐπισκύσσαιτο ἰδόντι·
> δύσζηλοι γάρ τ' εἰμὲν ἐπὶ χθονὶ φῦλ' ἀνθρώπων."
>
> (*Od.* 7.299–307)
>
> ["My friend, here is one proper thought that my daughter was not
> aware of, when she failed to bring you, with her attendants,
> here to our house. It was she to whom you first came as suppliant."

> Then resourceful Odysseus spoke in turn and answered him:
> "Hero, do not for my sake find fault with your blameless daughter.
> She did urge me to follow along with her serving maidens,
> but I for embarrassment and dread was not willing, for fear
> that something in this might stir your spirit to anger seeing us.
> For we who are people upon this earth are jealous in judgment."]

Odysseus' words here are usually explained in terms of his tact. He accepts the blame for Nausicaa's failed concern for his supplication. But things are more complex. For the truth, at first glance, hardly seems detrimental to Nausicaa. Her earlier refusal to accompany him was justified in terms that would seem to epitomize social propriety. She feared the reproaches of the Phaeacian men, who would be jealous of Odysseus as a rival. As a chaste maiden, she agreed that their words would be perfectly appropriate: a woman should not be seen in public with a man before marriage without the permission of her father (*Od.* 6.285 ff.). Odysseus "apologizes" for Nausicaa by transferring the *aidos* shown by her to him. It was he who felt shame, not her. What is so disquieting about the action of Nausicaa that Odysseus chooses to hide it?

We should contrast this show of "shame" and the shame exhibited at the start of book 6. There, the *aidos* shown by Nausicaa was immediately understood: nothing occurred behind the back of the all-knowing father. She had exhibited "desire" for men on Phaeacia in complete accordance with Alcinous' wishes. But the new situation is quite different. For Nausicaa has been confronted (for the first time) with the desire for a non-Phaeacian man. Her feelings of propriety are now opposed to the real possibility of transgression. The failure to bring Odysseus straight to Alcinous suggests that she is aware of this possibility; her shame now works to control this.[39] Before, there would have been no need to reflect on the dangers of bringing a stranger straight to her father, because she would have felt nothing inappropriate in so doing. Such transgression was literally unthinkable for Nausicaa. She articulates her first disapproval for the "mixing" with an outsider only once she dwells on the possibility of transgressing the prohibition. She tells Odysseus that an encounter with a man before marriage without her father's knowledge is inappropriate. The problem is that such an encounter with Odysseus has already happened behind her father's back. Her words of shame are too late: the totality of her father's knowledge is irrevocably punctured. Odysseus' "tact" now takes on a new light. If Alcinous were to find out that his daughter had refused to bring Odysseus to him because of shame, he would have to confront the fact of her desire for Odysseus that occurred behind his back. He would thus be forced to confront the limits of his *noos*.[40] Odysseus allows Alcinous to believe that the shame that occurred during the episode was exhibited by him, an outsider, and not by one of his subjects. He accordingly delays recognition of a wound already opened up on Phaeacia: he persuades Alcinous and delays the effect of the first *neikos* that comes into being as Nausicaa becomes a *parthenos*.

If critics have pounced on this particular Odyssean lie in book 7, they have been silent about another that is just as significant: the reason Odysseus gives for his awakening on the beach.

> εὗδον παννύχιος καὶ ἐπ' ἠῶ καὶ μέσον ἦμαρ·
> δείλετό τ' ἠέλιος, καί με γλυκὺς ὕπνος ἀνῆκεν.
> ἀμφιπόλους δ' ἐπὶ θινὶ τεῆς ἐνόησα θυγατρὸς
> παιζούσας, ἐν δ' αὐτὴ ἔην εἰκυῖα θεῇσι.
> τὴν ἱκέτευσ'· ἡ δ' οὔ τι νοήματος ἤμβροτεν ἐσθλοῦ . . .
> (*Od.* 7.288–92)

[I slept nightlong, and into the dawn, and on to the noonday;
the sun had passed its midpoint,[41] and then the sweet sleep released me.
Then I was aware of your daughter's attendant women playing
on the beach, and she, looking like the goddesses, went there among them.
I supplicated her, nor did she fail of the right decision . . .]

Odysseus' story focuses on the moment of his awakening, a moment already described in book 6. But he is conspicuously silent about the reason why he woke up. The sequence of events in book 6 is clear: Nausicaa drops the ball, the maidens cry out, and Odysseus hears them (*Od.* 6.116 ff.). Odysseus fails to mention the maidens' cries—the most important part of Athena's contrivance to waken him. But Odysseus' words also cannot help reminding us of them, for he tells Alcinous of the perfection of Nausicaa's *noos*: ἡ δ' οὔ τι νοήματος ἤμβροτεν ἐσθλοῦ [Nor did she *fail* of the right decision]. He repeats the most significant word used to describe the event that he chooses not to narrate. Nausicaa *fails* to hit her target with the *sphaira*: ἀμφιπόλου μὲν ἅμαρτε. Odysseus' "tact" prevents Alcinous from finding out about this incident of failure on Phaeacia. He portrays Nausicaa as if she remained a nondesiring woman, and he is silent about the act that introduced her to desire. Why?

The events on Phaeacia all occur with a shadow hanging over the civilization. The disavowal of the possibility of harm from Nausicaa is equivalent to Odysseus' denial of the emergence of self-reflective *aidos* or, indeed, to the Phaeacian flight into believing that their loss in the games was not utterly destructive of their society. The disaster has already happened, and the Phaeacians are living on borrowed time, yet they do not recognize this until after Odysseus leaves and the mountain arrives. The disaster takes place both because of their own disavowal of the change (e.g., Nausicaa's denial of the entrance of a Cyclops-like figure of *bie*) and because of the persuasive powers of Odysseus: Odysseus' *nostos* depends on the ongoing Phaeacian disavowal of the loss of their pseudocivilization.

Penelope as *Parthenos*

When we read the *Odyssey* teleologically, we slip into seeing the inevitable progression of Odysseus homeward. Such a reading, of course, depends on an identification with the poem's hero and leaves us with an adventure story. The hero overcomes every external obstacle that blocks his path homeward. Of course, Odysseus' return is not only to a home but also to a wife—Penelope, the epitome of fidelity, or so he presumably hopes.[1] If we agree that Penelope is thus the goal of Odysseus' *Odyssey*, the perfect representation of "woman" as normative ideal, then a teleological reading of the poem as a slow progression toward this normative goal of woman can be effortlessly constructed. It goes something like this: Odysseus is detained by lots of women on his way home, but insofar as they fall short of Penelope, his partner in his *oikos*, homestead at Ithaca, he cannot be satisfied by them for very long. Calypso detains him on her island, but because she is a goddess, their union is incapable of producing the children that are so essential to an *oikos*. Accordingly the union is barren, lacking in *human* meaning. The most alluring possibility is the appearance of the Phaeacian princess Nausicaa in *Odyssey* 6; the interaction between her and Odysseus suggests a mutual attraction, and indeed, her father explicitly suggests that Odysseus should stay in Phaeacia to marry. Yet if this is an offer of an *oikos*, it is not Odysseus' *oikos*, it is not a full replacement for the wife and son he has lost and now lacks.[2] The narrative depicts the satisfaction of Odysseus' desire, the filling of the lack of homecoming and wife emphasized in the proem (νόστου κεχρημένον ἠδὲ γυναικός [lacking his *nostos* and his wife], *Od.* 1.13).

If this is a story of the failure of the women Odysseus actually meets, there is a subtler—thought fundamentally similar—reading of the poem that emphasizes Penelope's differentiation from other women who have subverted the return (*nostos*) of other heroes. Crucial here is the importance of the figures of Clytemnestra and Helen. This supplementary story, the basis of a book by Katz, is constructed in roughly the following manner: Clytemnestra subverts Agamemnon's return, murdering her husband on his return home.[3] Helen is a figure who remains the epitome of infidelity, who left her husband, Menelaus, for Paris and caused the Trojan War. These figures are important insofar as they provide alternative subplots that threaten to undermine Odysseus' return home. Though Penelope remains faithful, she might yield to the desires of the suitors and thus become a Helen. Though Odysseus hopes to return to a faithful, waiting Penelope, there lurks the possibility that she will have changed into a murderous Clytemnestra. This reading emphasizes the split between return and wife noted in the proem (νόστου κεχρημένον ἠδὲ γυναικός). For Agamemnon's return proves that, in some circumstances, one might want a return without encountering a wife. With the same points of reference, Odysseus' prolonged encounter with the souls of the wives and daughters of princes in the underworld can be explained. Insofar as they provide alternative (per)versions of a woman's role in the *oikos*, they aid in Odysseus' understanding of what a normal woman is. This helps us understand the happiness of the ending, for the safe return of Odysseus to Penelope carries the force of a certain relief. Odysseus returns to a faithful Penelope, not a murderous Clytemnestra, an adulterous Helen, or, from Book 11, an incestuous Epicaste (who slept with her son Oedipus), a hateful Eriphyle (who sold her husband's life for gold), and so on. We have a typical structure of desire deferred (not her, or her, or her . . .) and finally satisfied (her!) in Penelope.

The problem with both of these readings of the poem is that they take into account only one of the Homeric views of gender outlined in the previous chapter. They depend on the symmetrical theory, with woman playing a contemporary role to man, and pay no heed to the asymmetrical one. If there is some agreement that the narrative success of the poem depends on the way it raises possibilities of infidelity as counternarratives, these possibilities are closed off by the poem's end. The figure of the *parthenos*, who acts out gendered roles in such a way as to demonstrate their contingency, is not taken into account. But if my argument in the last chapter has any weight, then this should be part of the analysis. It will also allow us to focus less on the normative content of what is desired and more on the process of desire itself, its peculiar logic.[4] To demonstrate this, let us look closely at where the teleological interpretations end: Penelope.

The logic that allows Penelope to function as the poem's telos is dependent on a moralizing divide of the category of woman into good and bad: a return to Penelope can only make sense if she is morally differentiated from others, if she is deemed worthy to return to. But this division of woman into good and evil is explicitly collapsed inside the poem in a pair of speeches delivered by Agamemnon. The words of Agamemnon have generally been dismissed as unthinking misogyny, and the speeches are of course misogynist. Yet this should not stop us from examining their logic. The first speech is delivered to Odysseus during Odysseus' trip to Hades. There, Agamemnon first tells of his murder at the hands of his wife and her lover, Aegisthus. Though Aegisthus seems at first to be the primary agent of murder, as Agamemnon recounts the tale, Clytemnestra's responsibility comes to the fore. This leads to a sweeping condemnation of all women.

> ὡς οὐκ αἰνότερον καὶ κύντερον ἄλλο γυναικός,
> ἥ τις δὴ τοιαῦτα μετὰ φρεσὶν ἔργα βάληται·
> οἷον δὴ καὶ κείνη ἐμήσατο ἔργον ἀεικές,
> κουριδίῳ τεύξασα πόσει φόνον. ἦ τοι ἔφην γε
> ἀσπάσιος παίδεσσιν ἰδὲ δμώεσσιν ἐμοῖσιν
> οἴκαδ' ἐλεύσεσθαι· ἡ δ' ἔξοχα λυγρὰ ἰδυῖα
> οἷ τε κατ' αἶσχος ἔχευε καὶ ἐσσομένῃσιν ὀπίσσω
> θηλυτέρῃσι γυναιξί, καὶ ἥ κ' εὐεργὸς ἔῃσιν.

(*Od.* 11.427–34)

[So there is nothing more deadly or more vile than a woman
who stores her mind with acts that are of such sort, as this one
did when she thought of this act of dishonor, and plotted
the murder of her lawful husband. See, I had been thinking
that I would be welcome to my children and thralls of my household
when I came home, but she with thoughts surpassingly grisly
splashed the shame on herself and the rest of her sex, on women
still to come, even on the one whose acts are virtuous.]

Interesting here is Agamemnon's refusal of the separation of women into categories of good and bad. Rather, even those who seem virtuous, through their virtuous acts, are already evil. For Agamemnon, women just *are* evil, in an existential judgment that cares little for the moral content of what they do. Odysseus replies by tacitly agreeing, mentioning the evil of Helen in addition to that of Clytemnestra.

> ὢ πόποι, ἦ μάλα δὴ γόνον Ἀτρέος εὐρύοπα Ζεὺς
> ἐκπάγλως ἤχθηρε γυναικείας διὰ βουλὰς
> ἐξ ἀρχῆς· Ἑλένης μὲν ἀπωλόμεθ' εἵνεκα πολλοί,
> σοὶ δὲ Κλυταιμνήστρη δόλον ἤρτυε τηλόθ' ἐόντι.

(*Od.* 11.436–39)

[Shame it is, how most terribly Zeus of the wide brows
from the beginning has been hateful to the seed of Atreus
through the schemes of women. Many of us died for the sake of Helen,
and when you were far, Klytaimnestra plotted treason against you.]

Odysseus' apparent affirmation of the guilt of women as a whole—Helen is added to Clytemnestra—remains conspicuously silent about Penelope, the obvious exception. The failure to mention Penelope prompts Agamemnon to qualify his misogyny; he modifies his earlier remarks by assuring Odysseus that the latter will never be murdered by his wife, for Penelope is "all too virtuous and her mind is stored with good thoughts" (*Od.* 11.445 ff.). But despite this apparent volte-face—which seems to assure Penelope entrance into the realm of virtue—Agamemnon produces a further surprise, which reinforces his previous argument. Despite Penelope's virtue, he goes on to emphasize that Odysseus should beware of her on his voyage home. Penelope, as a woman, cannot be trusted.

κρύβδην, μηδ' ἀναφανδά, φίλην ἐς πατρίδα γαῖαν
νῆα κατισχέμεναι, ἐπεὶ οὐκέτι πιστὰ γυναιξίν.

(*Od.* 11.455–56)

[When you bring your ship in to your own dear country, do it
secretly, not in the open. There is no trusting in women.]

One could perhaps try to explain Agamemnon's words in terms of the narrative progression of the poem. Though Penelope is given the benefit of the doubt and assumed to be virtuous, at this point in the narrative—with Odysseus still stuck on Phaeacia—her virtue remains unproved. Odysseus is thus forced to consider the possibility that Penelope might indeed turn out to be another Clytemnestra. Yet there is another twist to Agamemnon's misogyny. He repeats the condemnation of all women in almost exactly the same terms in the final book of the *Odyssey*, as he converses with the souls of the suitors murdered by Odysseus. At this point in the poem, there is no question about the success of Odysseus' return, for Penelope has proven herself to be virtuous. Yet though Agamemnon's words display an even more marked contrast between Penelope's virtue and the evils of women in general, Penelope is still tarred with the same brush as her species.

ὄλβιε Λαέρταο πάϊ, πολυμήχαν' Ὀδυσσεῦ,
ἦ ἄρα σὺν μεγάλῃ ἀρετῇ ἐκτήσω ἄκοιτιν·

ὡς ἀγαθαὶ φρένες ἦσαν ἀμύμονι Πηνελοπείῃ,
κούρῃ Ἰκαρίου, ὡς εὖ μέμνητ' Ὀδυσῆος,
ἀνδρὸς κουριδίου. τῶ οἱ κλέος οὔ ποτ' ὀλεῖται
ἧς ἀρετῆς, τεύξουσι δ' ἐπιχθονίοισιν ἀοιδὴν
ἀθάνατοι χαρίεσσαν ἐχέφρονι Πηνελοπείῃ,
οὐχ ὡς Τυνδαρέου κούρη κακὰ μήσατο ἔργα,
κουρίδιον κτείνασα πόσιν, στυγερὴ δέ τ' ἀοιδὴ
ἔσσετ' ἐπ' ἀνθρώπους, χαλεπὴν δέ τε φῆμιν ὀπάσσει
θηλυτέρῃσι γυναιξί, καὶ ἥ κ' εὐεργὸς ἔῃσιν.

(*Od.* 24.192–202)

[O fortunate son of Laertes, Odysseus of many devices,
surely you won yourself a wife endowed with great virtue.
How good was proved the heart that is in blameless Penelope,
Ikarios' daughter, and how well she remembered Odysseus,
her wedded husband. Thereby the fame of her virtue shall never
die away, but the immortals will make for the people
of earth a thing of grace in the song for prudent Penelope.
Not so did the daughter of Tyndareos fashions her evil
deeds, when she killed her wedded lord, and a song of loathing
will be hers among men, to make evil the reputation
of womankind, even for one whose acts are virtuous.]

The remarks at first seem to have the status of an obvious ideological disavowal. Agamemnon knows that some women are virtuous, yet his misogyny has so taken hold of him that he is ill equipped to recognize counterfactual examples. But in his very idiocy, he has stumbled upon an important insight, regardless of his own reasons for doing so. He gives the lie to any teleological reading of the poem based on the split of women into good and bad—"good" Penelope as end to be aimed for, "bad" Helen/Clytemnestra as end to be avoided. However noble, virtuous, and faithful Penelope is, it matters not one jot to Agamemnon. Insofar as she is a woman, she remains untrustworthy, inherently capable of evil. It is tempting to suggest that Agamemnon's words lay bare a hidden secret of patriarchal ideology, spoken more clearly here than in any other part of the poem. For patriarchy's power lies not in its unfair denigration of good women but in the unquestioned assumption of its ability to construct a separate morality of women (necessitating a determinate identity of "woman") in the first place. Indeed, precisely because of the clumsiness of the misogyny, Agamemnon's words contain an important insight. For try as anyone might to valorize a good Penelope, to produce an array of good feminine qualities with which to defend her, such a procedure will always run the risk of valorizing the process of categorization that assigns women virtues as women.

Agamemnon's words, together with the more general problem of Penelope's "exception" to the feminine rule, have produced interesting critical responses. In general, the more rabid the denunciations of Agamemnon are, the less critics are willing to appreciate the more salutary parts of his logic. For buried in his misogyny lies an important recognition of the contingency of identity and of the ultimate unreliability of fixed gender roles. The forcefulness of the moral denunciation of Agamemnon acts as a shield, protecting critics from a serious engagement with the anxiety Agamemnon exhibits. I will look at this in more detail shortly—suggesting that one of the reasons his words have been ignored is that his insight about Penelope is quite correct—and open up a plausible reading of the poem: Penelope indeed cannot be so easily separated from the "evil" women. Lurking beneath the apparent identity of "virtuous woman" are persistent narrative hints that this virtue is merely acted out for the sake of men; Penelope remains as untrustworthy as Clytemnestra and Helen.[5] But before I examine these hints, it is instructive to examine three separate ways in which critics have chosen to skirt Agamemnon's logic.

The classic approach is to fetishize Agamemnon's words, treating them as if they were the only examples of misogyny in the poem, and overlooking the more general constraints imposed on women. Consider the words of W. B. Stanford about Agamemnon: "Generalizing from his personal experience . . . as men are apt to do, he condemns the whole sex in words that are the first in a long series of anti-feminist gibes in Greek literature."[6] The problem with Stanford's argument is that, in the self-satisfaction generated by the moral denunciation of Agamemnon, any general questioning of the ideology of gender in the rest of the poem is put on hold. Such criticism can hardly avoid succumbing to the dominant ideology of the poem, which itself rests on the process of constructing a "good," "faithful" woman.

The approach of Felson-Rubin moves even further along the critical path of Stanford, by explicitly valorizing Penelope as a faithful wife against Agamemnon, who in turn displays "a flagrantly negative attitude toward womankind." On this interpretation, the poem offers a competitive dialogue about the nature of women, but it is clear who the winner is meant to be.

> [B]y the end of the performance, an invitation is extended to all listeners to transcend Agamemnon's limited perspective and adopt that of Odysseus. . . . If eventually *even he* is converted, then all skeptical males in Homer's audience can be cajoled into a kindly attitude toward faithful Penelope (and perhaps toward their own faithful wives).[7]

What underlies Felson-Rubin's critique of Agamemnon is a belief in the complementary roles of man and woman, of womankind as separate from "mankind" yet playing an equal role in the creation of a couple, a "one."⁸ This reading not only refuses to challenge the construction of a "feminine" identity; it acquiesces in this project. It tacitly affirms the "feminine" qualities of mothering and fidelity that are already on display on the poem's surface. But equally important is the way such an approach undermines any possibility of resistance; it seems to rule out in advance a feminist agency that is not always already the product of the social discourse that constructs women as women. For Felson-Rubin, Penelope's "agency" lies in her active assumption of the role as "faithful wife," her ability to play a full part in the voyage toward the oneness with Odysseus that is the apparent telos of the poem. I will return to the problem of assessing Penelope's agency. For now, it is enough to note that agency, for Felson-Rubin, is always already at the mercy of ideology—the options, for Penelope or Helen, are sketched out in advance—which means that it is a limited agency at best.⁹

A third reaction to Agamemnon, by Murnaghan, is subtler. It places Agamemnon's praise of the "faithful" Penelope in its patriarchal context.

> While the *Odyssey*'s portrait of Penelope is one of the most sympathetic in Greek literature, that portrait is also placed in wider context of misogyny through the self-representation of Penelope as an exception to the general rule. The poem self-consciously depicts the formation of a tradition of misogyny even as it places a counterexample at the center of its story.¹⁰

Murnaghan shows an awareness of a broader patriarchal strategy; Penelope's "virtue" is always already contained in a wider discourse that posits her as exception. As such, her sympathetic portrait is beside the point. Yet even here, Murnaghan notices the general logic of the poem but not the explicit words of Agamemnon. It is as if Agamemnon had argued that though most women were bad, Penelope is a notable exception. But this is only part of his argument; he also argues that any exception is irrelevant, undermined by the untrustworthy status of women as women. Thus, Agamemnon goes further than his critics, refusing to tie himself to the ideology that posits Penelope as an exception. The danger of giving in to the "sympathetic" portrait of Penelope is that there is already a yielding to the patriarchal logic that Murnaghan has so ably demonstrated. For Penelope is only sympathetic to the extent that she conforms to the notion of "good" woman, to the extent that she plays the role that is already carved out for her.

But what if Agamemnon is correct—what if Penelope is fundamentally similar to Helen and Clytemnestra? Here, the point is not simply the similarity itself—with the *Odyssey* knowingly pointing toward the possibility of a promiscuous Penelope—but what it signifies: the fragility of trust itself. Rather than directly providing evidence for the resemblance, I first consider the reason for Agamemnon's anxiety. An obvious answer lies in his personal misfortune: murdered by his own wife, he is naturally suspicious of other women. Yet this in itself does not explain the particular form his misogyny takes, which emphasizes not so much the cruelty of women but their deviousness, the impossibility of ever being able completely to trust them. Felson-Rubin suggests that Agamemnon fears an "autonomous female other,"[11] and I think she is at least partly correct. She is incorrect insofar as his fear has nothing to do with the "female" per se, but she is correct in that he is terrified by the prospect of a certain freedom in and of itself, a freedom that happens to be exhibited by Penelope. What terrifies Agamemnon is the possibility of Penelope's subjectivity, for she represents the possibility of a force that cannot be explained within his (or anyone's) ideological terms of reference. The problem with Penelope is not that she is "good" or "bad" but that her actions cannot be predicted. This unpredictability terrifies Agamemnon about women in general. Despite every system constructed to explain them, they still elude explanation and escape the parameters of the ideology that tries to ensnare them. So the similarity between Helen and Penelope exists not at the level of what they both do (as if Penelope, too, is promiscuous and adulterous, just as Helen is) but in that they both cannot be trusted.[12] In the terms of the last chapter, Agamemnon is aware of the possibility of Penelope as *parthenos*. Penelope's masks, as with the *parthenos*, seem to hide nothing; there is no motivation for them. This "nothing," the possibility of a subject not imprisoned by every determinate identity—and with it the possibility of an act performed on behalf of no particular ideological system—causes Agamemnon's anxiety.

Penelope as Nausicaa, Penelope as Arete

Let us now look at the manner in which the narrative signals Penelope as *parthenos*. Penelope becomes the figure Nausicaa is on the point of becoming for the Phaeacians as Odysseus leaves. We leave Phaeacia at the moment when the emergence of Nausicaa's desire threatens to disrupt the two roles assigned to females by patriarchal Phaeacian ideology: *parthenos* and *gyne*. Before Odysseus' appearance, Nausicaa had functioned as an idealized virgin maiden, Arete as an idealized *gyne*. Much of the complexity on show in Penelope's wiliness and apparent ambivalence toward Odysseus can be explained if we see her as a composite of both figures. For Odysseus, she appears to be a faithful wife and is treated as if she was an idealized *gyne*—like Arete. For the suitors, she appears as a virgin maiden, who teases by promising—yet only promising—marriage; she is treated as if she was a beautiful, alluring virgin—like Nausicaa. Because Penelope embodies both Arete and Nausicaa, complexities arise; the passage from virgin to *gyne* is meant to be a natural and progressive one. Young girls grow up to become what they naturally should be, wives. Marriage resolves the uncertainty implied in the moment of transition. Penelope undermines this transition. But she does this not simply by lingering on the point of indeterminacy when she is not fully either; rather, she is emphatically both. She appears as virgin and *gyne* to different people at the same time, and she thus clarifies that these are not natural states of being but roles that can be played out, masks to be worn.

Let us look at each of these roles in turn. In the closing books, as the scene is set for the slaughter of the suitors at the contest of the bow, Homer's narrative persistently draws attention to the parallels between the situation of Penelope and that of Nausicaa.[13] On Phaeacia, the emergence of Nausicaa's desire led to a quarrel (*neikos*) between the young Phaeacian men and Odysseus; the quarrel then led to the games of book 8, implicitly staged as a competition between the men for the right to marry Nausicaa. So, too, the gathering of the suitors around Penelope is described in terms of its potential for strife. Early in the poem, Eurymachus describes the gathering as an *eris* for the sake of Penelope's virtue (εἵνεκα τῆς ἀρετῆς ἐριδαίνομεν [we quarrel for the sake of her excellence], *Od.* 2.206). Later, Antinous suggests that the disguised Odysseus wants to string the bow because he is drunk. He compares the possible outcome to the legendary battle between the Centaurs and Lapiths at the marriage ceremony of Peirithoüs (*Od.* 21.293–98). That fight was provoked by the attempt of the drunken Centaur Eurytion to carry off Peirithoüs' bride. His reference to this *eris* over a woman anticipates the slaughter that will soon erupt after the bow contest.[14] More generally, the fears of the Phaeacians that Nausicaa might prefer to marry a stranger and might therefore put into question their status as *aristoi*[15] mirrors the concern of Eurymachus as he fails in his attempt to string the bow.

> Oh my sorrow. Here is a grief beyond all others;
> it is not so much the marriage I grieve for, for all my chagrin.
> There are many Achaian women besides, some of them close by
> in seagirt Ithaka, and some in the rest of the cities;
> but it is the thought, if this is true, that we can come so far short
> of godlike Odysseus in strength, so that we cannot even
> string his bow. A shame for men unborn to be told of.[16]
>
> (*Od.* 21.249–55)

Penelope as Parthenos 215

Just as the suspicion that Nausicaa was not interested in any of their number haunted the Phaeacians, so the suitors are threatened by the possibility that the bow contest will humiliate them. Further, it is not Penelope's worth that is in question; their humiliation comes from the manner in which her tricks constantly devalue their status as *aristoi*. She constantly undermines their claim to excellence.[17]

But if the suitors see Penelope as a Nausicaa, a woman who always threatens to become the source of a conflict, Odysseus sees her as an Arete, a figure of perfect virtue, who resolves quarrels rather than creates them. This is part of the point of the "reverse simile" used to describe Penelope in book 19, a simile that looks back to Arete.

> ὦ γύναι, οὐκ ἄν τίς σε βροτῶν ἐπ' ἀπείρονα γαῖαν
> νεικέοι· ἦ γάρ σευ κλέος οὐρανὸν εὐρὺν ἱκάνει,
> ὥς τέ τευ ἢ βασιλῆος ἀμύμονος, ὅς τε θεουδὴς
> ἀνδράσιν ἐν πολλοῖσι καὶ ἰφθίμοισιν ἀνάσσων
> εὐδικίας ἀνέχῃσι, φέρῃσι δὲ γαῖα μέλαινα
> πυροὺς καὶ κριθάς, βρίθῃσι δὲ δένδρεα καρπῷ,
> τίκτῃ δ' ἔμπεδα μῆλα, θάλασσα δὲ παρέχῃ ἰχθῦς
> ἐξ εὐηγεσίης, ἀρετῶσι δὲ λαοὶ ὑπ' αὐτοῦ.
>
> (*Od.* 19.107–14)

[Lady, no mortal man on the endless earth could have cause
to find fault with you; your fame goes up into the wide heaven,
as of some king who, as a blameless man and god-fearing,
and ruling as lord over many powerful people,
upholds the way of good government, and the black earth yields him
barley and wheat, his trees are heavy with fruit, his sheepflocks
continue to bear young, the sea gives him fish, because of
his good leadership, and his people prosper under him.]

The simile seems to be "reversed" because the would-be king, Odysseus, uses it to portray Penelope in the ruling role.[18] But this strangeness can be explained if we understand it as looking back to the peculiar social harmony that existed on Phaeacia. Alcinous, to be sure, is a classic example of the good king that Odysseus describes, but the harmony of his rule on Phaeacia was dependent on Arete's ability, as an idealized *gyne*, to resolve the quarrels between men formed in the competition for maidens (νείκεα λύει, *Od.* 7.74). The simile provides insight both into the sort of kingdom Odysseus believes to be ideal and into the gender relations he imagines to be at work—the idealized relations he describes elsewhere as *homophrosune*, "like-mindedness."[19] The world he describes resembles that of the Phaeacians, where gender identities are fixed and where the tensions created by marriageable maidens are resolved by marriage as soon as they arise. Odysseus' ideal is thoroughly nostalgic; he seeks to return to an idealized society that the narrative of his intervention on Phaeacia has already demonstrated as impossible. Odysseus is thus split in two, between what he objectively does to the Phaeacians—he engineers their introduction to loss—and what he seems not to know in the second half of the poem. For he will act as if he is unaware of the necessity of this kind of loss.

This motif of nostalgia lies behind Penelope's description of the actions of the suitors to the disguised Odysseus in book 18.

> νὺξ δ' ἔσται, ὅτε δὴ στυγερὸς γάμος ἀντιβολήσει
> οὐλομένης ἐμέθεν, τῆς τε Ζεὺς ὄλβον ἀπηύρα.
> ἀλλὰ τόδ' αἰνὸν ἄχος κραδίην καὶ θυμὸν ἱκάνει·
> μνηστήρων οὐχ ἥδε δίκη τὸ πάροιθε τέτυκτο,
> οἵ τ' ἀγαθήν τε γυναῖκα καὶ ἀφνειοῖο θύγατρα
> μνηστεύειν ἐθέλωσι καὶ ἀλλήλοις ἐρίσωσιν·
> αὐτοὶ τοί γ' ἀπάγουσι βόας καὶ ἴφια μῆλα
> κούρης δαῖτα φίλοισι, καὶ ἀγλαὰ δῶρα διδοῦσιν·
> ἀλλ' οὐκ ἀλλότριον βίοτον νήποινον ἔδουσιν.
>
> (*Od.* 18.272–80)

[And there will come that night when a hateful marriage is given
to wretched me, for Zeus has taken my happiness from me.
But this thing comes as a bitter distress to my heart and spirit:
the behavior of these suitors is not as it was in time past
when suitors desired to pay their court to a noble woman
and daughter of a rich man, and rival each other. Such men
themselves bring in their own cattle and fat sheep, to feast
the family of the bride, and offer glorious presents.
They do not eat up another's livelihood, without payment.]

Penelope looks back to a time of a good *eris;* suitors vied with each other (ἐρίσωσιν) in giving presents for a woman, a behavior in stark contrast to the present behavior of her suitors. Penelope's reference to this good *eris* comes close to the famous discussion of "two strifes" made by Hesiod in the *Works and Days:* for Hesiod, a praiseworthy *eris* encourages hard work through competition, while a shameful *eris* leads to the toil and suffering of war.[20] But Penelope's nostalgia for a former, trouble-free society can help clarify the difference between the two. In Phaeacia before the arrival of Odysseus, we have already seen a version of Penelope's idealized, conflict-free society from the mythical past. As it happens, there is also a showcasing of a "good *eris*" on Phaeacia, as the Phaeacian women vie with each other in washing the clothes.

εἵματα χερσὶν ἕλοντο καὶ ἐσφόρεον μέλαν ὕδωρ,
στεῖβον δ' ἐν βόθροισι θοῶς, <u>ἔριδα προφέρουσαι</u>.
αὐτὰρ ἐπεὶ πλῦνάν τε κάθηράν τε ῥύπα πάντα . . .

(*Od.* 6.91–93)

[[They] lifted the wash in their hands and carried it to the black water, and stamped on it in the basins, making a race and a game of it
until they had washed and rinsed all the dirt away . . .]

This conflict-free, playful competition is soon followed by the actual game played with the *sphaira*. But this game is complicated by the dropping of that ball, engineered by Athena, an event that introduces the Phaeacians to the possibility of loss.[21] We now have at least one reason why the initial *eris* over the washing is a good one; the competitors did not face the possibility of losing. So, too, Penelope looks back to a mythical past when games could be played honorably without any fear of defeat. Odysseus' later slaughter of the suitors is made in the hope of a return to this mythical past.

Penelope's Desire

If Penelope is an amalgam of masks, *gyne* and virgin maiden, hiding nothing, what is the importance of this for Penelope? We still need to consider the motivation for the wearing of these masks—the problem of her desire. A book by Marilyn Katz deals with the issue directly.[22] The title of the fourth chapter, which attempts to make sense out of Penelope's actions in books 18 and 19, poses the key question: "What Does Penelope Want?" Here Katz echoes the question that plagued Freud and that he confessed he was unable to answer. But before looking at Katz' answer, it is worth briefly affirming why this is a question in the first place.

Penelope's actions in these books are notoriously difficult to fathom. At the moment of Odysseus' return, she seems to give up her patient, twenty-year-long wait for him; she gives in to the demands of the suitors by instigating the contest of the bow. Her attitude toward the suitors is itself complex. Though professing disapproval of them, there is the ongoing suggestion that she might be willing to marry the "best" of them, and in a famous dream that she recounts to the disguised Odysseus, there is a suggestion that she sexually desires them.

ἀλλ' ἄγε μοι τὸν ὄνειρον ὑπόκριναι καὶ ἄκουσον.
χῆνές μοι κατὰ οἶκον ἐείκοσι πυρὸν ἔδουσιν
ἐξ ὕδατος, καί τέ σφιν ἰαίνομαι εἰσορόωσα·
ἐλθὼν δ' ἐξ ὄρεος μέγας αἰετὸς ἀγκυλοχείλης
πᾶσι κατ' αὐχέν' ἔαξε καὶ ἔκτανεν· οἱ δ' ἐκέχυντο
ἀθρόοι ἐν μεγάροισ', ὁ δ' ἐς αἰθέρα δῖαν ἀέρθη.
αὐτὰρ ἐγὼ κλαῖον καὶ ἐκώκυον ἔν περ ὀνείρῳ,
ἀμφὶ δ' ἔμ' ἠγερέθοντο ἐϋπλοκαμῖδες Ἀχαιαί,
οἴκτρ' ὀλοφυρομένην, ὅ μοι αἰετὸς ἔκτανε χῆνας.
ἂψ δ' ἐλθὼν κατ' ἄρ' ἕζετ' ἐπὶ προὔχοντι μελάθρῳ,
φωνῇ δὲ βροτέῃ κατερήτυε φώνησέν τε·
"θάρσει, Ἰκαρίου κούρη τηλεκλειτοῖο·
οὐκ ὄναρ, ἀλλ' ὕπαρ ἐσθλόν, ὅ τοι τετελεσμένον ἔσται.
χῆνες μὲν μνηστῆρες, ἐγὼ δέ τοι αἰετὸς ὄρνις
ἦα πάρος, νῦν αὖτε τεὸς πόσις εἰλήλουθα,
ὃς πᾶσι μνηστῆρσιν ἀεικέα πότμον ἐφήσω."
ὣς ἔφατ', αὐτὰρ ἐμὲ μελιηδὴς ὕπνος ἀνῆκε·
παπτήνασα δὲ χῆνας ἐνὶ μεγάροισι νόησα
πυρὸν ἐρεπτομένους παρὰ πύελον, ᾗχι πάρος περ.

(*Od.* 19.535–53)

[But come, listen to a dream of mine and interpret it for me.
I have twenty geese here about the house, and they feed on
grains of wheat from the water trough. I love to watch them.
But a great eagle with crooked beak came down from the mountain,
and broke the necks of them all and killed them. So the whole twenty lay
dead about the house, but he soared high in the bright air.
Then I began to weep—that was in my dream—and cried out
aloud, and around me gathered the fair-haired Achaian women
as I cried out sorrowing for my geese killed by the eagle.
But he came back again and perched on the jut of the gabled
roof. He now had a human voice and spoke aloud to me:
"Do not fear, O daughter of far-famed Ikarios.
This is no dream, but a blessing real as day. You will see it
done. The geese are the suitors, and I, the eagle, have been
a bird of portent, but now I am your own husband, come home,
and I shall inflict shameless destruction on the suitors."
So he spoke; and then the honey-sweet sleep released me,
and I looked about and saw the geese in my palace, feeding
on their grains of wheat from the water trough, just as they had been.]

The striking aspect of the dream that cries out for interpretation—and that has been avoided by those intent on preserving a pure, faithful, Arete-like Penelope—is the strength of her affection for the geese. Can this mean anything other than an unconscious sexual desire for the suitors, which can only contradict her professed intolerance of them?[23] I will return to this dream in due course. For now, it is worth pointing out that the difficulty in understanding the meaning of the dream parallels the difficulty in finding the motivations behind Penelope's actions; for she is emphatically a figure who does one thing while "her own mind has other intentions."[24]

What is Katz' answer to the question? Her first step is to reject all readings that rely on "psychological verisimilitude," readings that try to piece together out of the plethora of inconsistencies a "unified" character of Penelope. Instead (and it is easy to agree), she emphasizes the need for an approach that recognizes the inconsistencies. For her, such an approach is narratological: the exigencies of fiction far outweigh the importance of psychology.[25] Yet her narratological frame of reference itself has something to say about Penelope's character.

> It will be the burden of my reading overall, by contrast, to suggest that the indeterminacy around which the character of Penelope is constructed undermines this notion of a coherent, essential self and presents us with a notion of the person instead as constructed—invented on the spot, as it were—and ultimately brought into being as such by time, place, and circumstance.[26]

It is easy enough to detect a poststructuralist influence here. Rather than a naive notion of "unified character," there is the suggestion of a plurality of subject positions. In effect, there is no single Penelope but a multiplicity of Penelopes, whose desires change to fit in with the narrative construction of the poem. Katz therefore answers the question of Penelope's desire by simply denying its validity as posed. To solve the paradox of Penelope's desire, we need to stop thinking of a "single" Penelope. Penelope wants different things precisely insofar as she is a multiplicity of changing identities. The obvious value of Katz' thesis is that she refuses to provide any superficial resolution to the paradox constructed by Penelope's inconsistency. In short, she recognizes that all attempts to determine what Penelope wants by explaining away the empirical inconsistencies of what she desires are doomed to failure. I readily concede that what Penelope wants is inconsistent, but I think a more convincing answer to the problem can be found by looking more carefully at the wanting itself.

According to Anne Carson, who echoes Lacan, a central aspect of eros is that it does not want to be satisfied: "The unknown must remain unknown or the novel ends. As all paradoxes are, in some way, paradoxes *about* paradox, so all eros is, to some degree, desire *for* desire."²⁷ We can see how the problem of the inconsistency of the desire of the subject, rejected by Katz as doomed to failure, can be a significant subjective strategy. In the inconsistency of desire, we can see the desire for desire itself. Compare Lacan's formula "I demand that you refuse my demand, since it is not *that*." To return to Penelope, she would therefore not merely be at the mercy of her desire. Rather, her desire is staged for others, in order that she can sustain their interest in her. Indeed, what Antinous calls her *kleos* in keeping them at arm's length could just as easily be called her successful ability to sustain desire—both her own desire and the desire of those around her for her.

"I demand that you refuse my demand, since it is not *that*"—is this Lacanian formula not a perfect description of Penelope? She is constantly identified with a range of competing desires that, in the realm of the social world she inhabits, are quite clearly fulfillable. She could give in to any one of the suitors, or she could flatly reject them and await Odysseus. Instead, she shows an extraordinary willingness to procrastinate. Why? In the rejection of the multiplicity of possibilities that could fulfill her specific wants, she manifests desire for something beyond these wants. Her desire is not for any one thing but is purer: what Penelope wants is desire itself. Here, we can return to an analysis of the dream of the geese and Penelope's affection for them. A classic psychoanalytic interpretation was provided long ago by George Devereux.

> In fact, it is hard to understand how literary critics could have overlooked the obvious fact that a rapidly aging woman, denied for some twenty years the pleasures of sex and the company and support of a husband, would be unconsciously flattered by the attentions of young and highly eligible suitors, which is precisely what the chief suitor accuses her of in public.²⁸

Devereux' analysis continues be controversial insofar as it pulverizes the simplicity of any picture of a faithful, chaste Penelope.²⁹ Yet we can take it a step further. For what is crucial about Penelope's interactions with the suitors is her ongoing refusal of their attentions. So in sharp contrast to those who would reject Devereux' analysis, we should emphasize that Penelope's attraction to the suitors is quite obvious. There is nothing "unconscious" about it (as Devereux himself points out, she is accused of desiring the suitors in public, which suggests that this desire is an open secret). But recognition of her sexual desire for the suitors leads to an understanding of the general logic of her behavior, a logic of which she does seem to be unaware. If Penelope cries for her geese, it is not because the death of the suitors takes away the possibility of limitless sexual satisfaction; it is, rather, because the death of the suitors threatens to disrupt the economy of her desire. The suitors' deaths, to the extent that they entail the return of Odysseus, endanger the display of masks that seeks to capture their desire; their deaths remove her fellow actors from her stage. Penelope cries because Odysseus' return—made explicit in the dream—promises the death of her desire. It threatens to take away her desire for an unsatisfied desire, by offering the possibility of satisfaction.

If we understand Penelope in this way, then it is possible to see how both the suitors and Odysseus alike misread her. The suitors correctly read that her actions betray a sexual interest in them. But they fail to understand that, despite this attraction, she is not remotely interested in ending the game of courtship by marrying any one of them. Here is Penelope's most forceful rebuke of the suitors.

> κέκλυτέ μευ, μνηστῆρες ἀγήνορες, οἳ τόδε δῶμα
> ἐχράετ' ἐσθιέμεν καὶ πινέμεν ἐμμενὲς αἰεὶ
> ἀνδρὸς ἀποιχομένοιο πολὺν χρόνον, <u>οὐδέ τιν' ἄλλην
> μύθου</u> ποιήσασθαι ἐπισχεσίην ἐδύνασθε,
> <u>ἀλλ' ἐμὲ ἱέμενοι γῆμαι θέσθαι τε γυναῖκα</u>.
>
> (*Od.* 21.68–72)

[Hear me now, you haughty suitors, who have been using
this house for your incessant eating and drinking, though it
belongs to man who has been gone for a long time; never
have you been able to bring any other saying before me,
but only your desire to make me your wife and marry me.]

For Penelope, the suitors tell the same old story. They have no other *mythos* to offer her than the story so central to patriarchal Greek culture: the tale of the passage from virgin maiden to *gyne*. It is this tired story that Penelope resists, even as she is hooked on this resistance: she seems to say, "Desire me, so that I can resist your desire and so keep us both desiring!" With the suitors, she acts out the role of maiden, while promising (but only promising) to be a *gyne*. With Odysseus, the situation is fundamentally similar. She plays out the role of faithful *gyne*, but she does so with her husband safely away from Ithaca. She desires to be Odysseus' *gyne*, but only in his absence. His arrival poses the same threat to her as marriage to the suitors: the determinate identity of the *gyne*.

If Penelope's complaints to the suitors are double-edged, so, too, are her professions of faith to Odysseus. Zeitlin has suggested that competition for Penelope over the bow is a classic example of "mimetic" desire, that Odysseus' desire for Penelope is increased because others desire her.[30] But this brings with it an important consequence. It suggests that there is nothing objective about Penelope that makes her desirable; rather, her attractiveness is merely the effect of male desire. The contrast for Penelope takes place under the illusion (on the part of the suitors and Odysseus) that they are fighting for something. But Penelope comes to the brink of disrupting this illusion. Once more, this is not because she offers any alternative to what the men who compete for her want. Quite the opposite, she conforms all too exactly to what they want, raising the possibility that, with their fantasy construction of her removed, there will be nothing left of the "real" Penelope. Let us look at one of her protestations of fidelity.[31]

"ξεῖν', ἦ τοι μὲν ἐμὴν ἀρετὴν εἶδός τε δέμας τε
ὤλεσαν ἀθάνατοι, ὅτε Ἴλιον εἰσανέβαινον
Ἀργεῖοι, μετὰ τοῖσι δ' ἐμὸς πόσις ἦεν Ὀδυσσεύς.
εἰ κεῖνός γ' ἐλθὼν τὸν ἐμὸν βίον ἀμφιπολεύοι,
μεῖζόν κε κλέος εἴη ἐμὸν καὶ κάλλιον οὕτω.

(*Od.* 19.124–28)

[Stranger, all of my excellence, my beauty and figure,
were ruined by the immortals at that time when the Argives took ship
for Ilion, and with them went my husband, Odysseus.
If he were to come back to me and take care of my life, then
my reputation would be more great and splendid.]

Penelope's beauty, in her own words, is in itself nothing. It depends entirely on the quality of the men who vie for her. When Odysseus watches her, she is beautiful, but the beauty disappears as soon as the best men disappear.[32] There is a further disquieting note. If her beauty disappears with Odysseus, there is a suggestion that her beauty is staged for him. When Odysseus is not present, Penelope's virtue vanishes, suggesting that she merely acts out the vision of virtue Odysseus already expects to see; Odysseus' Penelope disappears from Ithaca the moment Odysseus leaves.

What is left of the subject behind the social mask that is worn? This perturbing question is central to the paradox of the self that the poem conjures up. It will be of special significance in the difficulties involved in the reunion of Penelope and Odysseus in the scene of the bed. If the self is just a series of masks, what can a reunion actually signify? Plainly, it cannot simply be a matter of any recognition of a normative content of the self. Before turning to book 23, let us see how these problems are already apparent when Penelope reacts to Odysseus' lying Cretan tales.

ἴσκε ψεύδεα πολλὰ λέγων ἐτύμοισιν ὁμοῖα·
τῆς δ' ἄρ' ἀκουούσης ῥέε δάκρυα, τήκετο δὲ χρώς.
ὡς δὲ χιὼν κατατήκετ' ἐν ἀκροπόλοισιν ὄρεσσιν,
ἥν τ' εὖρος κατέτηξεν, ἐπὴν ζέφυρος καταχεύῃ,
τηκομένης δ' ἄρα τῆς ποταμοὶ πλήθουσι ῥέοντες·
ὣς τῆς τήκετο καλὰ παρήϊα δάκρυ χεούσης,
κλαιούσης ἑὸν ἄνδρα, παρήμενον. αὐτὰρ Ὀδυσσεὺς
θυμῷ μὲν γοόωσαν ἑὴν ἐλέαιρε γυναῖκα,
ὀφθαλμοὶ δ' ὡς εἰ κέρα ἕστασαν ἠὲ σίδηρος
ἀτρέμας ἐν βλεφάροισι· δόλῳ δ' ὅ γε δάκρυα κεῦθεν.

(*Od.* 19.203–12)

[He knew how to say many things that were like true sayings.
As he listened *the tears ran, skin was melted,*
as the snow melts along the high places of the mountains
when the West Wind has piled it there, but the South Wind melts it,
and as it melts the rivers run full flood. It was even
so that her beautiful cheeks were streaming tears, as Penelope
wept for her man, who was sitting there by her side. But Odysseus
in his heart had pity for his wife as she mourned him,
but his eyes stayed, as if they were made of horn or iron,
steady under his lids. He hid his tears and deceived her.]

(translation modified)

Discussion of these lines has tended to center on the notorious paradox of saying "many things that were like true sayings" and on the problem that this poses for any discourse of sincerity. But Penelope's reaction contains its own difficulties. There are several noteworthy aspects of the passage. First, there is a pointed delay in revealing the identity of the weeper. In response to Odysseus' lies, we are given an image of tears falling, but only at line 208 do we get an indication that the tears belong to Penelope. The poetry lingers over a display of emotion, but it also refuses to anchor this emotion in a character, leaving us with free-floating tears between the two protagonists. This blurring of the lines between emotion and the identity of the self that produces these signs of emotion is accentuated by the details of the simile. For we see the shared rivers of water that the tears flow into, as if both are about to dissolve into the other. It is as if the problem of the nature of truth and lies opened up by Odysseus' deceit is given a physical context in the body of the two of them. Who is who? Indeed, even as Penelope is identified by the feminine τῆς in line 208, the edges of the self remain difficult to fix. Her cheeks themselves start to melt as she cries, a strange physical dissolution of not what is her but what is "beside her" (her cheeks, παρ-ήϊα), as she cries for the man who now happens to be beside her (παρ-ήμενον). So it is Penelope, but a Penelope in dissolution, who cries.[33]

The simile, if we push its correspondences, also give insight into the Homeric self as a kind of "open field of forces."[34] For the details raise a question about the source of her emotions. Odysseus comes and Odysseus goes—like the west wind that spreads snow and the south wind that melts it. The production of emotion seems almost Pavlovian, an automatic consequence of the presence and absence of Odysseus. We thus have a repetition of the problem of her beauty, which she claimed the gods removed when Odysseus left. But here, even the mediation of the gods has disappeared: her emotions are an effect of Odysseus' actions. So they are either not enough (automatic, so lacking in authenticity) or too much: there lurks the suspicion that they are staged. With this unease in mind, let us now turn to the difficulties of the most significant moment of the reunion, the scene of the bed.

From Proteus to Penelope

Any simple happiness in the final recognition scene between Odysseus and Penelope is haunted by a moment of doubt; Odysseus asks the maid Eurycleia to make up a bed, the emblem of sexual fidelity between the husband and wife.

> ἀλλ' ἄγε μοι, μαῖα, <u>στόρεσον λέχος</u>, ὄφρα καὶ αὐτὸς
> <u>λέξομαι</u>· ἦ γὰρ τῇ γε σιδήρεον ἐν φρεσὶν ἦτορ."
>   τὸν δ' αὖτε προσέειπε περίφρων Πηνελόπεια·
> "δαιμόνι', οὐ γάρ τι μεγαλίζομαι οὐδ' ἀθερίζω
> οὐδὲ λίην ἄγαμαι, μάλα δ' εὖ οἶδ' οἷος ἔησθα
> ἐξ Ἰθάκης ἐπὶ νηὸς ἰὼν δολιχηρέτμοιο.
> <u>ἀλλ' ἄγε οἱ στόρεσον πυκινὸν λέχος, Εὐρύκλεια,</u>
> <u>ἐκτὸς ἐϋσταθέος θαλάμου, τὸν ῥ' αὐτὸς ἐποίει·</u>
> ἔνθα οἱ ἐκθεῖσαι πυκινὸν λέχος ἐμβάλετ' εὐνήν,
> κώεα καὶ χλαίνας καὶ ῥήγεα σιγαλόεντα.
>
> (*Od.* 23.171–80)

["Come then, nurse, make me up a bed, so that I myself
will lie on it; for this woman has a heart of iron within her."
Circumspect Penelope said to him in answer:
"You are so strange. I am not being proud, nor indifferent,
nor puzzled beyond need, but I know very well what you looked like

when you went in the ship with the sweeping oars, from Ithaka.
Come then, Eurykleia, and make up a firm bed for him
outside the well-fashioned chamber: that very bed that he himself
built. Put the firm bed here outside for him, and cover it
over with fleeces and blankets, and with shining coverlets."]

(translation modified)

Infamously, Penelope tests Odysseus by hinting that the fixed *sema* of her fidelity to him has been moved. The return to a faithful Penelope promises to set the final seal on Odysseus' return to his *oikos* and thus to reestablish him as head of an ideal *oikos*. This moment of doubt, engineered by Penelope, poses a huge threat to Odysseus' sense of self. It opens the possibility that the entire premise of the *nostos*—the return to a faithful wife, the bedrock of a stable *oikos*—is an illusion. If Penelope's fidelity turns out to be a lie, what was the point of the *nostos?* This scene, with the promise of identity it provides, recalls an earlier episode in the poem that examines the difficulties of any concept of self-identity—the tricking of Proteus.

Let us briefly return to the Proteus story. The deception depended on the ambiguity between the aorist middle form of λέγω, meaning "count," from the aorist of λέχομα, meaning "lie down." The lying down of Proteus coincided with a moment of self-counting: to replace his lost seal, Proteus lay down among them at the same time that he counted himself (λέκτο καὶ αὐτός, *Od.* 4.453). The possibility of identity is premised on the loss of a seal: Proteus' belief in his identity is a fantasy, played out against the background of the void created by the disappearance of the seal. Proteus' later doubt about his polytropic capacity shows an awareness of the contingency of any notion of identity. Odysseus, when confronted with the moved bed, is forced into facing this possibility: any ownership of the *oikos* is only possible because it essentially belongs to no one. Until this moment, the series of tricks used to help him get back to Ithaca (his *metis*) and the many disguises used for self-preservation (his polytropy) were all premised on his role as husband to Penelope. The immovable bed is a symbol, for Odysseus, of the infallibility of their bond: it is the quilting point that stitches together and makes sense of the rest of his actions. His desire to himself lie down (ὄφρα καὶ αὐτὸς λέξομαι) is also a desire to count himself: if he lies successfully down on the bed with a faithful Penelope, he can convince himself that his identity as the husband of Penelope is secure. The bed (λέχος), fixed at the center of Odysseus' home, functions as the correlative to Odysseus' own fantasized belief that he has a centered, fixed identity.[35]

The possibility of the removal of the bed cannot help but undermine this belief of Odysseus; more accurately, it clarifies that it always was a fantasy. Proteus' self-counting, his belief in himself, is a fantasy projected onto the blank space opened up by the loss of the seal. So, too, Odysseus' belief in Penelope's fidelity occurs under the shadow of the suggestion that it is impossible to know whether she has been faithful or not. Underlying the shifting boundaries implied in the movement of the bed lies the attempt to find fixed parameters for the self, which provides added significance to the form of Penelope's test. She tells Eurycleia to move the bed outside her chamber (ἐκτὸς ἐϋσταθέος θαλάμου). The bed that Odysseus believed to be at the center of his world and that is the linchpin of his sense of self is removed. The sense of autonomy provided by Odysseus' own construction of the bed (τόν ῥ' αὐτὸς ἐποίει) is shown to be illusory because of the ruse of Penelope. Fidelity is a social relationship, irreducibly dependent on the actions of others. No amount of effort or toil from Odysseus can guarantee it.[36] But precisely because fidelity is the social relationship most clearly dependent on a leap of faith, it illustrates an important truth about any sense of self. There is no determinate identity, no unchanging kernel of the self, that can be separated from the external realm of social discourses. Nevertheless, all determinate identities are constructed against the background of this impossibility; they fill the blank screen created by this loss. Penelope's action provides Odysseus with a glimpse into his own emptiness, the void behind the series of *tropoi*, masks, he has worn (a self that his victims on Phaeacia and the island of the Cyclops had already glimpsed).

Not only the tricking of Proteus can help us read the bed scene. Odysseus replies to Penelope by describing at length the efforts he expended in constructing the bed, this "great sign" of their fidelity.

ὦ γύναι, ἦ μάλα τοῦτο ἔπος θυμαλγὲς ἔειπες.
τίς δέ μοι ἄλλοσε θῆκε λέχος; χαλεπὸν δέ κεν εἴη
καὶ μάλ' ἐπισταμένῳ, ὅτε μὴ θεὸς αὐτὸς ἐπελθὼν
ῥηϊδίως ἐθέλων θείη ἄλλῃ ἐνὶ χώρῃ.
ἀνδρῶν δ' οὔ κέν τις ζωὸς βροτός, οὐδὲ μάλ' ἡβῶν,
ῥεῖα μετοχλίσσειεν, ἐπεὶ μέγα σῆμα τέτυκται
ἐν λέχει ἀσκητῷ· τὸ δ' ἐγὼ κάμον οὐδέ τις ἄλλος.
θάμνος ἔφυ τανύφυλλος ἐλαίης ἕρκεος ἐντός,
ἀκμηνὸς θαλέθων· πάχετος δ' ἦν ἠΰτε κίων.
τῷ δ' ἐγὼ ἀμφιβαλὼν θάλαμον δέμον, ὄφρ' ἐτέλεσσα,
πυκνῇσιν λιθάδεσσι, καὶ εὖ καθύπερθεν ἔρεψα,
κολλητὰς δ' ἐπέθηκα θύρας, πυκινῶς ἀραρυίας.
καὶ τότ' ἔπειτ' ἀπέκοψα κόμην τανυφύλλου ἐλαίης,
κορμὸν δ' ἐκ ῥίζης προταμὼν ἀμφέξεσα χαλκῷ

εὖ καὶ ἐπισταμένως καὶ ἐπὶ στάθμην ἴθυνα,
ἑρμῖν' ἀσκήσας, τέτρηνα δὲ πάντα τερέτρῳ.
ἐκ δὲ τοῦ ἀρχόμενος λέχος ἔξεον, ὄφρ' ἐτέλεσσα,
δαιδάλλων χρυσῷ τε καὶ ἀργύρῳ ἠδ' ἐλέφαντι·
ἐν δ' ἐτάνυσσ' ἱμάντα βοὸς φοίνικι φαεινόν.
οὕτω τοι τόδε σῆμα πιφαύσκομαι· οὐδέ τι οἶδα,
ἤ μοι ἔτ' ἔμπεδόν ἐστι, γύναι, λέχος, ἦέ τις ἤδη
ἀνδρῶν ἄλλοσε θῆκε, ταμὼν ὕπο πυθμέν' ἐλαίης.

(*Od.* 23.183–204)

[What you have said, dear lady, has hurt me deeply. What man
has put my bed in another place? But it would be difficult
for even a very expert one, unless a god, coming
to help in person, were easily to change its position.
But there is no mortal man alive, no strong man, who lightly
could move the weight elsewhere. There is one particular feature
in the bed's construction. I myself, no other man, made it.
There was the bole of an olive tree with long leaves growing
strongly in the courtyard, and it was thick, like a column.
I laid down my chamber around this, and built it, until I
finished it, with close-set stones, and roofed it well over,
and added the compacted doors, fitting closely together.
Then I cut away the foliage of the long-leaved olive,
and trimmed the trunk from the roots up, planing it with a brazen
adze, well and expertly, and trued it straight to a chalkline,
making a bed post of it, and bored all holes with an augur.
I began with this and built my bed, until it was finished,
and decorated it with gold and silver and ivory.
Then I lashed it with thongs of oxhide, dyed bright with purple.
There is its character, as I tell you; but I do not know now,
dear lady, whether my bed is still in place, or if some man
has cut underneath the stump of the olive, and moved it elsewhere.]

Rick Newton has already argued that the elaborate description of the bed making is modeled on the craftsmanship exhibited by Hephaestus; in particular, it looks back to the trap he constructed for the adulterous Ares and Aphrodite in the second song of Demodocus in book 8. Newton also notes that Odysseus' skills as a craftsman are on show in his blinding of the Cyclops in book 9. But despite my general agreement that these passages are significant for our understanding of Odysseus' description of the making of the bed, I think we can read them differently. For Newton, the fidelity displayed between Odysseus and Penelope in book 23 contrasts with the infidelity of Ares and Aphrodite.

But amidst the many echoes between Demodocus' "Lay of Hephaestus and Aphrodite" and Homer's "Lay of Odysseus and Penelope" lies one essential difference: the Phaeacian song ends in the alienation and separation of Hephaestus and Aphrodite, while the Ithacan episode ends in the physical and spiritual reunion of husband and wife.[37]

The problem with this conclusion is that it fails to take adequate account of the peculiar nature of Odysseus' rhetoric of building in book 23 and of the consequent strength of the parallels to the other episodes of craftsmanship. Odysseus' speech is markedly self-contradictory; he begins by suggesting the impossibility of any other mortal man moving the immovable bedpost he has so laboriously constructed, even as he recognizes that a god might be able to move it. The elaborate description of the construction is then provided as evidence for this position. But he ends by recognizing that he does not know if a mortal has moved the bed. There is a blurring of the boundaries between the world of mortals and immortals. There is also a shift from certainty to doubt—a shift that exactly mirrors the narrative pattern of the Lay of Hephaestus and Aphrodite. Hephaestus is certain that the humiliating punishment he has so elaborately contrived for the lovers will ensure that no act of adultery will ever occur again. But this is so quickly undermined by the remark of Hermes to Apollo: Hermes would still sleep with Aphrodite, regardless of the punishment. I have already noted that this shift from boundary construction to boundary transgression is indicated by a pun on Hermes' name: for the word for bedpost is *hermis*. Hephaestus' efforts to construct a perfect circle around the bedpost (ἀμφὶ δ᾽ ἄρ᾽ ἑρμῖσιν χέε δέσματα κύκλῳ ἁπάντῃ, *Od.* 8.278) foreshadow the imminent failure of his enterprise, a failure suggested by Hermes. Odysseus' efforts to construct a similar, infallible bedpost (ἑρμῖν᾽ ἀσκήσας) cannot help but suggest the futility of his efforts, a futility his subsequent doubt acknowledges.

The theme of construction, shared with *Odyssey* 9, is also haunted by this anxiety about futility. Yes, the construction of the bedpost from olive wood mirrors the effort involved in the sharpening of the olive wood stake used to blind Polyphemus. But the wood plays a different role on each occasion. In book 9, Odysseus makes use of the stake to remove the eye of the Cyclops: the act deprives the Cyclops of his identity as a circle-eyed creature, creating a void in the center of his being. This act transformed the asocial Cyclops from an asocial monad into a *homo faber:* technological expertise is turned to in an attempt to find a cure for the incurable wound that is at the heart of mortal existence. Odysseus' illusion in book 23 lies in his apparent belief that Penelope can guarantee his identity and thus cure this wound. Odysseus' response to

Penelope's trick, suggested in the movement away from certainty toward the doubt expressed in the phrase οὐδέ τι οἶδα [I do not know] is thus a recognition not only of the lesson taught by Penelope but of the lesson he has taught others, including the Cyclops. Here, it is worth noting that Odysseus' initial claim that no mortal has the strength to move the immovable bed looks back to another immovable object—the boulder at the mouth of Polyphemus' cave, which Odysseus' *metis* succeeds in moving.[38]

Finally, Penelope's lesson is also a lesson in the nature of signs; for Odysseus' construction of the bed is also a construction of a "great sign" (μέγα σῆμα) which promises, for him, to ground the constantly shifting, indeterminate masks he has worn throughout the poem. This μέγα σῆμα functions as a master signifier for Odysseus, since his allegiance to Penelope promises to make sense of all his other actions. Every action throughout the poem is performed in the name of his relationship to Penelope. But does not the size of the sign point toward that other religious sign, the *colossos?* The thematic link between the bed as immovable and the immovable stone guarding the cave of the Cyclops already suggests a connection. The bed itself is also "large," covered over with stones (πυκνῇσιν λιθάδεσσι), and supposedly fixed (ἔμπεδόν). We are close to the identifying features of the senseless objects par excellence, the mute, massive stones that emerged as sublime objects in the world of the Phaeacians and the Cyclopes at the moment they doubted. The *mega sema* that at first seemed to guarantee Odysseus' identity is perilously close to the *sema* that signifies nothing.

The doubt acknowledged by Odysseus seems to be resolved by Penelope's later acceptance of him, as she seems to take back her suggestion that the bed could have moved. But her words of acceptance contain a host of complications of their own. She begins by identifying with Helen, the most important example of "evil," untrustworthy womanhood and the adulteress par excellence.

αἰεὶ γάρ μοι θυμὸς ἐνὶ στήθεσσι φίλοισιν
ἐρρίγει, μή τίς με βροτῶν ἀπάφοιτ' ἐπέεσσιν
ἐλθών· πολλοὶ γὰρ κακὰ κέρδεα βουλεύουσιν.
οὐδέ κεν Ἀργείη Ἑλένη, Διὸς ἐκγεγαυῖα,
ἀνδρὶ παρ' ἀλλοδαπῷ ἐμίγη φιλότητι καὶ εὐνῇ,
εἰ ᾔδη, ὅ μιν αὖτις ἀρήϊοι υἷες Ἀχαιῶν
ἀξέμεναι οἶκόνδε φίλην ἐς πατρίδ' ἔμελλον.
τὴν δ' ἦ τοι ῥέξαι θεὸς ὦρσεν ἔργον ἀεικές·
τὴν δ' ἄτην οὐ πρόσθεν ἑῷ ἐγκάτθετο θυμῷ
λυγρήν, ἐξ ἧς πρῶτα καὶ ἡμέας ἵκετο πένθος.

(*Od.* 23.215–24)

[For always the spirit deep in my very heart was fearful
that some one of mortal men would come my way and deceive me
with words. For there are many who scheme for wicked advantage.
For neither would the daughter born to Zeus, Helen of Argos,
have lain in love with an outlander from another country,
if she had known that the warlike sons of the Achaians would bring her
home again to the beloved land of her fathers.
It was a god who stirred her to do the shameful thing she
did, and never before had she had in her heart this terrible
wildness, out of which came suffering to us also.]

Lines 218–24 have often been athetized by critics who want to preserve the image of a chaste Penelope. It is not difficult to see why. The comparison to Helen and the implicit defense of her are quite unbearable.[39] There is also a parallel with Clytemnestra; for in Nestor's rendition of her adultery with Aegisthus, the tenuousness of the barrier separating the shameful, modest Clytemnestra from her "shameless" dark side is emphasized.[40] But it is the incoherence of the picture of Helen provided by Penelope that is most striking, especially as Penelope is supposedly demonstrating her fidelity. She ends her remarks by suggesting that Helen was in no way responsible for her actions—the "external" arrival of a god deprived her of her senses, took away any "choice" she might have had in the matter. Yet this is in stark contradiction to the first half of the defense of Helen, which emphasizes her initial *choice* to sleep with Paris. It is true that Helen's choice is then partially exonerated insofar as, with hindsight, Penelope claims Helen would not have made such a choice; yet even this claim is undermined by its utilitarian air. The choice is only wrong in hindsight, because Helen was finally dragged by force back to the house of Menelaus.

The split between pure agent and pure victim displayed in Penelope's words is characteristic of the whole myth of Helen.[41] But we can make more sense out of the description if we see it as another hint at the difficulties of understanding the motivations of the *parthenos*. The split marks the divide between Helen as player of roles, wearer of masks (to the extent that she merely fills roles that are always already created for her in the symbolic, she is pointedly not free, a victim of the "gods"), and something of Helen that evades these masks. What is left over is an inexplicable decision that manages to defy any of the roles allotted to her. Only with hindsight does she feel regret for undermining the laws of the *oikos* by escaping with Paris, and only because of the Greek expeditionary force, not because she recognizes that, as a woman, she is not meant to act in such a manner. We are thus left with the possibility that she could always defy the law again, just as Hermes would still want to sleep with Aphrodite after witnessing the penalty. In this way, we can understand the attribution of a "divine" cause for her actions as a necessary afterthought, covering over the horror of the possibility of the power of Helen's agency. If it is just an afterthought, then the scandal of Penelope's lines here has little to do per se with her identification with the sexual longings of Helen. They are scandalous insofar as Penelope aligns herself with a Helen who is something more than the multitude of masks she wears; even after the Trojan War, Helen cannot be fitted into any preconceived categories. But is not the same also true for Penelope?

Penelope's allusion to the complexities of Helen as agent at the end of book 23 is also related to the difficulties of determining Penelope's responsibility for the actions of the suitors—a theme that underlies the Ithacan narrative. For the verbal battles between Telemachus and the suitors center on the question of Penelope's control of the situation. When Antinous defends himself and the suitors against Telemachus' charges by diverting the blame onto Penelope, he does so in a way that can lead us back to a crucial scene in *Iliad* 3 where Priam absolves Helen of blame.

> σοὶ δ' οὔ τι μνηστῆρες Ἀχαιῶν αἴτιοί εἰσιν,
> ἀλλὰ φίλη μήτηρ, ἥ τοι περὶ κέρδεα οἶδεν.
>
> (*Od.* 2.87–88)

[And yet you have no cause to blame the Achaian suitors,
but it is your own dear mother, and she is greatly resourceful.]

> οὔ τί μοι αἰτίη ἐσσί, θεοί νύ μοι αἴτιοί εἰσιν
> οἵ μοι ἐφώρμησαν πόλεμον πολύδακρυν Ἀχαιῶν·
>
> (*Il.* 3.164–65)

[I am not blaming you: to me the gods are blameworthy
who drove upon me this sorrowful war against the Achaians.]

Helen flits between being viewed as the cause of the Trojan War and being considered one of its innocent victims.[42] So, too, Penelope appears to the suitors as the cause of the situation on Ithaca (in that she wears the mask of Nausicaa for the suitors) and to Odysseus as an innocent victim (the mask of Arete).

Equally interesting is the way that the "one/many" motif central to the role of Helen in the Trojan War—the war is fought by many for the sake of one—is replayed in the *Odyssey*.[43] At the moment when the killing of the mass of suitors is about to begin, Athena encourages Odysseus by referring back to the war fought over Helen.

ὣς φάτ', Ἀθηναίη δὲ χολώσατο κηρόθι μᾶλλον,
νείκεσσεν δ' Ὀδυσῆα χολωτοῖσιν ἐπέεσσιν·
  "οὐκέτι σοί γ', Ὀδυσεῦ, μένος ἔμπεδον οὐδέ τις ἀλκή,
οἵη ὅτ' ἀμφ' Ἑλένῃ λευκωλένῳ εὐπατερείῃ
εἰνάετες Τρώεσσιν ἐμάρναο νωλεμὲς αἰεί,
πολλοὺς δ' ἄνδρας ἔπεφνες ἐν αἰνῇ δηϊοτῆτι,
σῇ δ' ἥλω βουλῇ Πριάμου πόλις εὐρυάγυια.
πῶς δὴ νῦν, ὅτε σόν γε δόμον καὶ κτήμαθ' ἱκάνεις,
ἄντα μνηστήρων ὀλοφύρεαι ἄλκιμος εἶναι;

(Od. 22.224–32)

[He spoke, and Athene in her heart grew still more angry,
and she scolded Odysseus in words full of anger, saying:
"No longer, Odysseus, are the strength and valor still steady
within you, as when, for the sake of white-armed, illustrious
Helen, you fought nine years with the Trojans, ever relentless;
and by your counsel the wide-wayed city of Priam was taken.
How is it now, when you have come back to your own possessions
and house, you complain, instead of standing up to the suitors?"]

Athena's scolding leads to the eruption of the long anticipated, destructive *eris*. A long war over Helen is replayed in the short, violent massacre of the suitors over Penelope. Of course, the teleological reading of the poem depends on what Zeitlin has recently called the one "crucial and obvious difference" between the two: "Helen went away; Penelope did not."[44] But from a psychoanalytic perspective, what seems more significant is the similarity between these two wars, not the difference: one war is fought in the name of Helen's infidelity, the other in the name of Penelope's fidelity. But both are clearly wars fought as part of a futile attempt to guarantee fidelity—that is, they are intermale fights over the fantasy of what a woman should be. What this runs up against, in Zeitlin's words once more, is "the radical unknowability of the unexpressed secrets of a woman's desire."[45]

If Penelope's identification with Helen casts a shadow over her fidelity, her next rhetorical move brilliantly diverts us from the implications.

νῦν δ', ἐπεὶ ἤδη σήματ' ἀριφραδέα κατέλεξας
εὐνῆς ἡμετέρης, τὴν οὐ βροτὸς ἄλλος ὀπώπει,
ἀλλ' οἶοι σύ τ' ἐγώ τε καὶ ἀμφίπολος μία μούνη,
Ἀκτορίς, ἥν μοι δῶκε πατὴρ ἔτι δεῦρο κιούσῃ,
ἣ νῶϊν εἴρυτο θύρας πυκινοῦ θαλάμοιο,
πείθεις δή μευ θυμόν, ἀπηνέα περ μάλ' ἐόντα.

(Od. 23.225–30)

[But now, since you have given me accurate proof describing
our bed, which no other mortal man beside has ever seen,
but only you and I, and there is one serving woman,
Aktor's daughter, whom my father gave me when I came here,
who used to guard the doors for us in our well-built chamber;
so you persuade my heart, though it has been very stubborn.]

Through the trick of the bed, Penelope manages to reverse the roles that she and Odysseus play. Before the trick, the narrative centered on the question of Penelope's fidelity, but the possible movement of the bed shifts our attention to the ability of the skills of Odysseus as bed maker to guarantee her fidelity. We shift from concern with the referent of the *sema* (Penelope's fidelity) to the fidelity of *semata* in and of themselves. Odysseus no longer plays the role of accusing husband and is instead portrayed as someone engaged in persuading Penelope of his identity (πείθεις δή μευ θυμόν), which is in turn dependent on his ability to make the bed a sign of a safe, mutual pact. But the allure of this possibility is also undermined. Penelope's speech of recognition exhibits the same pattern as the speech of Odysseus. She begins by arguing that no other mortal could have seen the bed (just as Odysseus believed no other mortal could have moved it). But she undermines this certainty by the mention of a serving woman who shares the knowledge—a woman who appears nowhere else in the poem and whose identity seems a mystery.[46] Because another mortal has seen the bed, its secret is potentially available to anyone; Penelope's mention of Aktoris can only emphasize the tenuousness of the bond of faith that links her to Odysseus.

The reversal of roles engineered by Penelope's trick of the bed paves the way for a well-known reverse simile that describes their recognition scene.

> ὣς φάτο, τῷ δ' ἔτι μᾶλλον ὑφ' ἵμερον ὦρσε γόοιο·
> κλαῖε δ' ἔχων ἄλοχον θυμαρέα, κεδνὰ ἰδυῖαν.
> ὡς δ' ὅτ' ἂν ἀσπάσιος γῆ νηχομένοισι φανήῃ,
> ὧν τε Ποσειδάων εὐεργέα νῆ' ἐνὶ πόντῳ
> ῥαίσῃ, ἐπειγομένην ἀνέμῳ καὶ κύματι πηγῷ·
> παῦροι δ' ἐξέφυγον πολιῆς ἁλὸς ἤπειρόνδε
> νηχόμενοι, πολλὴ δὲ περὶ χροῒ τέτροφεν ἅλμη,
> ἀσπάσιοι δ' ἐπέβαν γαίης, κακότητα φυγόντες·
> ὣς ἄρα τῇ ἀσπαστὸς ἔην πόσις εἰσοροώσῃ,
> δειρῆς δ' οὔ πω πάμπαν ἀφίετο πήχεε λευκώ.
>
> (*Od.* 23.231–40)

[She spoke, and still more roused in him the passion for weeping.
He wept as he held his lovely wife, whose thoughts were virtuous.

> And as when the land appears welcome to men who are swimming,
> after Poseidon has smashed their strong-built ship on the open
> water, pounding it with the weight of wind and the heavy
> seas, and only a few escape the gray water landward
> by swimming, with a thick scurf of salt coated upon them,
> and gladly they set foot on the shore, escaping the evil;
> so welcome was her husband to her as she looked upon him,
> and she could not let him go from the embrace of her white arms.]

After an epic poem of Odyssean wandering, Penelope, not Odysseus, is compared to the sailor who finally reaches dry land. The reversal emphasizes the contingency of gender roles; if the *Odyssey* is the tale of a (male) wandering in search of a truth that rests on the knowledge of a woman, there is no reason why these gender roles could not be played by either sex. In the reversal of the simile, Odysseus occupies the (female) position of truth, and Penelope looks to him for a guarantee of her identity; she is the person journeying, while Odysseus is the haven to which she travels. There is also a wider thematic contrast between the certainty of a fixed abode on land that promises to set a limit to the uncertainties and flux of the sea. This in turn looks back to the fantasized worlds of the Cyclopes and Phaeacians. The Cyclopes lived a static existence on the tops of mountains and remained unaware of travel by sea; the perfection of Phaeacian ships meant that the Phaeacians had no concept of a limit to their ability to travel. Both species are introduced to the aspect of society that they themselves had lacked, which leads to the creation of a desire that will define them as humans. For should they fully identify with the mode of existence they lack, this can only come at the price of losing their current mode of existence; and to deny the desire for this alternate world is to enter the impossible, inhuman fantasized universes they had inhabited before Odysseus' arrival. So, too, Penelope and Odysseus hold out to each other the promise (but only the promise) of the satisfaction of desire. The *mega sema* of the bed is as much a divider as a uniter. For to look toward *semata* for a guarantee of unity between two selves is also to recognize that *semata* need to patch up a division already present.

Odysseus as Proteus, Penelope as Pandora

A further puzzle haunts the reunion of Penelope and Odysseus. Shortly after the recognition scene and before they turn to lovemaking, we find that this much anticipated end of the *Odyssey* is not to be *the* end. Instead, Odysseus remembers the prophecy of Teiresias that he must soon embark on another journey. Though I will not attempt to resolve the numerous problems associated with the specific form of Teiresias' prophecy,[47] some further parallels between Odysseus and Proteus and between Penelope and the figure of the *parthenos* can help us judge what is at stake.

Proteus' initial reaction to the trick that undermines his system of counting is to go on with business as usual. Only later (when he gives in to Menelaus) does he (retroactively) understand that his system of counting was always contingent, dependent on his arbitrary imposition of closure on the numerical chain. So, too, the challenge to Odysseus' ability to self-count and thus to impose a sense of closure on his travels is undermined by Penelope's trick. Though this provokes initial doubt, the recognition scene continues as if his doubt was not justified, as if the sign of the bed is certain. But in his later recollection of the prophecy of Teiresias, can we not see a belated understanding of the significance of Penelope's trick? Odysseus' belief in the bed as a sign of Penelope's fidelity coincided with his belief in his own identity. Penelope functioned as the telos of his voyage, which in turn promised to guarantee that he was the person he always thought he was. But just as Proteus came to realize that any telos imposed on the counting sequence was only a telos insofar as it was imposed by him, so, too, Odysseus belatedly realizes that the telos of Penelope is ultimately his own fantasy construction. Perhaps for this reason, Odysseus, as he remembers the prophecy of Teiresias, not only denies the possibility of closure but emphasizes that his future toils will be "immeasurable."

> ὦ γύναι, οὐ γάρ πω πάντων ἐπὶ πείρατ' ἀέθλων
> ἤλθομεν, ἀλλ' ἔτ' ὄπισθεν <u>ἀμέτρητος</u> πόνος ἔσται,
> πολλὸς καὶ χαλεπός, τὸν ἐμὲ χρὴ πάντα πελέσσαι.
>
> (*Od.* 23.248–50)

[Dear wife, we have not yet come to the limit of all our
trials. There is immeasurable labor left for the future,
both difficult and great, and all of it I must accomplish.]
(translation modified)

The phrase "immeasurable labor" not only anticipates toils to come but looks back to Odysseus' previous failure to measure the scope of his toils. His former belief that Penelope would be the telos of his journey, which in turn promised to guarantee the logic of his system of beliefs (all performed on her behalf), is swept aside. He is left at the same terrifying moment that confronted Proteus; his belief in himself is gone because the system on which his calculation of toils depended is undermined. Penelope's fidelity, together with his sense of self, is incalculable, and the recognition of this prompts him to recall Teiresias' prophecy.[48]

Odysseus' words are thus much more disturbing than has been realized; they hint at the destruction of his belief in his former world, replacing it with the worrying chaos of an incalculable world. Penelope's response is motivated by an awareness of this problem.

> εἰ μὲν δὴ γῆράς γε θεοὶ τελέουσιν ἄρειον,
> ἐλπωρή τοι ἔπειτα κακῶν ὑπάλυξιν ἔσεσθαι.
>
> (*Od.* 23.286–87)

[If the gods are accomplishing a more prosperous old age, then there is hope that you shall have an escape from your troubles.]

She first latches onto the apparent optimism implied in the old age prophesied by Teiresias. This single aspect of his highly enigmatic pronouncements then forms the basis of a message of hope, ἐλπωρή. The final words uttered by Penelope are in stark contrast to her actions as *parthenos*, which destroyed Odysseus' self-belief. The destruction of any belief in any system of counting, of language's ability to guarantee identity, is replaced by the hope that, nevertheless, meaning can be constructed. In the appearance of hope following in the wake of destruction, it is possible to detect a story familiar from the mythical tale of the first *parthenos*, Pandora. For in Hesiod's tale, though Pandora lets evils from Zeus' jar loose on the world of the mortals, Ἐλπίς, "Hope," is allowed to remain.[49] The narrative of the *Odyssey* uses the figure of the *parthenos* to highlight the logical difficulties involved in the presumption of a fixed, calculable identity (and accordingly the difficulties of the social systems that promise to confer such identity). But it also leaves open the hope, if only the hope, that some sense can be constructed out of the human condition.

Notes

INTRODUCTION

1. Goldhill 1995, 196.

2. For the consensus, see, among many other works, Finley 1977; Goldhill 1991; Vidal-Naquet 1986; Morris 1986; Said 1979.

3. Quint (1993, chap. 1) discusses the antagonistic relationship between epic teleology and romance narratives. See also Pucci 1995, esp. the introduction.

4. For a Bakhtinian approach, see Peradotto 1990, esp. chap. 2. For feminist approaches, see Katz 1991; Zeitlin 1996.

5. The *Odyssey* thus comes close to realizing a fantasy of Achilles in the *Iliad:* that he and Patroclus alone would exult over the fallen Troy, with all Greeks and Trojans dead (*Il.* 16.97 ff.). In chap. 7, I discuss this episode and the more general way the *Odyssey* realizes other Iliadic fantasies.

6. Paradigmatic, in my interpretation, will be the cases of the Phaeacians and the Cyclopes, to be discussed at some length in chaps. 1–2.

7. For an attempt to chart some of these complexities, see Hartog 2001. The poem itself knows very well that desire can be radically relativized. Consider only Menelaos' tale of Helen, the figure of desire par excellence, taking on the voices of the wives of the Greeks embedded within the Trojan Horse (*Od.* 4.279 ff.). An apparent objective beauty is here given a subjective twist, with the result that it becomes utterly unclear where beauty might lie. In individual fantasy? In the changing persona of Helen herself? In her ability to manipulate individual fantasies? At any rate, the episode itself should encourage us to complicate our ideas of what desire might mean in this poem.

8. Cedric Whitman's analysis of Achilles' as a seeker of the "absolute" (1958) remains very relevant. For a recent critique of Whitman, see Gill 1996 (chap. 1), a book that itself builds on the arguments of Martin 1989. Both Gill and Martin seek to downplay the scale of Achilles' challenge to the world, his nihilism, by relating his speech of book 9 to specific cultural codes.

9. Cf. the analysis of Martin (1989, 207 ff.), who sees this passage in terms of conflicting genres of speech, with a discourse of politeness running alongside one of threat. This kind of ambiguity in genre is heightened by the difficulty in understanding the reference to death—split between "I would rather die" and "I would rather kill you."

10. For Socrates (*Hippias Minor*), the Achilles of book 9 is the true liar. Unsure of what he wants, even as he claims his own certainty, Achilles gives his guests a contradictory picture of his own intentions, first suggesting that he will leave Troy immediately, then later affirming that he will only avoid battle until the Greeks face fire at their ships.

11. Of course, to make use of psychoanalysis is not simplistically to identify an ancient with a modern self and is still less to reduce ancient and modern selves to some transhistorical key that will always yield the correct answer. I use psychoanalysis as a kind of conceptual tool aiding a research project, providing guidelines for certain lines of inquiry rather than raiding the past to exemplify its truths. As such, I have little desire to mount any defense against the supposed "ahistoricism" of psychoanalysis, a defense that has anyway already been waged: see the sensible remarks of Janan (1994, intro.). I have tried to explain relevant psychoanalytic terminology as the argument progresses, providing references to psychoanalytic literature for further reading for those interested.

12. This is perhaps most poignantly on view in the death of Odysseus' dog, Argos, in *Odyssey* 17. For does not Argos die at the very moment he gets what he wants? Thus is he not only the sure knower of Odysseus but also the perfect foil for Odysseus.

13. To complete the circle, we might imagine another ending to the *Odyssey:* Odysseus is at home for seven years already, looking out toward the sea, imagining the island of Calypso, the excitement of his travels, when Penelope comes to him, and so on.

14. The terror, especially on the part of Telemachus, at the loss of the household's goods cause us to overlook the massive wealth of a household that has sustained the revelry of the suitors for years and seems well equipped to continue to sustain it.

15. Their obsession with the marriage of Penelope is reason enough that any simple critical denunciation of the suitors fails. To tease out the comparison with Achilles, we could say that the suitors are faithful to the letter of the law (the need for Penelope to marry to preserve a male leader of the *oikos*), while failing to obey its spirit. Achilles does the opposite: he violates the authority of the lawgiver Agamemnon in the name of a fidelity to the spirit of the laws of heroism that holds the Greeks together. I discuss this more fully in chaps. 6–7.

16. Indeed, a move out of their world of indecision in either direction open to them—either an open disregard for the law and a more concerted effort to oppose Telemachus with violence, or a stronger effort to enforce Penelope's wedding—would have saved them. They are significantly halfhearted in both enterprises.

17. See Detienne and Vernant 1991, 223–25.

18. Here, it is worth noting that the *Odyssey*'s counterstory, the return of Orestes, offers an example of this kind of race, followed by a failure. Menelaus lingers too long in Egypt, amasses wealth, but loses the ability to avenge his brother—and this loss retroactively makes the wealth meaningless.

19. Achilles' argument with Agamemnon in the opening of the *Iliad*, by arguing for a return, would thus preserve the place of Argos/Greece as the place of return and undermine the increasing grip that day-to-day life in Troy has on their fantasies. It provokes the kind of remembrance of home that is in danger of being forgotten, just as Odysseus remembers Ithaka at the start of the *Odyssey*.

20. On this, see, e.g., the opening chapters of Vidal-Naquet 1986 and Goldhill 1991.

21. Katz 1991, 9.

22. The reverse might be the case. Any knowledge of one's genetic identity, the mere fact that two people had sex and thus produced a child, is just as likely to be traumatic as comforting. Comfort can occur, but not directly, because of the genetic fact; rather, it can occur indirectly, because of the ability to trust the assurances of a parent who confirms this fact.

23. This in part explains the recognition scene in book 16, when Telemachus only recognizes his father after his father has authoritatively told him that no other Odysseus would arrive. If we pay attention to what he *does,* it seems Telemachus is looking just as much for that paternal authority as he is for any truth about his genetic makeup.

24. The Lacanian Other is the symbolic system that any human confronts as he or she becomes a speaking being, the world of symbols and language that predate him or her, where he or she must ultimately find a home. In a well-known pun, we can speak of a child's entrance to language coinciding with the replacement of the mother (a figure who satisfies all the child's needs) with the Other (a social, symbolic system of rules/regulations where the child must find a place for himself or herself). Of course, this system is only available to the child through the words of the parents and is only ever incompletely available. As such, it is connected to desire—a failure to know it all and a concomitant desire to know it all.

25. See Zizek 1989 for a discussion of this Lacanian point.

26. Perhaps the most famous occurrence is the trick of Hera in *Iliad* 14.

27. I borrow the title of the fine recent book of Haubold (2000).

CHAPTER 1

1. It is true that Zeus refers to Polyphemus by name in the first book of the poem (1.68 ff.), but this is after the blinding has occurred.

2. The reaction of the Cyclopes to Polyphemus' blinding can be contrasted with the reaction to adversity exhibited by the Kikonians earlier in Odysseus' narrative. When attacked by Odysseus' men, the Kikonians immediately come to each other's aid, calling out to each other: Κίκονες Κικόνεσσι γεγώνευν (Od. 9.47). The immediacy of this response highlights their status as a community linked by a common language. This status is in marked contrast to the lack of such group solidarity exhibited by the Cyclopes.

3. This is the assumption of Austin (1980). He is eager to counter the notion of "barbarism" attached to the Cyclops by structuralist-inspired criticism. Accordingly, he tries to emphasize both the brutality of Odysseus and the aspects of Cyclopean civilization that appear to put them in a more charitable light. For Austin, the efforts of other Cyclopes to come to the help of Polyphemus are one such example. I agree that the Cyclopes' efforts suggest civilization, and there is certainly great merit in Austin's efforts to rethink the Cyclopes' barbarism; but I want to stress that this is the first act of "civilization" that occurs for the species. In short, Austin makes an unwarranted generalization, believing that this single act of civilization means that the Cyclopes were civilized before this act.

4. For this stabbing and the importance of the wordplay between Οὖτις and οὐτάω, see Peradotto 1990, 143 ff.

5. This "significant" aspect of Polyphemus' name has been noted by both Burkert (1979, 33) and Ahl (1991, 228).

6. For elaboration of the concept of kleos as repeated speech, see Pucci 1995, 13 ff.

7. Lynn-George 1988, 122.

8. Cf. the words of Whitman (1958, 187) on Achilles: "All human relationships require compromise; their very nature, committed as they are to mortality, imply violation and loss, by death, if nothing else." Lacan's term for the loss we all (men *and* women) suffer on entrance to language is *symbolic castration*. Lynn-George (1994, 238 ff) argues that it is significant that Peradotto ignores the name *Polyphemus,* and he suggests that "some particularly disturbing aspects of language are unleashed in Odysseus' stratagem for survival." The disturbing aspects of language referred to by Lynn-George are presumably linked in some way to the violence of the blinding, which in my reading of this episode functions as the basis of language. Only this fundamental loss produces passage into the realm of the contested field of language. However, Lynn-George's insight into the "disturbing aspects" of language unleashed by Odysseus, breaking with so many humanist readings of the poem that remain faithful to their identification with Odysseus, is very important and will form the basis for much of my later analysis of Odysseus as "destroyer of the people."

9. Burkert 1979, 33; Vidal-Naquet 1986, 18 ff.

10. This is noted by Crotty (1994, 146): "To eat human flesh is so horrific as to be utterly beyond such codes [of hospitality]. To accuse Polyphemus of 'not scrupling' to eat 'his guests' is an unwarranted importing of one culture's ethics into another realm, where ethics can have no meaning." This fundamental insight of Crotty has too often been ignored and is crucial to the episode. But rather than turn away in horror—and run back to the safety of a position of supposed ethical agreement (where ethics can have a meaning)—it is perhaps better to linger over the amoralism of the Cyclops. For it can open up a space from which to make judgments on the ethical codes of hospitality, at least signaling their incompleteness.

11. Consider the following remarks of Bruce Fink (1995, 103) about the relationship of the child to language, which apply equally well to the Cyclops: "Why would a child ever bother to learn to speak if all of its needs were anticipated, if its caretakers fed it, changed it, adjusted the temperature, and so on before it even had a chance to feel hunger, wetness, cold, or any other discomfort? Or if the breast or bottle were almost immediately placed in its mouth as soon as it began to cry? If nourishment is never missing, if the desired warmth is never lacking, why would the child take the trouble to speak?"

12. Peradotto 1990.

13. Searle 1967, 488, quoted in Peradotto 1990, 97.

14. Zizek 1989, 89 ff. My debt to Zizek's reworking of the debate will soon become obvious.

15. Quoted in Zizek 1989, 92.

16. Zizek 1989, 93.

17. In the *Odyssey,* the Cyclops remembers the prophecy of Telemus.

18. In fact, Searle's tribe is much closer to another of Homer's tribes, the Phaeacians. I explore this in chap. 2.

19. See Heubeck's commentary in Heubeck, West, and Hainsworth 1988, 84. The relevant fragment of Aristotle referred to by West is fr. 172 Rose, which comes from the H.Q. scholiast at *Od.* 9.106: ζητεῖ Ἀριστοτέλης πῶς ὁ Κύκλωψ ὁ Πολύφημος μήτε πατρὸς ὢν Κύκλωπος· Ποσειδῶνος γὰρ ἦν· μήτε μητρός, Κύκλωψ ἐγένετο αὐτός [Aristotle questioned how the Cyclops Polyphemus himself became a Cyclops, since he was born neither from a Cyclopean father (Poseidon was his father) nor from a Cyclopean mother].

20. This raises an important problem. The Cyclops is "defined" as a one-eyed being; but for whom? The obvious answer is only for us, as human beings, who read the episode through the eyes of that other human being, Odysseus. For the Cyclopes themselves, definition can never be their concern—and the moment they do begin to define themselves as Cyclopes, it is already too late; they make themselves human. We should also ask a related question: what is the cause of the trauma that emerges on the island? It is not simply that one Cyclops loses an eye: it is that this loss is registered by the other Cyclopes, who answer his call for help. If his cry had not been registered, nothing need have changed: the Cyclopes could have stayed on their mountaintops. This means that the loss of the eye is just as traumatic for them: they see that a fellow Cyclops loses an eye, which suggests that they, too, can lose their eye. Their defining feature comes into being when it has been witnessed as lost and thus as only contingently, not naturally, theirs.

21. Lacan, 1982, 81. For a general elaboration of these concepts, see Rose's introduction to the same volume (32 ff.).

22. The emphasis on this emergence of the Cyclops' voice as a scream is already enough to complicate the deconstructive readings of the poem that see the voice as the primary provider of the illusion of self-presence and identity. Pucci (1995, 96) refers to "the decisive importance of the voice above all other signs in the epic tradition." Consider also the following typical remark: "The self-identity of this voice, whatever disguise and situation a man is in, must intimate that this voice 'mirrors' or bespeaks what is immutable (essential) in man" (Pucci 1995, 76–77). There is certainly much of value in this insight. But the scream of the Cyclops suggests something quite different and unsettling about the voice, which we can pinpoint by referring to its objectlike nature. For the Cyclops' scream suggests that the voice is not simply the neutral medium that allows characters to achieve a whole identity. Here, the voice's isolated scream underlines its radical incompatibility with the sense of language necessary for a subject's belief in his or her consistency. For the Cyclops, his scream signifies the way he has been torn from a universe where everything seemed to be whole. Whenever the Cyclops now speaks, using his voice, it will be linked to the traumatic scream that was his first quasi-linguistic act. Because of this excessive and unsettling nature of the voice, Lacan categorized it, within psychoanalytic parlance, as a "partial object." It is part of a mythical "lost object," which signifies the primal, lost unity the child experienced with the mother (for Melanie Klein, the breast and faeces were the partial objects par excellence). Insofar as we unconsciously try to restore that lost unity, we seek out such partial objects. If we are attracted to someone, what they say to us might be less important than the unquantifiable way that they say it. The voice is that material part of their utterance that exceeds anything their words might mean. See Salecl and Zizek 1996.

23. We can ask a further important question: who is the subject of this scream? It cannot yet be "Polyphemus," because the act of naming has not yet occurred. It is not a Cyclops, if we define the Cyclopes in terms of their defining quality, their one eye. For this is a Cyclops who has just lost his eye and is thus no longer properly a Cyclops. The subject of the scream is no one, which announces the entrance of the subject as such to Cyclopean civilization.

24. On the significance of the term οἶος as a marked term, against μοῦνος as a more general, "unmarked" term, see Kahane's commentary in Kahane and Bakker 1997, 118 ff. Also relevant is the original status of οἶος as a numeral—the Cyclops becomes "one" individual as he is introduced to the "manyness" of language.

25. Before the blinding, we can thus imagine a hypothetical Cyclopean response to Telemachus' doubt concerning paternity: "'No one knows his father.' Who cares?" The desire to know one's father only makes sense in a world where knowledge itself is missing and desire is operative, where the father promises such knowledge.

26. Goldhill 1991, 10.

27. Goldhill (1991, 11) notes the tautology with the following statement, which he italicizes: "*Recognition is part of the relationship (to be) recognized.*" We merely need to take this a step further: in the case of father and son, it is not simply *part* of the relationship; it is the *essence* of the relationship. This is not the only instance of such wordplay in the poem: cf. Nestor's words at *Od.* 3.122–23—πατὴρ τεός, εἰ ἐτεόν γε / κείνου ἔκγονός ἐσσι—which play on the credibility of any assertion of paternity.

28. This picture of Odysseus as able to do anything and yet unable to get what he wants is fundamental to Pucci's deconstructive reading of the poem.

29. Note that Polyphemus' cry for help dragged the other Cyclopes from their "immortal night" [νύκτα δι' ἀμβροσίην] (*Od.* 9.404). We should also note the symbolic importance of the wine given by Odysseus to the Cyclops in order to guarantee the success of his trick. The text is careful to stress its exceptionality (*Od.* 9.196 ff.), and it quickly captivates the Cyclops. But what is crucial is that its strength causes the Cyclops to liken it to ambrosia (9.359). The ambrosian liquid allows the mortal hero to approach, and render vulnerable, a quasi-divine being.

30. Zizek 1989, 94.

31. For a brief summary of the problem, with bibliographical references to the debate, see Heubeck, West, and Hainsworth 1988, 19 ff.

32. Hesiod *Theog.* 139 ff.

33. The connection between wandering and blinding is emphasized by underlying wordplays on "wandering"/"blinding"/"avoiding" (ἀλύω / ἀλαόω / ἀλέομαι). See, e.g., 9.398, 411, 453, 516. This vocabulary of blinding and wandering is integrated into a wider vocabulary of alterity, connecting this wandering and blinding to Polyphemus' (recently discovered) dependence on others (ἄλλοι). Consider in particular 9.115, 129, 192. For the division between the blinded Cyclops and the others, see 9.401, 493. Before his blinding, the Cyclops had no concept of wandering (because he lived in a universe without doubt) or alterity (because he was perfectly self-sufficient). Both this very wandering and Polyphemus' new status as a man of "much speech" organized around a central loss, a nothing, should begin to remind us of Odysseus *polytropos*, endless wanderer and explorer par excellence.

34. The episode thus reverses the usual way of thinking of blindness. We might naively believe that we need to be able to see where we are going in order to discover new things. But without a fundamental blindness—which renders us unsure of ourselves and thus equipped with the desire to find out more about ourselves—we would never begin the process of searching in the first place.

35. Austin 1980, 22.

36. Austin 1980, 26–27. The shift from indicative to optative starts at *Od.* 9.126.

37. The world of Goat Island functions as a blank screen that allows fantasized self-projection—a screen that did not exist for the Cyclopes before the blinding.

CHAPTER 2

1. *Od.* 6.4–5.
2. The opposition is now widely recognized. See Hainsworth 1993, 293.
3. *Od.* 8.557 ff.
4. This, paradoxically, makes the Phaeacians similar to their apparent opposites, the Cyclopes. For because the Phaeacians can go anywhere, they are in no real sense explorers: there is simply nothing new for them to discover.
5. The adjective is only extant in the dative, in the phrase ἐν σχερῶι, meaning "uninterruptedly, successively." See LSJ, s.v. Cf. Pind. *Nem.* 1.69.
6. See in particular *Od.* 7.201–2: αἰεὶ γὰρ τὸ πάρος γε θεοὶ φαίνονται ἐναργεῖς / ἡμῖν [For always in time past the gods have shown themselves clearly to us]; 7.205–6: οὔ τι κατακρύπτουσιν, ἐπεί σφισιν ἐγγύθεν εἰμέν, / ὥς περ Κύκλωπες . . . [They make no concealment, as we are very close to them, as are the Cyclopes . . .].
7. See Rose 1969. Rose's arguments have undermined the efforts by certain scholars to view the Phaeacians as one-dimensionally perfect.
8. We can also make a connection between the Phaeacian's unconscious knowledge of the prophecy and their behavior. They constantly need to show themselves to be perfect hosts in order to prove the error of the prophecy; they are accordingly ruled by it, enslaved to it insofar as they base their actions around avoiding it.
9. There seems to be a difference between the form of disavowal of Alcinous and that of the rest of the Phaeacians. Alcinous, unlike the other Phaeacian men, does not have a name that reflects the qualities of a seaman. He seems to have conscious access to the prediction of Nausithous (a knowledge implied in the meaning of his name, "Strong *noos*"), which makes his disavowal sharper. It is as if he says, "I know very well that we are destined to be destroyed, but still I go on as if I didn't." The other Phaeacians seem to have repressed this knowledge, which reappears in their unfriendliness. Alcinous thus appears as simultaneously more trusting and more asinine than the others.

It is also worth emphasizing that readers are aware of this "unconscious knowledge" of the Phaeacians as not simply something hidden within them (and thus pure speculation) but, rather, as "objective." We, as readers/listeners, know that they are both perfect and destined to be destroyed by the entrance of Odysseus. Their "unfriendliness" is a symptomatic way (a compromise formation) of recognizing their own impossible status as perfect hosts.

10. Most 1989.
11. However, as Dolar (1993) has argued, the example may be misleading in that "it suggests that one might actually have possessed 'life with money' before being presented with the choice." The crucial point is that this possibility is retroactively produced by the act of choosing itself. This initial "forced choice" is precisely what opens up the possibility of "choice" in general. The Phaeacians represent this impossible "wholeness" of "life and money"—of life without loss.
12. The italics indicate where I have modified the translation of Lattimore.
13. The verb ἐκτελέσειεν here retains some of its literal sense of "bring an end to" rather than merely meaning "accomplish." Cf. *Od.* 10.41.
14. Note the undermining of Alcinous' initial confidence. He begins by inviting the com-

petitors to take part in "all the games" in which the Phaeacians surpass others (*Od.* 8.101 ff.). Alcinous quickly modifies this after Odysseus' victory, limiting his boast to games of speed.

15. The aetiological aspect of Odysseus' interactions with the Phaeacians is mentioned in passing by Nagler (1990). The importance of the theme of firstness is emphasized by Athena's earlier remark about the discus throw, which is "by far the first" [πολὺ πρῶτον]. The general question of the importance of the numerical sequence and the role of "firstness" will be explored in much greater detail in the next chapter, when I consider the tricking of *Proteus*.

16. On this aspect of the symbolic, see Zizek 1991, 11. This opening of a gap allows the Phaeacians to become aware (self-consciously) of the impossibility of their society, something that they already knew unconsciously (exhibited in their unfriendliness). Of course, in the *Odyssey*, they become self-conscious too late to preserve their identities as Phaeacians.

17. The italics indicate where I have changed the translation of Lattimore. For the problems of the phrase, see Stanford 1965, ad loc.

18. For extensive references to the debate in antiquity, together with discussion, see Most 1989, 15.

19. See *Od.* 13.291. Note the retroactive confirmation of Phaeacian concern about Odysseus' status as a god.

20. This aspect of Homer's literary ruse seems to have been understood by Virgil, who needs to invent a companion who was left behind by Odysseus in order to rewrite the tale (and reopen the case of the species of Cyclopes) in *Aeneid* 3. The suggestion that Odysseus unwittingly left one man behind is an implicit literary challenge to the perfection of Odysseus' ruse, even as it acknowledges it by altering Odysseus' story. For, at least as *Odysseus* tells the tale in the *Odyssey*, the story of the Cyclopes is brought to an end.

21. On this passage, see the superb discussion of Peradotto 1990, 80 ff.

22. Perhaps this is the point of the cry of despair that is uttered at the loss of sight of the ship (*Od.* 13.169), which before its petrifaction was entirely visible (καὶ δὴ προὐφαίνετο πᾶσα [*Od.* 13.169]).

23. Goldhill 1991, 35.

24. Peradotto 1990, 161.

25. Or, to compare them to the Cyclopes, what is missing on Phaeacia is the moment when words are produced in a response to the absence of identity—the scenario for the naming of the blinded Cyclops.

CHAPTER 3

1. For some preliminary work on counting and classification, see the suggestive article of Henderson (1997).

2. The translation is Muellner's (1996, 14).

3. Muellner 1996, 16.

4. See, e.g., Vidal-Naquet 1986, chap. 1.

5. *Od.* 9.334 ff.

6. In the specification of Proteus as Aegyptian (*Od.* 4.385), it is tempting to see a connection, at the level of the signifier, to Aegyptius, the father obsessed with his fifth son.

7. Note how the simile νομεὺς ὣς πώεσι μήλων signposts the connection to the tricking of Polyphemus in *Odyssey* 9, where a real shepherd will be deprived of his flocks. I discuss the similarity of the two tricks in greater detail in chap. 7.

8. πέμπε is Aeolic for πέντε. See Stanford 1965, ad loc. The meaning of the word is obscure enough to merit comment by the scholiasts: κατὰ πεντάδας μετρῆσι, ἀριθμήσηι. πεμπάζειν γὰρ λέγεται τὸ κατὰ πεντάδας μετρεῖν. παρὰ δὲ τοῖς Δωριεῦσι πέμπε τὰ πέντε κατονομάζονται [He measures, counts in fives. For πεμπάζειν means to measure in fives. For the Dorians call πέμπε "five"] (A); κατὰ πέντε ἀριθμήσει. τὰ γὰρ πέντε πέμπε λέγουσιν Αἰολεῖς [He counts in fives. For the Aeolians call πέμπε "five"] (P.Q.) The definition in LSJ (s.v.) strengthens the likelihood that πεμπάσσεται means "count in fives" by appealing to "counting on one's fingers"—of which there are, for most people, five. There is no verb τεσσαράζω for "counting in fours," though there is a verb τριάζω for counting in threes, which seems to be associated with wrestling, in which "three falls" are required for victory. This suggests that πεμπάσσεται does not mean "number every fifth one." I am grateful to Ann Hanson for pointing this out to me and just as grateful to Sally Humphreys for raising it as an objection. That Homer's characters might count on their fingers, in multiples of five, has actually long been recognized. See Wood 1775, 255–56 for a discussion of πεμπάσσεται.

9. See West's commentary in Heubeck, West, and Hainsworth 1988, 221. Though the pun is noted, it is not interpreted. This follows the scholiasts, who merely note that Homer uses the same word to signify different things: ὅτι τῆι αὐτῆι λέξει παραλλήλως οὐκ ἐπὶ τοῦ αὐτοῦ σημαινομένου κέχρηται (P.Q.).

10. Cf. another Egyptian tale with the same structure, the story of how Psammetichus came to power (Herodotus 2.147.4 ff). At a time when Egypt was divided up evenly between twelve kings, an oracle declared that the one who should pour a libation from a bronze cup in the temple of Hephaestus would become master of the entire country. When, later, all the kings were about to pour a libation in the temple, it so happened that the priest brought one cup too few. Psammetichus, because he lacked a cup, having no idea what he was doing, took his own helmet off to serve as a cup, and the oracle was fulfilled. Something goes missing, and someone (unwittingly) moves into the void opened up by the missing object.

11. On the manner in which Saussure grappled with the problem, see Porter 1986.

12. Copjec 1994, 174. Copjec is emphasizing the points made by Jacques-Alain Miller (1978) in his important article "Suture (Elements of the Logic of the Signifier)."

13. Cf. Zizek 1989, 87 ff, for a discussion of the Lacanian concept of the master signifier.

14. Fink 1995, 52.

15. The problem of counting and accounting is replayed in the sheep trick of *Odyssey* 9, where Odysseus undermines Polyphemus' control over his sheep and his ability to account for them, even as he submerges the remainder of his own men *into* the sheep of Polyphemus. This vocabulary of herding for men will reappear in the group killing of another set of men—the suitors, later in the poem. The politics of closeness to an animal acted out on the physical level in both these tricks (Menelaus and his men wrapped in sealskins, Odysseus' men attached to sheep) raises questions about the difference between humans and animals.

16. Cf. Detienne and Vernant 1991, 264: "The fact is that Proteus was deceived by the seal-disguise Menelaus and his companions adopted when they dressed up in the freshly flayed skins of these sea monsters; and the reason he was deceived is undoubtedly that the distance between man and seal is one that is easily crossed." Though there is a great deal of

interest in the overall discussion of the similarity of humans to seals—in particular, in the question of the shared five fingers of both creatures—I maintain that these authors have alighted on a kind of alluring red herring in this story.

17. It is possible to understand this episode in the simpler way, as depending on the confusion of sign and referent. If it was possible for πεμπάσσεται to mean "number every fifth one," then the problem of "four seals" could be resolved if we were to presume that Eidothea killed four of Proteus' seals in order to get the skins for Menelaus and his men. This interpretation was initially suggested to me by Professor H. D. Cameron and underpins the suggestion of Professor Humphreys. The interpretation I offer seems more powerful, however, because it explains aspects of the text that otherwise remain puzzling, in particular the punning on λέγω and the emphasis on counting. There is no obvious reason why the tale (if interpreted in the simpler manner) needs to involve four people. One dead seal and Menelaus alone in a sealskin would be sufficient for it to work.

18. Of course, it is a "logical" seal that is missing. In reality, the number of Proteus' seals may well remain the same.

19. The endlessness of Proteus' system of counting, its lack of limits, might remind us of the endless series of guests who arrived at Phaeacia. Proteus had no idea of who was counting (a figure of pure sense) until he lost one of his seals. His counting was in an important sense automatic; it went on without any doubt on the part of any subject. It thus resembles the relationship between the Phaeacians and their ships, which pass people onto their destination automatically.

20. I here read λέκτο as from λέχομαι.

21. The classic text is "Jokes and Their Relation to the Unconscious."

22. On the time of epiphany, see Hinds 1988.

23. The immortalizing aspect of ambrosia is clear in its etymology as "immortal." See Chantraine 1984–90, s.v. "ambrosia."

24. Peradotto 1990, 113. Peradotto provides the example of Odysseus' dog, Argus—motionless, dying, yet called "Flash."

25. Lacan, Seminar X, 1957–58, Nov. 6. Quoted in Dor 1997, 197.

26. This would give a novel spin to Eidothea's formulaic phrase at 4.387: "And *they say* also he is my father, that he begot me." Others need to tell Eidothea that Proteus is her father, because he remains silent. This also gives more retroactive significance to the pun on λέγω and λέχομαι. For λέγω is also the most common verb used to mean "to speak."

27. As such, this miscommunication—between a human who believes a god still to be divine and a god who has just become human—previews the difficulty of recognition that Telemachus will encounter with Odysseus in book 16; for there, too, Telemachus clings to the belief that his shape-shifting father is a god. The problem Odysseus faces with Telemachus is itself of broader significance. In the first half of the poem, his tricks are responsible for opening up the divides between gods and mortals by introducing them to loss. In the second half, he not only falls victim to the failings of his own power but seems unaware of the lessons he has taught others.

28. Lacan 1997, 302.

29. Here there is an obvious similarity to Oedipus, so crucial to Freud not because he slept with his mother but because he did not know who he was.

30. See Fink 1977, chap. 8.

31. See Henderson 1997 for the most sublimely obsessive attempt yet made to come to terms with counting in the *Odyssey*. I have learned a great deal from this attempt.

32. For some obvious examples that are central to the narratives of both poems, consider the catalog of ships in *Iliad* 2, which follows Odysseus' ordering and counting of each division of troops earlier in the book. Also, Odysseus is careful to chart in some detail the gradual loss of his own soldiers in the story of his wanderings to the Phaeacians; the loss of his men leads to ongoing restructuring of the group. In both cases, the way humans become part of a social group is put under the microscope. I take up this problem at length in chaps. 6–7.

33. For a discussion of this Lacanian point, also well understood by Marx, see Zizek 1989, 46 ff.

34. For this "experiment," I beg the reader's indulgence; whether it is viable for the poem will ultimately depend on the extent to which one believes that the *Odyssey* is constantly engaged in questioning the limits that separate humans from animals. In chap. 7, I explore the ways in which human and animal life are strangely intertwined; see esp. my discussion of the transformation of men into animals on Circe's island. At any rate, the metaphor of animal herding for people is central to the epic idea of what constitutes a people. Haubold (2000, 17 ff.) argues for the centrality of "shepherding," embedded in the phrase ποιμὴν λαῶν, to the epic construction of the "people." Crucial for me is less the specificity of shepherding than the general principle of "herding" as a metaphor for the control of a human population—a metaphor that can slip from sheep to other animals, such as seals. This centrality of the metaphor has an important consequence—and here I part company with Haubold. When we move into actual descriptions of the herding of animals, the epic poems may well be literalizing (and thus redefining) the nature of the metaphor itself, telling us more about its underlying dynamics; that is, the metaphorical use of "shepherding" can allow us to see, in any act of real herding, a redefinition of the problem of what a leader of the people is doing.

35. The dilemma I have traced for the seals is structurally similar to the problem faced by Odysseus' men as they consider the possibility of rebellion from Odysseus, a rebellion suggested by Eurylochus in book 10.

36. Goldhill 1991, 4.

37. On the allures and dangers of a teleological criticism, see Porter 1990.

38. This is one of the central issues examined by Peradotto (1990).

39. Here, we might see a connection with the traditional phrase ὤλεσε λαόν. It is certainly true that much of the second half of the *Odyssey* will play with the possibility that Odysseus is just such a people-destroyer. But in these tales, he does something more profound: he introduces the possibility of absolute loss, the utter contingency of any communal identity, to a species that had not encountered such a possibility before. On the importance of this dynamic, see Haubold 2000.

CHAPTER 4

1. Haubold 2000, 43.

2. In terms of exchange, we can also see the episode as dramatizing an exchange of wonder itself. Odysseus arrives on Phaeacia and sees a wondrous civilization that seems quite ordinary to the local inhabitants. What they end up with, after his departure, is the

possibility for amazement and wonder they hitherto have lacked. For Odysseus' wonder, see *Od.* 7.43, 45.

3. *Theog.* 453 ff.

4. πρῶτον δ' ἐξήμησε λίθον, πύματον καταπίνων (*Theogony* 497). For insightful comments on this pattern and its relationship to the rest of the *Theogony*, see Zeitlin 1996, 80 ff.

5. Apollodorus *Bibliotheca* 1.47–48.

6. On the way the autonomous workings of language subjugates the subject, consider only Freud's case study of the Rat Man's psychic organization, as summarized by Fink (1995, 22): "As a child, the Rat Man identified with rats (*Ratten*) as biting creatures that are often treated cruelly by humans, he himself having been severely beaten by his father for having bitten his nurse. Certain ideas then become part of the 'rat complex' due to meaning: rats can spread diseases such as syphilis, just like a man's penis. Hence rat = penis. But other ideas become grafted onto the rat complex due to the word *Ratten* itself, not its meanings: *Raten* means installments, and leads to the equation of rats and florins; *Spielratte* means gambler, and Rat Man's father, having incurred a debt gambling, becomes drawn into the rat complex. Freud refers to these links as 'verbal bridges' (SE X, p. 213); they have no meaning per se, deriving entirely from literal relations among words. Insofar as they give rise to symptomatic acts involving payment (for the pince-nez/father's debt), it is the signifier itself that subjugates the Rat Man, not meaning." Lacan refers to this subjugation as the "agency of the letter."

7. Vernant 1983, 306.

8. Vernant 1983, 314–15.

9. The metaphorical range of the term "head" is well traced in Ford 1994.

10. So Alcinous claims at *Od.* 8.557 ff.

11. This seems to be represented in the lack of an agent of movement in ἐλαυνομένην. The ship moves without a mover.

12. Hainsworth (1993, 174) so translates the pluperfect βεβήκει (*Od.* 13.164). Poseidon introduces a paradoxical moment of presence/absence. He arrives and is gone at the very moment he arrived. My phrase "followed by" is thus in itself a little misleading.

13. Here, the parallel with the birth of Zeus in the *Theogony* offers itself. For the Phaeacians, the last of their old visitors, Odysseus, is the origin of their new society. Zeus, too, is straddled between old and new worlds, eaten last, vomited forth first. But again, the difference is crucial. The agent, connecting old and new civilizations, disappears from Phaeacian civilization; all that replaces him is a sign they cannot entirely understand (the stone ship) and a second sign hinting at their possible obliteration (the mountain). On Olympus, continuity is preserved in the person of Zeus: he links old and new orders. But the means by which he usurped the old order (the stone ingested by Kronos in his place), itself a sign of the fragility of any order is displaced onto the human world.

14. Language is synchronic not just because it is frozen, atemporal, but because it freezes different times into its own structure, thus disrupting any linear, temporal chain of cause and effect.

15. *Od.* 13.163–64: ἅς μιν λᾶαν θῆκε καὶ ἐρρίζωσεν ἔνερθε / χειρὶ καταπρηνεῖ ἐλάσας· ὁ δὲ νόσφι βεβήκει.

16. In the passage, Odysseus' discus is referred to first as *lithos* then as *laos*, previewing the more explicit etymologizing play between "stones" and "people" in book 13.

17. It is worth pausing over the evidence for the situation on Phaeacia prior to

Odysseus' arrival. Athena's remarks about Phaeacian unfriendliness and general suspicion of strangers (*Od.* 7.32 ff.) suggest both that they do regularly receive strangers and that they are nervous about their presence. Alcinous also boasts of the Phaeacians ability to pass every stranger on to their destination, and he suggests that this is a regular occurrence (*Od.* 8.32 ff.). Given the typical nature of the scenario, with strangers routinely arriving and routinely being passed on, it is surely reasonable to assume that the games are part of this routine. Normal strangers arrive, compete in the games, lose, and are sent home. This allows the Phaeacians to continue believing in their own infallibility. But Odysseus is not normal; he is the agent of Nausithous' prophecy.

18. It is tempting to link this "headless" mountain, a torso without a top, to the ship on Phaeacia. There, we have the shape of a ship, which may or may not link itself to a time when the ships moved freely. The "decapitated" mountain could perhaps function, mythically, in the same way—as a reminder of the days when the mountain was whole and had a top. This argument might be strengthened by a "naturalizing" interpretation of the episode, seeing the beheaded mountain as the origin of the volcano on Sicily—an interpretation that seems to be picked up in Virgil's depiction of the Cyclops in *Aeneid* 3.

19. It is not that the Cyclops has simply become less strong because of the blinding: it is that despite his limitless strength, he is unable to get what he wants. The first stone lands before the ship; the second, when he uses his limitless strength, lands behind the ship. In short, we are dealing with the problem of desire. It is interesting to recall here Lacan's defense of Zeno's paradox of Achilles and the tortoise. Lacan's point is that it is, after all, quite obvious that Achilles can pass the tortoise. But that is precisely the problem. He can fail to reach him or can overtake him, but he can never reach the point of identity with him. Can we not see this with the throws of the Cyclops? He can get closer and closer to the ship, a little behind, a little before, but—for him—it proves impossible to hit it.

20. Thanks to Ann Hanson for suggesting this line of inquiry.

21. Poseidon's precinct is at the heart of the Phaeacian assembly (*Od.* 6.266 ff.); their seamanship is declared as a gift of Poseidon at *Od.* 7.34 ff.

22. Critical reactions, ancient and modern, to the action of Poseidon are explored by Peradotto (1990, 79 ff.).

23. Zizek 1991, 134.

24. Cf. *Il.* 24.253 ff. Cf. also Aegyptius in *Od.* 2.21 ff., where the loss of one of his sons, a companion of Odysseus, seems to make him forget his other sons.

CHAPTER 5

1. Lynn-George 1994, 238. See also the astute remarks of Kennedy (1984), who shows how a shared ideology of contemporary critics influences how we understand the relationship of literature to ideology. In Lacan's terms, this is a phenomenon of the Imaginary—our narcissistic desire to see doubles of ourselves.

2. Peradotto 1990, 90–91.

3. Of course, such an identification with the Phaeacians brings its own dangers. Is this no more than a pathetic, retroactive rationalizing of loss—a paranoid attempt to make sense out of a loss that could never have been avoided, thus a way of clinging to it?

4. On the connection between Odysseus and bards and on the role of bards in general, see Segal 1994, chaps. 6–7.

5. A staging of separate songs that provide a different picture of the same event or person is clearly part of Homeric technique. The competing—indeed, contradictory—songs of Menelaus and Helen about Odysseus in book 4 of the *Odyssey* are the most obvious example. The competition between Odysseus and Demodocus is fundamentally similar.

6. On the latter split, see Nagy 1979, chap. 12, 222 ff. The question of deception raises the possibility that even generic performance markers such as "praise poetry" can be unreliable; that is, they might not mean what they say. In short, it calls into question the power of genre itself to provide reliable meaning.

7. *Od.* 8.72 ff.

8. Nagy 1979, chap. 3.

9. For a discussion of the attempts, see Clay 1983, 98 ff.; Hainsworth 1993, 351, at *Od.* 8.75.

10. Cf. Nagy's argument (1979, chap. 19) that *eris* is constitutive of human society. Phaeacia is a society without *eris*—or, rather, it is a society where conflicts are immediately (and, for the Phaeacians, unproblematically) resolved by Arete. I offer more on this in chap. 8.

11. *Od.* 8.158. The link has been noted by Braswell. His 1982 article notices much of the thematic significance of the songs of Demodocus; my additions and modifications to his important insights are largely based on the assumption of the aetiological significance of Odysseus' stay on Phaeacia.

12. Martin (1984, 43 ff.) argues that Odysseus' victory in the games completely resolves the *neikos*. By contrast, I suggest that Odysseus' victory opens the possibility of a *neikos* without resolution on Phaeacia by introducing the Phaeacians to loss, even as his rhetoric fools them into thinking no such loss has occurred.

13. Peradotto 1990, 170.

14. Does it not also show what is lacking on the island of the Cyclopes? The emphasis is on pushing a rock to a peak (λόφον) and transcending the summit (ἄρκον ὑπερβαλέειν). This is usefully glossed at *Od.* 11.593 by scholiast B, who explains the punishment in terms of the failure to reach the top of a mountain (ἡ τιμωρία τούτου ἦν ἵνα λίθον μέγαν ἀναβιβάσῃ ἐν κορυφῇ ὄρους). The effort to attain the missing "peak" of a mountain is unnecessary for the Cyclopes until the first mountaintop is broken off by Polyphemus' throw at Odysseus. The story of Sisyphus can thus be seen as an attempt to return to the mountain the peak that was severed from it—but that, as with the Cyclops' failure to heal his wounded eye, is destined never to be returned to its former wholeness.

15. As an anonymous reader has pointed out to me, the emotional reaction to the song also succeeds in drawing attention away from the song itself to Odysseus' reactions to it. His tears succeed in positioning himself as privileged interpreter of the song. The poem dramatizes the way a certain emotional perspective illuminates the song for the Phaeacians, who read it through Odysseus' tears.

16. *Od.* 8.93 ff.

17. Calhoun 1939, 11 ff.

18. There is a close parallel between Odysseus' false modesty here and his later treatment of the beggar Iros. When forced to fight Iros, he chooses to hit him lightly in order to

ensure that the suitors do not suspect his identity. They therefore do not entertain the possibility of destruction (*Od.* 18.93 ff). Both the Phaeacians and the suitors choose to continue to believe in their own infallibility, which makes them want to believe in the relative weakness of Odysseus.

19. I offer this as a footnote to the well-argued claims offered by Nagy on behalf of the sophistication of traditional poetry. See Nagy 1996, chap. 4.

20. *Od.* 8.219: "There was Philoctetes alone who surpassed me in archery..."

21. Haft (1990, 52) mentions Odysseus' theft of the Palladium, his capture of the prophet Helenus, his bringing Neoptolemus to Troy, and the killing of Rhesus in the Doloneia.

22. On the identification of Hephaestus with Odysseus, cf. Braswell 1982; Newton 1987. Critics normally take it for granted that Achilles and Odysseus have separate qualities, suggested by their epithets; consider the following words of Lowenstam (1993, 44): "As is often pointed out, we have 'fleet-footed' Achilleus, on the one hand, who hates deceit as much as the gates of Hades and whose greatest deed in the epic tradition is achieved with the aid of his swift feet. On the other hand, Odysseus 'of the many wiles' is renowned for his shrewdness while he admits his limitation in running." Lowenstam seems to presume that because Odysseus lacks the speed of foot of Achilles, this constitutes a fundamental limitation to his powers. But it is part and parcel of his *metis* that it can make up for the speed he lacks. Demodocus' song suggests that any Achillean "victory" that Achilles' swiftness of foot promises to provide will be a hollow one. Consider also the following suggestion by Zeitlin (1995, 150 n. 42) on the funeral games in the *Iliad:* "Achilles, of course, is best known for his swiftness of foot, and if Odysseus wins the footrace in *Iliad* 23, it is because Achilles presides over the games." But more needs to be said here. In the race, Odysseus defeats Ajax, a figure who already surpasses Odysseus in his swiftness of foot; he does this through Athena's trick. The suggestion is surely that Achilles' speed would be useless against Odyssean guile (unless, of course, we follow Socrates in the *Hippias Minor* and see Achilles as the cunning one: Odysseus thinks he is showcasing his *metis* but only does so because Achilles allows him to showcase it, a ruse worthy of Odysseus himself). This episode also looks back to the previous book, which depicted Achilles' greatest heroic act, the killing of Hector. It is often noted that there is a certain appropriateness to the chase scene that precedes Achilles' killing of Hector, since it showcases the key quality of his major epithet, *podarkes,* "swift-footed" (and, as Nagy [1979, 326 ff.] demonstrates, swiftness is thematically linked to *bie*). Von Reden (1995, 31) has emphasized the *bie* aspect of Achilles' victory by claiming that "he kills Hector . . . in an open battle rather than an attack launched from an ambush." But this ignores the crucial point that *Iliad* 22 also showcases the limitations of Achilles' speed; for Achilles is unable to catch Hector until Athena intervenes to trick Hector into giving up his flight. She persuades him to give up his attempt to escape; this gives added significance to the link between *bie* and speed suggested by Nagy. I here quote the relevant lines, with Nagy's translation.

ἠθεῖ' ἦ μάλα δή σε <u>βιάζεται ὠκὺς</u> Ἀχιλλεὺς
ἄστυ πέρι Πριάμοιο <u>ποσὶν ταχέεσσι</u> διώκων.

(*Il.* 22.229–30)

[Dear brother, indeed swift Achilles uses **bie** against you,
as he chases you <u>swift feet</u> around the city of Priam.]

The *bie*, "strength," of Achilles succeeds only because Athena tricks Hector into thinking that this strength is irresistible. Until her intervention, Hector was happily holding his own. Athena's later intervention, which sends Ajax into the dung and wins the footrace for Odysseus, is thematically linked to her intervention here. In both cases, her trick undermines the pretensions of speed. *Metis* overpowers *bie*, even in the *Iliad*. Achilles not only needs a trick but seems happy to take advantage of it.

23. I change Lattimore's "from every direction" to the more literal "in a perfect circle." I discuss the importance of the circle imagery later.

24. See Detienne and Vernant 1991.

25. *Od.* 8.339 ff. Hermes is of course the god of the liminal, the preserver of doorways, but he performs this role because he himself is the ultimate thief, the transgressor of boundaries par excellence: "In the house, his place is at the door, protecting the threshold, repelling thieves because he is himself the thief . . . for whom no lock, no barricade, no frontier exists. He is the wall-piercer who is pictured in the 'Hymn to Hermes' as 'gliding edgeways through the keyhole of the hall like autumn breeze, even as mist'" (Vernant 1983, 129). Vernant (chap. 5) explores the transgressive role of Hermes in his relationship to Hestia. See also the Bakhtinian reading of Peradotto (1990, 56 ff). In chap. 6, I further discuss the similarity between Odysseus and Hermes. The word used for "bedpost" here, *hermis*, only occurs at one other point in the poem, in the crucial scene where Penelope and Odysseus confront each other over the mutability of Odysseus' bed. That scene and its relationship to the song of Ares and Aphrodite is discussed further in chap. 9.

26. See Haft 1990.

27. Cf. 13.152, 158: μέγα δέ σφιν ὄρος πόλει ἀμφικαλύψαι [[I would] cover over their city with a great mountain].

28. As I suggested in the last chapter, their eventual punishment at the hands of Poseidon appears to the Phaeacians as utterly senseless.

29. *Od.* 9.460.

30. In terms of the Phaeacians' process of reading, they again read the *Apologoi* of Odysseus too literally. They read these tales as part of an identifying description that is to be attached to the name *Odysseus*. They fail to read the tale of the blinding of the Cyclops allegorically, as the tale of loss as the sine qua non of language but also its point of failure, because their symbolic identity depends on their belief in language's infallibility, its lack of ambiguity.

31. Foley (1978, 20) talks of Odysseus' "special ability to comprehend and respond to the female consciousness" and of his affinity with "non-masculine heroism." Cf. Goldhill 1991, 53 ff.

CHAPTER 6

1. See Adkins 1960.

2. On *Il.* 9.186 ff. see also Nagy 1996, 72 ff. Nagy believes that Patroclus is about to insert the "glories of men" that Achilles sings into the entire heroic tradition of song and that we have an enactment here, self-consciously, of what he calls the "esthetics of rhapsodic sequencing." This is certainly possible, but if so, I would add that the episode seems to play,

just as self-consciously, with the limits of song, since Achilles' song is no simple repository of cultural memory but is always already complicit with the suffering of the Greeks. Further, if it is one possibility that Patroclus could, hypothetically, reply to Achilles' song with a widening of the song into the "Homeric tradition" itself, Achilles' speech in book 16 suggests the possibility of the closure of the "Homeric tradition" into itself, at least in the persons of Achilles and Patroclus.

3. Scodel 1982.

4. Scodel 1982, 42–43.

5. We might also notice that Achilles is also imagining himself and Patroclus in the position of Zeus and Poseidon in Odyssey 13, as they debated the total eradication of Phaeacia.

6. Peradotto 1990, 169.

7. Dolar (1993) provides a Lacanian critique of Althusser's theory of ideological interpellation. A subject is confronted with a seemingly all-powerful force (the realm of the law) that demands his or her obedience. But there remains the possibility of a questioning of this power; for if it is truly all-powerful, then why does it need the subject's obedience? The command to obey is in itself evidence of its failure.

8. Zizek 1994, 98. For a good discussion of the "carnivalesque" aspect of Bakhtinian reversals and of a relationship to studies of Old Comedy, see Goldhill 1991, 176–85.

9. This malevolent aspect of the superego has been noted by Redfield (1990).

10. Recall the pun lurking in the "Nom du Père" (Name-of-the-Father) and utilized by Lacan. The "Nom" (name) of the father is also the "Non" of the father. Paternal authority's ability to structure a group rests on common renunciation of individual desires, on the obedience to this "Non."

11. Let me be explicit: the social order is built on the premise that the spoils of war must be shared. The Greeks kill in a controlled manner because they have given up (on entrance to the social pact under Agamemnon) the right to kill without control. Achilles strips away the spirit of renunciation. It matters little whether the Greeks, in the cold light of day, would be horrified at these superegoic acts. The crucial point is that, in their everyday deeds, they act as if this is what they want. Achilles' actions provide us with access to the fantasy structure that regulates the Greeks' everyday behavior.

12. Haft 1990, 38.

13. Haft (1990) argues that the expression πτολίπορθος Ὀδυσσεύς, used at Il. 2.278 and 10.363, is proleptic, anticipating Odysseus' role as sacker of Troy. She also argues that the Doloneia looks forward to the dolos of the Trojan horse.

14. On this connection, see Hainsworth's introduction to book 10 (1993, 152 ff.).

15. On the symbolic importance of the scepter, cf. Lynn-George 1988, 47–49.

16. Haft notes that the Odysseus of Iliad 2 "blends a keen understanding of his men . . . with a genuine concern for Agamemnon's reputation" (1990, 43), but she seems to miss the irony of Odysseus' supplanting of the "one king."

17. Zizek 1994, 98.

18. On this ability of Odysseus, see Haft 1990, 52.

19. We can compare Odysseus to the Phaeacians before he reached Scheria. They, too, are eerie, because they always succeed in passing on voyagers to their destination.

20. Stanford (1963, 15) believed that these words epitomized Odysseus' polytropic

tact—his ability to act in a socially cohesive manner by avoiding any excess of praise or blame. Though I agree that Odysseus' words help solidify the realm of the social, they do so in a much more perturbing manner than Stanford believed.

21. Odysseus replaces Diomedes' "tactlessness" with tact, referring to what everyone knows as merely "these things" [ταῦτα]. He provides a pronoun without any obvious referent, silencing the attempt to produce such a referent.

22. Diomedes is likened to a lion advancing against a helpless herd (*Il.* 10.485). The helplessness of the sleeping warriors is emphasized (10.471 ff.).

23. Vernant 1991, 50 ff. One might say that the Doloneia, in allowing us to see what happens at night, is showing us the limitations of what can and cannot be seen during the daytime. The paradox is that the limitations of what heroic ideology lets its subjects see in the daytime is only visible via a detour through what happens in the dark.

24. Of course, though I am using psychoanalytic vocabulary to articulate the peculiar nature of the Doloneia and its relationship to heroic ideology, it is worth emphasizing that the Doloneia itself sticks out, or draws attention to itself, as "antiepic," in its perversion of official epic values. Because of the way that this episode of the poem is put on display as exceptional (leading to ongoing attempts to excise it from the poem, most recently by Taplin [1992], I suggest that there is a challenge to heroic ideology within the poem. In principle, it could be possible for a modern critic to find the blind spots of heroic ideology, the "structured silences" (to use the term of the Marxist critic Pierre Macherey) that it reveals to us but that are inconceivable for those within that ideology. But what should be clear from my analysis is that this reading of epic enjoyment is already Homer's. The *Iliad* does not need the Doloneia; the fact that it is there, as an integral part of the poem, and the fact that it suggests a reading of the poem, are highly significant.

25. Peradotto 1990, 100–101.

26. On the transgressive aspects of Achilles, see Goldhill 1991, 89 ff.

27. Lynn-George 1988, 88. On Achilles' "need," see also Rabel 1991.

28. Wathelet 1989.

29. Wathelet (1989, 227 ff.) explores the connection between Rhesus, Odysseus, and the sun god.

30. On the linkage between *noos* and the trickster, see Nagy 1979, 51.

31. See Euripides *Rhesus* 600–606; schol. L at *Od.* 10.435. Haft (1990) explores the relevance of this myth for interpretation of the Doloneia. She argues that the defeat by Odysseus of Rhesus—a warrior destined to be superior to Achilles if he survives for one day—is part of the traditional battle waged between Achilles and Odysseus over the title of *aristos* throughout the Homeric poems. I comment on this later in this chapter.

32. On Hermes, cf. Vernant 1983, chap. 3; Kahn 1979.

33. I modify the Lattimore translation of φέρτεροι from "stronger" to "better"—a translation that Lattimore uses elsewhere for the word.

34. The horses that "are even better" [πολὺ φέρτεροί εἰσιν] recall the quarrel between Agamemnon and Achilles, where the significance of Achilles as the "better" man lies at the center of their argument.

35. Note the parallel between Odysseus' words here and his words to the Cyclops at *Od.* 9.525, where he emphasizes that it is useless for the Cyclops to expect his father to cure the problem of his desire.

36. Wathelet 1989, 218 ff.
37. Gernet 1981, chap. 6; Davidson 1979.
38. These are Gernet's terms.
39. On the relationship between Hermes and Autolycus, see Stanford 1963, chap. 2. Jeanmaire (1939, 400 ff.) has noted the similarity between this Autolycan cap worn by Odysseus in the Doloneia and the "Cap of Hades," which renders the wearer invisible and is worn by Athena to help defeat Ares in *Iliad* 5.845 ff.
40. Davidson 1979, 64 (emphasis in the original).
41. Nagy 1990, chap. 8.
42. Frame 1978, chap. 1.
43. This phrase is Lynn-George's. The phrase in the header, "Obscurist of all," belongs to Hainsworth, quoted in Lynn-George 1988, 123.
44. Agamemnon's offer of the bronze and gold occurs at *Il.* 9.137 and is repeated by Odysseus at 9.279. Achilles rejects this at 9.365. See Lynn-George 1988, 115 ff.
45. *Il.* 9.624 ff.
46. For the way Achilles exults in killing, consider the way he delights in telling Lycaon of the fate in store for him (*Il.* 21.122 ff.); forcing Lycaon to listen to a preview of his imminent mutilation is a crucial part of Achilles' general cruelty. I thank Simon Goldhill for first emphasizing this aspect of Achilles to me.
47. Two recent treatments, with bibliography, are those of Crotty (1994, 84–85) and Lynn-George (1988, 201–7). An influential earlier treatment by Griffin (1980, 55 ff.) emphasizes the depth of the friendship between Achilles and Lycaon as companions in death. The danger in this sort of humanist criticism is that by glorifying the "shared humanity" in death, it simultaneously glorifies the destructive vision of Achilles and thus can only apologize for the destructive, superegoic dimensions of Achilles' actions. Consider Griffin's following observation: "Achilles kills in a passionate revenge, but not in blind ferocity. He sees his action in the perspective of human life and death as a whole, the perspective which puts slayer and slain on a level . . ." (55). As a former teacher once commented to me, "Tell that to Lycaon."
48. Note Achilles' words at *Il.* 21.54 ff. "Here is a strange thing that my eyes look on. Now the great-hearted Trojans, even those I have killed already, will stand up and rise again out of the gloom and the darkness . . ." Note also the marked similarity in Diomedes' argument when he rejects the supplication of Dolon at *Il.* 10.447 ff.: "Do not, Dolon, have in your mind any thought of escape, now that you have got in our hands, though you brought us an excellent message. For if we let you get away now, or set you free, later you will come back again to the fast ships of the Achaians either to spy on us once more, or to fight strongly with us." Diomedes' words once more subvert the public law, but they can do so because they are uttered under the cover of darkness.
49. Griffin recognizes this, if obliquely.

CHAPTER 7

1. Pucci 1982, 42.
2. See Saïd 1979 for such an argument.

3. Nagler 1990, 344–45.

4. This desire comes close to breaking through in book 10, where Eurylochus challenges Odysseus' authority and nearly gets beheaded.

5. *Od.* 20.29 ff: "[S]o he was twisting and turning back and forth, meditating / how, though he was one alone against many, he could lay hands on / the shameless suitors."

6. Detienne and Vernant 1991).

7. Alongside Pucci, Segal is perhaps the most influential of such critics—though it is interesting that he does not dismiss the dark side of the poem. See the concluding remarks to his 1994 collection of essays on the *Odyssey* (224 ff.). These concluding remarks (as he well realizes) cannot help but complicate his general praise of Odysseus as an "everyman" figure, an ethical hero. My analysis begins where Segal's suggestively ends.

8. The quoted phrase is Heubeck's (from Heubeck, Russo, and Fernandez-Galiano 1992, 356). Note, too, that there appears to be no effort made to distinguish the supposedly ethically evil suitors from the heroes. Agamemnon treats them as heroes and makes no unfavorable comment on their behavior. Rather, it is suggested that the best young men of Ithaca are quite at home with the victims of the war.

9. See *Hymn to Hermes* 13: παῖδα πολύτροπον, αἱμυλομήτην; also, 439. Peradotto (1990, 116) remarks that it is "no accident that, in our extant evidence, the only other bearer of the epithet *polytropos* is the volatile divine crosser of boundaries, Hermes." A link between Hermes and Odysseus is suggested by Pucci (1982, 50 ff.). He notes that the proem may attribute "some divine, Hermes-like power" to Odysseus. The crucial question remains: what sort of power is this?

10. See Nagler 1990. Nagler argues for a split between the deaths of the suitors and the deaths of Odysseus' comrades, in order to emphasize the "transgressive" aspect of the killings of the suitors as Odysseus crosses a fatal boundary into his own *oikos*. This leads Nagler to find "ethical anxiety" in the proem. I agree with the diagnosis of ethical anxiety, but, as will become clearer, I think the split between deaths inside/outside Ithaca is more complicated. The relationship between Odysseus and his men is further analyzed later in this chapter.

11. For both epithets, see, e.g., *Hymn to Demeter* 9, 17–18. See also Richardson 1974, ad loc.

12. Nagler 1990, 337 ff.

13. Indeed, Peradotto (1990, 76 n. 17) remarks that the lying tales Odysseus provides to Penelope and Eumaeus (*Od.* 14.314 ff., 19.269 ff.) seem far more appropriate to the promise of the proem than anything that occurs in the actual narrative.

14. On the Phaeacians as "ferrymen of Elysium," see Cook 1992. On the notion of "ultimate destination," see the famous discussion of Lacan (1991, 191 ff.) on Poe's *The Purloined Letter*, with Lacan's closing claim that a letter always arrives at its destination. For an elaboration of the ominous aspects of the phrase, which suggests the necessity of mortality, see Zizek 1992, chap. 2.

15. For the motif of death—"the homeless journey"—in *Iliad* 24, see Lynn-George 1988, 233 ff.; Whitman 1958, 217 ff.

16. Herein lurks a weakness in Lynn-George's critique (1994) of Peradotto's work on the *Odyssey*. The power of his criticsm of Peradotto's dismissal of the "*Iliad*'s great achieve-

ment" (as a poem that self-reflects on death) is undermined by his own underestimation of the ethical anxiety present in the *Odyssey*.

17. The adjective ἄγριος, "hard," is used throughout *Odyssey* 9 of the Cyclops. Note esp. 9.215. The Cyclops is also σχέτλιος, "harsh" (9.295, 351). For the separation of one Cyclops from another, see 9.113 ff.

18.
αἴ γάρ πως αὐτόν με μένος καὶ θυμὸς ἀνήη
ὤμ' ἀποταμνόμενον κρέα ἔδμεναι, οἷα ἔοργας...

(*Il*. 22.346–47)

[I wish only that my spirit and fury would drive me
to hack your meat away and eat it raw for the things that you have done to
   me . . .]

19. This pun is written into Achilles' very name: Ἀχ-ιλλεύς.

20. Whitman 1958, 182. Whitman's treatment of Achilles remains deeply insightful and is especially sensitive to the hero's savagery.

21. The comments of Austin (1980, 34 n. 9) are apt: "Any anthropological analysis of the Cyclopeia, structuralist or otherwise, which ignores the person of the central actor in the episode must do injustice both to the story and to its particular shaping of the concepts of barbarism and civilization. The trickster-hero violates every code of civilized behavior, as nowhere else in the *Odyssey*, and does so before the Cyclops demonstrates any deviant behavior."

22. On the violence of the law, see Salecl 1994. Note also the remarks of Pucci (1995, 175 ff.) on the ambiguity of *Od*. 17.287–89, where Eumaeus is told by Odysseus that "on account of the destructive stomach, well-benched ships are fitted out for the barren sea to bring evils on one's enemies." The reference can be both to pirates and to the Trojan War. Cf. Crotty 1994, 137 ff.

23. This seemingly paradoxical aspect of Odysseus is, I think, crucial to his status in myth. Consider the heritage of Autolycus: he is both an "enemy" of society and a trickster. The association brings with it a major problem. How can one ever tell them apart? The ability of a leader to cement (via *metis*) the realm of the social is precisely what renders him an "outsider." This takes us to the heart of the relationship between superego and ego ideal—the ego ideal is not separate from superego (as if they had nothing to do with each other). Rather, the very success of the operations of the public law renders it superegoic—just as Athena's offer to kill the suitors all at once is obviously connected to (an extension of) Odysseus' desire to kill them with *metis*. The situation of Autolycus on the cusp of the civilized—his ability to exercise the power of the defining element of civilization (*metis*) turns him into an enemy of civilization—provides a matrix with which we can understand three of the figures considered in detail so far: Dolon, the Cyclops, and Achilles. Dolon's trickery remains attached to the pursuit of prestige: he is not yet an "enemy" of society, an outsider. Achilles lingers over the possibility of rejecting the law entirely (i.e., he flirts with psychosis) before giving in to a superego imperative and thus becoming fanatically devoted to the law. The Cyclops is perhaps most Autolycan of all, in that he simply rejects society

(though this means that he has no opportunity to exercise *metis*); we should note that the Cyclops lives as Autolycus does on the top of a mountain, they are both *agrios*, and both have no concern for the gods. But the Cyclops' rejection of society in effect means that he is not a figure of *metis*, because his rejection of society is complete.

24. On the punning on Οὖτις and οὐτάω, see Peradotto 1990, 149 ff. Peradotto connects the verb of "spearing," via the pun, with "nobody."

25. Nagler (1990, 344) notes, "A refrain that punctuates the Adventures in mantic space could be paraphrased: 'We got out, regretting the loss of our companions but grateful to have escaped with our own skins.'" The "we" is inexorably reduced to Odysseus.

26. See Austin 1972; Peradotto 1990, 117.

27. Peradotto 1990, 130–34.

28. This interpretation also allows us to reread the peculiar identity of the Phaeacians as providers of escorts, as πομπαί, "senders." For they also have an infallible record as dispatchers of their guests, which allows them to remain safe in their belief that they are perfect senders of guests, until they are forced to perform one unusual form of πομπή (for Odysseus), which will utterly change the way they send people in the future.

29. Stanford 1965, ad loc. Stanford notes the parallel to *Hymn to Hermes* 542.

30. Burkert 1979, 33.

31. I owe this suggestion to Flora Diaz, who helped me think through much of this episode.

32. See, e.g., Segal 1994, chap. 10; Nagler 1990.

33. It is worthy of note that the verb μήδομαι is etymologically connected to *metis*.

34. Frame 1978, 69.

35. The inconsistency of this weakness of the omniscient god led Aristarchus to athetize lines 374–90. But questioning the lines does nothing to explain the failure to prevent the killing of the cattle. Stanford (1965, ad loc.) defends the lines, noting that "omniscience is anomalously treated elsewhere in Homer" and referring to the tricking of Proteus. The treatment is not so much "anomalous" as a sustained exploration of the manner in which humans are defined in their relationship to omniscience.

36. I modify the translation of Lattimore, who translates μέγα ἔργον ἐμητίσαντο as "dared a deed that was monstrous."

37. On this pattern, see Nagler 1990, 344.

38. Heubeck (Heubeck and Hoekstra 1989, 66) at *Od.* 10.431.

39. Cf. the famous words of Andromache to Hector at *Il.* 6.429–30, which illustrate her pathetic dependence on him.

> Hektor, thus you are father to me, and my honoured mother,
> you are my brother, and you it is who are my young husband.

40. For μέσσαυλος in this sense, cf. *Il.* 11.548, and the definition in LSJ.

41. As Stanford (1965, ad loc.) argues, with the agreement of Heubeck (Heubeck and Hoekstra 1989), ἔρξ is best taken from ἔργω, meaning "confine."

42. Frame 1979, 50 ff.

43. *Od.* 10.240.

44. However, the creatures' monstrous appearance, with its particular pulling power, might itself be part of Circe's ruse to lure the Greeks into her trap.

45. See Saïd 1979; Reece 1993, chap. 8

46. I have much more to say on *aidos* in the following chapter, when I consider the complications of the *aidos* of Nausicaa.

47. This word is ultimately "no," the "non du père."

48. It is worth noting the difficulties of Penelope's words. How are we to understand εἴ ποτ' ἔην γε'? Penelope looks back to a time of perfect authority, but it is unsure if such an Odysseus (as symbolic father) ever existed. It is tempting to suggest that Penelope is quite right, that Odysseus as Name-of-the-Father had no ontological existence, because the power of any real father depends on his ability to play the role of the idealized, symbolic father (which is why the Name-of-the-Father is a metaphor, a constant displacement of any real father). Insofar as Odysseus functioned as Name-of-the-Father, he did not exist. I thank Jim Porter for making this suggestion.

But there may be a darker side to Penelope's words. She refers to the ability of Odysseus to receive strangers and pass them on to their destination, returning us to the Phaeacians, but also looking forward to the destination to which the suitors will be dispatched. In this regard, it is interesting to recall that one of the epithets of Hades is *polysemantor* (one who gives instructions to many).

49. Note the significance of Diomedes' words to Dolon at 10.448 (they preview the later *aristeia* of Achilles).

50. See *Od.* 21.231 ff. for Odysseus' plans to trap the suitors within the hall. Note also that as they are enclosed, they are likened to livestock, as were Odysseus' companions. See *Od.* 22.229 ff., where the suitors hunted down by Odysseus charge around like stampeding cattle.

51. On the symbolic significance of eclipses in general, see Stanford 1965, ad loc.

52. On the unusual "synaesthetic" metaphor, see Stanford 1965, ad loc. The "blazing" of the wailing occurs in the absence of the fire of the sun: cf. Odysseus' alleged ability to return from "blazing fire" in the Doloneia. I have changed Lattimore's translation of οἰμωγὴ δὲ δέδηε to reflect the metaphor.

53. Zizek 1992.

54. Nagler 1990, 351.

55. On the killing of the suitors as Iliadic, see also Segal 1994, 224 ff.

56. See chap. 6 on the bronze/gold motif as raised by the Doloneia.

57. Nowhere else in either epic does a line begin οὐδέ κεν ὣς ἔτι.

58. The choice between two deaths for Achilles is echoed by the impossible choice confronting the suitors—to flee and die or to fight and die.

59.

> ἔστι γὰρ ἔνδον
> χαλκός τε χρυσός τε πολύκμητός τε σίδηρος,
> τῶν κ' ὔμμιν <u>χαρίσαιτο</u> πατὴρ ἀπερείσι' ἄποινα
> εἴ κεν ἐμὲ ζωὸν πεπύθοιτ' ἐπὶ νηυσὶν Ἀχαιῶν.

(*Il.* 10.378–81)

[In my house
there is bronze, and gold, and difficultly wrought iron,
and my father would make you glad with abundant ransom
were he to hear that I am alive by the ships of the Achaians.]

60. On Odysseus' ἄχος, see *Od.* 18.348, 20.256. On the association of Achilles with ἄχος, see Nagy 1979, chap. 6.

61. Heubeck in Heubeck, Russo, and Fernandez-Galiano 1992, 290. Because of the incongruity, the lines have been thought spurious. Heubeck provides a good defense of their authenticity.

62. See Segal 1994, 223 ff., for the view that it is Odyssean restraint and thus part of his moral rectitude.

63. Crotty has recently argued for what I believe is a significantly different view of this censoring. For Crotty (1994, 155), the words to Eurycleia are not a "denial of responsibility" but, rather, evidence that Odysseus "seems to understand the troubling features of his slaughter, and to give expression—above all, by his call for silence—to his understanding of the complexity of the suitors' deaths." This leads Crotty to suggest that Odysseus "expresses the viewpoint not of the victor but of the slain." As I have already argued, I am deeply suspicious of this identification of Odysseus with "the viewpoint of the slain." Perhaps a greater danger is the way that Crotty's rhetoric comes close to repaying the humanist rhetoric of Griffin, who is concerned with discovering the supposed ethical depth of Achilles in the midst of his killing spree. This rhetoric of Griffin tries as best it can not only to apologize in terms of the moral development of the hero for indiscriminate slaughter but also to allow the slaughterer to take the moral high ground by illustrating the lessons learned. For some astute remarks on the ability of contemporary humanist criticism to justify mass slaughter (in this case, the Vietnam War) within a rhetoric of ethical and aesthetical complexity, see Said 1983, 23 ff. However, despite my criticism of Crotty, I quite agree with him that Odysseus' silence (and silencing) once again (as in the Doloneia) is highly significant. It is also worth emphasizing that Crotty at least is well aware of the moral ambiguity of the suitors' deaths, in contrast to a host of critics who see no moral problem at all.

CHAPTER 8

1. See Van Nortwick 1979; Segal 1994, chap. 1.

2. See, e.g., Gross 1976.

3. Woodhouse 1929, 64.

4. For this "troubling" aspect of gender in recent feminist debates, see Butler 1990, with the criticism of Zizek 1993b, 265.

5. The myth is related at *Prt.* 320c7 ff.

6. *Prt.* 322c4 ff. All translations of Plato's *Protagoras* are those of Taylor 1976.

7. See *Prt.* 323a6 ff. "In the case of the other skills, as you say, if anyone says he's a good flute-player or good at anything else when he isn't, they either laugh at him or get angry at him, and his family come and treat him like a madman. But in the case of justice and the rest of the excellence of a citizen, even if they know someone to be unjust, if he him-

self admits it before everyone, they regard that sort of truthfulness as madness, though they called it sound sense before." We have here a vanishing point of truth for any political community. Indeed, it is less a question of truth than of what a community must agree on for any regime of truth to work. For in dealing with questions of justice, the "truth-value" of what a citizen says no longer applies. Subjective sincerity no longer applies—the unjust man is presumably being sincere. No referential truth applies: it hardly matters if the man who admits he is unjust is objectively the most just of all.

8. See *Od*. 6.5–7.

9. Indeed, in Plato, Protagoras slides (without being aware of it, it seems) from a discussion of humanity, *anthropoi*, and of the need for all *anthropoi* to have a share in justice to a discussion of *andres*. See *Prt.* 323a, where the slippage occurs. This ambiguity is central to the drama of Sophocles' *Antigone*, where Creon seems to be aware of the possibility of a male threat to his rule (he consistently imagines that a man has buried Polyneices' corpse) but unaware of the internal female threat.

10. In Lacanian terms, an Imaginary identity.

11. Loraux 1993, 76.

12. The translation is from Loraux 1993, 73.

13. Loraux 1993, 77.

14. Pucci 1977, chap. 4.

15. Loraux 1993, 81.

16. For a fine description of the cultural significance and complexities of this moment in Greek representations of women, see King 1985. The terminology is complicated because *parthenos* signifies both "maiden," referring to a biological status, and the role of woman as "mask wearer." The latter interpretation undermines the naturalness of any biological definition of a young woman by suggesting that this is a social role.

17. Loraux 1993, 82.

18. In *Moses and Monotheism*, Freud provides a useful example of the manner in which a symptom works as a compromise formation. A boy, when a small child, heard his parents having sex. Later, after his first semen emission, he is unable to get to sleep: "This disturbance was a true compromise symptom: on the one hand the expression of defense against his nocturnal observations, on the other hand the endeavor to reestablish the wakefulness which had enabled him to listen to those experiences."

19. This double reading corresponds to the twin possibilities I have earlier offered for understanding the counting system of Proteus. He is either an immortal with a perfect system of counting or a human whose counting is an obsessive denial of his status as human.

20. We can contrast the power of Arete to heal wounds in the social with Odysseus' barbed remark to the blinded Cyclops that his eye (the wound incurred on entrance to the social) could never be healed by his father. Arete functions as the (nonexistent) figure of authority who promises to heal this wound for the Phaeacians.

21. Zizek 1989, 21.

22. On the significance of the name of Alcinous, see Nagy 1990, 205.

23. We cannot apply to her any of the phrases used by Lacan to get at what is essential about desire, such as "It's not always what people ask you to give them that they want" or "I demand that you refuse what I ask of you, because that's not what I want!" This kind of ongoing lack of satisfaction is foreign to her.

24. The limitless nature of Alcinous' knowledge about Nausicaa's desires is parallel to the limitless nature of Phaeacian society, Scheria.

25. What we have here is a context (the peculiar society of the Phaeacians) that forces us to reevaluate the use of a common Greek term whose meaning is relatively clear. Can "shame" make any sense when no one seriously entertains the possibility of a transgression of the law and when the law has never been broken? We need to pay attention to the circumstances in which this "shame" is enunciated. Just as Alcinous' remark about the ubiquity of naming was not a neutral statement but was related to his status as a Phaeacian, so, too, Nausicaa's shame is a Phaeacian shame—a shame that is not properly a human shame.

26. The playing with balls is certainly erotically charged. See Carson 1986, 20.

27. The scholiasts (at *Od.* 6.116) nicely confirm this in their commentary on the significance of βαθείῃ: the detail emphasizes the fact that the ball is out of the reach of the person who threw it, irretrievable.

28. Sappho 105a is probably the locus classicus for this aspect of desire.

> οἶον τὸ γλυκύμαλον ἐρεύθεται ἄκρωι ἐπ' ὔσδωι,
> ἄκρον ἐπ' ἀκροτάτωι, λελάθοντο δὲ μαλοδρόπηες,
> οὐ μὰν ἐκλελάθοντ', ἀλλ' οὐκ ἐδύναντ' ἐπίκεσθαι
>
> [Just as a sweet apple becomes red on the top of a branch
> the top of the topmost branch, and the apple pickers forgot . . .
> they didn't forget, they couldn't reach . . .]

29. I infer these defeats [which admittedly are not mentioned in the text] from the general logic of the narrative on Phaeacia. We know that the Phaeacians have always passed on to his destination, with an escort, every voyager who lands on their island (cf. *Od.* 8.30–31). We know they believe themselves to be infallible transporters and also surely superior to the human guests they transport. (Their ships never fail, they have a closer relationship to the gods, etc. In contrast, their guests are by definition less powerful because they *need* transportation.) This suggests that ongoing victory in the games is part of their belief in their own infallibility. This can help explain the exceptionality of Odysseus. He is not only the traveler who will bring an end to their civilization but also one who is (to their great surprise) superior to them at games.

30. The hurling of the discus by Odysseus will later perform the same function for the Phaeacian men.

31. Freud 1912, 188–89, quoted in Lacan 1982, 6.

32. *Od.* 6.94–95. The clothes are dried by the seashore, where pebbles are washed ashore.

33. Though I have stated (without discussion) that Odysseus is awakened by the sun, I should acknowledge that there are deep textual difficulties at 7.289. I discuss these problems in detail in n. 41.

34. Perhaps it recalls not just any rape but, rather, a specific mythical one. The innocence of the dancing maidens recalls the innocence of another maiden, Persephone. Her rape by Hades is another mythical tale of origins, which seeks to explain the changing of the seasons—and therefore the entrance of mortality—to the human world.

35. See, e.g., Hainsworth's discussion (1993) at *Od.* 6.71–84.

36. He destroys the identity of Phaeacians as perfect transporters of ships, the peculiar, inhuman aspect of their civilization. His intervention also creates a properly human society, which is subject to the possibility (but not certainty) of destruction: this is the significance of the threat of the mountain.

37. Nausicaa's initial desire of Odysseus also heralds the end of Phaeacia as an endogamous society. Note, in particular, the possible sexual connotation of ἐπιμίσγεται at 6.205 (and later at 6.241). There is also a parallel between the dropped balls on Phaeacia, which set in motion new forms of looking, and the loss of the Cyclops' eyeball, which has a similar effect. The problem with the Phaeacians is that, though they have a desire to look, there is nothing in the world outside that they do not already see. Their mode of vision changes when something is extracted from the world around them—the ball that disappears into the swirling water, the discus that sails beyond their frame of reference. We also know that this mode of looking is itself false, because there is something they cannot bear looking at, which sustains their ability to look at everything else: the civilization of the violent Cyclopes. So the emergence of a hole in their sense of reality coincides with a violent, external intrusion. The Cyclops, by way of contrast, pays no attention to the world around him until the loss of his eye. Only this loss sets off a search for it in the world outside, although the object is not actually there. But both species seek lost balls.

38. Loraux 1993, 76.

39. For an interesting account of the "static electricity" generated in the relationship between *aidos* and *eros,* see Carson 1986, 20 ff. I would emphasize that this "electricity" is generated from the recognition that something is being violated.

40. So, ultimately, the games on Phaeacia turn out to be (highly symptomatic) ways of domesticating the problem of desire. To ensure that the "best man" always wins the girl is to match up the measuring of "best" with the desire of the woman. They are social modes of reassurance about "what a woman wants."

41. I provide my own translation at line 7.289, reading δείλετό τ' ἠέλιος (the reading of Aristarchus) rather than the manuscripts' δύσετο. As Stanford (1965, ad loc.) points out, δύσετο makes little sense because so much happens between Odysseus' wakening and nightfall. One problem with Aristarchus' reading is that δείλετο is not attested elsewhere. It does, however, seem to refer to the Homeric division of the day into morning, midday, and evening (Stanford quotes *Il.* 21.111, ἠὼς ἢ δείλη ἢ μέσον ἦμαρ). If it is correct, the time of Odysseus' awakening would be particularly significant. He would have been awakened the moment after the time for epiphany had passed—the moment after the dropping of the ball by Nausicaa signaled her descent into mortal society.

CHAPTER 9

1. Recent versions of this teleological narrative, with Penelope confirmed as faithful wife, include Fredericksmeyer and, more forcefully, Gregory.

2. See Goldhill 1984, 183 ff., for a longer, persuasive version of this structuralist-inspired thesis. However, with its link to the perspective of Odysseus, this kind of thesis also has something of a humanist flavor.

3. In fact, the poem is unclear as to whether Clytemnestra or her lover, Aegisthus, is the actual murderer. See Katz 1991, esp. chap. 1, for a discussion of the implications of this.

4. The recent bibliography on Penelope, which has been sparked in part by a reconsideration of her conflicting desires, is immense. I concentrate on the recent books of Katz (1991) and Felson-Rubin (1994), who themselves provide useful surveys of the literature.

5. Agamemnon's nostalgia for a lost *pistis* has something of the flavor of the elegies to lost *pistis* in the corpus of Theognis.

6. Stanford 1965, at *Od.* 11.441 ff.

7. Felson-Rubin 1994, 93.

8. The valorization of womankind in the poem explicitly mirrors Felson-Rubins' critical approach (1994), which advocates a "female," more "emotional" approach to reading literature.

9. The issue of "Penelope as moral agent" is also discussed, in a similar manner, in Foley 1995. For Foley, Penelope makes "a fully conscious choice and autonomous decision" to reject "hope and desire for obedience to social responsibilities." In effect, Penelope acts out a paradox, choosing not to be free. The central difficulty here lies in the compatibility of "autonomy" with responsibilities that are emphatically social. In what follows, I suggest that the "obedience" of Penelope is more complex. She lingers over the choice between what she wants and what she is expected to do, allowing us to see her desire to desire both at the same time. Consequently, her eventual obedience is both overdetermined and disturbing. In general, this suggests that, in what she does, there is an unconscious refusal of social dictates, rather than merely conscious obedience. She puts into question the very categories implied in "social responsibilities."

10. Murnaghan 1987, 124.

11. Felson-Rubin 1994, 107.

12. It seems reasonable to assume, however, that the poem shows some awareness of the "Arcadian" tradition of Penelope as linked to Pan and fertility. On this in general, see Fredricksmeyer, who agrees that there is awareness of a common Helen/Penelope tradition but that the Penelope of the *Odyssey* rejects it. But the crucial question is, how reliable is Penelope in her rejection of that tradition? Agamemnon puts this question onto our critical agendas.

13. On this parallel, see Van Nortwick 1979.

14. The poem continually portrays the possible victory over the suitors as the victory of Odysseus as athlete. Menelaus associates the successful punishment of the suitors with the image of Odysseus as a wrestler (4.343 ff.). Menelaus' words are later repeated by Telemachus to Penelope (17.134 ff.).

15. *Od.* 6.282 ff.

16. It is worth noting in passing how Eurymachus' logic here alludes to and in an important sense surpasses Achilles' famous arguments against the Trojan War. Achilles realizes the surface stupidity in the fight over a single woman, when there are "many others." The rejection of the war for Helen is reinforced in his rejection of the symbolic importance of the daughter of Agamemnon as wife (*Il.* 9.388 ff.; cf. his remarks at 9.340–42). For Eurymachus, however, the women in and of themselves are of no importance. They are merely the pretext for the battle for prestige between men.

17. In this sense, the contest of the bow replaces the weaving of the shroud. However, there are complications. Despite all the apparent desire of the suitors for Penelope to marry one of them, they seem hooked, at the level of what they do, on not knowing who is best. For this allows them to continue to court her. Later, Antinous will halt the bow contest before all of them have tried it—thereby keeping the contest open. This hope for a contest without a winner is destroyed by Odysseus, just as the trick of the shroud is foiled by the maidservants. But it is worth noticing that both the suitors (as a collective, if not individually) and Penelope act as if they want to maintain the status quo. Penelope wins *kleos* from both her tricks and the attention of the suitors. The suitors maintain an official posture of wanting male, competitive glory but are a curious parody of this zero-sum culture. This strange symbiosis is disrupted from the outside—first by the maidservants and later by Odysseus.

18. See Foley 1978, 11 ff.

19. Cf. his words to Nausicaa outlining an ideal of marriage at *Od.* 6.181 ff.

20. Hesiod *Works and Days* 11 ff. The problem of this split in *eris* is negotiated in Odysseus' offer of a competition in work to Eurymachus in book 18.

21. It also previews the "bad *eris*" that will arise from the games. Odysseus' later attempt to patch up the effect of his discus throw involves a denunciation of any man who would bring *eris* to the games. His language, uttered at the moment when the possibility of innocent competition disappears on Phaeacia, recalls the *eris* between the washers (ἔριδα προφέρουσαι).

> ἄφρων δὴ κεῖνός δε καὶ οὐτιδανὸς πέλει ἀνήρ,
> ὅς τις ξεινοδόκῳ <u>ἔριδα προφέρηται</u> ἀέθλων ...
>
> (*Od.* 8.209–10)
>
> Any man can be called mad and a nobody
> who brings forth an *eris* in the games to his host ...
>
> (translation modified)

22. Katz 1991.

23. This is the thesis of Devereux 1957.

24. The formulaic phrase here is νόος δέ οἱ ἄλλα μενοινᾷ. Specific examples of the phrase include 18.281 ff., 13.381 (where the description is Athena's), and 2.90 ff. (where Antinous describes the famous ruse of the weaving—Penelope promises to marry the suitors when she has finished weaving a shroud for Laertes; she then weaves during the day, but undoes her work during the evening).

25. Katz, 1991, 11: "[T]he long-standing problem of Penelope's character is better addressed from the perspective of narrative fiction than from that of psychological verisimilitude."

26. Katz 1991, 94.

27. Carson 1986, 109.

28. Devereux 1957, 382. Peradotto has recently defended Devereux' insight.

29. See, e.g., the analysis of Pratt 1994. Despite its interesting observation that the

number of the geese might signify the time of Odysseus' departure, Pratt's article falls victim to the urge to keep Penelope simple. Pratt mentions that "the *obvious* surface meaning of the text" is that "she mourns for her geese," and Pratt tries to use this to exclude her desire for the suitors (148). It is quite possible that the twenty geese might refer to the twenty-year absence of Odysseus and to her attempt to stay faithful to him. But it is equally clear that the signification is open (otherwise, why bother asking for interpretation?) and that the dream itself makes an unequivocal connection between the geese and the suitors. Pratt's reading thus destroy the dilemma that Odysseus as dream interpreter is presented with: insofar as Odysseus presses the connection between geese and suitors (in order to realize his own desire, their death), he is forced to drag along with him the affection of Penelope for them.

30. Zeitlin 1995, 141. See in particular *Od.* 18.158 ff., where Athena encourages Penelope to appear before the suitors.

31. These lines to the disguised Odysseus are a near repetition of her earlier lines to Eurymachus at *Od.* 18.251 ff.

32. There is already a strange comparison to Helen here, as if the Greek men are caught up in a competition of two beautiful Greek women for their shows of affections. In Troy, Helen is the center of attention, until the attention shifts back to Ithaca.

33. To make matters worse, her dissolution comes not at the prospect of the continued absence of Odysseus but at a story about his imminent arrival, as if her choice is between a kind of subjective consistency that keeps Odysseus at bay and utter dissolution at the prospect of his presence.

34. Redfield 1994, 21.

35. In a sense, it is indeed the *axis mundi*, but only subjectively, for Odysseus' world. One could also see it as the knot that ties together those conceptual opposites Hestia and Hermes. See the pathbreaking essay of Vernant (1969). The play on "counting" and "lying," which links the fixity of the bed/lying to the fluidity and trickery of numerical schemes, is also active in the puns on *lechos* and *lochos*, "bed" and "ambush." This is already at work in Hesiod's account of Kronos' ambush of his father, Ouranos, in the *Theogony*. On this, see Loraux 1995, chap. 1. Indeed, in book 23 of the *Odyssey*, we have the presentation of a single bed, on whose integrity lies the issue of two "wars" (the Trojan War and the killing of the suitors).

36. In response to this, one might understand the famous "Arcadian" myth about Penelope—that she slept with all the suitors and gave birth to Pan—as less a shocking counterstory than allowing a certain amount of relief for this toil. If Penelope has slept with all of them, then at least there is nothing left to protect.

37. Newton 1987, 18.

38. There is, once more, a verbal parallel: ῥεῖα μετοχλίσσειεν (*Od.* 23.188) (lightly could move it). οὐκ ἂν τόν γε δύω καὶ εἴκοσ' ἄμαξαι / ἐσθλαὶ τετράκυκλοι ἀπ' οὔδεος ὀχλίσσειαν· (*Od.* 9.241–42) (twenty-two of the best wagons could not have moved it from the ground).

39. These lines are central to the argument of Devereux, who sees them as further indication of the simmering, unconscious sexual desire of Penelope that is only barely kept under wraps in the poem itself. While agreeing, once more, that Penelope displays a sexual desire here, I would again emphasize that there is nothing unconscious about this.

40. See *Od.* 3.265 ff. Nestor emphasizes both that at first Clytemnestra was faithful—

"for her own nature was honest"—and that she only gave in to Aegisthus after he had murdered a singer, appointed by Agamemnon to look after her.

41. Cf. Porter 1993, in particular the remarks on Homer's Helen (278).

42. Note also the similar streak of self-destructiveness that both Helen and Penelope seem to show, as suggested in their common desire for death. Penelope's desire to be snatched off by storm winds rather than to face an inferior husband (*Od.* 20.61 ff.) looks back to Helen's desire (*Il.* 6.345 ff.) not to have been born but, rather, to have been snatched away by a storm wind. In Helen's case, of course, this desire is tempered by her willingness elsewhere to sleep with the worse man, Paris, which in turn cannot help but call into question Penelope's fidelity.

43. On Helen and the "one/many" motif, cf. Porter 1993. The parallel between Penelope and Helen as women who are fought over by many men is suggested by Nestor at *Od.* 3.212—"many suitors are in your palace for the sake of your mother." Cf. Achilles words on Helen at *Il.* 9.343 ff.

44. Zeitlin 1995, 144.

45. Zeitlin (1996, 43) is acutely aware of the way the problems of the narrative itself defy easy interpretation.

46. See Stanford 1965, ad loc., for a discussion of the problem.

47. For a discussion of the problem, see Peradotto 1990, chap. 3.

48. Here, it is worth noting the similarity of the prophecy of Teiresias to the prophecies of Nausithous to the Phaeacians and of Telemus to the Cyclops. All three prophecies are ignored by their listeners, and all three are remembered "too late," at the time when their victims confront the loss of their identity. Odysseus, after he reaches the telos of Penelope, recalls the prophecy of Teiresias, which had already predicted that Penelope was not his ultimate telos. Throughout the poem, Odysseus acts as if he had ignored this prophecy, as if Penelope was his telos. The destruction of his identity enables a new reading of the prophecy, which his former sense of self prohibited. Odysseus rereads the prophecy of Teiresias; in this regard, it is interesting that Teiresias himself makes no mention of "immeasurable toil": these are the words of Odysseus. The "truth" of the prophecies in each case is created by the specific reading their victims provide.

49. Hesiod *Works and Days* 94 ff. The meaning of this passage is notoriously difficult to fathom. For a discussion of the problem, see West 1978, ad loc. For my present purposes, I go along with West's suggestion that *Elpis* must be intended as a good thing, countering the evils emitted from the jar (however paradoxical this "good" may be).

References

Adkins, A. W. H. 1960. *Merit and Responsibility*. Oxford.
———. 1970. *From the Many to the One*. Ithaca.
Ahl, Frederick M. 1991. *Sophocles' Oedipus: Evidence and Self-Conviction*. Ithaca.
Austin, N. 1972. "Name Magic in the *Odyssey*." *California Studies in Classical Antiquity* 5: 1–19.
———. 1980. "Odysseus and the Cyclops: Who is Who." In *Approaches to Homer*, ed. Carl A. Rubino and Cynthia W. Shelmardine, 3–37. Austin.
Bergren, Ann L. T. "Language and the Female in Early Greek Thought." *Arethusa* 16:69–95.
Braswell, K. 1982. "The Song of Ares and Aphrodite: Theme and Relevance to *Odyssey* 8." *Hermes* 110:129–37.
Burkert, Walter. 1979. *Structure and History in Greek Mythology and Ritual*. Berkeley.
Butler, Judith. 1990. *Gender Trouble*. New York.
Carson, Anne, 1986. *Eros the Bittersweet*. Princeton.
Calhoun, G. M. 1939. "Homer's Gods: Myth and Märchen." *AJP* 60: 1–28.
Chantraine, Pierre. 1984–90. *Dictionnaire etymologique de la langue grecque*. Paris.
Claus, David. 1981. *Toward the Soul*. New Haven.
Clay, Jenny Strauss. 1983. *The Wrath of Athena*. Princeton.
Cook, E. 1992. "Ferrymen of Elysium and the Homeric Phaeacians." *Journal of Indo-European Studies* 20:239–67.
Copjec, Joan. 1994. *Read My Desire: Lacan against the Historicists*. Cambridge, Mass.
Crotty, Kevin. 1994. *The Poetics of Supplication*. Ithaca.
Davidson, O. M. 1979. "Dolon and Rhesus in the *Iliad*." *QUCC* 30:61–66.
Detienne, Marcel, and Jean-Pierre Vernant. 1991. *Cunning Intelligence in Greek Culture and Society*. Chicago.
Devereux, G. 1957. "Penelope's Character." *Psychoanalytic Quarterly* 26:378–86.
Dolar, Mladen. 1993. "Beyond Interpellation." *Qui Parle* 6, no. 2:75–96.
Dor, Joel. 1997. *Introduction to the Reading of Lacan*. Northvale, N.J.
Edwards, Anthony E. 1985. "Odysseus against Achilles: The Role of Allusion in the Homeric Epic." *Beiträge zur klassischen Philologie* 171.
Felson-Rubin, Nancy. 1994. *Regarding Penelope*. Princeton.

Fenik, B. 1964. *"Iliad X," and the "Rhesus": The Myth.* Brussels.
Fink, Bruce. 1995. *The Lacanian Subject.* Princeton.
———. 1997. *A Clinical Introduction to Lacanian Psychoanalysis.* Cambridge.
Finley, M. I. 1977. *The World of Odysseus.* 2d ed. London.
Flaumenhaft, M. 1982. "The Undercover Hero: Odysseus from Dark to Daylight." *Interpretation: A Journal of Political Philosophy* 10:9–41.
Foley, H. 1978. "'Reverse Similes' and Sex Roles in the *Odyssey.*" *Arethusa* 11:7–26.
———. 1995. "Penelope as Moral Agent." In *The Distaff Side*, ed. Beth Cohen, 93–115. Oxford.
Ford, Andrew. 1994. "Protagoras' Head: Interpreting Philosophic Fragments in *Theaetetus.*" *AJP* 155, no. 2:199–218.
Fowler, Don. 2000. *Roman Constructions: Readings in Postmodern Latin.* Oxford.
Frame, Douglas. 1978. *The Myth of Return in Early Greek Epic.* New Haven.
Fredricksmeyer, Hardy C. 1997. "*Penelope Polutropos:* The Crux at *Odyssey* 23.218–24." *AJP* 118, no. 4:487–97.
Gernet, Louis. 1981. *The Anthropology of Ancient Greece.* Baltimore.
Gill, Christopher. 1996. *Personality in Greek Epic, Tragedy, and Philosophy: The Self in Dialogue.* Oxford.
Goldhill, Simon. 1984. *Language, Sexuality, Narrative, the* Oresteia. Cambridge.
———. 1986. *Reading Greek Tragedy.* Cambridge.
———. 1988. "Reading Differences: *The Odyssey* and Recognition." *Ramus* 17:1–31.
———. 1991. *The Poet's Voice.* Cambridge.
———. 1995. "Review of Peter Rose, *Sons of the Gods, Children of the Earth.*" *CJ* 90, no. 2:195–98.
Gregory, Elizabeth. 1996. "Unravelling Penelope: The Construction of the Faithful Wife in Homer's Heroines." *Helios* 23, no. 1:3–20.
Griffin, Jasper. 1980. *Homer on Life and Death.* Oxford.
Gross, N. 1976. "Nausikaa: A Female Threat." *CW* 69:311–17.
Habermas, J. 1983. *Philosophical-Political Profiles.* Trans. Frederick G. Lawrence. Cambridge, Mass.
Haft, Adele. 1990. "'The City-sacker Odysseus' in *Iliad* 2 and 10." *TAPA* 120:37–56.
Hainsworth, Bryan. 1993. *The Iliad: A Commentary.* Vol. 3, *Books 9–12.* Cambridge.
Halperin, David M., John J. Winkler, and Froma I. Zeitlin, eds. 1990. *Before Sexuality.* Princeton.
Hanson, Ann Ellis. 1994. "A Division of Labor." *Thamyris* 1, no. 2:157–202.
Hartog, F. *Memories of Odysseus.* 2001. Chicago.
Haubold, Johannes. 2000. *Homer's People.* Cambridge.
Henderson, John. 1986. "Becoming a Heroine (1st): Penelope's Ovid . . ." *LCM* 11:7–10, 25–28, 37–40, 67–70, 82–85, 114–21.
———. 1997. "The Name of the Tree: Recounting *Odyssey* 24 340–42." *JHS* 97:87–116.
Heubeck, A., and A. Hoekstra. 1989. *A Commentary on Homer's* Odyssey. Vol. 2. Oxford.
Heubeck, A., J. Russo, and M. Fernandez-Galiano. 1992. *A Commentary on Homer's* Odyssey. Vol. 3. Oxford.
Heubeck, A., S. West, and J. B. Hainsworth. 1988. *A Commentary on Homer's* Odyssey. Vol. 1. Oxford.

Hinds, Stephen. 1988. "Generalising about Ovid." In *Imperial Muse: Ramus Essays on Roman Literature of the Empire*, ed. A. J. Boyle, 4–31. Burwick, Australia.
Janan, Micaela. 1994. *When the Lamp Is Shattered*. Carbondale.
Jeanmaire, H. 1939. *Couroi et courètes*. Lille and Paris.
Kahane, Ahuvia, and Egbert Bakker, eds. 1997. *Written Voices, Spoken Signs: Tradition, Performance, and the Epic Test*. Cambridge.
Kahn, L. 1979. "Hermès, la frontière et l'identité ambigue." *Ktema* 4:201–11.
Katz, Marilyn. 1991. *Penelope's Renown*. Princeton.
Kennedy, Duncan. 1984. "Review of Woodman and West: Poetry and Politics in the Age of Augustus." *LCM* 9:157–60.
———. 1993. *The Arts of Love*. Cambridge.
King, Helen. 1985. "*From Παρθένος to Γυνή.*" Ph.D. diss., University College, London.
Knox, B. M. W. 1961. "The *Ajax* of Sophocles." *HSCP* 65:1–37.
Lacan, Jacques. 1977. *Ecrits: A Selection*. New York.
———. 1978. *The Four Fundamental Concepts of Psychoanalysis*. New York.
———. 1982. *Feminine Sexuality*. Ed. Juliet Mitchell and Jacqueline Rose. New York.
———. 1991. *The Seminar of Jacques Lacan, Book II: The Ego in Freud's Theory and in the Technique of Psychoanalysis 1954–55*. New York.
Lloyd, G. E. R. 1987. *The Revolutions of Wisdom*. Berkeley and Los Angeles.
Loraux, Nicole. 1986. *The Inventions of Athens*. Cambridge, Mass.
———. 1993. *The Children of Athena*. Princeton.
———. 1995. *The Experiences of Tiresias*. Princeton.
Lowenstam, Steven. 1993. *The Scepter and the Spear*. Lanham, Md.
Lynn-George, Michael. 1988. *Epos: Word, Narrative, and the* Iliad. Atlantic Highlands, N.J.
———. 1993. "Aspects of the Epic Vocabulary of Vulnerability." *Colby Quarterly* 29, no. 3:197–221.
———. 1994. "'The Stem of the Full-Blown Flower': Homeric Studies and Literary Theory." *Phoenix* 47, no. 3:226–53.
Martin, Richard P. 1984. "Hesiod, Odysseus, and the Instruction of Princes." *TAPA* 114:29–48.
———. 1989. *The Language of Heroes*. Ithaca.
———. 1993. "Telemachus and the Last Hero Song." *Colby Quarterly* 29, no. 3:222–40.
Martindale, Charles. 1993. *Redeeming the Text*. Cambridge.
Marx, Karl. 1973. *Grundrisse*. London.
Miller, Jacques-Alain. 1978. "Suture (Elements of the Logic of the Signifier)." *Screen* 18, no. 4.
Morris, Ian. 1986. "The Use and Abuse of Homer." *Classical Antiquity* 5:81–138.
Most, G. 1989. "The Structure and Function of Odysseus' *Apologoi*." *TAPA* 119:15–30.
Muellner, L. 1990. "The Simile of the Cranes and Pygmies: A Study of Homeric Metaphor." *Harvard Studies in Classical Philology* 93:59–101.
———. 1996. *The Anger of Achilles*. Ithaca.
Murnaghan, S. 1987. *Disguise and Recognition in the* Odyssey. Princeton.
Nagler, Michael. 1990. "Odysseus: The Proem and the Problem." *Classical Antiquity* 9, no. 2:335–56.
Nagy, Gregory, 1979. *The Best of the Achaeans*. Baltimore.

———. 1990. *Greek Mythology and Poetics*. Ithaca.
———. 1996. *Homeric Questions*. Austin.
Newton, R. 1987. "Odysseus and Hephaestus in the *Odyssey*." *CJ* 83:12–20.
Parry, A. 1956. "The Language of Achilles." *TAPA* 87:1–7.
Peradotto, John. 1990. *Man in the Middle Voice*. Princeton.
Petegorsky, Dan. 1982. "Context and Evocation: Studies in Early Greek and Sanskrit Poetry." Ph.D. diss., University of California at Berkeley.
Porter, J. I. "Saussure and Derrida on the Figure of the Voice." *MLN* 101:871–94.
———. 1990. "Patterns of Perception in Aeschylus." In *Cabinet of the Muses*, ed. M. Griffith and D. J. Mastronarde, 31–56. Atlanta.
———. 1993. "The Seductions of Gorgias." *Classical Antiquity* 12, no. 2:267–99.
Pratt, Louise M. 1993. *Lying and Poetry from Homer to Pindar*. Ann Arbor.
———. 1994. "Odyssey 19.535–50: On the Interpretation of Dreams and Signs in Homer." *Classical Philology* 89, no. 2:147–52.
Pucci, Pietro. 1977. *Hesiod and the Language of Poetry*. Baltimore.
———. 1982. "The Proem of the *Odyssey*." *Arethusa* 15:39–62.
———. 1995. *Odysseus Polutropos: Intertextual Readings in the* Iliad *and the* Odyssey. Ithaca.
Quint, David. 1993. *Epic and Empire*. Princeton.
Rabel, Robert J. 1991. "The Theme of Need in *Iliad* 9–11." *Phoenix* 45:283–95.
Redfield, James. 1990. "From Sex to Politics: The Rites of Artemis Triklaria and Dionysos Aisymnetes at Patras." In *Before Sexuality*, ed. David M. Halperin, John J. Winkler, and Froma I. Zeitlin, 115–34.
———. 1994. *Nature and Culture in the* Iliad. Durham.
Reece, Steve. 1993. *The Stranger's Welcome*. Ann Arbor.
Richardson, Nicholas James. 1974. *The Homeric Hymn to Demeter*. Oxford.
Rose, Gilbert P. 1969. "The Unfriendly Phaeacians." *TAPA* 100:387–406.
Rose, Peter W. 1992. *Sons of the Gods, Children of the Earth: Ideology and Literary Form in Ancient Greece*. Ithaca.
Rosenmeyer, T. G. 1963. *The Masks of Tragedy*. Austin.
Said, Edward. 1983. *The World, the Text, and the Critic*. Cambridge, Mass.
Saïd, S. 1979. "Les crimes des prétendants, la maison d'Ulysse et les festins de l'*Odyssée*." In *Etudes de littérature ancienne*, 9–49. Paris.
Salecl, Renata. 1994. *The Spoils of Freedom*. London and New York.
Salecl, Renata, and Slavoj Zizek, eds. 1996. *Gaze and Voice as Love Objects*. Durham, N.C., and London.
Scodel, Ruth. 1982. "The Achaean Wall and the Myth of Destruction." *HSPh* 84:33–53.
Searle, J. R. 1967. "Proper Names and Descriptions." In *The Encyclopedia of Philosophy*, ed. Paul Edwards, 6:487–91. New York and London.
Segal, Charles. 1981. *Tragedy and Civilization: An Interpretation of Sophocles*. Cambridge, Mass.
———. 1994. *Singers, Heroes, and Gods in the* Odyssey. Ithaca.
Snell, Bruno. 1953. *The Discovery of the Mind: The Greek Origins of European Thought*. Oxford.
Stanford, William Bedell. 1939. *Ambiguity in Greek Literature*. Oxford.

———. 1950. "Homer's Use of Personal *polu*-Compounds." *CP* 45:108–10.
———. 1963. *The Ulysses Theme.* Oxford.
———, ed. 1965. *The Odyssey of Homer.* 2 vols. 2d ed. London and New York.
Stinton, T. C. W. 1990. *Collected Papers on Greek Tragedy.* Oxford.
Taplin, Oliver. 1992. *Homeric Soundings.* Oxford.
Taylor, C. C. W., trans. 1976. *Plato's* Protagoras. Oxford.
Van Nortwick, T. 1979. "Penelope and Nausikaa." *TAPA* 109:269–76.
Vernant, Jean-Pierre. 1969. "Hestia-Hermes: The Religious Expression of Social Space and Movement among the Greeks." Trans. H. Piat. *Social Sciences Information* 8, no. 4:131–68.
———. 1983. *Myth and Thought among the Greeks.* London.
———. 1991. *Mortals and Immortals.* Princeton.
Vicaire, Paul. 1960. *Platon, critique littéraire.* Paris.
Vidal-Naquet, Pierre. 1986. *The Black Hunter.* Baltimore.
Von Reden, Sitta. 1995. *Exchange in Ancient Greece.* London.
Wathelet, P. 1989. "Rhésos, ou la quête de l'immortalité." *Kernos* 2:213–31.
Wees, Hans Van. 1992. *Status Warriors.* Amsterdam.
West, M. L. 1978. *Hesiod: Works and Days.* Oxford.
Whitman, Cedric Hubbell. 1951. *Sophocles: A Study of Heroic Humanism.* Cambridge, Mass.
———. 1958. *Homer and the Heroic Tradition.* Cambridge, Mass.
Williams, Bernard. 1973. *Problems of the Self: Philosophical Papers, 1956–1972.* Cambridge.
———. 1985. *Ethics and the Limits of Philosophy.* Cambridge, Mass.
———. 1993. *Shame and Necessity.* Berkeley.
Wood, Robert. 1775. *On the Original Genius of Homer.* London.
Woodhouse, W. J. 1929. *The Composition of Homer's* Odyssey. Oxford.
Zeitlin, Froma. 1995. "Figuring Fidelity in Homer's *Odyssey.*" In *The Distaff Side*, ed. Beth Cohen, 117–52. Oxford.
———. 1996. *Playing the Other: Gender and Society in Classical Greek Literature.* Chicago.
Zizek, Slavoj. 1989. *The Sublime Object of Ideology.* London.
———. 1991. *For They Know Not What They Do: Enjoyment as a Political Factor.* London.
———. 1992. *Enjoy Your Symptom! Jacques Lacan in Hollywood and Out.* New York.
———. 1993a. "From Courtly Love to *The Crying Game.*" *New Left Review* 202:95–100.
———. 1993b. *Tarrying with the Negative.* Durham, N.C.
———. 1994. *The Metastases of Enjoyment: Six Essays on Women and Causality.* London.

Index

Achilles, 3, 5–7, 60, 107–10, 174, 178; anger *(menis)* of, 112, 174, 176; argument with Agamemnon, 115, 175–76, 177, 238n. 19; argument with Odysseus, 92–93, 96–97, 101, 103; and Cyclops compared, 143–45; and death of Lycaon, 6, 131; destructive fantasy of, 107, 109–10, 112–13, 122, 132, 136, 255nn. 47–48; fame *(kleos)* of, 6, 21; indecision of, 6–7, 9, 10–11; language of, 21; mortality of, 130; and Patroclus, 108, 110, 252n. 2; strength *(bie)* of, 92–93, 101, 103, 147, 251–52n. 22; violence of, 16

Adkins, A. W. H., 107

Aegisthus, 208, 230

Aegyptius, 52

Agamemnon, 7, 11–12, 60, 96–97, 122; Achilles' rejection of, 112, 144, 175–76, 177; and the Doloneia, 115–21; misogyny of, 188, 208–13; murder of, 207, 208, 213; Odysseus' challenge to, 113, 114–15, 149; and public law, 113–15, 130, 133–34, 176

aidos. See shame *(aidos)*

Ajax, 98–99, 101, 121, 144, 251n. 22

Alcinous, 43, 48, 73, 83, 215, 243n. 9; and Nausicaa, 194–95, 202, 203–4; and Odysseus' tales, 44–45, 46; and patriarchy, 37–38; and songs of Demodocus, 96, 97–98

Amphinomos, 172, 173

anger *(menis)*, 51, 112, 174, 176

anthropomorphism, 155

antidescriptivism. *See* naming theory controversy

Antilochus, 98–99

Antinous, 51–52, 191–92, 214, 220, 231, 265n. 17

Aphrodite, 101, 102, 227–28, 231

Apollo, 51, 52, 97

Apollodorus, 76

Apologoi (Odysseus), 135, 148, 157, 171, 181; companions of Odysseus in, 54, 65, 143, 147, 159; and Phaeacians, 40, 44, 45–46, 80, 103, 252n. 30; structure of, 151. *See also* Polyphemus, blinding of; Proteus

archery contest, 100

Ares, 100–102, 227–28

Arete, 186, 190–93, 201, 213–14, 215

aristoi (martial power), 56, 118, 120, 127, 214–15; and leadership of Agamemnon, 112, 117, 149

Athena, 12, 41, 83, 86, 192; and funeral games in *Iliad*, 98, 251–52n. 22; and killing of the suitors, 2, 135–36, 232; and Nausicaa, 195–96, 217; and Pandora, 188–89

Austin, Norman, 35, 239n. 3, 257n. 21

Bakhtinian reading, 2, 110, 111

baptism, 24–25, 33–34. *See also* naming

bed scene, 17, 224–35; and construction theme, 227–29; wonder *(sema)* of fidelity in, 224–28, 229, 233, 234, 235

bow contest, 139–40, 174, 191–92, 214–15, 217, 265n. 17; and public law, 179–80

Bryseis, 11
Burkert, Walter, 22, 154

Calchas, 153
Calhoun, G. M., 97
Calypso, 7–8, 206
cannibalism, 22, 46, 144, 240n. 10
Carson, Anne, 219–20
cattle of the Sun, 3, 155–61, 170–71
Cephallenians, 137, 138, 165–66
chariot of the Sun, 123
choice, 40, 230, 243n. 11. *See also* indecision
Chryseis, 11
Circe, magic of, 161–66
civilization, piracy and, 146
closure, 1, 70, 235
Clytemnestra, 11, 12, 207, 208–9, 211, 230
Colossos, 79–81, 85
communication, 25, 108; of Cyclopes, 20, 23, 46; failure of, 66, 93; of Phaeacians, 37, 38, 44, 74. *See also* language
companions of Odysseus, 142–43, 152; allegiance of, 144, 153–54; and cattle of the Sun, 155, 158, 160, 170; and Circe's magic, 161–64, 165; death of, 3, 16, 113, 134–35, 136, 147, 158, 159, 171; and suitors compared, 167–68, 170
contests/competition, 135, 202; bow contest, 139–40, 174, 179–80, 191–92, 214–15, 217, 265n. 17; discus throw, 83, 86, 179, 196, 265n. 21; funeral games, 99, 251–52n. 22; of Phaeacians, 42–43, 83, 86, 97, 139–40, 191–92
counting system, 50–52, 55, 59, 67–68, 152
Cyclopes, 14, 50, 71, 164, 234, 239n. 3; cannibalism of, 22, 46, 144, 240n. 10; and cattle of Sun compared, 157–58; communication of, 20, 23, 46; infallibility of, 15; and paternal law, 29–33; Penelope's suitors compared to, 52–53; and Phaeacians, 36–37, 38, 44, 48–49, 85–88, 179, 192, 198, 199–200; and Poseidon, 18, 29, 30, 31–32, 33, 36; rejection of morality by, 22–23; self-sufficiency of, 19, 20–21, 28–29, 35, 84; surprise of, 19–20; tricking of, 104. *See also* Polyphemus, blinding of

Davidson, O. M., 125, 126
death, 1, 25; acceptance of, 6–7; of companions of Odysseus, 3, 16, 113, 134–35, 136, 147, 158, 159, 171; hero and, 139; of Lycaon, 6, 131, 255n. 47; of Patroclus, 6–7, 16, 122, 145; of Penelope's suitors, 113, 134–36, 137, 166–80, 220–21, 231–32, 260n. 63
deception, 6. *See also* trickery *(metis)*
decision making. *See* choice; indecision
demand, 27–28, 195, 220
Demodocus, songs of, 42, 92–106, 153, 227–28; on myth of Sisyphus, 94, 95–96; and Phaeacian games, 96, 97–98; on quarrel between Odysseus and Achilles, 92–93, 96–97; on sacking of Troy, 103–5; on trickery of Hephaestus, 100–102
descriptivist-antidescriptivist controversy, 23–27, 33
desire, 5, 8–9, 12, 197–200, 234; of Achilles, 145; complexity of, 4; Doloneia as drama of, 122–28, 159; economy of, 53; and gender, 181–82, 197–98; and identity, 19, 34; Lacan on, 195, 219–20, 261n. 23; and language, 33, 34; narrative of, 15; of Nausicaa, 197–98, 203, 204, 214, 263n. 37; of Odysseus, 18, 159; origin of, on Phaeacia, 72, 83; of Other, 13–14, 65, 66–67, 239n. 24; of Patroclus, 52; for return, 8–9; sexual, 17, 197, 219; unconscious, 67–68
destruction: Achilles' fantasy of, 107, 109–10, 112–13, 122, 132, 136, 255nn. 47–48; Odysseus as agent of, 81, 91, 104, 105, 138; of self, 10. *See also* Nausithous, prophecy of
Detienne, Marcel, 136, 245n. 16
Deucalion and Pyrrha myth, 73, 76–78, 79–80, 110; gender issues in, 182, 183–84, 190
Devereux, George, 220
Diomedes, 118, 123, 124, 126, 177, 255n. 48; Odysseus' silencing of, 119–20, 121, 131, 169, 178
disaster myths, 4, 109, 204–5. *See also* destruction; Nausithous, prophecy of
discus throw, 83, 86, 179, 196, 265n. 21
Dolon, 117–18, 120, 124–25, 126–29, 166

Doloneia, 118–32, 169, 178, 254n. 24; as dark side of warfare, 129–30; as drama of desire, 122–29, 159; Odysseus' trickery in, 117, 118–21, 149; wolf motif in, 125–26, 128. *See also* public law

doubt, 32, 63–64, 140, 141, 174. *See also* indecision

Ehoeae (Hesiod), 109

Eidothea, trickery of, 59, 63–65, 68, 198; and Menelaus, 50, 53–54, 55; and Proteus' self-consciousness, 61, 62, 152

emotional display, 223–24

encirclement motif, 153, 164, 169

enjoyment, deferral of, 168, 169, 171, 179, 180

Epimetheus, 4, 190

eris. *See* primal strife *(eris)*

eros and desire, 219–20

eroticism, 198. *See also* sexual desire; sexual love *(philotes)*

esthlos (noble), 145–46, 169

ethics, 10, 22, 35, 113. *See also* moral code

Eupeithes, 2–3

Euryalus, 40, 93, 97, 190

Eurycleia, 178, 260n. 63

Eurylochus, 155, 156–57, 162, 163–66

Eurymachus, 53, 172, 174–76, 214, 264n. 16

Eurymedon, 77

evil *(kakos)*, 145–46, 168–69; of women, 208, 229

fallibility, 118, 160. *See also* infallibility

fame *(kleos)*, 21, 131, 145, 220, 265n. 17; undying, 6, 25

fantasy, 4, 52; of return *(nostos)*, 3, 5, 8, 10. *See also* destruction, Achilles' fantasy of

father: Agamemnon as, 112, 130; rule of, 185–86; symbolic power of, 174. *See also* Name-of-the Father; paternal law/authority; patriarchal ideology

Felson-Rubin, Nancy, 211–12, 213

female identity, 187, 189, 212. *See also* gender; maiden *(parthenos)*; woman *(gyne)*

fidelity, of Penelope, 207, 209–11, 212, 222, 232, 235; bed as symbol of, 224–28, 229, 233

flood myth. *See* Deucalion and Pyrrha myth

force *(bie)*, 120, 156–57, 200; of Achilles, 92–93, 101, 103, 147

Four Fundamental Concepts of Psychoanalysis (Lacan), 40

Frame, Douglas, 128, 157

freedom, 110–11, 140–41, 145, 213

Freud, Sigmund, 5, 61–62, 197, 217, 248n. 6; on compromise, 192, 261n. 18; on unconscious, 67

games. *See* contests/competition

gender, 16–17, 181–205, 207, 234; and Arete as *gyne*, 190–93; and desire, 181–82, 197–98; in Deucalion and Pyrrha myth, 182, 183–84, 190; and identity, 183–84, 186, 190, 197–98, 201–2; ideology of, 182, 211; in Phaeacian ideal society, 181–82, 215–17; in Plato's *Protagoras*, 182, 184–86; and sexual symmetry, 186–87, 202; and shame of Nausicaa, 194–95, 197, 202–5

generational order, 25, 74, 76. *See also* paternal law/authority

genetic inheritance, 12–14

Gernet, Louis, 125

Goldhill, Simon, 31, 70

group identity, 60, 69, 150

guest-friendship ritual *(xenia)*, 37, 146

gyne. *See* woman *(gyne)*

Hades, 138, 147, 160; journey to, 32, 124, 127, 137, 142–43. *See also* death

Haft, Adele, 113

Halitherses, 9, 172–73

Haubold, Johannes, 73, 247n. 34

Hector, 127, 144; killing of, 88, 111, 122, 251–52n. 22

Helen, 13, 106, 201; Penelope compared to, 207, 208–9, 211, 229–32, 267n. 42

Helios (Sun): cattle of, 155–61, 170–71; chariot of, 123

Hephaestus, 100–102, 153, 154, 159, 227–28; and Pandora, 188–89

Hera, 141

Hermes, 123–25, 127, 143, 165; and Aphrodite, 102, 231; and justice, 184–85; Odysseus compared to, 123,

Hermes (*continued*)
  125, 127, 138, 141, 142, 147, 252n. 25; as *psychopomp*, 123–24, 137, 138, 140, 141
Herodotus, 2
heroic contest *(aethlos)*, 135. *See also* contests/competition
heroism: code of, 60, 113, 169; ideology of, 113, 120, 121, 254n. 24; limits of, 109
Hesiod, 33; *Ehoeae*, 109; Pandora story of, 182, 186–90, 236; *Theogony*, 75, 187, 248n. 13; *Works and Days*, 216
Heubeck, A., 162
homo faber tradition, 34, 228
hope, 236
household *(oikos)*, 1–2, 4, 7, 10, 53; of Agamemnon, 11–12; fantasy of, 37, 206; law of, 168, 230; Odysseus as head of, 134, 176, 182, 225
humanity *(anthropoi)*, 187, 188. *See also* Deucalion and Pyrrha myth

identification, 91, 119, 155, 170; with hero, 3, 4–5, 6; with the law, 111–12
identity, 33–34; and blinding of Polyphemus, 19–23, 241n. 22; and desire, 19, 34; female, 187, 189, 212; gendered, 183–84, 186, 190, 197–98, 201–2; herd/group, 60, 69, 150; lack of, 127, 128; of Odysseus, 39, 103, 225, 233, 267n. 48; Odysseus as "No one" *(Outis)*, 10, 31, 71, 148–49; of Penelope, 219, 233, 234; Phaeacian, 74, 81, 84, 90–91, 97; riddle of, 14; social, 70; symbolic, 44; of Telemachus, 13. *See also* naming
ideology, 2, 3, 60, 61; in the Doloneia, 118, 119; gender, 182, 211; heroic, 113, 120, 121, 254n. 24; patriarchal, 210, 212, 213; workings of, 16
Iliad (Homer), 51; anger *(menis)* in, 51, 112; death in, and *Odyssey* compared, 133, 136–38, 174; funeral games of, 98–99, 251–52n. 22; Helen's role in, 231; Odysseus' persuasion in, 153; sacking of Troy in, 100, 103–5, 141, 149. *See also* Achilles; Agamemnon; Doloneia
immortality, 123
indecision, 9, 192; of Achilles, 6–7, 10–11
infallibility, 15, 225; of Phaeacians, 92, 193; of Proteus, 55, 56, 61, 63, 65

initiation rites, Zeus Lykaios, 126, 128
innocence, 139; loss of, 101, 197
Ithaca, fantasy of, 3, 8, 176. *See also* Odysseus, return of *(nostos)*

justice, 184–86

kakos. See evil *(kakos)*
katabasis motif, 118, 127, 198
Katz, Marilyn, 13, 207, 217, 219
kleos. See fame *(kleos)*
knowledge *(noos)*, 45, 123, 128, 140, 165; of Alcinous, 141, 194, 203, 243n. 9; and *metis* (trickery), 90, 159; self-, 12, 40, 81
Kronos, 75

Lacan, Jacques, 5, 27, 64, 185, 240n. 8; on choice, 40; on desire, 195, 219–20, 261n. 23; on the fool, 69; on Name-of-the-Father, 25, 87; on the Other, 14, 239n. 24; signifier of, 25, 58, 62; on superego, 130; symbolic order of, 32, 58–59, 64; on unconscious, 67, 77–78
Laertes, 2, 3
Lampetia, 159
language, 27; of Achilles, 21; and blinding of Polyphemus, 32, 240n. 8; and choice, 40; of Cyclopes, 23, 143, 240n. 11; and desire, 33, 34; and identity, 21, 236; and naming theory, 25; and Phaeacians, 44–49; of Proteus, 63–68, 70–71; of supplication *(charis)*, 177; *tropoi* of, 139; unconscious, 77–78. *See also* communication; signifier
Laodamas, 40, 41, 93
law: household *(oikos)*, 168, 230; and justice, 184–86; and shame, 262n. 25. *See also* paternal law/authority; public law
Leodes, 176–77, 178
limits, 59; of desire, 195, 198; and Phaeacians, 40–44, 140, 196
Loraux, Nicole, 187–90, 192, 201
loss, 21, 65, 140, 192–93; fear of, 16; and gender, 181; of Phaeacians, 71, 196, 217; survival of, 77; and trickery, 89, 90
lost balls *(sphaira)*, 196–97, 217, 263n. 37
love, demand for, 27. *See also* desire
Lycaon, death of, 6, 131, 255n. 47

Lynn-George, Michael, 89–90, 122, 127, 142, 145, 240n. 8; on Achilles' language, 21, 145

madman, 185–86, 200, 260n. 7
maiden *(parthenos)*, 192, 207, 230; Nausicaa as, 197, 201, 202, 213–15; Pandora as, 189–90; Penelope as, 207, 213; and woman *(gyne)*, 194–95, 197, 221
marriage, 189, 214
martial power. *See aristoi* (martial power)
masks *(polytropoi)* of Odysseus, 54, 71, 125, 142, 153, 225, 226. *See also* No one *(Outis)*, Odysseus as
Menelaus, 50, 53–57, 62, 65–66, 117; and Helen, 207, 230
menis (anger), 51, 112, 174, 176
metis. See trickery *(metis)*
misogyny, 188, 208–13
moral code, 9–10, 22–23. *See also* ethics
moral status, 69
mortality, 130, 140; and Cyclops, 32–33, 148. *See also* death
Muellner, Leonard, 51–52, 56
Murnaghan, S., 212

Nagler, Michael, 134, 139–40, 166–67, 174, 179
Nagy, Gregory, 92, 128, 140–41
Name-of-the-Father, 26, 38, 88, 171, 179, 259n. 48; Lacan on, 25, 87. *See also* paternal law/authority
naming, 33–34, 48–49, 67, 138. *See also* baptism; identity
naming theory controversy, 23–27, 33
Nausicaa, 17, 186, 187, 194–205; desire of, 197–98, 203, 204, 214, 263n. 37; Penelope as, 213–15; shame of, 194–95, 202–5; as wife for Odysseus, 37, 182, 206
Nausithous, 77, 199; prophecy of, 38–39, 40, 46–48, 76, 81, 91, 105
necessity and freedom, 110–11
neikos. See quarrel *(neikos)*
Nekuia, 137, 142–43, 170
Nestor, 118, 122, 124, 146, 230
Newton, Rick, 227
noble *(esthlos)*, 145–46, 169
No one *(Outis)*, Odysseus as, 10, 31, 71, 110–11, 139; and Cyclops, 31, 104, 110, 147, 151, 154
noos. See knowledge *(noos)*
nostalgia, 5, 15, 216
nostos. See Odysseus, return of *(nostos)*; return *(nostos)*

Odysseus, 149; as agent of destruction, 81, 91, 104, 105, 138; bestiality of, 198–99; censorship of Diomedes by, 119–20, 121; discus throw of, 83, 86, 179, 196, 265n. 21; as figure of death, 123–24; and Hermes compared, 123, 125, 127, 138, 141, 142, 147, 252n. 25; lies to Alcinous, 202–3; and Nausicaa, 187, 194, 201; as "No one" *(Outis)*, 10, 31, 71, 104, 110–11, 139, 147; Penelope as faithful wife to, 17, 214, 215, 221; persuasive powers of, 113, 114–15; polytropic masks of, 54, 71, 125, 142, 153, 225, 226; and Proteus compared, 60–61, 69–71; reply to Calypso, 7–8; and suitors compared, 9; and Telemachus, 30–31, 246n. 27; warning to Achilles, 144–45. *See also Apologoi* (Odysseus); trickery *(metis)* of Odysseus
Odysseus, return of *(nostos)*, 1, 3–4, 8–9, 12, 142; fantasy of, 3, 5, 8, 10; and Penelope, 206, 221, 225; and Phaeacians, 41, 90–91; prophecy of, 172–73
Odysseus and Cyclops. *See* Polyphemus, blinding of
Odysseus and Phaeacians. *See* Phaeacians
oikos. See household *(oikos)*
Other, 42, 173, 213; desire of, 13–14, 65, 66–67, 239n. 24
Outis. See No one *(Outis)*, Odysseus as
Ovid, 183–84

Pandora, 182, 186–90, 236
paradox, 1, 6, 220, 222
Paris, 230
paternal law/authority, 167, 171, 173, 188; of Alcinous, 194–95; of Cyclopes, 26, 29–33, 38, 87, 200; on Ithaca, 3; Phaeacian, 37–38, 44, 87. *See also* Name-of-the-Father; public law
paternity, 25, 30–31
patriarchal ideology, 210, 212, 213

Patroclus, 10–11, 51, 52, 55, 130, 136; and Achilles' song, 108, 110, 252n. 2; death of, 6–7, 16, 122, 145
Peleus, 10–11
Penelope, 2, 8, 206–36, 259n. 48; and Agamemnon's misogyny, 208–13; as Arete, 213–14; and bed scene, 224–34; compared to Helen, 207, 208–9, 211, 229–32, 267n. 42; courtship of, 51–52; desire of, 217–24; dream of, 218–19, 220–21, 266n. 29; emotional display by, 223–24; fidelity of, 207, 209–11, 212, 222, 224–28, 229, 235; multiple identities of, 219; as Nausicaa, 213–15; obedience of, 264n. 9; Odysseus' return to, 17, 182, 222–24, 233–34; trickery of, 215, 228–29, 235, 265n. 17. *See also* suitors of Penelope
Peradotto, John, 23, 91, 110–12, 122, 141; on myth of Sisyphus, 95, 96; on Odysseus as *Outis*, 110–11, 140; on Odysseus as trickster, 121; on Proteus, 64, 152
Phaeacians, 14–15, 36–49, 50, 71; and Arete as *gyne*, 190–93; contests of, 42–43, 83, 86, 97, 139–40, 191–92; and Cyclopes, 36–37, 38, 44, 48–49, 85–88, 179, 192, 198, 199–200; freedom of, 140–41; gender harmony among, 181–82, 215–17; and identity, 90–91, 97; infallibility of, 92, 193; introduction of limits to, 40–44, 140, 196, 234; justice and, 185; and language, 44–49; and Nausithous' prophecy, 38–39, 40, 46–48, 76, 81, 91, 105; and Odysseus' trickery, 40, 89–91, 97–101, 181; and paternal authority, 37–38, 44; punishment of, 36, 80–81, 86–88, 91; return of madman to, 186; transportation of, 38, 262n. 29; unfriendliness of, 38–40, 73, 76, 91, 193. *See also* Demodocus, songs of; Nausicaa
Phaeacians and stones, 16, 72–88, 229; and birth of Zeus, 75; and Colossos, 79–81; and Deucalion and Pyrrha myth, 73, 76–78, 79–80; and identity, 74, 81, 84; and myth of Sisyphus, 94, 95–96; as objects of wonder *(sema)*, 73, 74, 75, 78; and Poseidon's punishment, 80–83
Phemius, 177–78

Philoctetes, 98, 100
piracy and law, 146–47
Plato, 6, 23; *Protagoras*, 182, 184–86, 200
Polyphemus, blinding of, 18–35, 42, 45–46, 83, 159, 240n. 8; Achilles compared to, 143–45; and appeal to fathers, 29–33, 86, 87; and Cyclopean split, 34–35, 242n. 33; demand/scream of, 27–28, 241nn. 22–23; as *homo faber*, 34, 228; and identity, 19–23; lost monadic status of, 85; mortality of, 148; and naming theory, 23–27, 33–34; Odysseus' trickery in, 102, 150–51, 154–55; and Penelope's trick compared, 228–29; self-sufficiency, 20–21, 28–29; stone throwing by, 72, 84, 85–86, 249n. 19; and tricking of Proteus compared, 149, 152–53. *See also* Cyclopes
polytropoi. *See* masks *(polytropoi)* of Odysseus
Poseidon: and Cyclopes, 18, 29, 30, 31–32, 33, 36; and Phaeacians, 38–39, 47, 73, 74, 80–83, 86–88, 98
prestige, 127, 131, 176. *See also* fame *(kleos)*
Priam, 88, 231
primal strife *(eris)*, 93, 104, 214, 216–17, 232, 265n. 21
Protagoras (Plato), 182, 184–86, 200
Proteus, 14, 245–46nn. 16–19; counting system of, 50, 55–56, 59–60, 67–68, 152, 235; Eidothea's trick on, 50, 53–54, 55, 59, 61, 62, 63–65, 198; infallibility of, 55, 56, 61, 63, 65; and limits of language, 63–68, 70–71; and Menelaus, 50, 53–57, 62, 65–66; and Odysseus compared, 60–61, 69–71, 225–26, 235; structuralist theory and, 57–59; subjectivization of, 68–69; and tricking of Cyclops compared, 149, 152–53
psychoanalytic themes, 5, 7, 195, 238n. 11. *See also* closure; desire; destruction; Freud; Lacan; loss; trauma
psychopomp, Hermes as, 123–24, 137, 138, 140, 141
public law, 111–15, 128, 131, 177–78, 257n. 23; Achilles' rejection of, 111, 122, 143, 177, 238n. 15; Agamemnon and, 133–34, 176; and companions of Odysseus, 136;

deficiencies in, 119–20; and Odysseus' *metis,* 120–21; and paternal law, 167; in Phaeacia, 179; piracy and, 146–47; splitting of, 113–15, 117; suitors' disdain for, 168–69, 174

Pucci, Pietro, 133, 174, 188, 241n. 22

punishment, of Phaeacians, 36, 80–81, 86–88, 91

puns and wordplay, 61–62, 63, 76, 77–78, 145

quarrel *(neikos),* 93, 190–93

renunciation, 168, 169, 185–86, 192, 195

return *(nostos),* 1, 4, 128; fantasy of, 3, 5, 8–9. *See also* Odysseus, return of *(nostos)*

Rhea, 75

Rhesus, death of, 123, 124, 130, 159

riddle *(griphos),* 70

romance tradition, 1

sacred power, 79

sacrifice to gods, 193

Saussure, Ferdinand de, 57

Scheria, 37, 80, 90, 199. *See also* Phaeacians

Scodel, Ruth, 109

Searle, John, 23–26

self, 110–11, 225; concept of, 10; and desire, 14, 145; fantasies of, 4; free, 110, 141; knowledge of, 12, 40, 81; paradox of, 222; plural, 70. *See also* identity

self-consciousness, 61, 62, 100, 110, 152

self-deception, 154–55

self-destruction, 10

self-knowledge, 12, 40, 81

self-sufficiency, 108; of Cyclopes, 19, 20–21, 28–29, 35, 84

sema. See wonder *(sema)*

sexual desire, 17, 197, 219. *See also* desire

sexual difference, 17. *See also* gender

sexual love *(philotes),* 187

sexual symmetry, 186–87, 202

shame *(aidos),* 167, 214, 262n. 25; of Nausicaa, 194–95, 197, 202–5

signifier, 27, 33, 60, 77–78, 229; master, 25, 68; and signified, 57–59, 61, 62, 64, 78, 139, 150

Sisyphus, myth of, 94, 95–96

social rank, 131

Solon, 2

Stanford, William Bedell, 153

stones. *See* Phaeacians and stones

structuralism, 22, 57–59

subject, 59, 68–69

suitors of Penelope, 216, 217, 231; appeal of Leodes, 176–77; and contest of the bow, 139–40, 180, 191–92; and Cyclops compared, 52–53; disdain for law, 168–69, 174, 238n. 15; eating excesses of, 9; enjoyment of, 168; Eurymachus' plea, 174–76; killing of, 113, 134–36, 137, 166–80, 220–21, 231–32, 260n. 63; and Odysseus' companions compared, 167–68, 170; in Penelope's dream, 218–19, 220–21, 266n. 29; and plot to kill Telemachus, 172, 173; warning of Theoclymenus to, 169–70

superego, 112, 130, 131, 180, 257n. 23

surprise, 4, 14, 19–20

suturing concept, 58

symbolic authority, 115–16, 171–72, 173, 177, 180. *See also* father; public law

symbolic structure, 15, 32, 58–59, 61, 64; Other as, 66

Teiresias' prophecy, 2, 4, 70, 235–36, 267n. 48

Telemachus, 2, 3, 30–31, 33, 146, 231, 246n. 27; genetic identity of, 12–14, 239n. 23; suitors' plot to murder, 172, 173

Telemus' prophecy, 158

teleological readings, 4, 206

teleological structure, 1, 7

Theoclymenus, 169–70, 171

Theogony (Hesiod), 75, 187, 248n. 13

Thersites, 115

Thracians, killing of, 120, 130, 178

timing *(kairos)* of action, 10

trauma, 16, 26; narratives of, 4, 14–15, 21

trickery *(metis):* in birth of Zeus, 76; of Dolon, 117, 118, 120, 124–25, 126–29; in Doloneia, 115–21; of Hephaestus, 100–102, 153, 154; of Penelope, 215, 228–29, 235, 265n. 17. *See also* Eidothea, trickery of trickery *(metis)* of Odysseus, 16, 31, 53, 105, 123, 257n. 23; and Achilles' force *(bie)*, 92–93, 96–97, 101, 103, 251–52n. 22; and cattle of the Sun, 158–61; and cowardly killing, 133–34; and Cyclops, 144, 150–51, 154–55, 160, 181; in Doloneia, 117, 118–21, 166; and Eurylochus' force, 156–57; head-veiling and tears as, 93–94, 105; and Hermes compared, 123, 125, 127, 138; and heroic code, 169; in killing of Penelope's suitors, 134–36; and the law, 131; and leadership, 113; Penelope's reaction to, 222–24; and Phaeacians, 40, 89–91, 97–101, 181; and *polytropoi* (masks), 54, 71, 125, 142, 153, 225, 226; self-inflicted suffering as, 106; Trojan horse, 103–4. *See also* Polyphemus, blinding of

Trojan horse, 103–4

Troy, sack of, 100, 103–5, 141, 149. See also *Iliad* (Homer)

truthfulness, 45

unconscious, 67–68, 77–78

Vernant, Jean-Pierre, 79, 85, 120, 136, 245n. 16

victims. *See* companions of Odysseus; suitors of Penelope

Vidal-Naquet, Pierre, 22

violence, 16, 146–47

virgin. *See* maiden *(parthenos)*

Wathelet, P., 123, 124, 127

Whitman, Cedric Hubbell, 145

wolf motif, 125–26, 128

woman *(gyne)*, 189–95; Arete as, 190–93, 213–14, 215; and misogyny, 188, 208–13. *See also* female identity; gender; maiden *(parthenos)*

wonder *(sema)*, 127–28, 140, 167, 173, 229; and *noos,* 141; of Odysseus, 42, 43–44, 48; of Penelope's fidelity, 225, 233; stones as, 73, 74, 75, 78

Works and Days (Hesiod), 216

wounding, 14, 101. *See also* trauma

xenia (guest ritual), 37, 146

Zeitlin, Froma, 221, 232, 251n. 22

Zeus, 14, 47, 96, 113, 141; birth of, 75, 248n. 13; and Cyclops, 29, 33, 53; and flood myth, 76; and Helios, 160; law of, 22, 26, 28, 146, 184–85; Lykaios, 125–26, 128; and Pandora, 188, 189–90, 236; and Phaeacian myths, 73, 74, 80

Zizek, Slavoj, 24–25, 33, 112, 117, 193